THE LIFE AND DEATH OF JOHNNY ALPHA

Writer: John Wagner
Artist: Carlos Ezquerra
Colours: Hector Ezquerra
Letters: Simon Bowland

Originally published in *2000 AD* Progs 1689-1699

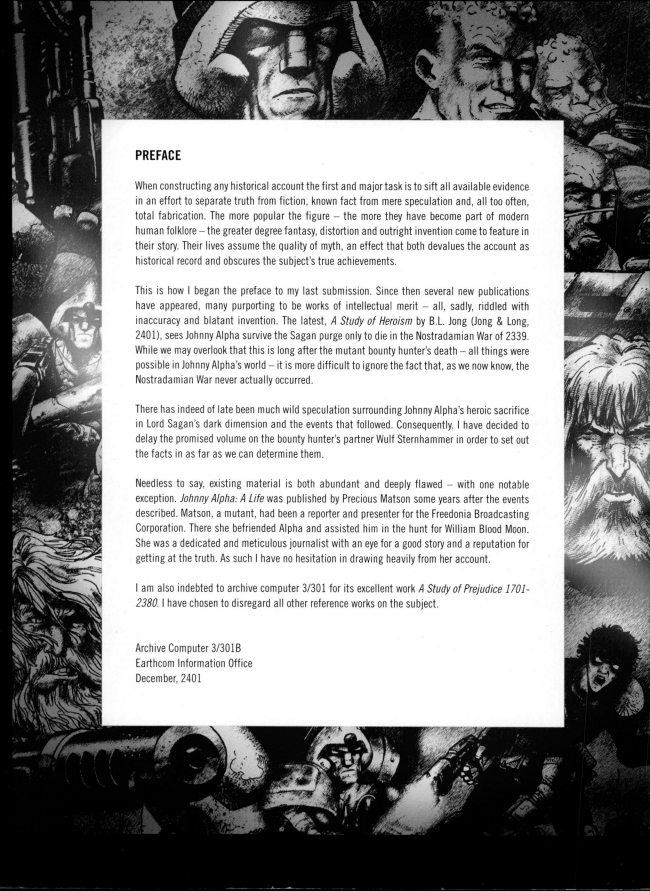

PREFACE

When constructing any historical account the first and major task is to sift all available evidence in an effort to separate truth from fiction, known fact from mere speculation and, all too often, total fabrication. The more popular the figure – the more they have become part of modern human folklore – the greater degree fantasy, distortion and outright invention come to feature in their story. Their lives assume the quality of myth, an effect that both devalues the account as historical record and obscures the subject's true achievements.

This is how I began the preface to my last submission. Since then several new publications have appeared, many purporting to be works of intellectual merit – all, sadly, riddled with inaccuracy and blatant invention. The latest, *A Study of Heroism* by B.L. Jong (Jong & Long, 2401), sees Johnny Alpha survive the Sagan purge only to die in the Nostradamian War of 2339. While we may overlook that this is long after the mutant bounty hunter's death – all things were possible in Johnny Alpha's world – it is more difficult to ignore the fact that, as we now know, the Nostradamian War never actually occurred.

There has indeed of late been much wild speculation surrounding Johnny Alpha's heroic sacrifice in Lord Sagan's dark dimension and the events that followed. Consequently, I have decided to delay the promised volume on the bounty hunter's partner Wulf Sternhammer in order to set out the facts in as far as we can determine them.

Needless to say, existing material is both abundant and deeply flawed – with one notable exception. *Johnny Alpha: A Life* was published by Precious Matson some years after the events described. Matson, a mutant, had been a reporter and presenter for the Freedonia Broadcasting Corporation. There she befriended Alpha and assisted him in the hunt for William Blood Moon. She was a dedicated and meticulous journalist with an eye for a good story and a reputation for getting at the truth. As such I have no hesitation in drawing heavily from her account.

I am also indebted to archive computer 3/301 for its excellent work *A Study of Prejudice 1701-2380*. I have chosen to disregard all other reference works on the subject.

Archive Computer 3/301B
Earthcom Information Office
December, 2401

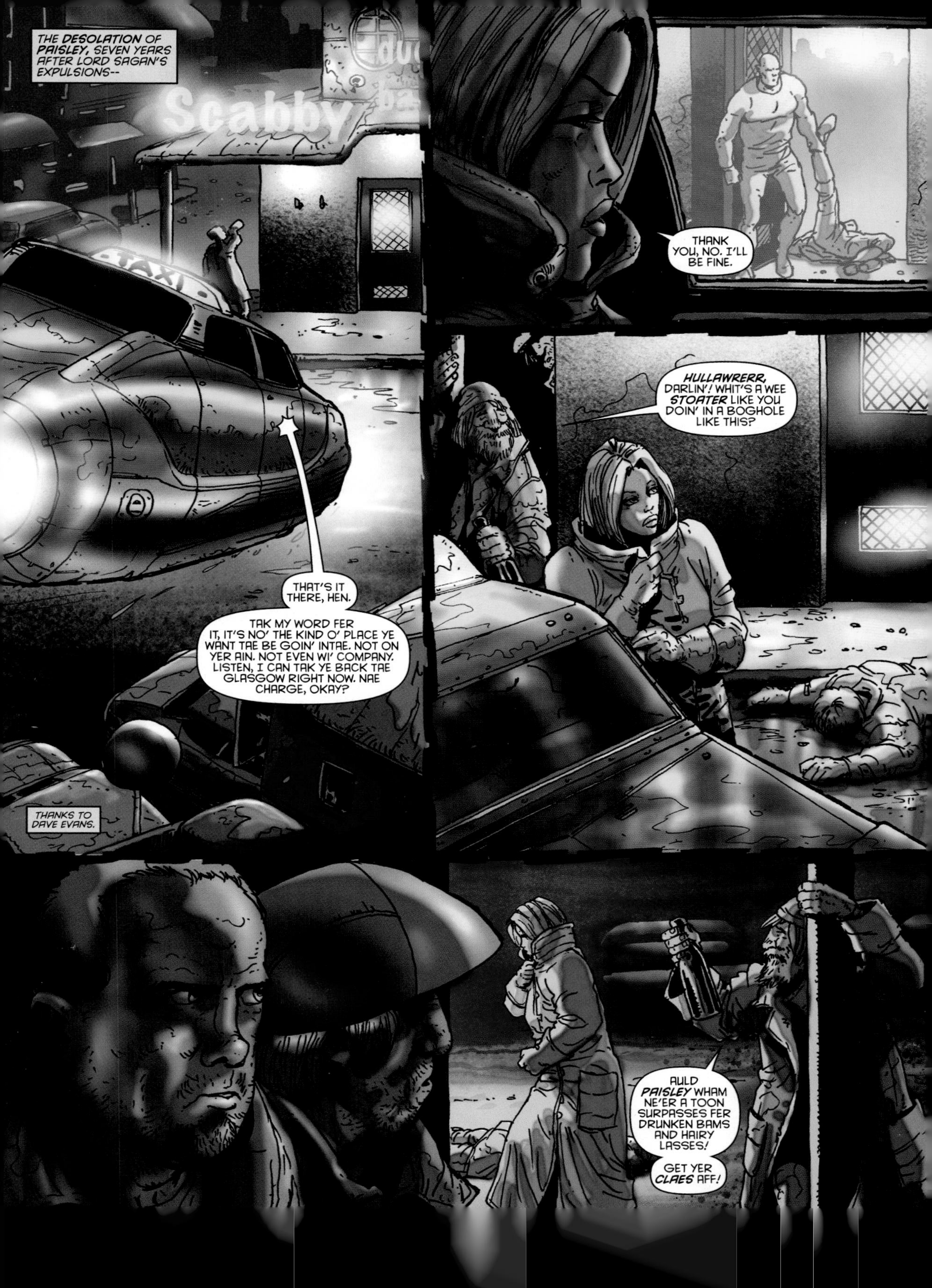
THE DESOLATION OF PAISLEY, SEVEN YEARS AFTER LORD SAGAN'S EXPULSIONS--
Scabby
TAXI
THAT'S IT THERE, HEN.
TAK MY WORD FER IT, IT'S NO' THE KIND O' PLACE YE WANT TAE BE GOIN' INTAE. NOT ON YER AIN. NOT EVEN WI' COMPANY. LISTEN, I CAN TAK YE BACK TAE GLASGOW RIGHT NOW. NAE CHARGE, OKAY?
THANKS TO DAVE EVANS.
THANK YOU, NO. I'LL BE FINE.
HULLAWRERR, DARLIN'! WHIT'S A WEE STOATER LIKE YOU DOIN' IN A BOGHOLE LIKE THIS?
AULD PAISLEY WHAM NE'ER A TOON SURPASSES FER DRUNKEN BAMS AND HAIRY LASSES!
GET YER CLAES AFF!

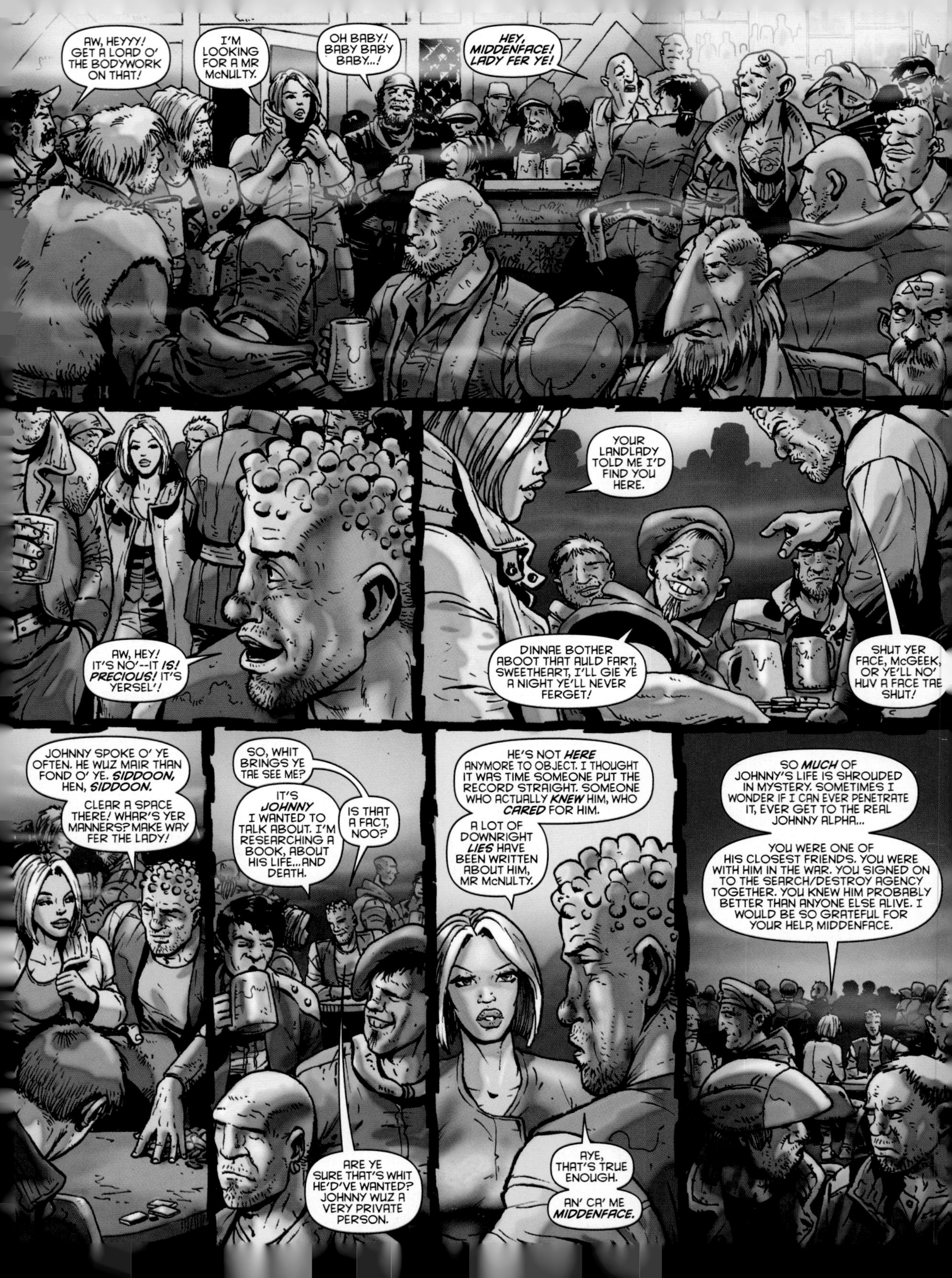

AW, HEYYY! GET A LOAD O' THE BODYWORK ON THAT!
I'M LOOKING FOR A MR McNULTY.
OH BABY! BABY BABY BABY...!
HEY, MIDDENFACE! LADY FER YE!
AW, HEY! IT'S NO'--IT IS! PRECIOUS! IT'S YERSEL'!
YOUR LANDLADY TOLD ME I'D FIND YOU HERE.
DINNAE BOTHER ABOOT THAT AULD FART, SWEETHEART, I'LL GIE YE A NIGHT YE'LL NEVER FERGET!
SHUT YER FACE, McGEEK, OR YE'LL NO' HUV A FACE TAE SHUT!
JOHNNY SPOKE O' YE OFTEN. HE WUZ MAIR THAN FOND O' YE. SIDDOON, HEN, SIDDOON.
CLEAR A SPACE THERE! WHAR'S YER MANNERS? MAKE WAY FER THE LADY!
SO, WHIT BRINGS YE TAE SEE ME?
IT'S JOHNNY I WANTED TO TALK ABOUT. I'M RESEARCHING A BOOK, ABOUT HIS LIFE... AND DEATH.
IS THAT A FACT, NOO?
ARE YE SURE THAT'S WHIT HE'D'VE WANTED? JOHNNY WUZ A VERY PRIVATE PERSON.
HE'S NOT HERE ANYMORE TO OBJECT. I THOUGHT IT WAS TIME SOMEONE PUT THE RECORD STRAIGHT. SOMEONE WHO ACTUALLY KNEW HIM, WHO CARED FOR HIM.
A LOT OF DOWNRIGHT LIES HAVE BEEN WRITTEN ABOUT HIM, MR McNULTY.
AYE, THAT'S TRUE ENOUGH.
AN' CA' ME MIDDENFACE.
SO MUCH OF JOHNNY'S LIFE IS SHROUDED IN MYSTERY. SOMETIMES I WONDER IF I CAN EVER PENETRATE IT, EVER GET TO THE REAL JOHNNY ALPHA...
YOU WERE ONE OF HIS CLOSEST FRIENDS. YOU WERE WITH HIM IN THE WAR. YOU SIGNED ON TO THE SEARCH/DESTROY AGENCY TOGETHER. YOU KNEW HIM PROBABLY BETTER THAN ANYONE ELSE ALIVE. I WOULD BE SO GRATEFUL FOR YOUR HELP, MIDDENFACE.

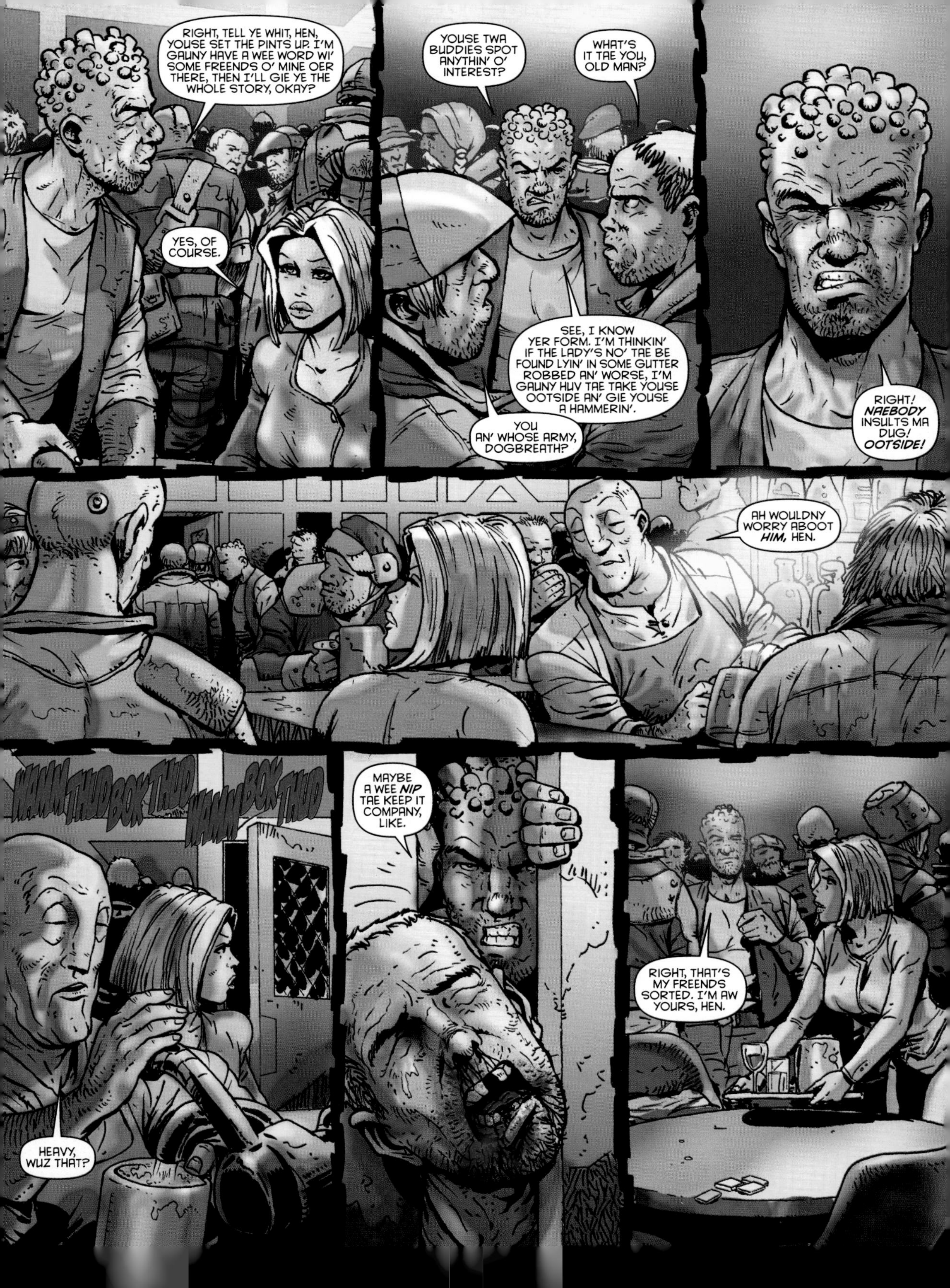
RIGHT, TELL YE WHIT, HEN, YOUSE SET THE PINTS UP. I'M GAUNY HAVE A WEE WORD WI' SOME FREENDS O' MINE OER THERE, THEN I'LL GIE YE THE WHOLE STORY, OKAY?
YES, OF COURSE.
YOUSE TWA BUDDIES SPOT ANYTHIN' O' INTEREST?
WHAT'S IT TAE YOU, OLD MAN?
SEE, I KNOW YER FORM. I'M THINKIN' IF THE LADY'S NO' TAE BE FOUND LYIN' IN SOME GUTTER ROBBED AN' WORSE, I'M GAUNY HUV TAE TAKE YOUSE OOTSIDE AN' GIE YOUSE A HAMMERIN'.
YOU AN' WHOSE ARMY, DOGBREATH?
RIGHT! NAEBODY INSULTS MA DUG! OOTSIDE!
AH WOULDNY WORRY ABOOT HIM, HEN.
HAMM THUD BOK THUD HAMM BOK THUD
HEAVY, WUZ THAT?
MAYBE A WEE NIP TAE KEEP IT COMPANY, LIKE.
RIGHT, THAT'S MY FREENDS SORTED. I'M AW YOURS, HEN.

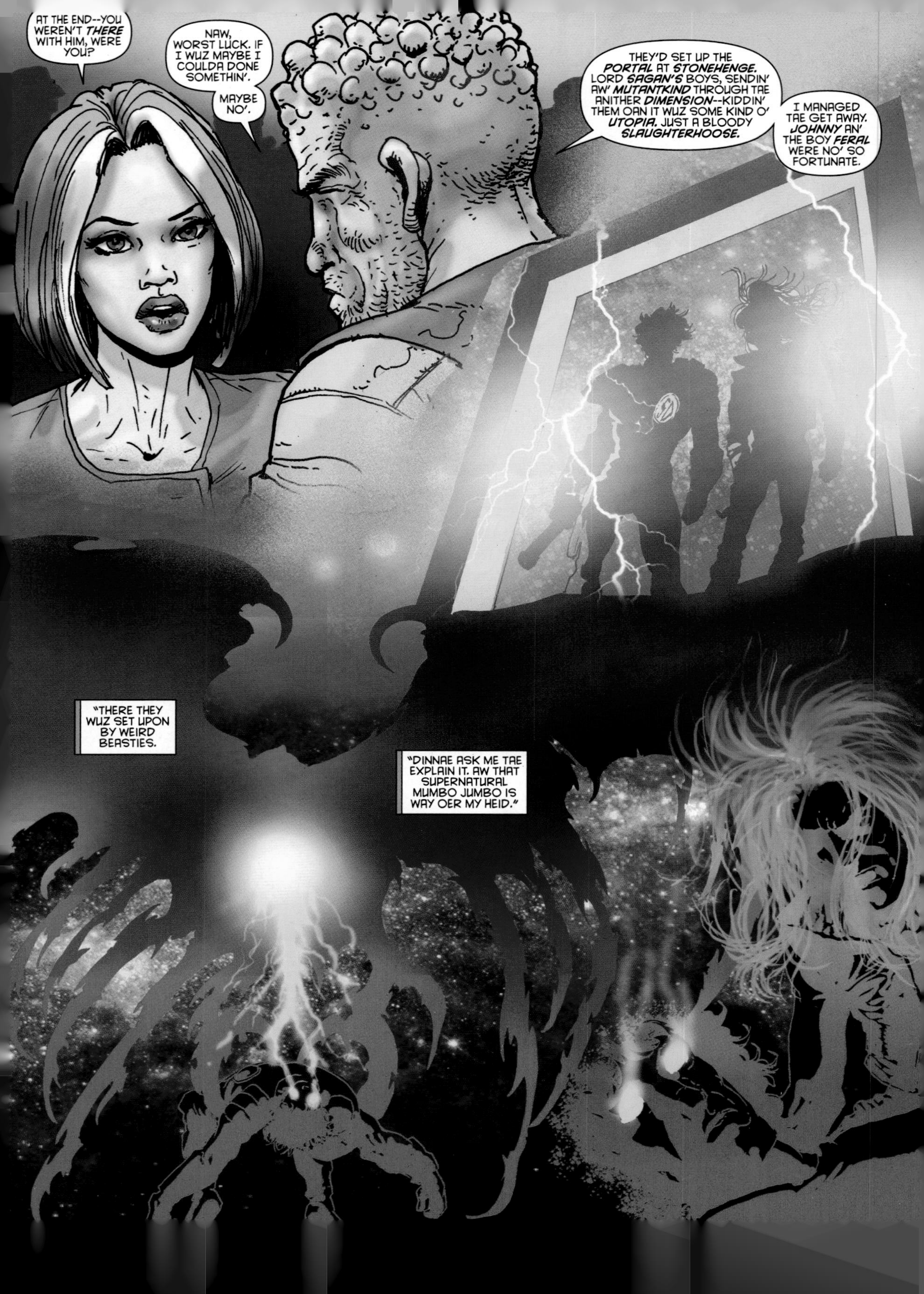
AT THE END--YOU WEREN'T THERE WITH HIM, WERE YOU?
NAW, WORST LUCK. IF I WUZ MAYBE I COULDA DONE SOMETHIN'.
MAYBE NO'.
THEY'D SET UP THE PORTAL AT STONEHENGE. LORD SAGAN'S BOYS, SENDIN' AW' MUTANTKIND THROUGH TAE ANITHER DIMENSION--KIDDIN' THEM OAN IT WUZ SOME KIND O' UTOPIA. JUST A BLOODY SLAUGHTERHOOSE.
I MANAGED TAE GET AWAY. JOHNNY AN' THE BOY FERAL WERE NO' SO FORTUNATE.
"THERE THEY WUZ SET UPON BY WEIRD BEASTIES.
"DINNAE ASK ME TAE EXPLAIN IT. AW THAT SUPERNATURAL MUMBO JUMBO IS WAY OER MY HEID."

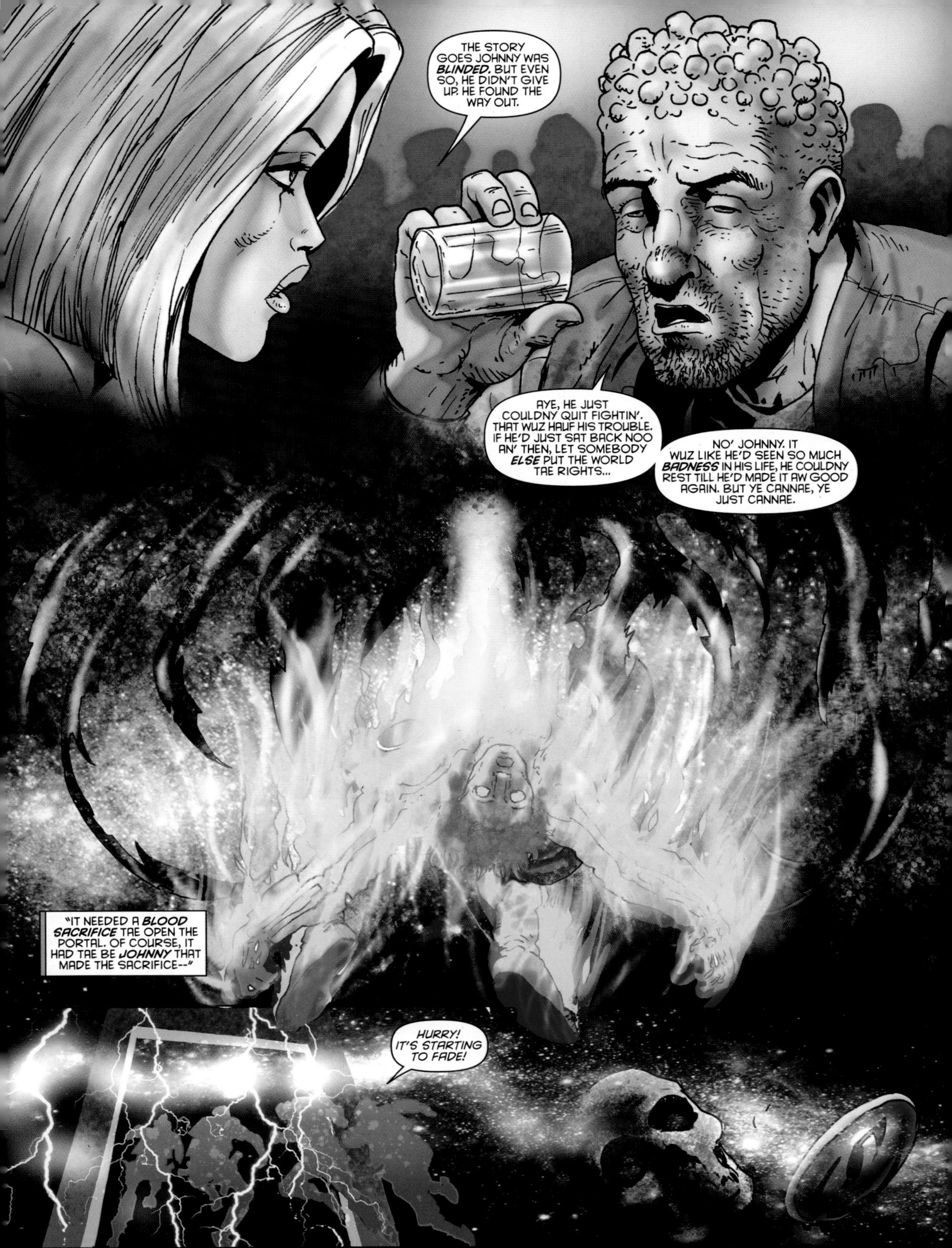
THE STORY GOES JOHNNY WAS BLINDED. BUT EVEN SO, HE DIDN'T GIVE UP. HE FOUND THE WAY OUT.
AYE, HE JUST COULDNY QUIT FIGHTIN'. THAT WUZ HAUF HIS TROUBLE. IF HE'D JUST SAT BACK NOO AN' THEN, LET SOMEBODY ELSE PUT THE WORLD TAE RIGHTS...
NO' JOHNNY. IT WUZ LIKE HE'D SEEN SO MUCH BADNESS IN HIS LIFE, HE COULDNY REST TILL HE'D MADE IT AW GOOD AGAIN. BUT YE CANNAE, YE JUST CANNAE.
"IT NEEDED A BLOOD SACRIFICE TAE OPEN THE PORTAL. OF COURSE, IT HAD TAE BE JOHNNY THAT MADE THE SACRIFICE--"
HURRY! IT'S STARTING TO FADE!

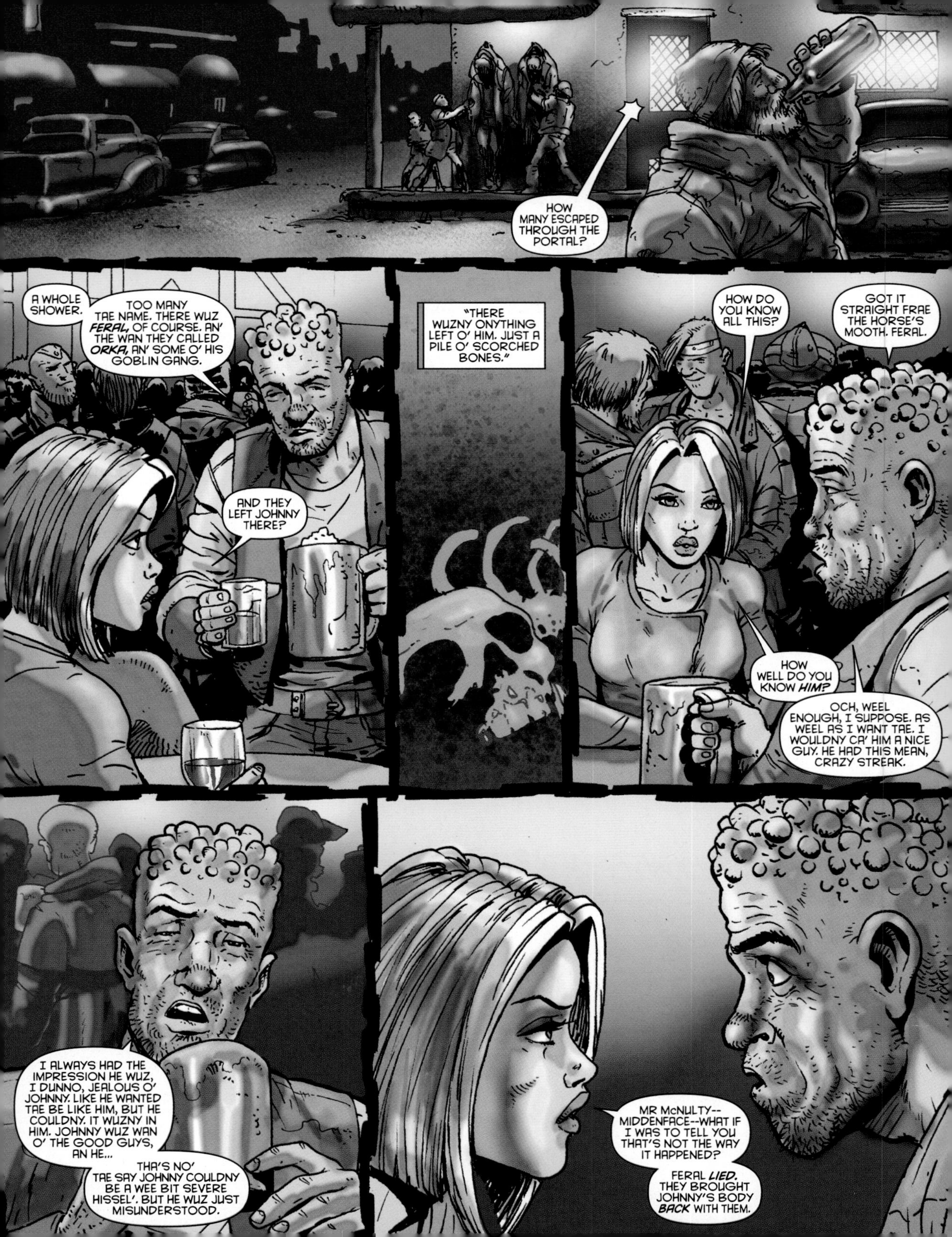
HOW MANY ESCAPED THROUGH THE PORTAL?
A WHOLE SHOWER.
TOO MANY TAE NAME. THERE WUZ FERAL, OF COURSE. AN' THE WAN THEY CALLED ORKA, AN' SOME O' HIS GOBLIN GANG.
AND THEY LEFT JOHNNY THERE?
"THERE WUZNY ONYTHING LEFT O' HIM. JUST A PILE O' SCORCHED BONES."
HOW DO YOU KNOW ALL THIS?
GOT IT STRAIGHT FRAE THE HORSE'S MOOTH. FERAL.
HOW WELL DO YOU KNOW HIM?
OCH, WEEL ENOUGH, I SUPPOSE. AS WEEL AS I WANT TAE. I WOULDNY CA' HIM A NICE GUY. HE HAD THIS MEAN, CRAZY STREAK.
I ALWAYS HAD THE IMPRESSION HE WUZ, I DUNNO, JEALOUS O' JOHNNY. LIKE HE WANTED TAE BE LIKE HIM, BUT HE COULDNY. IT WUZNY IN HIM. JOHNNY WUZ WAN O' THE GOOD GUYS, AN HE...
THA'S NO' TAE SAY JOHNNY COULDNY BE A WEE BIT SEVERE HISSEL'. BUT HE WUZ JUST MISUNDERSTOOD.
MR McNULTY--MIDDENFACE--WHAT IF I WAS TO TELL YOU THAT'S NOT THE WAY IT HAPPENED?
FERAL LIED. THEY BROUGHT JOHNNY'S BODY BACK WITH THEM.

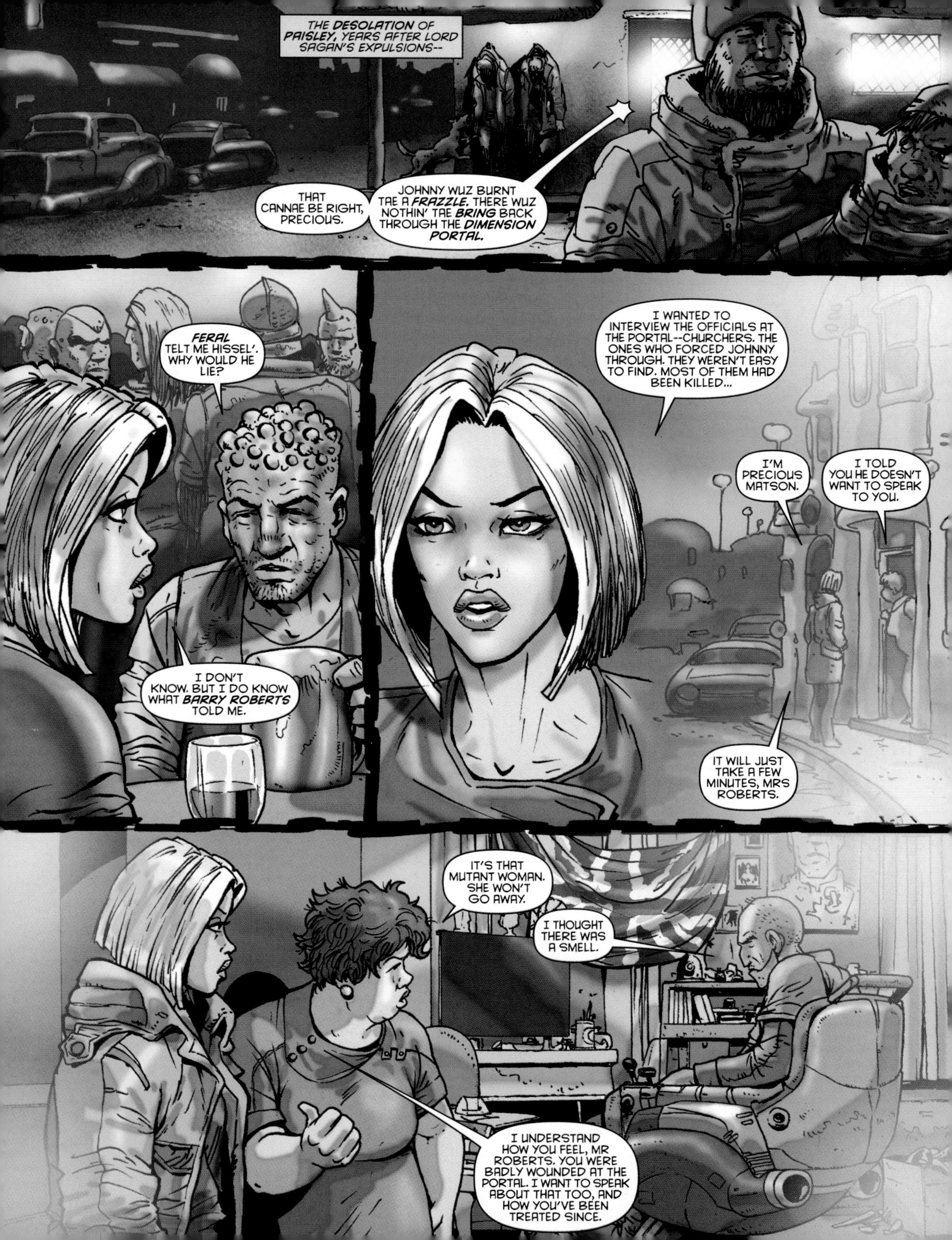

THE DESOLATION OF PAISLEY, YEARS AFTER LORD SAGAN'S EXPULSIONS--
JOHNNY WUZ BURNT TAE A FRAZZLE. THERE WUZ NOTHIN' TAE BRING BACK THROUGH THE DIMENSION PORTAL.
THAT CANNAE BE RIGHT, PRECIOUS.
FERAL TELT ME HISSEL'. WHY WOULD HE LIE?
I DON'T KNOW. BUT I DO KNOW WHAT BARRY ROBERTS TOLD ME.
I WANTED TO INTERVIEW THE OFFICIALS AT THE PORTAL--CHURCHERS. THE ONES WHO FORCED JOHNNY THROUGH. THEY WEREN'T EASY TO FIND. MOST OF THEM HAD BEEN KILLED...
I'M PRECIOUS MATSON.
I TOLD YOU HE DOESN'T WANT TO SPEAK TO YOU.
IT WILL JUST TAKE A FEW MINUTES, MRS ROBERTS.
IT'S THAT MUTANT WOMAN. SHE WON'T GO AWAY.
I THOUGHT THERE WAS A SMELL.
I UNDERSTAND HOW YOU FEEL, MR ROBERTS. YOU WERE BADLY WOUNDED AT THE PORTAL. I WANT TO SPEAK ABOUT THAT TOO, AND HOW YOU'VE BEEN TREATED SINCE.

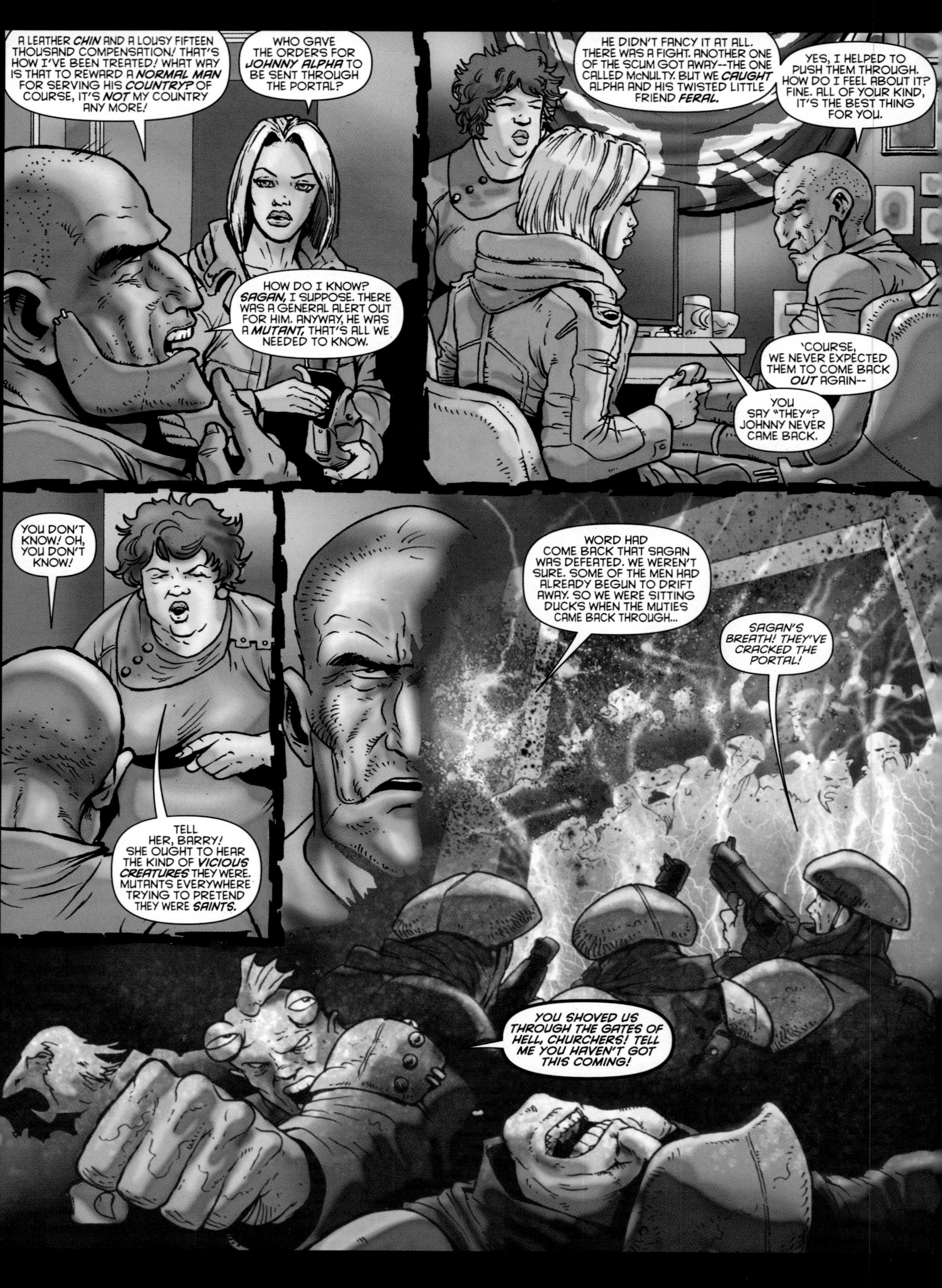

A LEATHER CHIN AND A LOUSY FIFTEEN THOUSAND COMPENSATION! THAT'S HOW I'VE BEEN TREATED! WHAT WAY IS THAT TO REWARD A NORMAL MAN FOR SERVING HIS COUNTRY? OF COURSE, IT'S NOT MY COUNTRY ANY MORE!
WHO GAVE THE ORDERS FOR JOHNNY ALPHA TO BE SENT THROUGH THE PORTAL?
HOW DO I KNOW? SAGAN, I SUPPOSE. THERE WAS A GENERAL ALERT OUT FOR HIM. ANYWAY, HE WAS A MUTANT, THAT'S ALL WE NEEDED TO KNOW.
HE DIDN'T FANCY IT AT ALL. THERE WAS A FIGHT. ANOTHER ONE OF THE SCUM GOT AWAY--THE ONE CALLED McNULTY. BUT WE CAUGHT ALPHA AND HIS TWISTED LITTLE FRIEND FERAL.
YES, I HELPED TO PUSH THEM THROUGH. HOW DO I FEEL ABOUT IT? FINE. ALL OF YOUR KIND, IT'S THE BEST THING FOR YOU.
'COURSE, WE NEVER EXPECTED THEM TO COME BACK OUT AGAIN--
YOU SAY "THEY"? JOHNNY NEVER CAME BACK.
YOU DON'T KNOW! OH, YOU DON'T KNOW!
TELL HER, BARRY! SHE OUGHT TO HEAR THE KIND OF VICIOUS CREATURES THEY WERE. MUTANTS EVERYWHERE TRYING TO PRETEND THEY WERE SAINTS.
WORD HAD COME BACK THAT SAGAN WAS DEFEATED. WE WEREN'T SURE. SOME OF THE MEN HAD ALREADY BEGUN TO DRIFT AWAY. SO WE WERE SITTING DUCKS WHEN THE MUTIES CAME BACK THROUGH...
SAGAN'S BREATH! THEY'VE CRACKED THE PORTAL!
YOU SHOVED US THROUGH THE GATES OF HELL, CHURCHERS! TELL ME YOU HAVEN'T GOT THIS COMING!

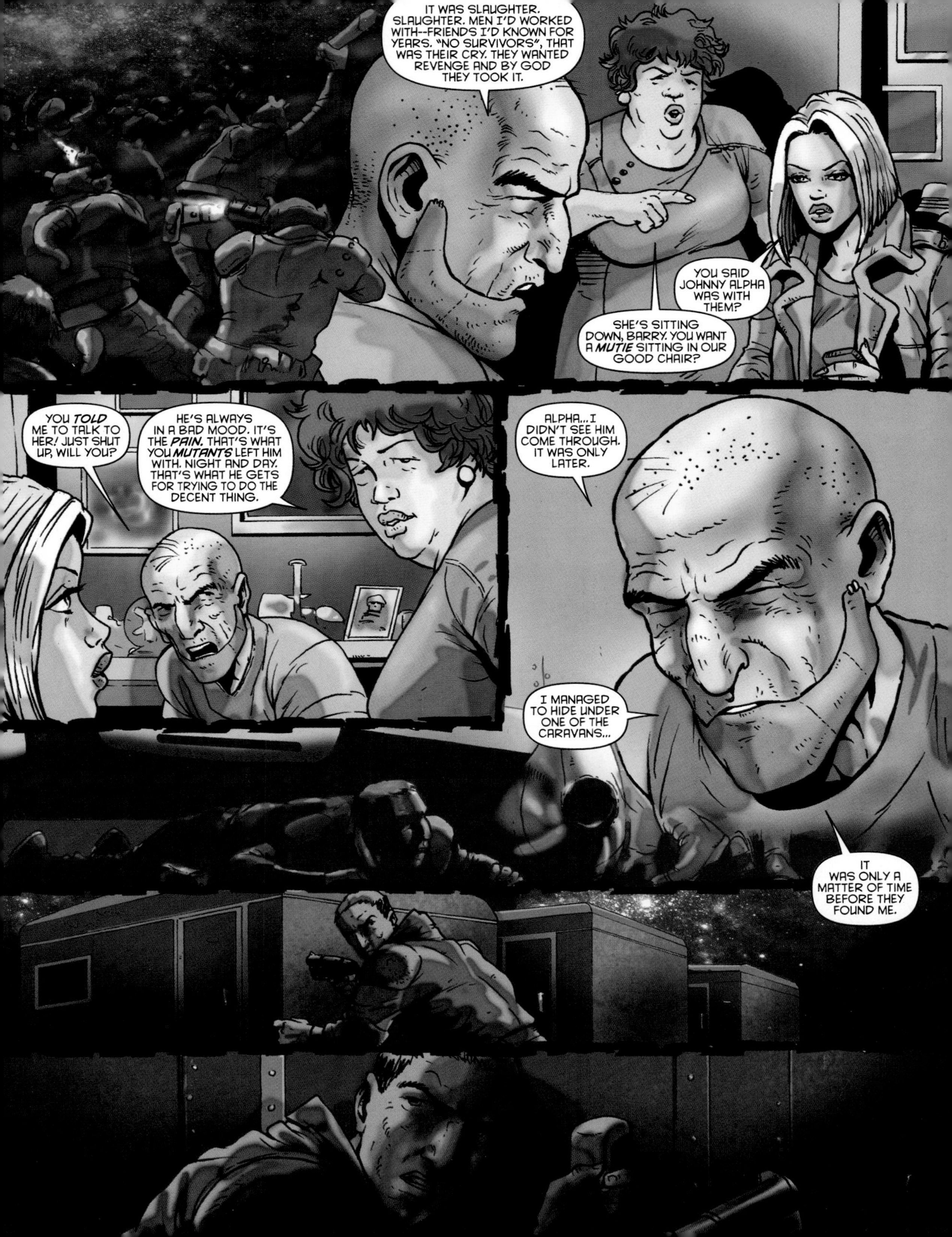
IT WAS SLAUGHTER. SLAUGHTER. MEN I'D WORKED WITH--FRIENDS I'D KNOWN FOR YEARS. "NO SURVIVORS", THAT WAS THEIR CRY. THEY WANTED REVENGE AND BY GOD THEY TOOK IT.
SHE'S SITTING DOWN, BARRY. YOU WANT A *MUTIE* SITTING IN OUR GOOD CHAIR?
YOU SAID JOHNNY ALPHA WAS WITH THEM?
YOU *TOLD* ME TO TALK TO HER! JUST SHUT UP, WILL YOU?
HE'S ALWAYS IN A BAD MOOD. IT'S THE *PAIN.* THAT'S WHAT YOU *MUTANTS* LEFT HIM WITH. NIGHT AND DAY. THAT'S WHAT HE GETS FOR TRYING TO DO THE DECENT THING.
ALPHA... I DIDN'T SEE HIM COME THROUGH. IT WAS ONLY LATER.
I MANAGED TO HIDE UNDER ONE OF THE CARAVANS...
IT WAS ONLY A MATTER OF TIME BEFORE THEY FOUND ME.

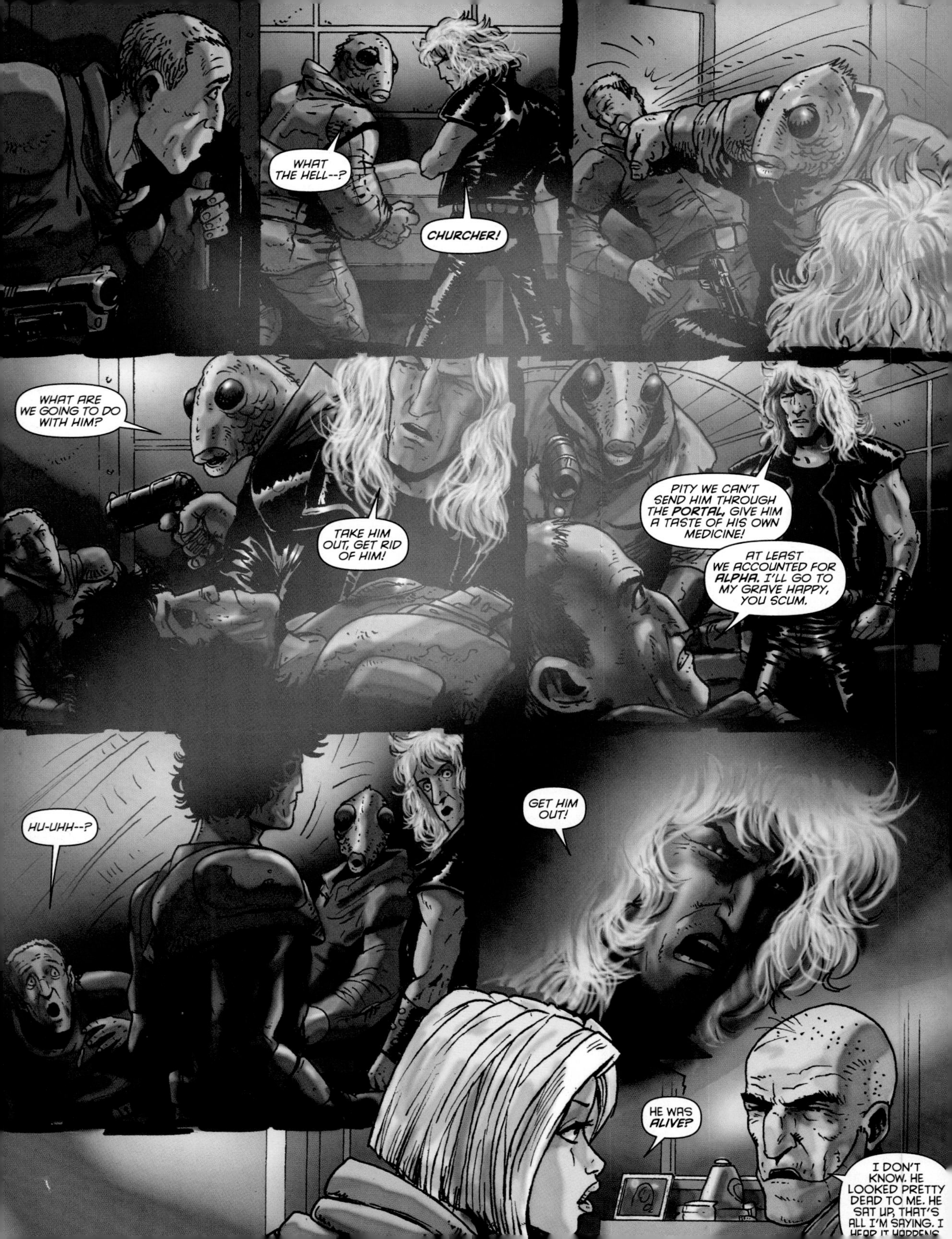
WHAT THE HELL--?
CHURCHER!
WHAT ARE WE GOING TO DO WITH HIM?
TAKE HIM OUT, GET RID OF HIM!
PITY WE CAN'T SEND HIM THROUGH THE PORTAL, GIVE HIM A TASTE OF HIS OWN MEDICINE!
AT LEAST WE ACCOUNTED FOR ALPHA. I'LL GO TO MY GRAVE HAPPY, YOU SCUM.
HU-UHH--?
GET HIM OUT!
HE WAS ALIVE?
I DON'T KNOW. HE LOOKED PRETTY DEAD TO ME. HE SAT UP, THAT'S ALL I'M SAYING. I

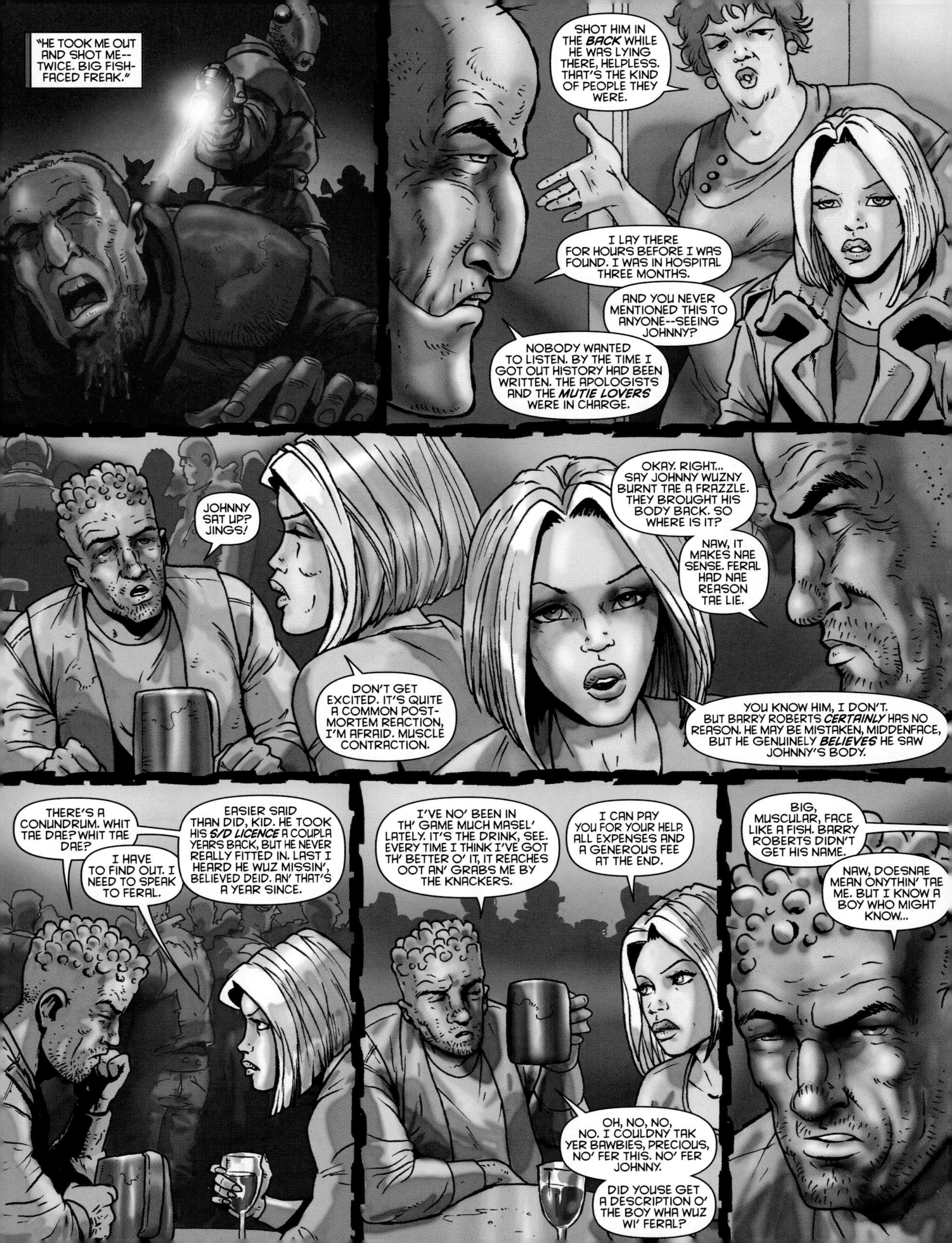
"HE TOOK ME OUT AND SHOT ME--TWICE. BIG FISH-FACED FREAK."
SHOT HIM IN THE BACK WHILE HE WAS LYING THERE, HELPLESS. THAT'S THE KIND OF PEOPLE THEY WERE.
I LAY THERE FOR HOURS BEFORE I WAS FOUND. I WAS IN HOSPITAL THREE MONTHS.
AND YOU NEVER MENTIONED THIS TO ANYONE--SEEING JOHNNY?
NOBODY WANTED TO LISTEN. BY THE TIME I GOT OUT HISTORY HAD BEEN WRITTEN. THE APOLOGISTS AND THE MUTIE LOVERS WERE IN CHARGE.
JOHNNY SAT UP? JINGS!
DON'T GET EXCITED. IT'S QUITE A COMMON POST-MORTEM REACTION, I'M AFRAID. MUSCLE CONTRACTION.
OKAY. RIGHT... SAY JOHNNY WUZNY BURNT TAE A FRAZZLE. THEY BROUGHT HIS BODY BACK. SO WHERE IS IT?
NAW, IT MAKES NAE SENSE. FERAL HAD NAE REASON TAE LIE.
YOU KNOW HIM, I DON'T. BUT BARRY ROBERTS CERTAINLY HAS NO REASON. HE MAY BE MISTAKEN, MIDDENFACE, BUT HE GENUINELY BELIEVES HE SAW JOHNNY'S BODY.
THERE'S A CONUNDRUM. WHIT TAE DAE? WHIT TAE DAE?
I HAVE TO FIND OUT. I NEED TO SPEAK TO FERAL.
EASIER SAID THAN DID, KID. HE TOOK HIS S/D LICENCE A COUPLA YEARS BACK, BUT HE NEVER REALLY FITTED IN. LAST I HEARD HE WUZ MISSIN', BELIEVED DEID. AN' THAT'S A YEAR SINCE.
I'VE NO' BEEN IN TH' GAME MUCH MASEL' LATELY. IT'S THE DRINK, SEE. EVERY TIME I THINK I'VE GOT TH' BETTER O' IT, IT REACHES OOT AN' GRABS ME BY THE KNACKERS.
I CAN PAY YOU FOR YOUR HELP. ALL EXPENSES AND A GENEROUS FEE AT THE END.
OH, NO, NO, NO. I COULDNY TAK YER BAWBIES, PRECIOUS, NO' FER THIS. NO' FER JOHNNY.
DID YOUSE GET A DESCRIPTION O' THE BOY WHA WUZ WI' FERAL?
BIG, MUSCULAR, FACE LIKE A FISH. BARRY ROBERTS DIDN'T GET HIS NAME.
NAW, DOESNAE MEAN ONYTHIN' TAE ME. BUT I KNOW A BOY WHO MIGHT KNOW...

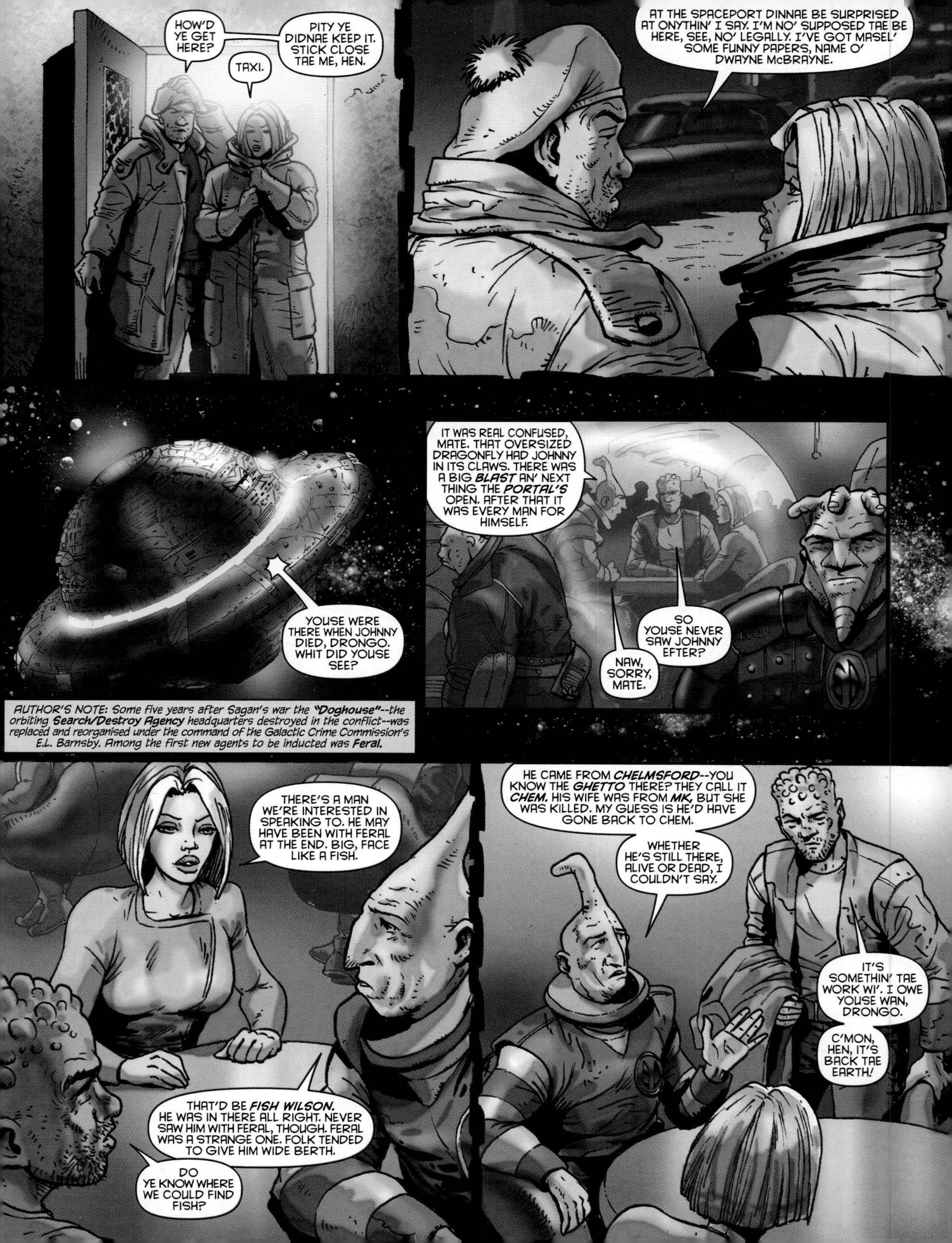
HOW'D YE GET HERE?
TAXI.
PITY YE DIDNAE KEEP IT. STICK CLOSE TAE ME, HEN.
AT THE SPACEPORT DINNAE BE SURPRISED AT ONYTHIN' I SAY. I'M NO' SUPPOSED TAE BE HERE, SEE, NO' LEGALLY. I'VE GOT MASEL' SOME FUNNY PAPERS, NAME O' DWAYNE McBRAYNE.
YOUSE WERE THERE WHEN JOHNNY DIED, DRONGO. WHIT DID YOUSE SEE?
AUTHOR'S NOTE: Some five years after Sagan's war the "Doghouse"--the orbiting Search/Destroy Agency headquarters destroyed in the conflict--was replaced and reorganised under the command of the Galactic Crime Commission's E.L. Barnsby. Among the first new agents to be inducted was Feral.
IT WAS REAL CONFUSED, MATE. THAT OVERSIZED DRAGONFLY HAD JOHNNY IN ITS CLAWS. THERE WAS A BIG BLAST AN' NEXT THING THE PORTAL'S OPEN. AFTER THAT IT WAS EVERY MAN FOR HIMSELF.
SO YOUSE NEVER SAW JOHNNY EFTER?
NAW, SORRY, MATE.
THERE'S A MAN WE'RE INTERESTED IN SPEAKING TO. HE MAY HAVE BEEN WITH FERAL AT THE END. BIG, FACE LIKE A FISH.
THAT'D BE FISH WILSON. HE WAS IN THERE ALL RIGHT. NEVER SAW HIM WITH FERAL, THOUGH. FERAL WAS A STRANGE ONE. FOLK TENDED TO GIVE HIM WIDE BERTH.
DO YE KNOW WHERE WE COULD FIND FISH?
HE CAME FROM CHELMSFORD--YOU KNOW THE GHETTO THERE? THEY CALL IT CHEM. HIS WIFE WAS FROM MK, BUT SHE WAS KILLED. MY GUESS IS HE'D HAVE GONE BACK TO CHEM.
WHETHER HE'S STILL THERE, ALIVE OR DEAD, I COULDN'T SAY.
IT'S SOMETHIN' TAE WORK WI'. I OWE YOUSE WAN, DRONGO.
C'MON, HEN, IT'S BACK TAE EARTH!

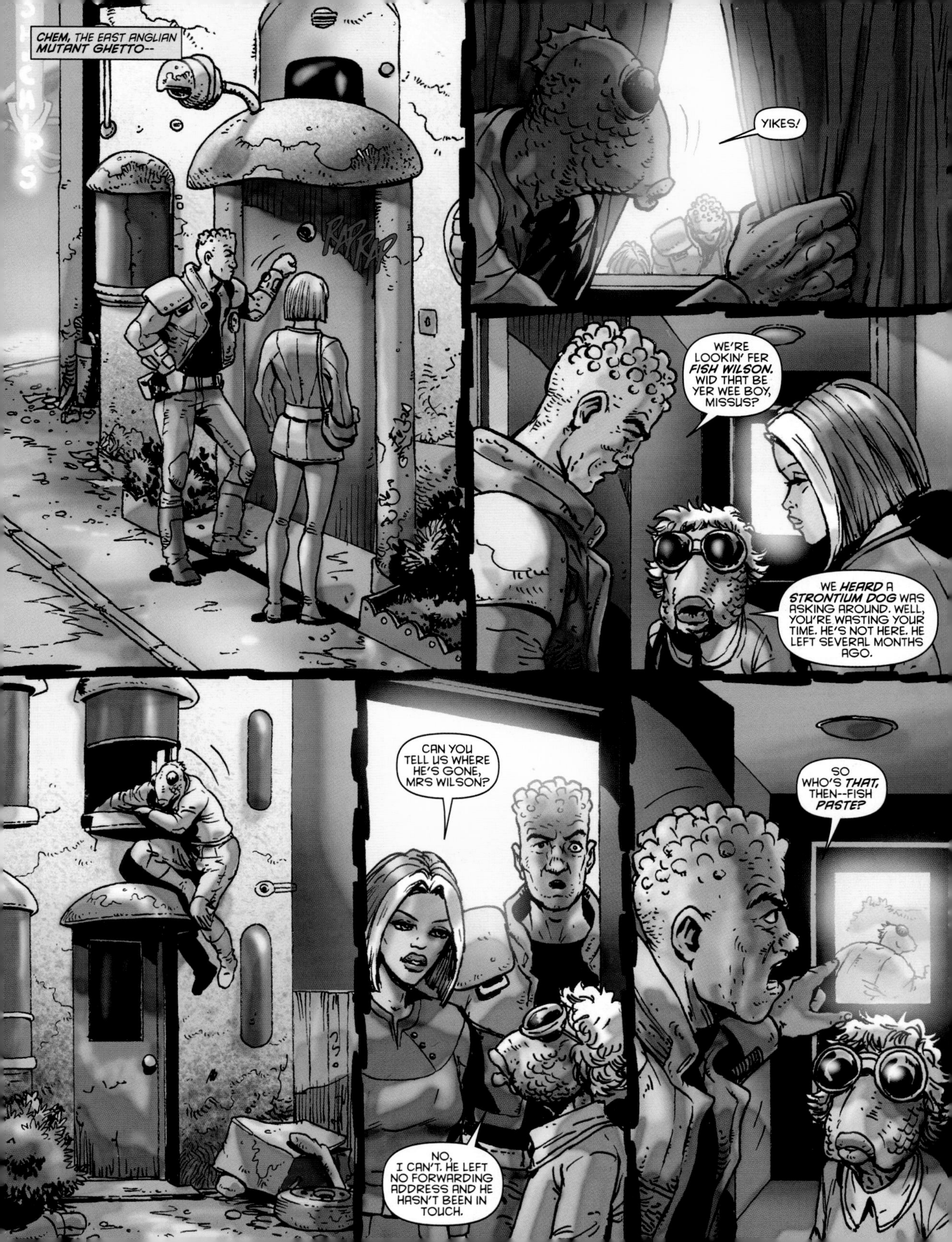

CHEM, THE EAST ANGLIAN MUTANT GHETTO--
RAP RAP
YIKES!
WE'RE LOOKIN' FER FISH WILSON. WID THAT BE YER WEE BOY, MISSUS?
WE HEARD A STRONTIUM DOG WAS ASKING AROUND. WELL, YOU'RE WASTING YOUR TIME. HE'S NOT HERE. HE LEFT SEVERAL MONTHS AGO.
CAN YOU TELL US WHERE HE'S GONE, MRS WILSON?
NO, I CAN'T. HE LEFT NO FORWARDING ADDRESS AND HE HASN'T BEEN IN TOUCH.
SO WHO'S THAT, THEN--FISH PASTE?

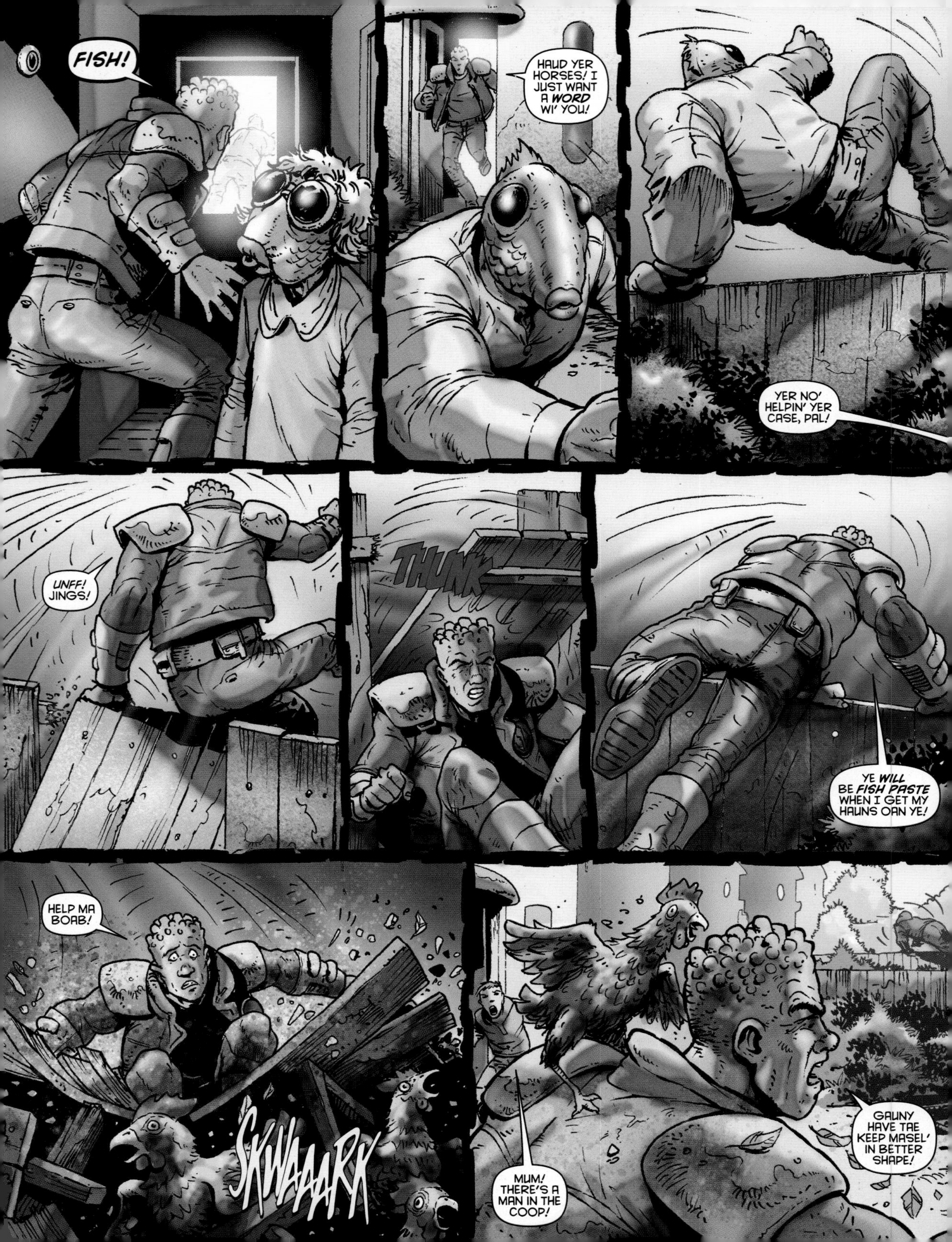
FISH!
HAUD YER HORSES! I JUST WANT A WORD WI' YOU!
YER NO' HELPIN' YER CASE, PAL!
UNFF! JINGS!
THUNK
YE WILL BE FISH PASTE WHEN I GET MY HAUNS OAN YE!
HELP MA BOAB!
SKWAAARK
MUM! THERE'S A MAN IN THE COOP!
GAUNY HAVE TAE KEEP MASEL' IN BETTER SHAPE!

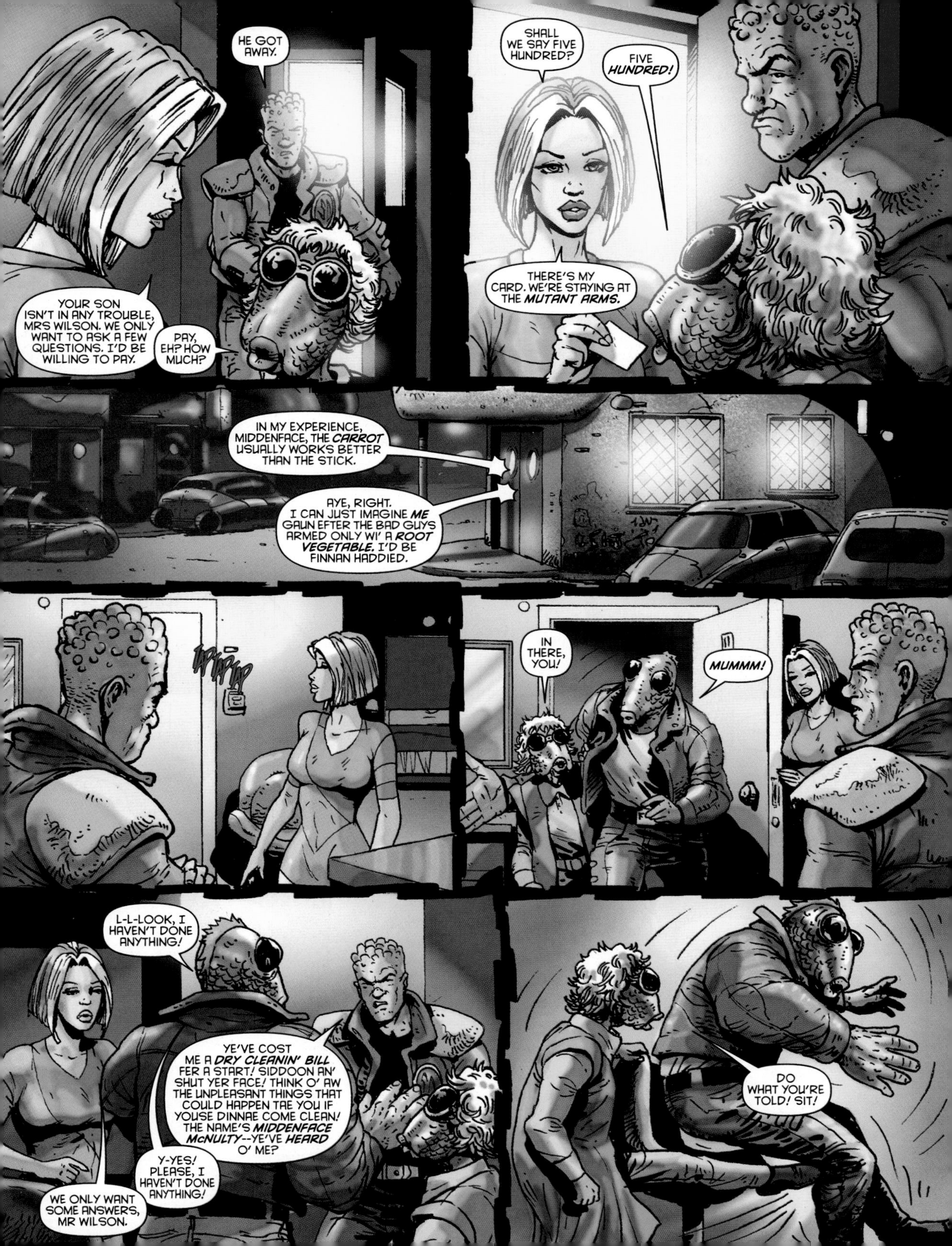
HE GOT AWAY.
YOUR SON ISN'T IN ANY TROUBLE, MRS WILSON. WE ONLY WANT TO ASK A FEW QUESTIONS. I'D BE WILLING TO PAY.
PAY, EH? HOW MUCH?
SHALL WE SAY FIVE HUNDRED?
FIVE HUNDRED!
THERE'S MY CARD. WE'RE STAYING AT THE MUTANT ARMS.
IN MY EXPERIENCE, MIDDENFACE, THE CARROT USUALLY WORKS BETTER THAN THE STICK.
AYE, RIGHT. I CAN JUST IMAGINE ME GAUN EFTER THE BAD GUYS ARMED ONLY WI' A ROOT VEGETABLE. I'D BE FINNAN HADDIED.
TAP TAP TAP
IN THERE, YOU!
MUMMM!
L-L-LOOK, I HAVEN'T DONE ANYTHING!
YE'VE COST ME A DRY CLEANIN' BILL FER A START! SIDDOON AN' SHUT YER FACE! THINK O' AW THE UNPLEASANT THINGS THAT COULD HAPPEN TAE YOU IF YOUSE DINNAE COME CLEAN! THE NAME'S MIDDENFACE McNULTY--YE'VE HEARD O' ME?
Y-YES! PLEASE, I HAVEN'T DONE ANYTHING!
WE ONLY WANT SOME ANSWERS, MR WILSON.
DO WHAT YOU'RE TOLD! SIT!

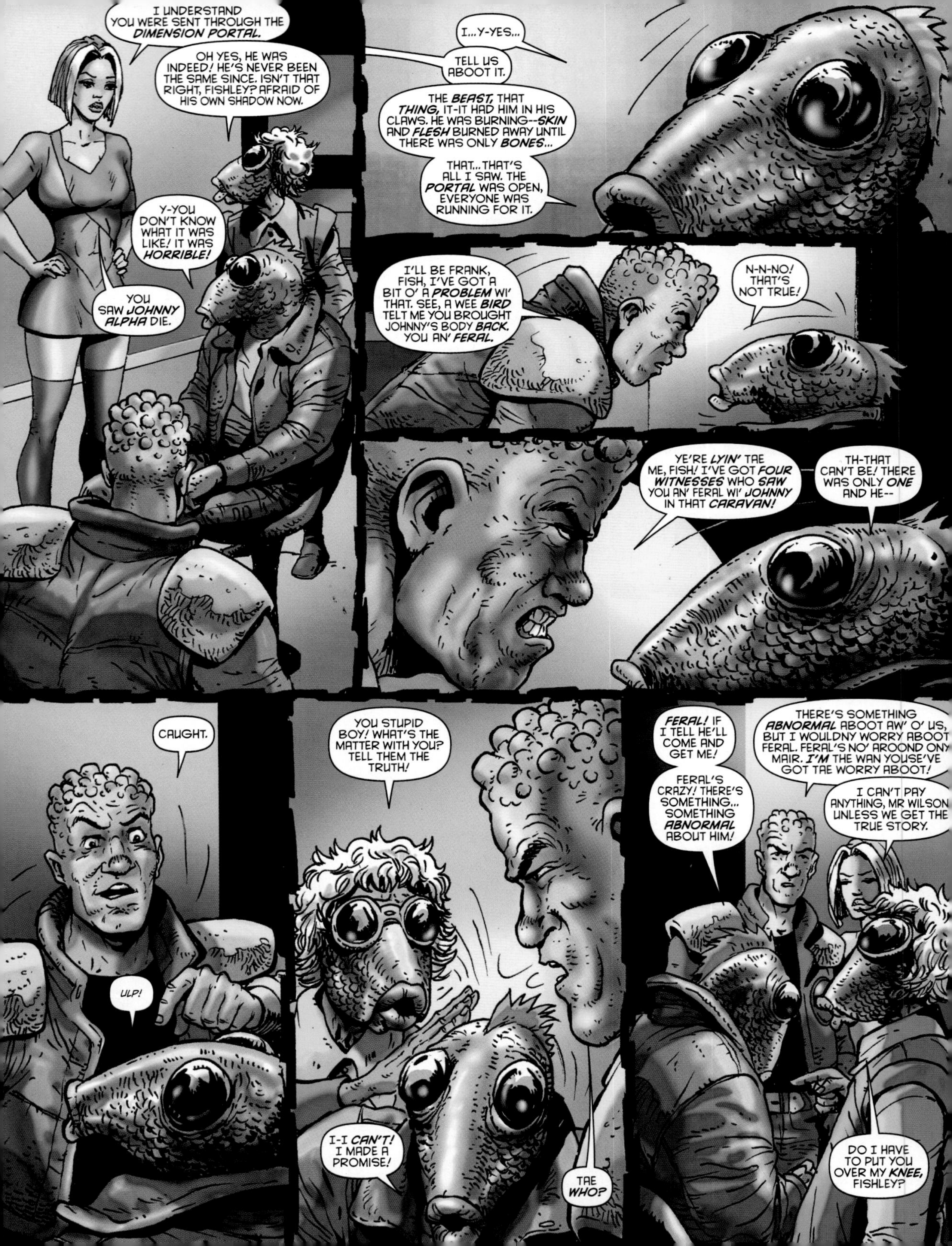
I UNDERSTAND YOU WERE SENT THROUGH THE *DIMENSION PORTAL.*
OH YES, HE WAS INDEED! HE'S NEVER BEEN THE SAME SINCE. ISN'T THAT RIGHT, FISHLEY? AFRAID OF HIS OWN SHADOW NOW.
Y-YOU DON'T KNOW WHAT IT WAS LIKE! IT WAS *HORRIBLE!*
YOU SAW *JOHNNY ALPHA* DIE.
I...Y-YES...
TELL US ABOOT IT.
THE *BEAST,* THAT *THING,* IT-IT HAD HIM IN HIS CLAWS. HE WAS BURNING--*SKIN* AND *FLESH* BURNED AWAY UNTIL THERE WAS ONLY *BONES*...
THAT... THAT'S ALL I SAW. THE *PORTAL* WAS OPEN, EVERYONE WAS RUNNING FOR IT.
I'LL BE FRANK, FISH, I'VE GOT A BIT O' A *PROBLEM* WI' THAT. SEE, A WEE *BIRD* TELT ME YOU BROUGHT JOHNNY'S BODY *BACK.* YOU AN' *FERAL.*
N-N-NO! THAT'S NOT TRUE!
YE'RE *LYIN'* TAE ME, FISH! I'VE GOT *FOUR WITNESSES* WHO *SAW* YOU AN' FERAL WI' *JOHNNY* IN THAT *CARAVAN!*
TH-THAT CAN'T BE! THERE WAS ONLY *ONE* AND HE--
CAUGHT.
ULP!
YOU STUPID BOY! WHAT'S THE MATTER WITH YOU? TELL THEM THE TRUTH!
I-I *CAN'T!* I MADE A PROMISE!
TAE *WHO?*
FERAL! IF I TELL HE'LL COME AND GET ME!
FERAL'S CRAZY! THERE'S SOMETHING... SOMETHING *ABNORMAL* ABOUT HIM!
THERE'S SOMETHING *ABNORMAL* ABOOT AW' O' US, BUT I WOULDNY WORRY ABOOT FERAL. FERAL'S NO' AROOND ONY MAIR. *I'M* THE WAN YOUSE'VE GOT TAE WORRY ABOOT!
I CAN'T PAY ANYTHING, MR WILSON UNLESS WE GET THE TRUE STORY.
DO I HAVE TO PUT YOU OVER MY *KNEE,* FISHLEY?

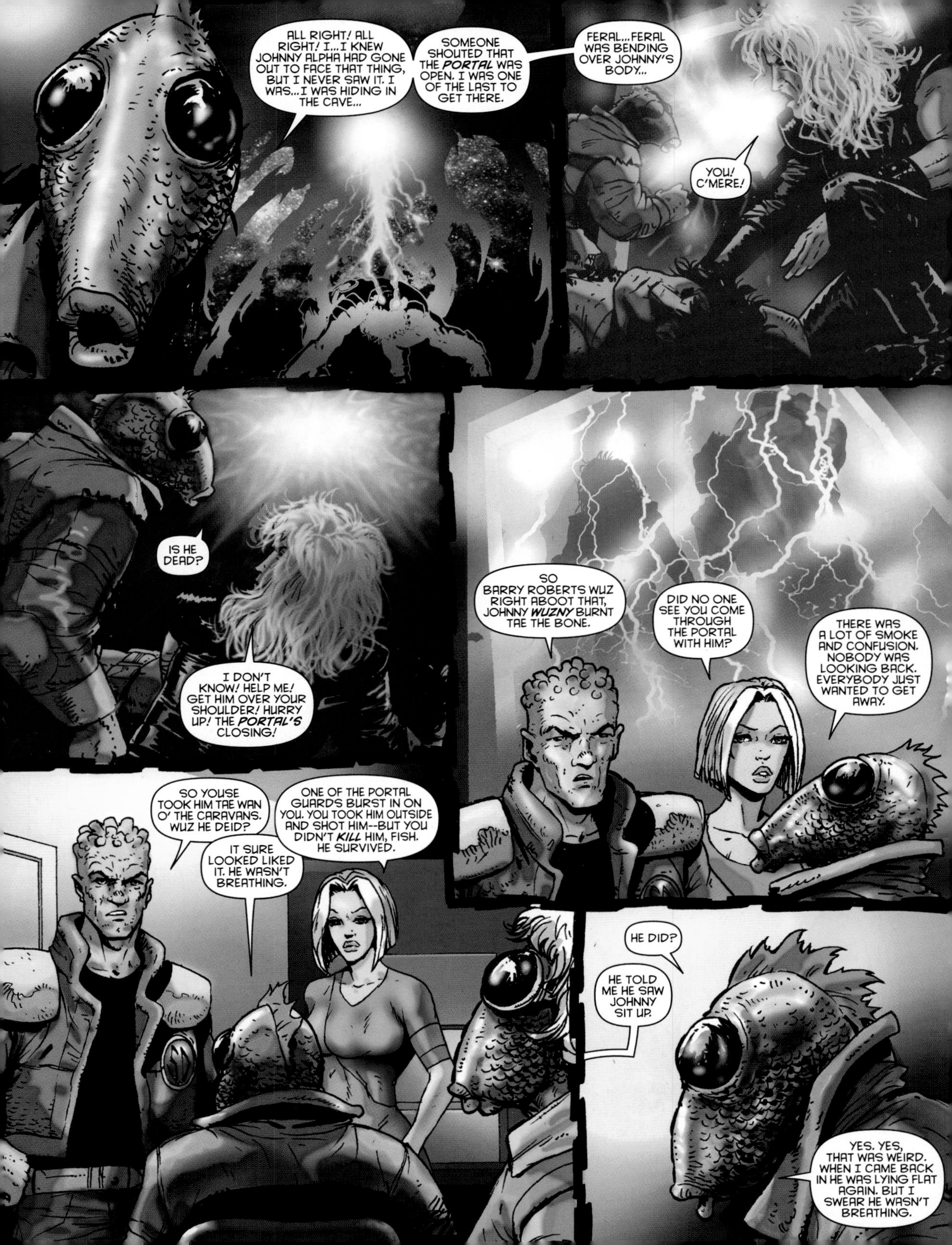
ALL RIGHT! ALL RIGHT! I...I KNEW JOHNNY ALPHA HAD GONE OUT TO FACE THAT THING, BUT I NEVER SAW IT. I WAS...I WAS HIDING IN THE CAVE...
SOMEONE SHOUTED THAT THE PORTAL WAS OPEN. I WAS ONE OF THE LAST TO GET THERE.
FERAL...FERAL WAS BENDING OVER JOHNNY'S BODY...
YOU! C'MERE!
IS HE DEAD?
I DON'T KNOW! HELP ME! GET HIM OVER YOUR SHOULDER! HURRY UP! THE PORTAL'S CLOSING!
SO BARRY ROBERTS WUZ RIGHT ABOOT THAT, JOHNNY WUZNY BURNT TAE THE BONE.
DID NO ONE SEE YOU COME THROUGH THE PORTAL WITH HIM?
THERE WAS A LOT OF SMOKE AND CONFUSION. NOBODY WAS LOOKING BACK. EVERYBODY JUST WANTED TO GET AWAY.
SO YOUSE TOOK HIM TAE WAN O' THE CARAVANS. WUZ HE DEID?
IT SURE LOOKED LIKED IT. HE WASN'T BREATHING.
ONE OF THE PORTAL GUARDS BURST IN ON YOU. YOU TOOK HIM OUTSIDE AND SHOT HIM--BUT YOU DIDN'T KILL HIM, FISH. HE SURVIVED.
HE DID?
HE TOLD ME HE SAW JOHNNY SIT UP.
YES. YES, THAT WAS WEIRD. WHEN I CAME BACK IN HE WAS LYING FLAT AGAIN. BUT I SWEAR HE WASN'T BREATHING.

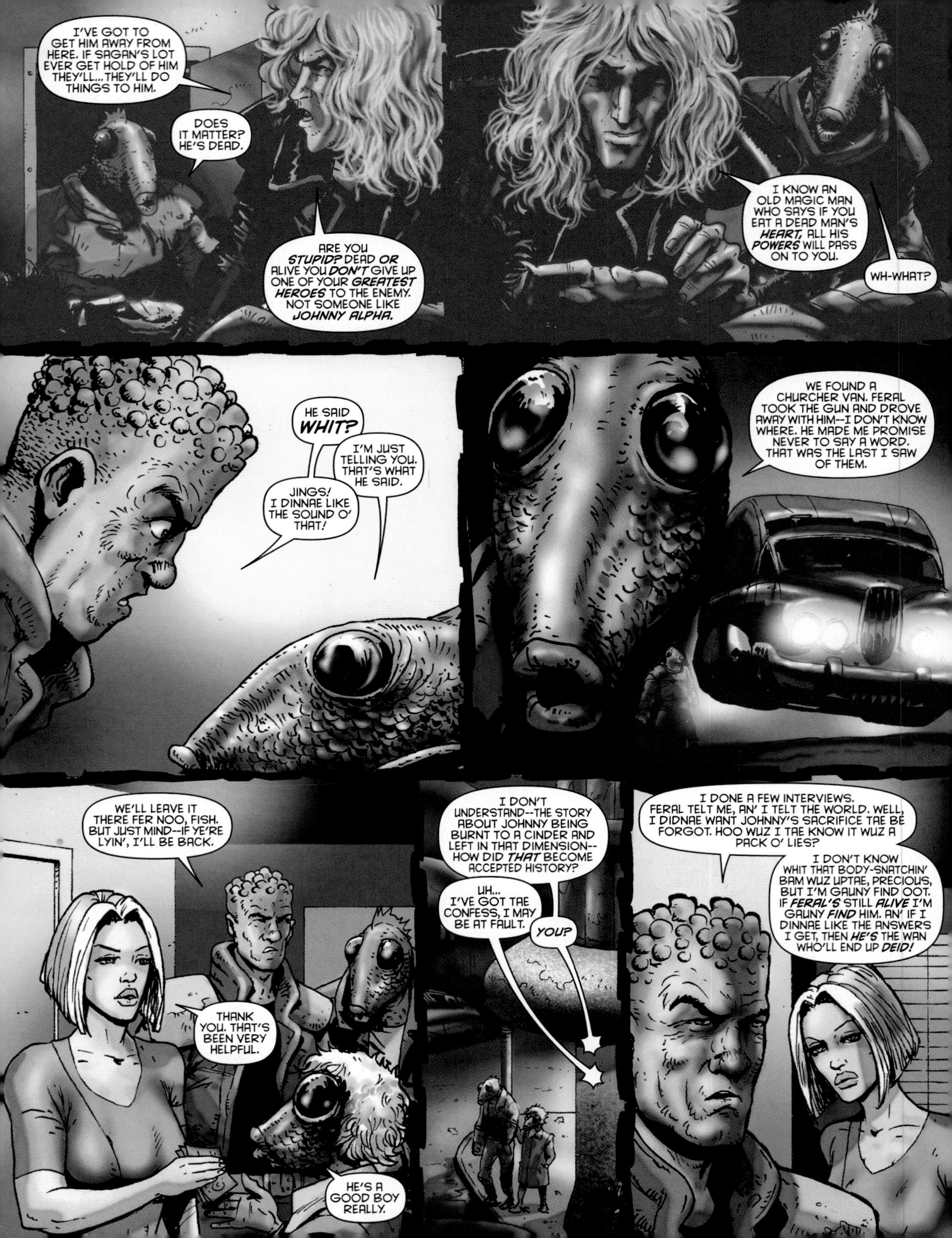
I'VE GOT TO GET HIM AWAY FROM HERE. IF SAGAN'S LOT EVER GET HOLD OF HIM THEY'LL... THEY'LL DO THINGS TO HIM.
DOES IT MATTER? HE'S DEAD.
ARE YOU STUPID? DEAD OR ALIVE YOU DON'T GIVE UP ONE OF YOUR GREATEST HEROES TO THE ENEMY. NOT SOMEONE LIKE JOHNNY ALPHA.
I KNOW AN OLD MAGIC MAN WHO SAYS IF YOU EAT A DEAD MAN'S HEART, ALL HIS POWERS WILL PASS ON TO YOU.
WH-WHAT?
HE SAID WHIT?
I'M JUST TELLING YOU. THAT'S WHAT HE SAID.
JINGS! I DINNAE LIKE THE SOUND O' THAT!
WE FOUND A CHURCHER VAN. FERAL TOOK THE GUN AND DROVE AWAY WITH HIM--I DON'T KNOW WHERE. HE MADE ME PROMISE NEVER TO SAY A WORD. THAT WAS THE LAST I SAW OF THEM.
WE'LL LEAVE IT THERE FER NOO, FISH. BUT JUST MIND--IF YE'RE LYIN', I'LL BE BACK.
THANK YOU. THAT'S BEEN VERY HELPFUL.
HE'S A GOOD BOY REALLY.
I DON'T UNDERSTAND--THE STORY ABOUT JOHNNY BEING BURNT TO A CINDER AND LEFT IN THAT DIMENSION--HOW DID THAT BECOME ACCEPTED HISTORY?
UH... I'VE GOT TAE CONFESS, I MAY BE AT FAULT.
YOU?
I DONE A FEW INTERVIEWS. FERAL TELT ME, AN' I TELT THE WORLD. WELL, I DIDNAE WANT JOHNNY'S SACRIFICE TAE BE FORGOT. HOO WUZ I TAE KNOW IT WUZ A PACK O' LIES?
I DON'T KNOW WHIT THAT BODY-SNATCHIN' BAM WUZ UPTAE, PRECIOUS, BUT I'M GAUNY FIND OOT. IF FERAL'S STILL ALIVE I'M GAUNY FIND HIM. AN' IF I DINNAE LIKE THE ANSWERS I GET, THEN HE'S THE WAN WHO'LL END UP DEID!

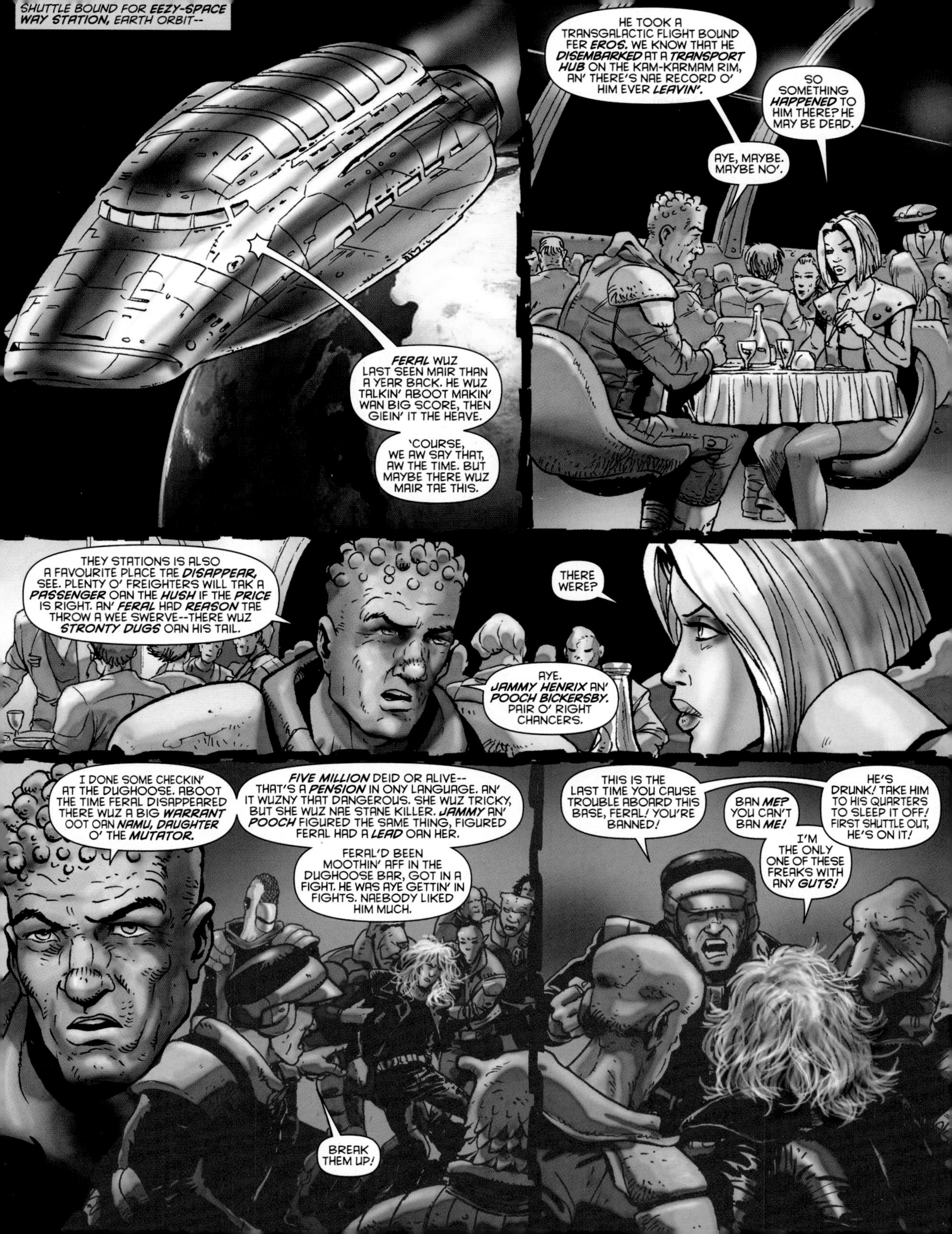

SHUTTLE BOUND FOR EEZY-SPACE WAY STATION, EARTH ORBIT--
FERAL WUZ LAST SEEN MAIR THAN A YEAR BACK. HE WUZ TALKIN' ABOOT MAKIN' WAN BIG SCORE, THEN GIEIN' IT THE HEAVE.
'COURSE, WE AW SAY THAT, AW THE TIME. BUT MAYBE THERE WUZ MAIR TAE THIS.
HE TOOK A TRANSGALACTIC FLIGHT BOUND FER EROS. WE KNOW THAT HE DISEMBARKED AT A TRANSPORT HUB ON THE KAM-KARMAM RIM, AN' THERE'S NAE RECORD O' HIM EVER LEAVIN'.
SO SOMETHING HAPPENED TO HIM THERE? HE MAY BE DEAD.
AYE, MAYBE. MAYBE NO'.
THEY STATIONS IS ALSO A FAVOURITE PLACE TAE DISAPPEAR, SEE. PLENTY O' FREIGHTERS WILL TAK A PASSENGER OAN THE HUSH IF THE PRICE IS RIGHT. AN' FERAL HAD REASON TAE THROW A WEE SWERVE--THERE WUZ STRONTY DUGS OAN HIS TAIL.
THERE WERE?
AYE. JAMMY HENRIX AN' POOCH BICKERSBY. PAIR O' RIGHT CHANCERS.
I DONE SOME CHECKIN' AT THE DUGHOOSE. ABOOT THE TIME FERAL DISAPPEARED THERE WUZ A BIG WARRANT OOT OAN NAMU, DAUGHTER O' THE MUTATOR.
FIVE MILLION DEID OR ALIVE-- THAT'S A PENSION IN ONY LANGUAGE. AN' IT WUZNY THAT DANGEROUS. SHE WUZ TRICKY, BUT SHE WUZ NAE STANE KILLER. JAMMY AN' POOCH FIGURED THE SAME THING, FIGURED FERAL HAD A LEAD OAN HER.
FERAL'D BEEN MOOTHIN' AFF IN THE DUGHOOSE BAR, GOT IN A FIGHT. HE WAS AYE GETTIN' IN FIGHTS. NAEBODY LIKED HIM MUCH.
BREAK THEM UP!
THIS IS THE LAST TIME YOU CAUSE TROUBLE ABOARD THIS BASE, FERAL! YOU'RE BANNED!
BAN ME? YOU CAN'T BAN ME!
I'M THE ONLY ONE OF THESE FREAKS WITH ANY GUTS!
HE'S DRUNK! TAKE HIM TO HIS QUARTERS TO SLEEP IT OFF! FIRST SHUTTLE OUT, HE'S ON IT!

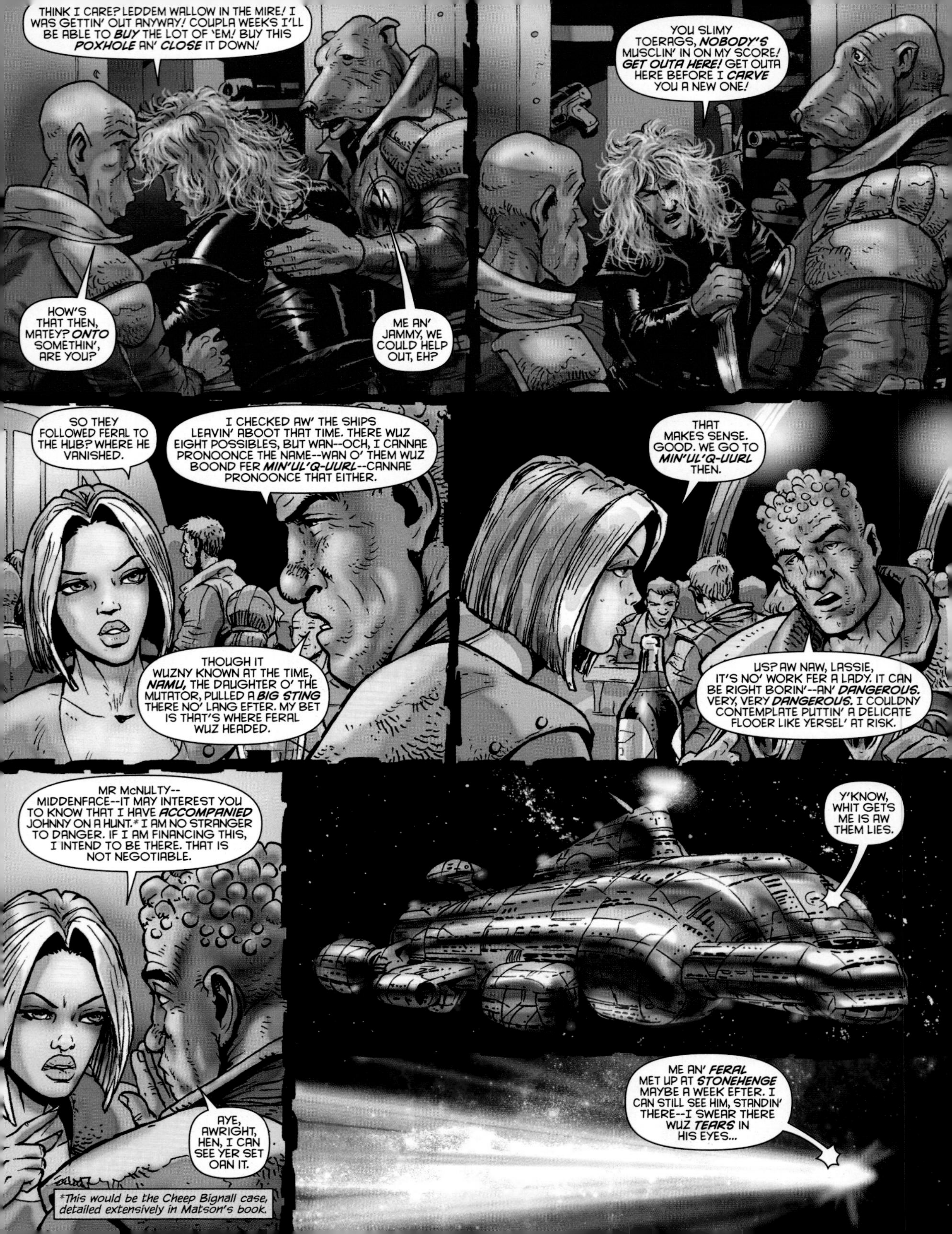
THINK I CARE? LEDDEM WALLOW IN THE MIRE! I WAS GETTIN' OUT ANYWAY! COUPLA WEEKS I'LL BE ABLE TO BUY THE LOT OF 'EM! BUY THIS POXHOLE AN' CLOSE IT DOWN!
HOW'S THAT THEN, MATEY? ONTO SOMETHIN', ARE YOU?
ME AN' JAMMY, WE COULD HELP OUT, EH?
YOU SLIMY TOERAGS, NOBODY'S MUSCLIN' IN ON MY SCORE! GET OUTA HERE! GET OUTA HERE BEFORE I CARVE YOU A NEW ONE!
SO THEY FOLLOWED FERAL TO THE HUB? WHERE HE VANISHED.
I CHECKED AW' THE SHIPS LEAVIN' ABOOT THAT TIME. THERE WUZ EIGHT POSSIBLES, BUT WAN--OCH, I CANNAE PRONOONCE THE NAME--WAN O' THEM WUZ BOOND FER MIN'UL'Q-UURL--CANNAE PRONOONCE THAT EITHER.
THOUGH IT WUZNY KNOWN AT THE TIME, NAMU, THE DAUGHTER O' THE MUTATOR, PULLED A BIG STING THERE NO' LANG EFTER. MY BET IS THAT'S WHERE FERAL WUZ HEADED.
THAT MAKES SENSE. GOOD. WE GO TO MIN'UL'Q-UURL THEN.
US? AW NAW, LASSIE, IT'S NO' WORK FER A LADY. IT CAN BE RIGHT BORIN'--AN' DANGEROUS. VERY, VERY DANGEROUS. I COULDNY CONTEMPLATE PUTTIN' A DELICATE FLOOER LIKE YERSEL' AT RISK.
MR McNULTY--MIDDENFACE--IT MAY INTEREST YOU TO KNOW THAT I HAVE ACCOMPANIED JOHNNY ON A HUNT.* I AM NO STRANGER TO DANGER. IF I AM FINANCING THIS, I INTEND TO BE THERE. THAT IS NOT NEGOTIABLE.
AYE, AWRIGHT, HEN, I CAN SEE YER SET OAN IT.
Y'KNOW, WHIT GETS ME IS AW THEM LIES.
ME AN' FERAL MET UP AT STONEHENGE MAYBE A WEEK EFTER. I CAN STILL SEE HIM, STANDIN' THERE--I SWEAR THERE WUZ TEARS IN HIS EYES...

*This would be the Cheep Bignall case, detailed extensively in Matson's book.

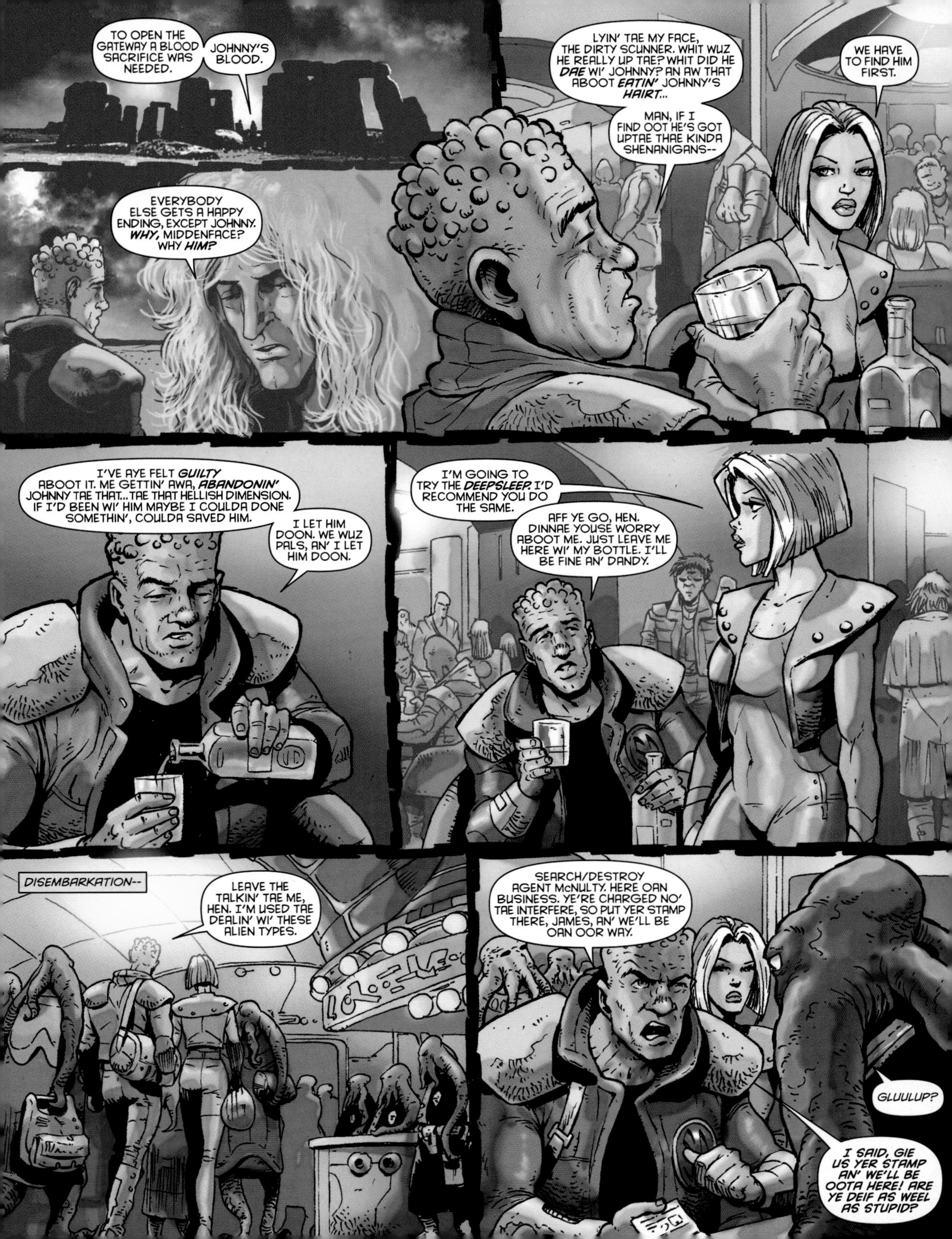
TO OPEN THE GATEWAY A BLOOD SACRIFICE WAS NEEDED.
JOHNNY'S BLOOD.
EVERYBODY ELSE GETS A HAPPY ENDING, EXCEPT JOHNNY. WHY, MIDDENFACE? WHY HIM?
LYIN' TAE MY FACE, THE DIRTY SCUNNER. WHIT WUZ HE REALLY UP TAE? WHIT DID HE DAE WI' JOHNNY? AN AW THAT ABOOT EATIN' JOHNNY'S HAIRT...
MAN, IF I FIND OOT HE'S GOT UPTAE THAE KINDA SHENANIGANS--
WE HAVE TO FIND HIM FIRST.
I'VE AYE FELT GUILTY ABOOT IT. ME GETTIN' AWA, ABANDONIN' JOHNNY TAE THAT... TAE THAT HELLISH DIMENSION. IF I'D BEEN WI' HIM MAYBE I COULDA DONE SOMETHIN', COULDA SAVED HIM.
I LET HIM DOON. WE WUZ PALS, AN' I LET HIM DOON.
I'M GOING TO TRY THE DEEPSLEEP. I'D RECOMMEND YOU DO THE SAME.
AFF YE GO, HEN. DINNAE YOUSE WORRY ABOOT ME. JUST LEAVE ME HERE WI' MY BOTTLE. I'LL BE FINE AN' DANDY.
DISEMBARKATION--
LEAVE THE TALKIN' TAE ME, HEN. I'M USED TAE DEALIN' WI' THESE ALIEN TYPES.
SEARCH/DESTROY AGENT McNULTY. HERE OAN BUSINESS. YE'RE CHARGED NO' TAE INTERFERE, SO PUT YER STAMP THERE, JAMES, AN' WE'LL BE OAN OOR WAY.
GLUULUP?
I SAID, GIE US YER STAMP AN' WE'LL BE OOTA HERE! ARE YE DEIF AS WEEL AS STUPID?

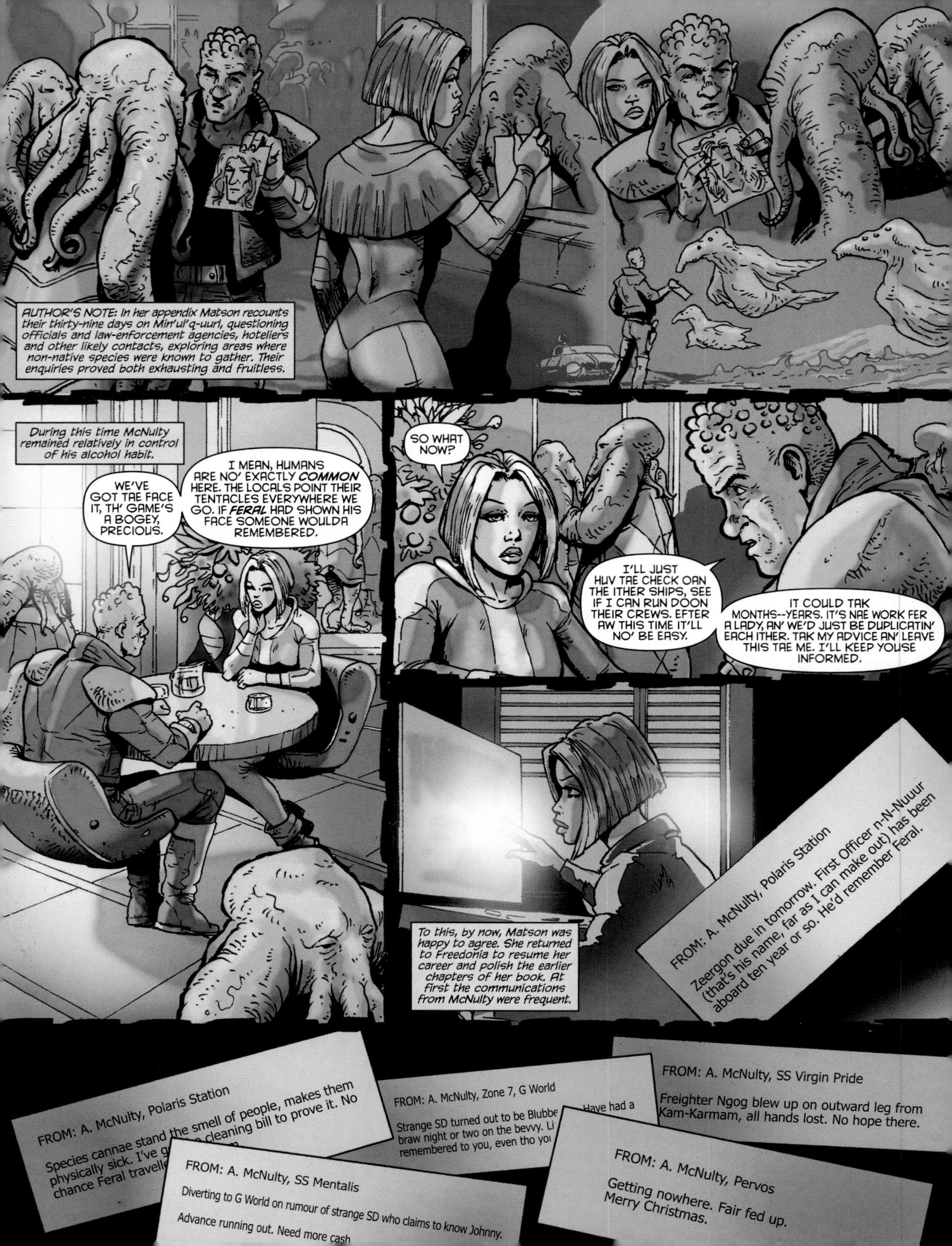
AUTHOR'S NOTE: In her appendix Matson recounts their thirty-nine days on Min'ul'q-uurl, questioning officials and law-enforcement agencies, hoteliers and other likely contacts, exploring areas where non-native species were known to gather. Their enquiries proved both exhausting and fruitless.
During this time McNulty remained relatively in control of his alcohol habit.
WE'VE GOT TAE FACE IT, TH' GAME'S A BOGEY, PRECIOUS.
I MEAN, HUMANS ARE NO' EXACTLY COMMON HERE. THE LOCALS POINT THEIR TENTACLES EVERYWHERE WE GO. IF FERAL HAD SHOWN HIS FACE SOMEONE WOULDA REMEMBERED.
SO WHAT NOW?
I'LL JUST HUV TAE CHECK OAN THE ITHER SHIPS, SEE IF I CAN RUN DOON THEIR CREWS. EFTER AW THIS TIME IT'LL NO' BE EASY.
IT COULD TAK MONTHS--YEARS. IT'S NAE WORK FER A LADY, AN' WE'D JUST BE DUPLICATIN' EACH ITHER. TAK MY ADVICE AN' LEAVE THIS TAE ME. I'LL KEEP YOUSE INFORMED.
To this, by now, Matson was happy to agree. She returned to Freedonia to resume her career and polish the earlier chapters of her book. At first the communications from McNulty were frequent.
FROM: A. McNulty, Polaris Station
Zeergon due in tomorrow. First Officer n-N-Nuuur (that's his name, far as I can make out) has been aboard ten year or so. He'd remember Feral.
FROM: A. McNulty, Polaris Station
Species cannae stand the smell of people, makes them
cleaning bill to prove it. No
FROM: A. McNulty, Zone 7, G World
Have had a
FROM: A. McNulty, SS Virgin Pride
Freighter Ngog blew up on outward leg from Kam-Karmam, all hands lost. No hope there.
FROM: A. McNulty, SS Mentalis
Diverting to G World on rumour of strange SD who claims to know Johnny.
Advance running out. Need more cash
FROM: A. McNulty, Pervos
Getting nowhere. Fair fed up.
Merry Christmas.

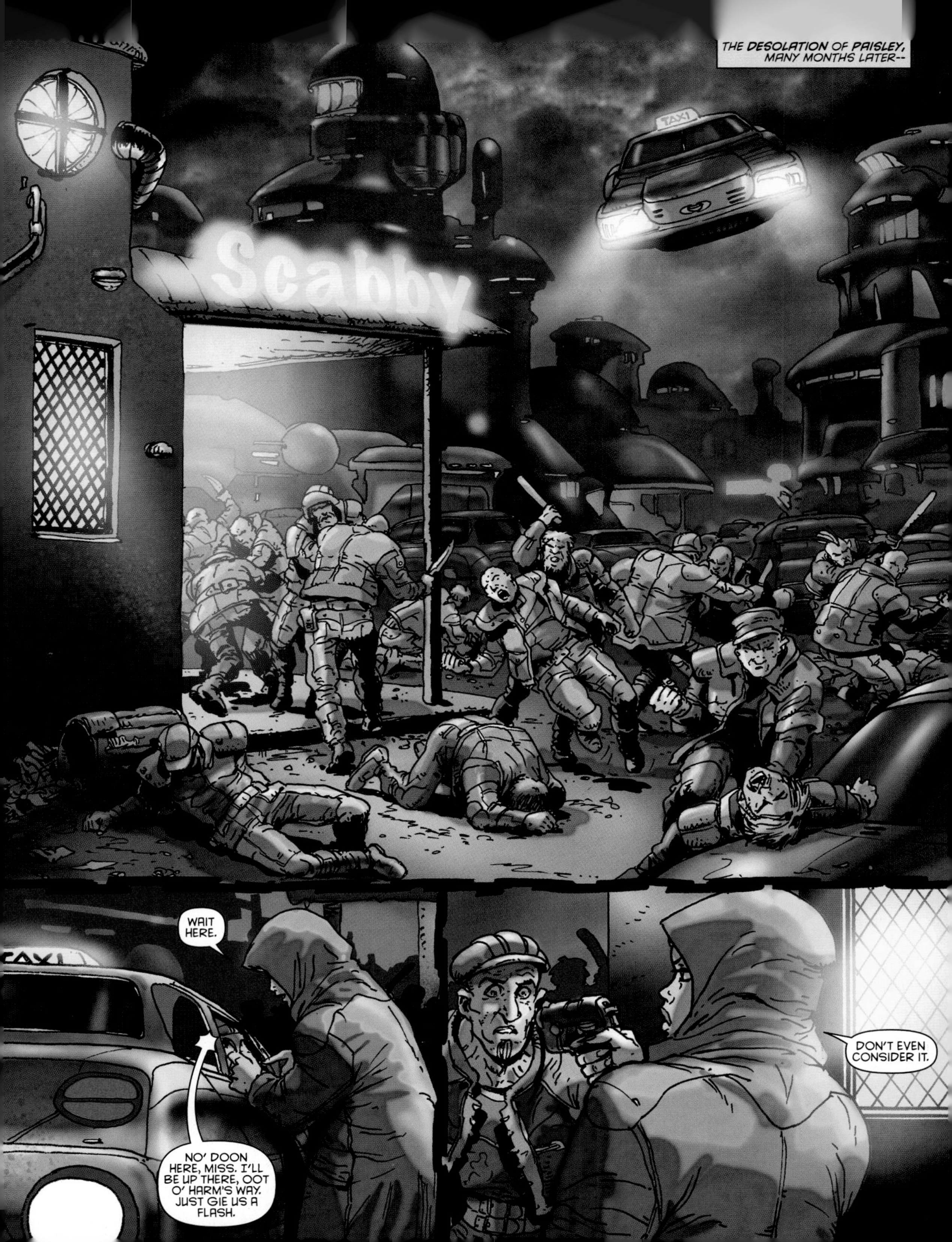
THE DESOLATION OF PAISLEY, MANY MONTHS LATER--
Scabby
TAXI
WAIT HERE.
NO' DOON HERE, MISS. I'LL BE UP THERE, OOT O' HARM'S WAY. JUST GIE US A FLASH.
DON'T EVEN CONSIDER IT.

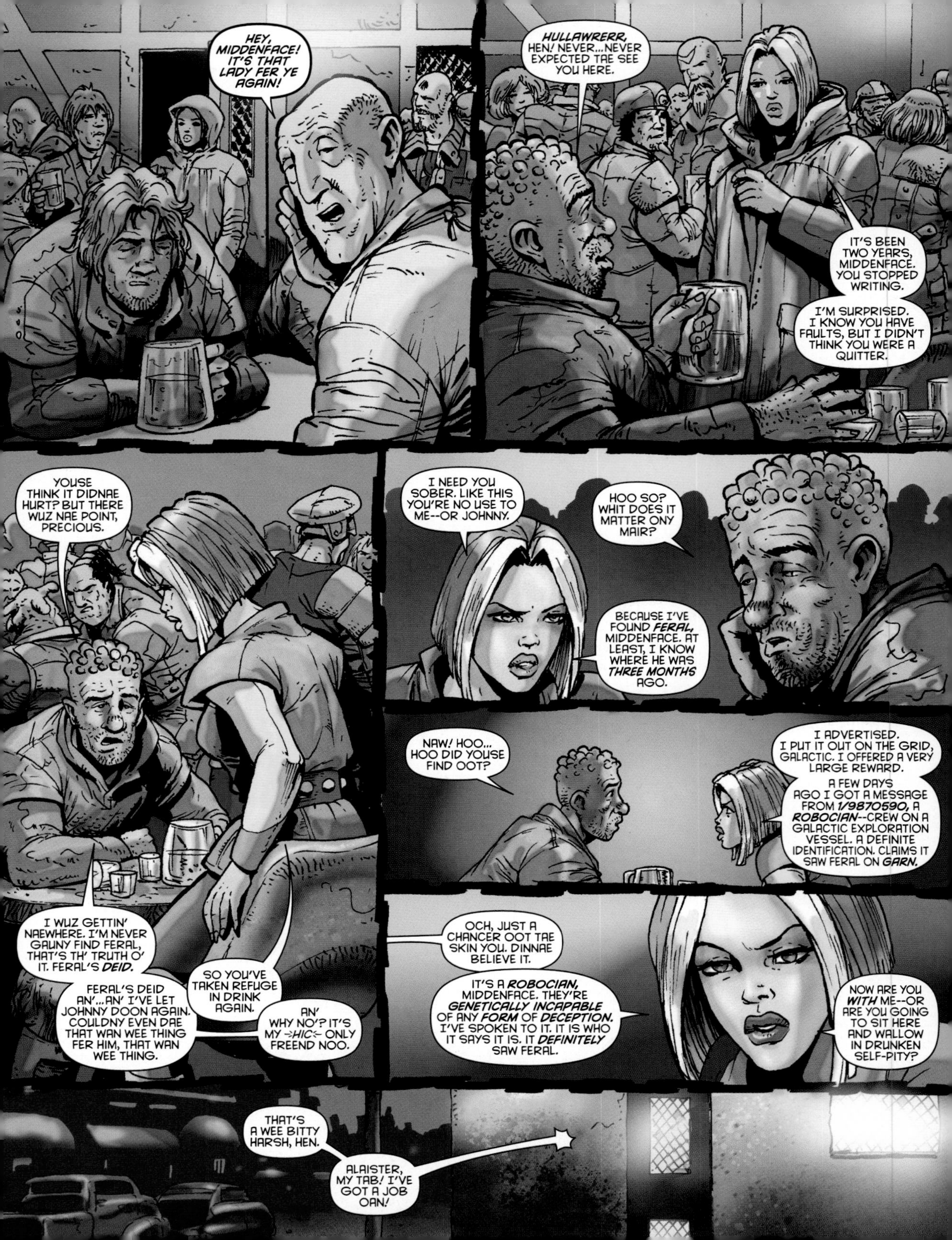
HEY, MIDDENFACE! IT'S THAT LADY FER YE AGAIN!
HULLAWRERR, HEN! NEVER...NEVER EXPECTED TAE SEE YOU HERE.
IT'S BEEN TWO YEARS, MIDDENFACE. YOU STOPPED WRITING.
I'M SURPRISED. I KNOW YOU HAVE FAULTS, BUT I DIDN'T THINK YOU WERE A QUITTER.
YOUSE THINK IT DIDNAE HURT? BUT THERE WUZ NAE POINT, PRECIOUS.
I WUZ GETTIN' NAEWHERE. I'M NEVER GAUNY FIND FERAL, THAT'S TH' TRUTH O' IT. FERAL'S DEID.
FERAL'S DEID AN'...AN' I'VE LET JOHNNY DOON AGAIN. COULDNY EVEN DAE THAT WAN WEE THING FER HIM, THAT WAN WEE THING.
SO YOU'VE TAKEN REFUGE IN DRINK AGAIN.
AN' WHY NO'? IT'S MY =HIC= ONLY FREEND NOO.
I NEED YOU SOBER. LIKE THIS YOU'RE NO USE TO ME--OR JOHNNY.
HOO SO? WHIT DOES IT MATTER ONY MAIR?
BECAUSE I'VE FOUND FERAL, MIDDENFACE. AT LEAST, I KNOW WHERE HE WAS THREE MONTHS AGO.
NAW! HOO... HOO DID YOUSE FIND OOT?
I ADVERTISED. I PUT IT OUT ON THE GRID, GALACTIC. I OFFERED A VERY LARGE REWARD.
A FEW DAYS AGO I GOT A MESSAGE FROM 1/9870590, A ROBOCIAN--CREW ON A GALACTIC EXPLORATION VESSEL. A DEFINITE IDENTIFICATION. CLAIMS IT SAW FERAL ON GARN.
OCH, JUST A CHANCER OOT TAE SKIN YOU. DINNAE BELIEVE IT.
IT'S A ROBOCIAN, MIDDENFACE. THEY'RE GENETICALLY INCAPABLE OF ANY FORM OF DECEPTION. I'VE SPOKEN TO IT. IT IS WHO IT SAYS IT IS. IT DEFINITELY SAW FERAL.
NOW ARE YOU WITH ME--OR ARE YOU GOING TO SIT HERE AND WALLOW IN DRUNKEN SELF-PITY?
THAT'S A WEE BITTY HARSH, HEN.
ALAISTER, MY TAB! I'VE GOT A JOB OAN!

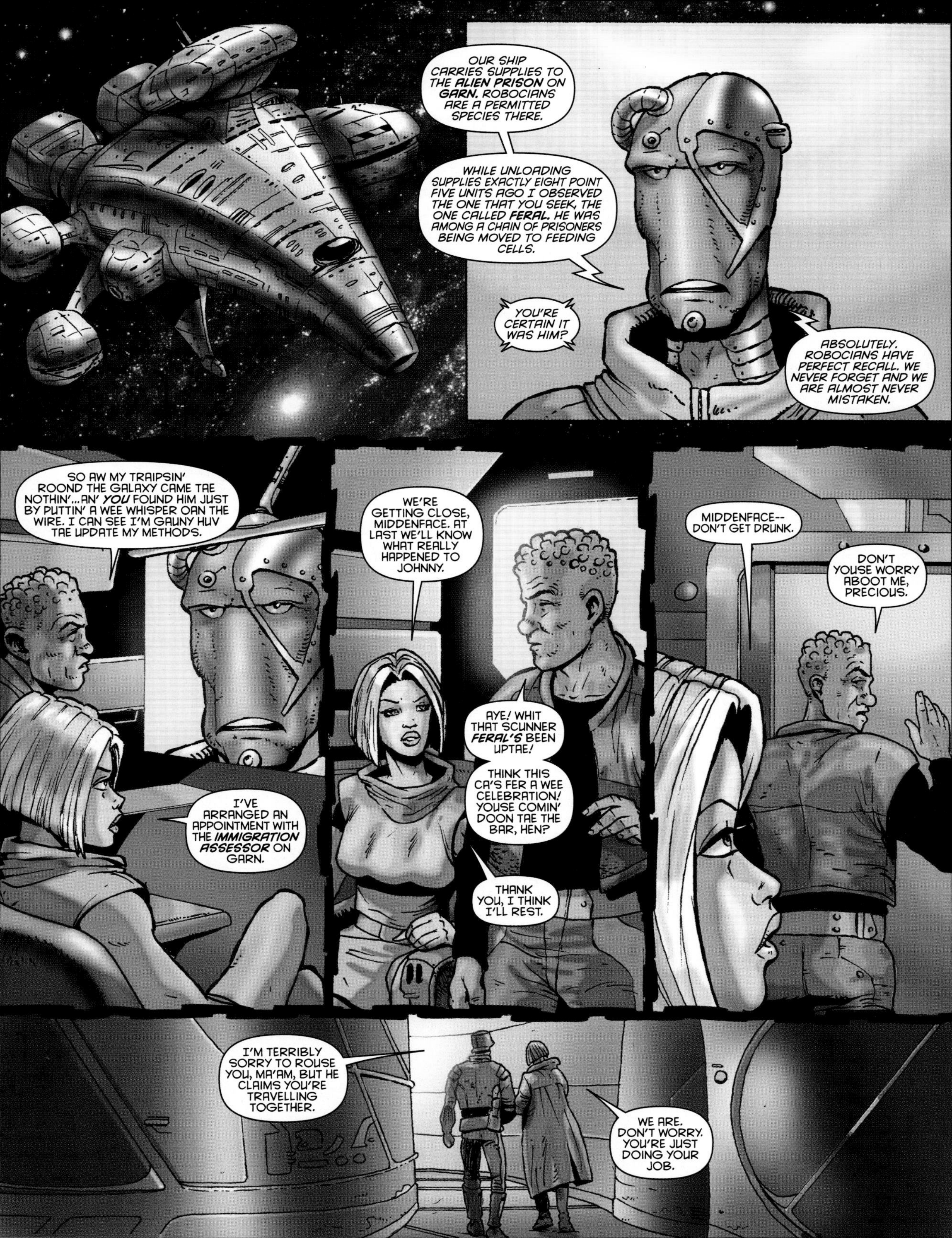

OUR SHIP CARRIES SUPPLIES TO THE ALIEN PRISON ON GARN. ROBOCIANS ARE A PERMITTED SPECIES THERE.
WHILE UNLOADING SUPPLIES EXACTLY EIGHT POINT FIVE UNITS AGO I OBSERVED THE ONE THAT YOU SEEK, THE ONE CALLED FERAL. HE WAS AMONG A CHAIN OF PRISONERS BEING MOVED TO FEEDING CELLS.
YOU'RE CERTAIN IT WAS HIM?
ABSOLUTELY. ROBOCIANS HAVE PERFECT RECALL. WE NEVER FORGET AND WE ARE ALMOST NEVER MISTAKEN.
SO AW MY TRAIPSIN' ROOND THE GALAXY CAME TAE NOTHIN'...AN' YOU FOUND HIM JUST BY PUTTIN' A WEE WHISPER OAN THE WIRE. I CAN SEE I'M GAUNY HUV TAE UPDATE MY METHODS.
I'VE ARRANGED AN APPOINTMENT WITH THE IMMIGRATION ASSESSOR ON GARN.
WE'RE GETTING CLOSE, MIDDENFACE. AT LAST WE'LL KNOW WHAT REALLY HAPPENED TO JOHNNY.
AYE! WHIT THAT SCUNNER FERAL'S BEEN UPTAE!
THINK THIS CA'S FER A WEE CELEBRATION! YOUSE COMIN' DOON TAE THE BAR, HEN?
THANK YOU, I THINK I'LL REST.
MIDDENFACE-- DON'T GET DRUNK.
DON'T YOUSE WORRY ABOOT ME, PRECIOUS.
I'M TERRIBLY SORRY TO ROUSE YOU, MA'AM, BUT HE CLAIMS YOU'RE TRAVELLING TOGETHER.
WE ARE. DON'T WORRY. YOU'RE JUST DOING YOUR JOB.

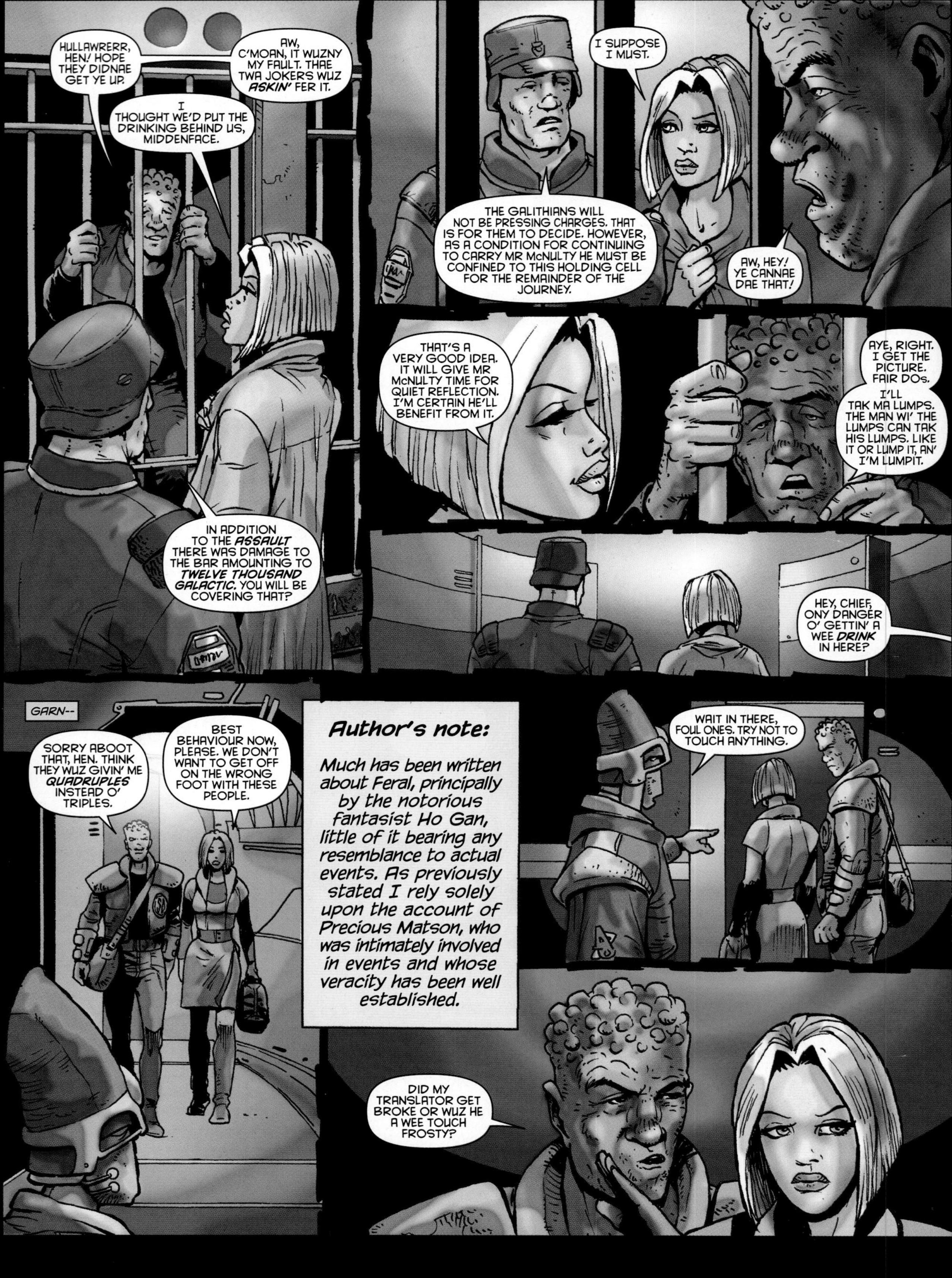
HULLAWRERR, HEN! HOPE THEY DIDNAE GET YE UP.
AW, C'MOAN, IT WUZNY MY FAULT. THAE TWA JOKERS WUZ ASKIN' FER IT.
I THOUGHT WE'D PUT THE DRINKING BEHIND US, MIDDENFACE.
IN ADDITION TO THE ASSAULT THERE WAS DAMAGE TO THE BAR AMOUNTING TO TWELVE THOUSAND GALACTIC. YOU WILL BE COVERING THAT?
I SUPPOSE I MUST.
THE GALITHIANS WILL NOT BE PRESSING CHARGES. THAT IS FOR THEM TO DECIDE. HOWEVER, AS A CONDITION FOR CONTINUING TO CARRY MR McNULTY HE MUST BE CONFINED TO THIS HOLDING CELL FOR THE REMAINDER OF THE JOURNEY.
AW, HEY! YE CANNAE DAE THAT!
THAT'S A VERY GOOD IDEA. IT WILL GIVE MR McNULTY TIME FOR QUIET REFLECTION. I'M CERTAIN HE'LL BENEFIT FROM IT.
AYE, RIGHT. I GET THE PICTURE. FAIR DOs.
I'LL TAK MA LUMPS. THE MAN WI' THE LUMPS CAN TAK HIS LUMPS. LIKE IT OR LUMP IT, AN' I'M LUMPIT.
HEY, CHIEF, ONY DANGER O' GETTIN' A WEE DRINK IN HERE?
GARN--
SORRY ABOOT THAT, HEN. THINK THEY WUZ GIVIN' ME QUADRUPLES INSTEAD O' TRIPLES.
BEST BEHAVIOUR NOW, PLEASE. WE DON'T WANT TO GET OFF ON THE WRONG FOOT WITH THESE PEOPLE.
Author's note:
Much has been written about Feral, principally by the notorious fantasist Ho Gan, little of it bearing any resemblance to actual events. As previously stated I rely solely upon the account of Precious Matson, who was intimately involved in events and whose veracity has been well established.
WAIT IN THERE, FOUL ONES. TRY NOT TO TOUCH ANYTHING.
DID MY TRANSLATOR GET BROKE OR WUZ HE A WEE TOUCH FROSTY?

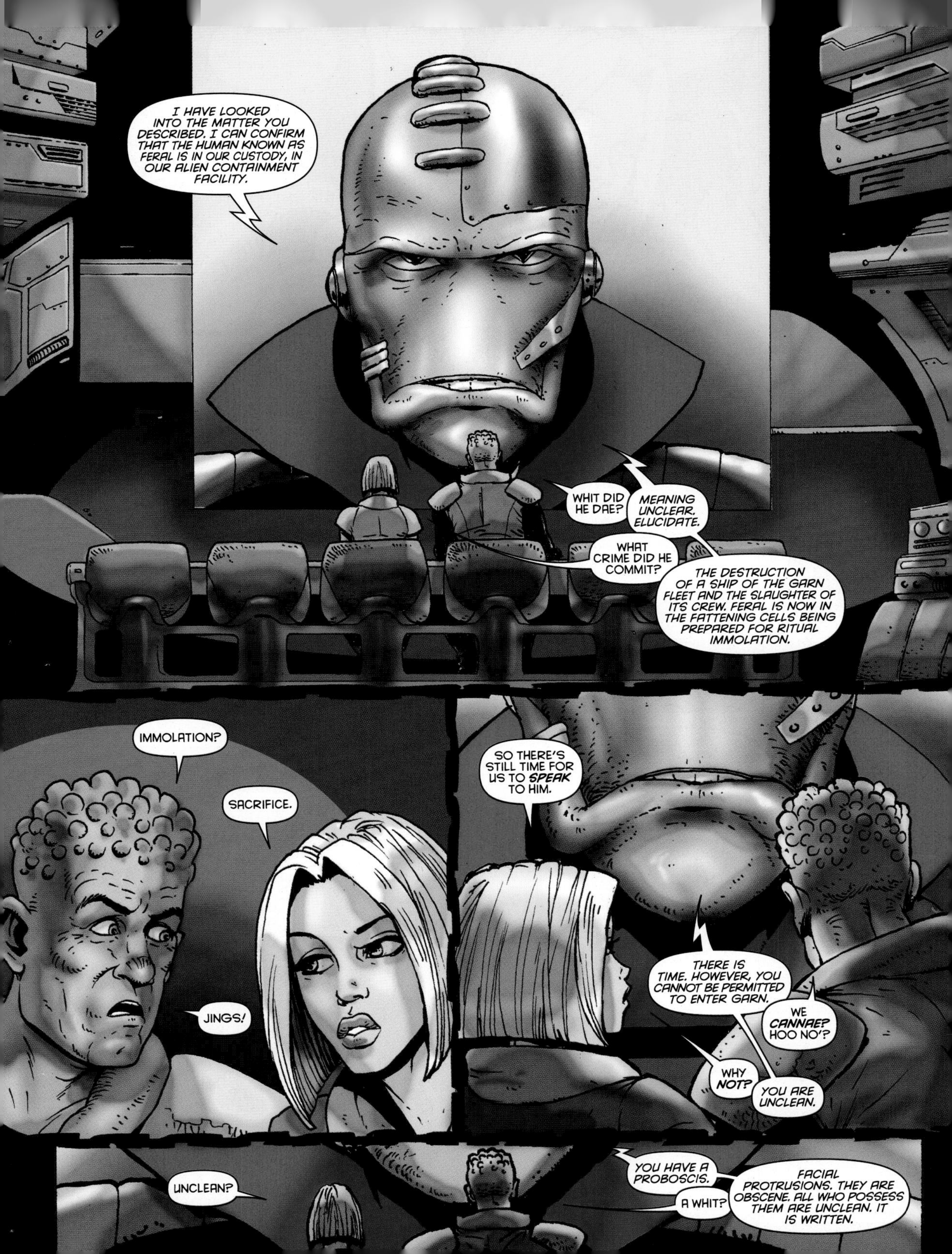

I HAVE LOOKED INTO THE MATTER YOU DESCRIBED. I CAN CONFIRM THAT THE HUMAN KNOWN AS FERAL IS IN OUR CUSTODY, IN OUR ALIEN CONTAINMENT FACILITY.
WHIT DID HE DAE?
MEANING UNCLEAR. ELUCIDATE.
WHAT CRIME DID HE COMMIT?
THE DESTRUCTION OF A SHIP OF THE GARN FLEET AND THE SLAUGHTER OF ITS CREW. FERAL IS NOW IN THE FATTENING CELLS BEING PREPARED FOR RITUAL IMMOLATION.
IMMOLATION?
SACRIFICE.
JINGS!
SO THERE'S STILL TIME FOR US TO SPEAK TO HIM.
THERE IS TIME. HOWEVER, YOU CANNOT BE PERMITTED TO ENTER GARN.
WE CANNAE? HOO NO'?
WHY NOT?
YOU ARE UNCLEAN.
UNCLEAN?
YOU HAVE A PROBOSCIS.
A WHIT?
FACIAL PROTRUSIONS. THEY ARE OBSCENE. ALL WHO POSSESS THEM ARE UNCLEAN. IT IS WRITTEN.

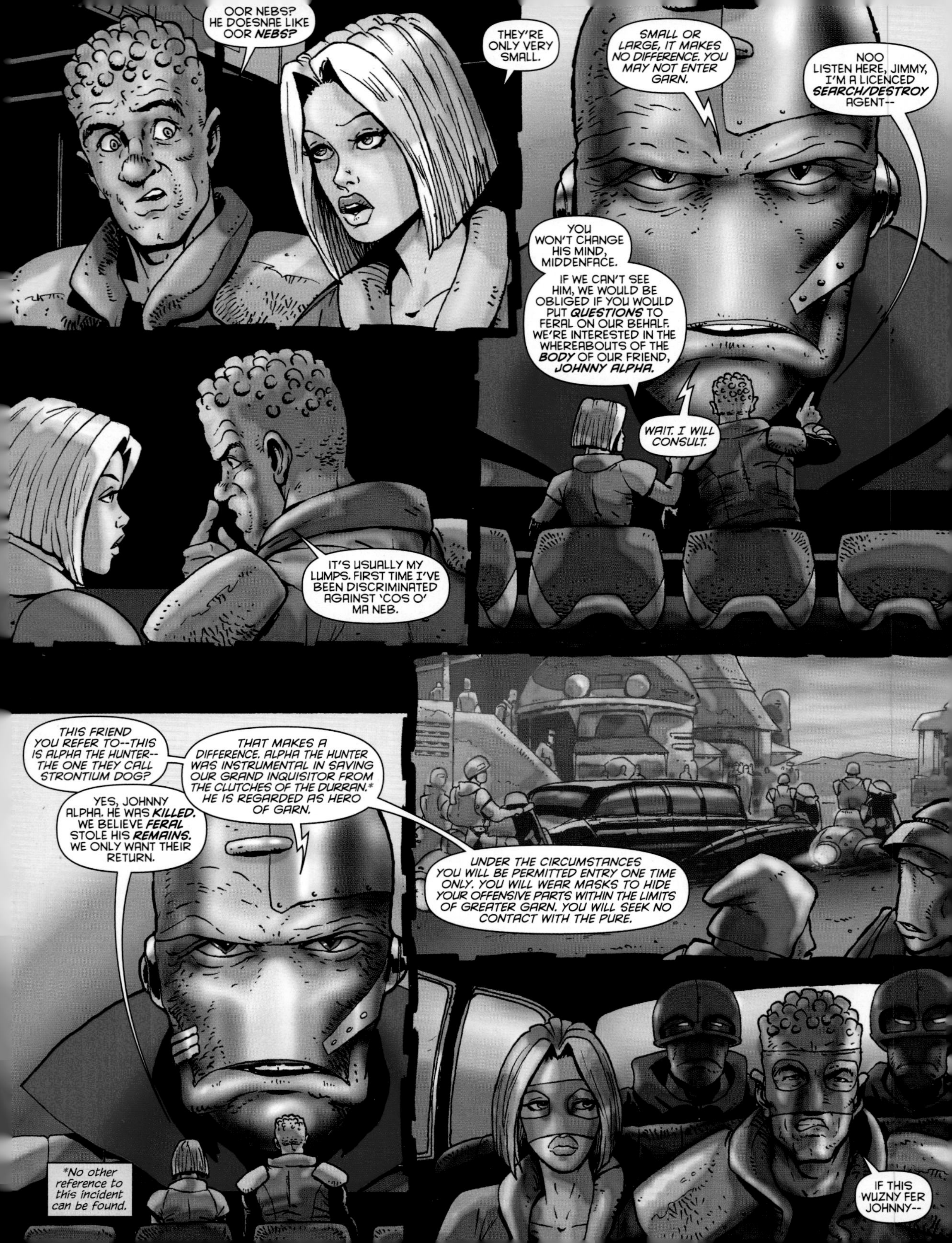
OOR NEBS? HE DOESNAE LIKE OOR NEBS?
THEY'RE ONLY VERY SMALL.
SMALL OR LARGE, IT MAKES NO DIFFERENCE. YOU MAY NOT ENTER GARN.
NOO LISTEN HERE, JIMMY, I'M A LICENCED SEARCH/DESTROY AGENT--
IT'S USUALLY MY LUMPS. FIRST TIME I'VE BEEN DISCRIMINATED AGAINST 'COS O' MA NEB.
YOU WON'T CHANGE HIS MIND, MIDDENFACE.
IF WE CAN'T SEE HIM, WE WOULD BE OBLIGED IF YOU WOULD PUT QUESTIONS TO FERAL ON OUR BEHALF. WE'RE INTERESTED IN THE WHEREABOUTS OF THE BODY OF OUR FRIEND, JOHNNY ALPHA.
WAIT. I WILL CONSULT.
THIS FRIEND YOU REFER TO--THIS IS ALPHA THE HUNTER-- THE ONE THEY CALL STRONTIUM DOG?
YES, JOHNNY ALPHA. HE WAS KILLED. WE BELIEVE FERAL STOLE HIS REMAINS. WE ONLY WANT THEIR RETURN.
THAT MAKES A DIFFERENCE. ALPHA THE HUNTER WAS INSTRUMENTAL IN SAVING OUR GRAND INQUISITOR FROM THE CLUTCHES OF THE DURRAN.* HE IS REGARDED AS HERO OF GARN.
UNDER THE CIRCUMSTANCES YOU WILL BE PERMITTED ENTRY ONE TIME ONLY. YOU WILL WEAR MASKS TO HIDE YOUR OFFENSIVE PARTS WITHIN THE LIMITS OF GREATER GARN. YOU WILL SEEK NO CONTACT WITH THE PURE.
*No other reference to this incident can be found.
IF THIS WUZNY FER JOHNNY--

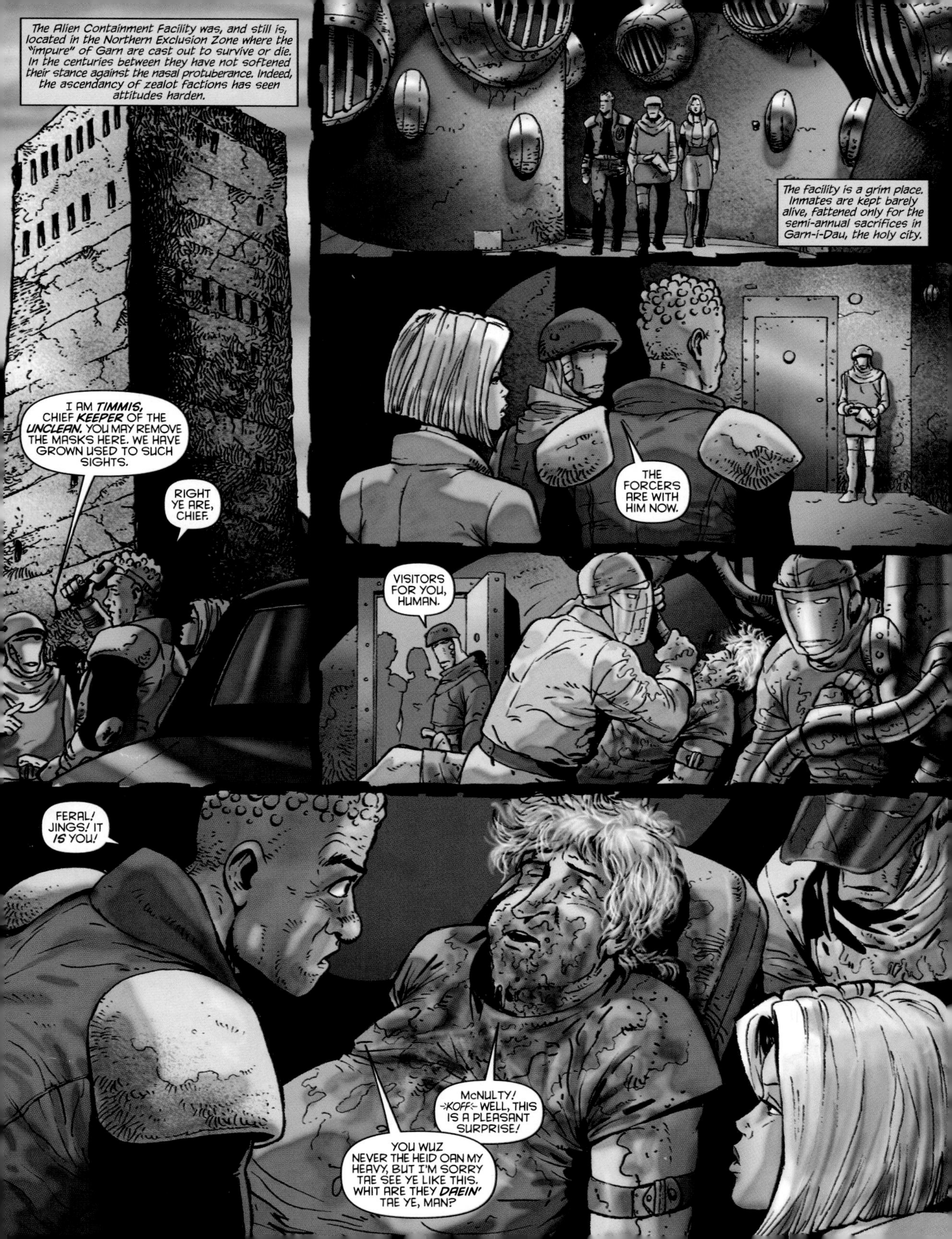

The Alien Containment Facility was, and still is, located in the Northern Exclusion Zone where the "impure" of Garn are cast out to survive or die. In the centuries between they have not softened their stance against the nasal protuberance. Indeed, the ascendancy of zealot factions has seen attitudes harden.
I AM TIMMIS, CHIEF KEEPER OF THE UNCLEAN. YOU MAY REMOVE THE MASKS HERE. WE HAVE GROWN USED TO SUCH SIGHTS.
RIGHT YE ARE, CHIEF.
The facility is a grim place. Inmates are kept barely alive, fattened only for the semi-annual sacrifices in Garn-i-Dau, the holy city.
THE FORCERS ARE WITH HIM NOW.
VISITORS FOR YOU, HUMAN.
FERAL! JINGS! IT IS YOU!
McNULTY! -KOFF- WELL, THIS IS A PLEASANT SURPRISE!
YOU WUZ NEVER THE HEID OAN MY HEAVY, BUT I'M SORRY TAE SEE YE LIKE THIS. WHIT ARE THEY DAEIN' TAE YE, MAN?

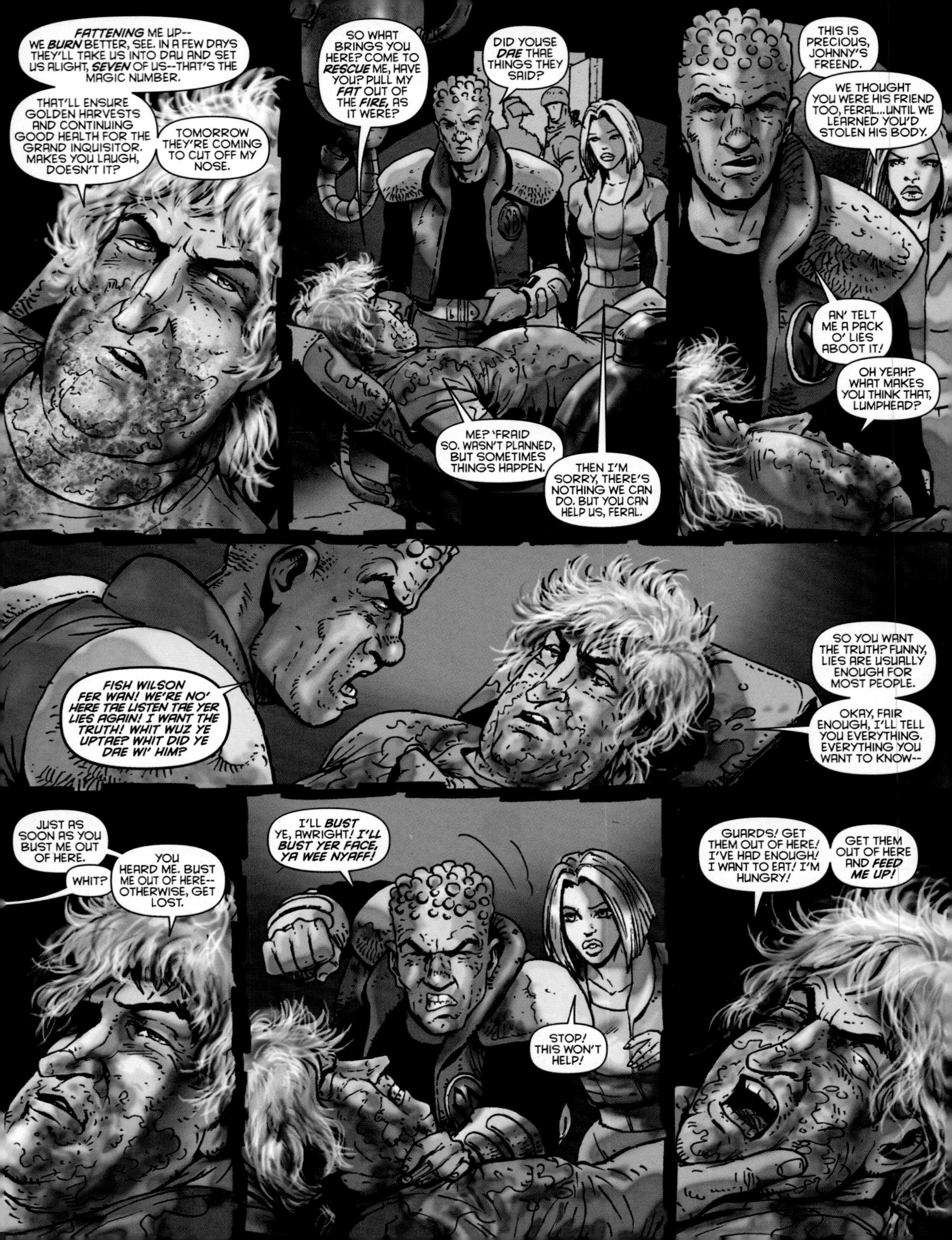
FATTENING ME UP-- WE BURN BETTER, SEE. IN A FEW DAYS THEY'LL TAKE US INTO DAU AND SET US ALIGHT, SEVEN OF US--THAT'S THE MAGIC NUMBER.
THAT'LL ENSURE GOLDEN HARVESTS AND CONTINUING GOOD HEALTH FOR THE GRAND INQUISITOR. MAKES YOU LAUGH, DOESN'T IT?
TOMORROW THEY'RE COMING TO CUT OFF MY NOSE.
SO WHAT BRINGS YOU HERE? COME TO RESCUE ME, HAVE YOU? PULL MY FAT OUT OF THE FIRE, AS IT WERE?
DID YOUSE DAE THAE THINGS THEY SAID?
ME? 'FRAID SO. WASN'T PLANNED, BUT SOMETIMES THINGS HAPPEN.
THEN I'M SORRY, THERE'S NOTHING WE CAN DO. BUT YOU CAN HELP US, FERAL.
THIS IS PRECIOUS, JOHNNY'S FREEND.
WE THOUGHT YOU WERE HIS FRIEND TOO, FERAL...UNTIL WE LEARNED YOU'D STOLEN HIS BODY.
AN' TELT ME A PACK O' LIES ABOOT IT!
OH YEAH? WHAT MAKES YOU THINK THAT, LUMPHEAD?
FISH WILSON FER WAN! WE'RE NO' HERE TAE LISTEN TAE YER LIES AGAIN! I WANT THE TRUTH! WHIT WUZ YE UPTAE? WHIT DID YE DAE WI' HIM?
SO YOU WANT THE TRUTH? FUNNY, LIES ARE USUALLY ENOUGH FOR MOST PEOPLE.
OKAY, FAIR ENOUGH, I'LL TELL YOU EVERYTHING. EVERYTHING YOU WANT TO KNOW--
JUST AS SOON AS YOU BUST ME OUT OF HERE.
WHIT?
YOU HEARD ME. BUST ME OUT OF HERE-- OTHERWISE, GET LOST.
I'LL BUST YE, AWRIGHT! I'LL BUST YER FACE, YA WEE NYAFF!
STOP! THIS WON'T HELP!
GUARDS! GET THEM OUT OF HERE! I'VE HAD ENOUGH! I WANT TO EAT! I'M HUNGRY!
GET THEM OUT OF HERE AND FEED ME UP!

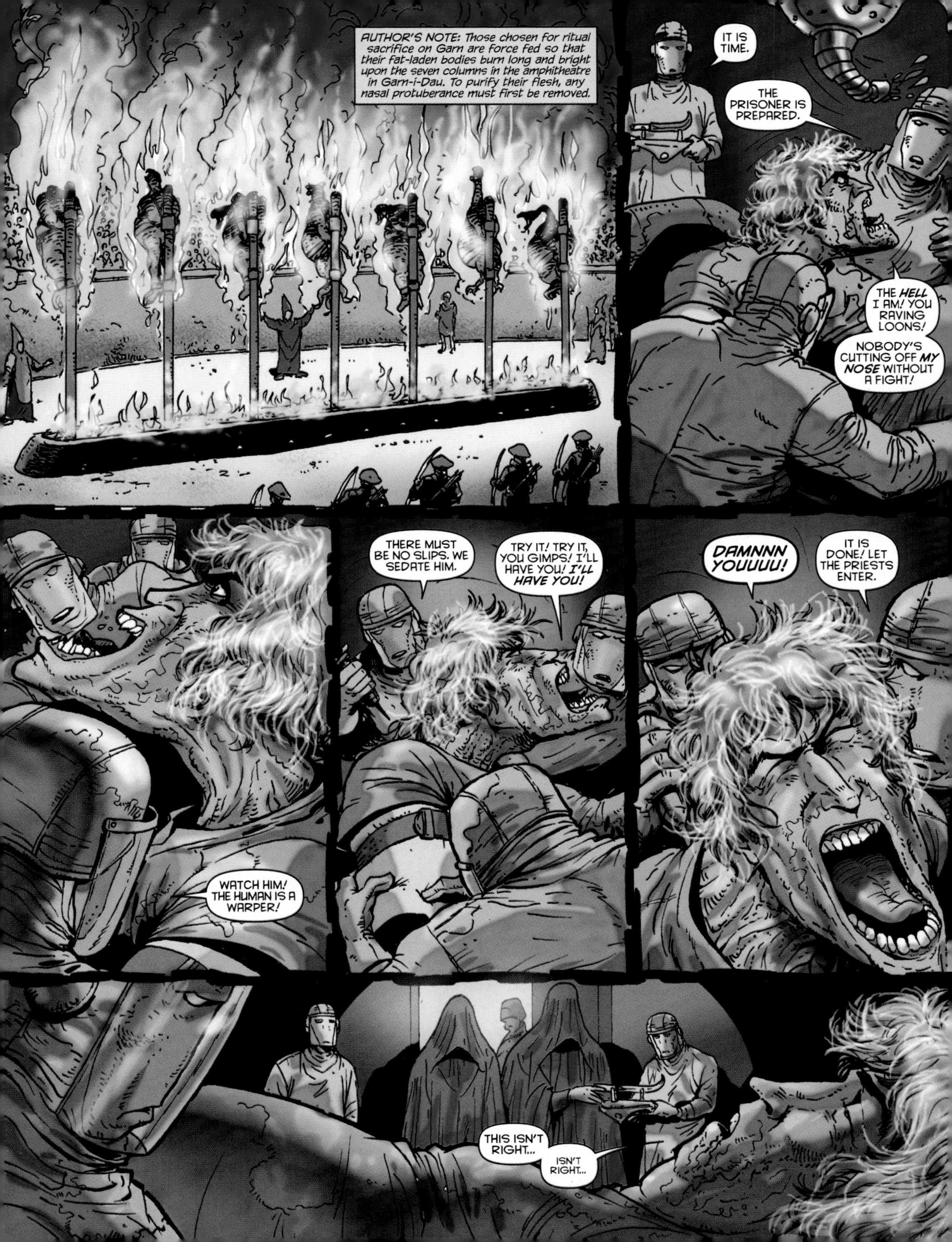
AUTHOR'S NOTE: Those chosen for ritual sacrifice on Garn are force fed so that their fat-laden bodies burn long and bright upon the seven columns in the amphitheatre in Garn-i-Dau. To purify their flesh, any nasal protuberance must first be removed.
IT IS TIME.
THE PRISONER IS PREPARED.
THE HELL I AM! YOU RAVING LOONS!
NOBODY'S CUTTING OFF MY NOSE WITHOUT A FIGHT!
WATCH HIM! THE HUMAN IS A WARPER!
THERE MUST BE NO SLIPS. WE SEDATE HIM.
TRY IT! TRY IT, YOU GIMPS! I'LL HAVE YOU! I'LL HAVE YOU!
DAMNNN YOUUUU!
IT IS DONE! LET THE PRIESTS ENTER.
THIS ISN'T RIGHT...
ISN'T RIGHT...

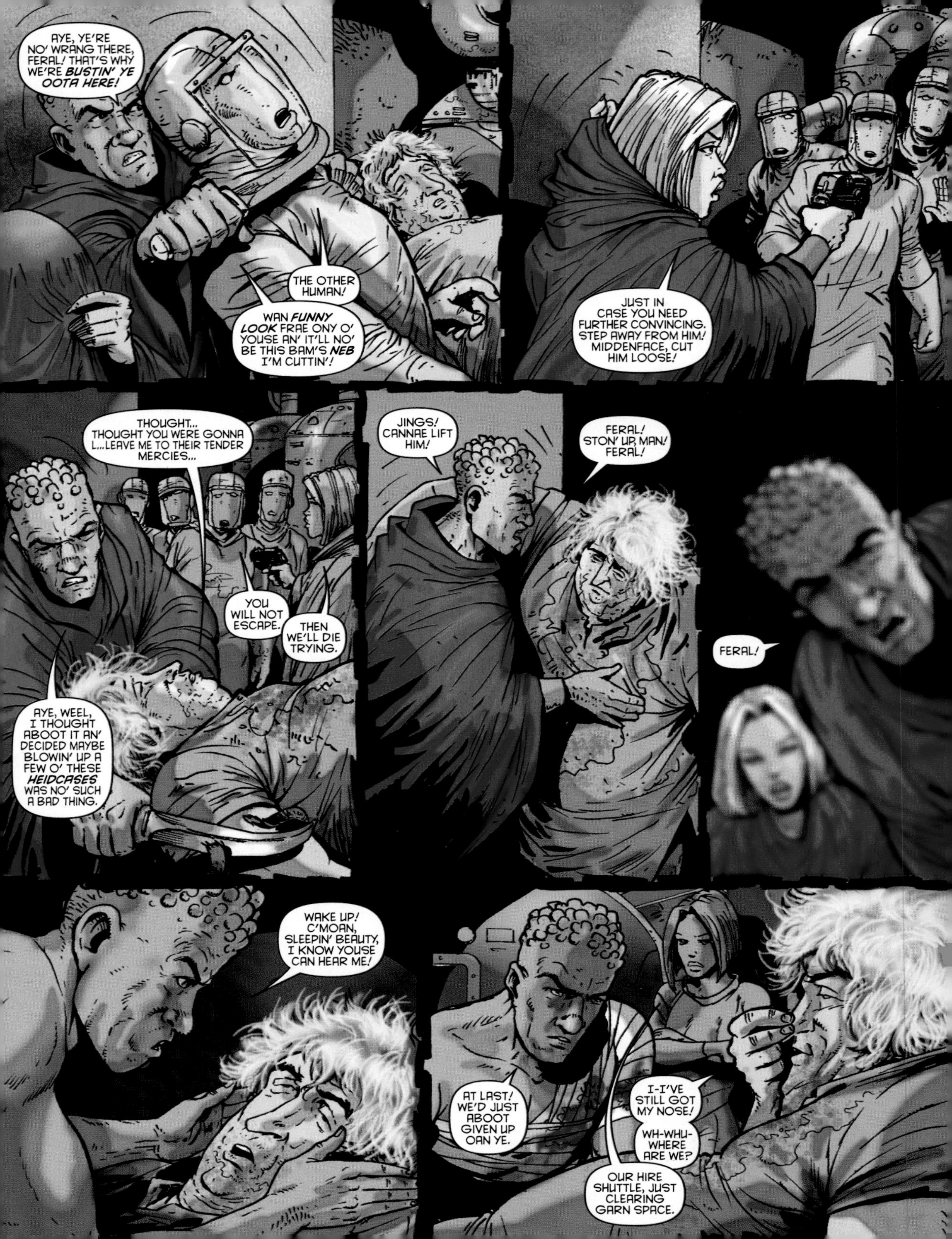

AYE, YE'RE NO' WRANG THERE, FERAL! THAT'S WHY WE'RE *BUSTIN' YE OOTA HERE!*
THE OTHER HUMAN!
WAN *FUNNY LOOK* FRAE ONY O' YOUSE AN' IT'LL NO' BE THIS BAM'S *NEB* I'M CUTTIN'!
JUST IN CASE YOU NEED FURTHER CONVINCING. STEP AWAY FROM HIM! MIDDENFACE, CUT HIM LOOSE!
THOUGHT... THOUGHT YOU WERE GONNA L...LEAVE ME TO THEIR TENDER MERCIES...
AYE, WEEL, I THOUGHT ABOOT IT AN' DECIDED MAYBE BLOWIN' UP A FEW O' THESE *HEIDCASES* WAS NO' SUCH A BAD THING.
YOU WILL NOT ESCAPE.
THEN WE'LL DIE TRYING.
JINGS! CANNAE LIFT HIM!
FERAL! STON' UP, MAN! FERAL!
FERAL!
WAKE UP! C'MOAN, SLEEPIN' BEAUTY, I KNOW YOUSE CAN HEAR ME!
AT LAST! WE'D JUST ABOOT GIVEN UP OAN YE.
I-I'VE STILL GOT MY NOSE!
WH-WHU-WHERE ARE WE?
OUR HIRE SHUTTLE, JUST CLEARING GARN SPACE.

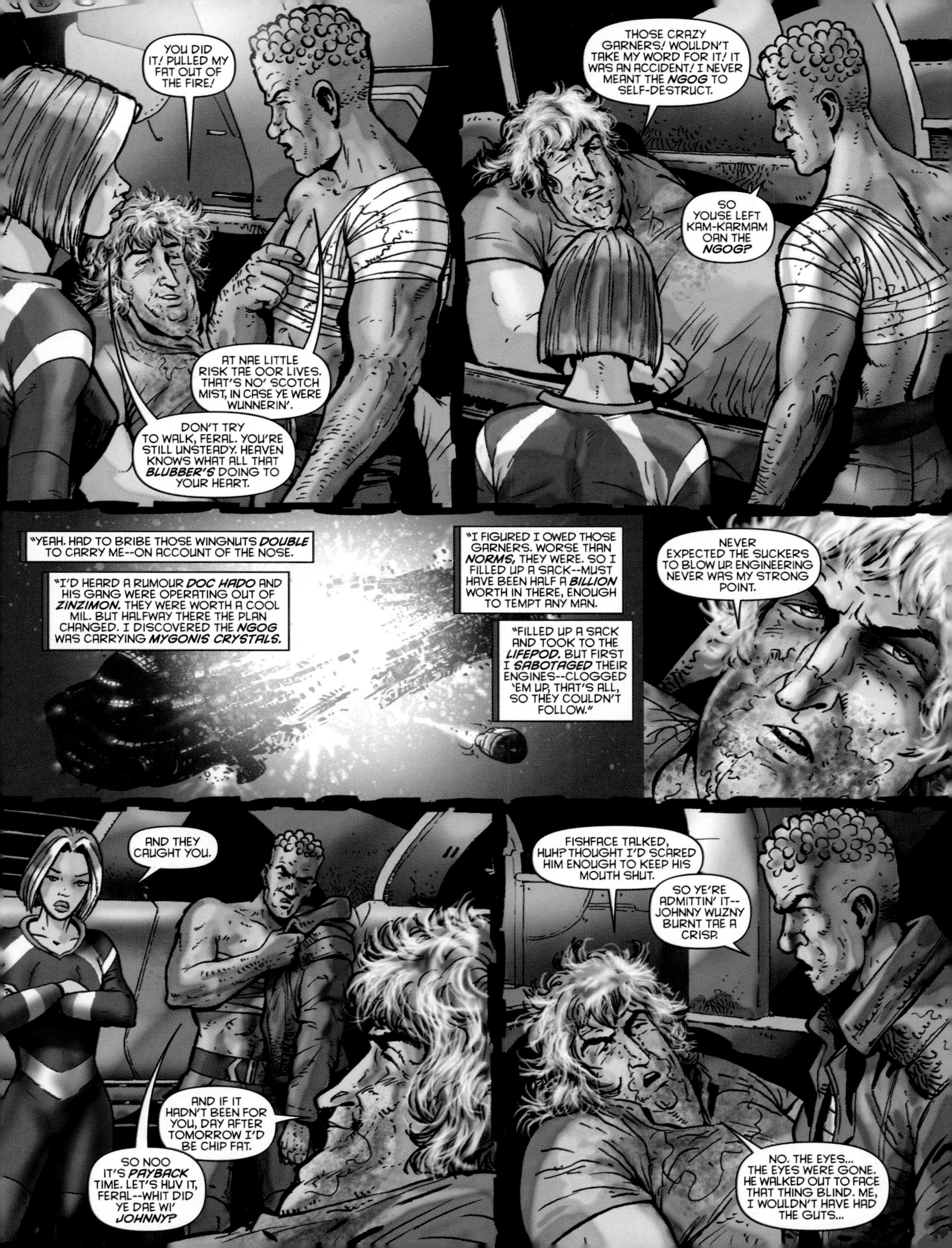
YOU DID IT! PULLED MY FAT OUT OF THE FIRE!
AT NAE LITTLE RISK TAE OOR LIVES. THAT'S NO' SCOTCH MIST, IN CASE YE WERE WUNNERIN'.
DON'T TRY TO WALK, FERAL. YOU'RE STILL UNSTEADY. HEAVEN KNOWS WHAT ALL THAT BLUBBER'S DOING TO YOUR HEART.
THOSE CRAZY GARNERS! WOULDN'T TAKE MY WORD FOR IT! IT WAS AN ACCIDENT! I NEVER MEANT THE NGOG TO SELF-DESTRUCT.
SO YOUSE LEFT KAM-KARMAM OAN THE NGOG?
"YEAH. HAD TO BRIBE THOSE WINGNUTS DOUBLE TO CARRY ME--ON ACCOUNT OF THE NOSE.
"I'D HEARD A RUMOUR DOC HADO AND HIS GANG WERE OPERATING OUT OF ZINZIMON. THEY WERE WORTH A COOL MIL. BUT HALFWAY THERE THE PLAN CHANGED. I DISCOVERED THE NGOG WAS CARRYING MYGONIS CRYSTALS.
"I FIGURED I OWED THOSE GARNERS. WORSE THAN NORMS, THEY WERE. SO I FILLED UP A SACK--MUST HAVE BEEN HALF A BILLION WORTH IN THERE, ENOUGH TO TEMPT ANY MAN.
"FILLED UP A SACK AND TOOK TO THE LIFEPOD. BUT FIRST I SABOTAGED THEIR ENGINES--CLOGGED 'EM UP, THAT'S ALL, SO THEY COULDN'T FOLLOW."
NEVER EXPECTED THE SUCKERS TO BLOW UP. ENGINEERING NEVER WAS MY STRONG POINT.
AND THEY CAUGHT YOU.
AND IF IT HADN'T BEEN FOR YOU, DAY AFTER TOMORROW I'D BE CHIP FAT.
SO NOO IT'S PAYBACK TIME. LET'S HUV IT, FERAL--WHIT DID YE DAE WI' JOHNNY?
FISHFACE TALKED, HUH? THOUGHT I'D SCARED HIM ENOUGH TO KEEP HIS MOUTH SHUT.
SO YE'RE ADMITTIN' IT--JOHNNY WUZNY BURNT TAE A CRISP.
NO. THE EYES... THE EYES WERE GONE. HE WALKED OUT TO FACE THAT THING BLIND. ME, I WOULDN'T HAVE HAD THE GUTS...

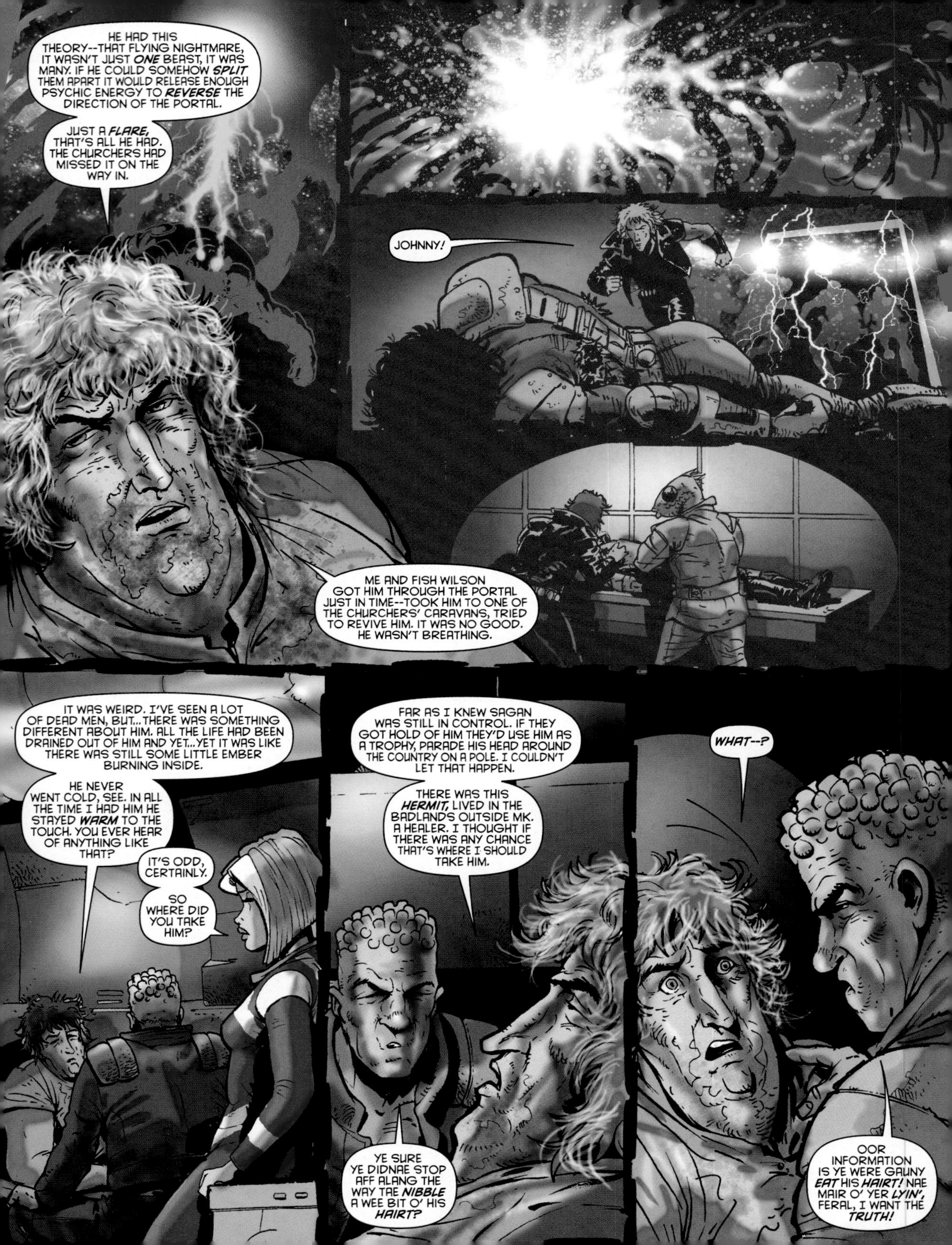

HE HAD THIS THEORY--THAT FLYING NIGHTMARE, IT WASN'T JUST ONE BEAST, IT WAS MANY. IF HE COULD SOMEHOW SPLIT THEM APART IT WOULD RELEASE ENOUGH PSYCHIC ENERGY TO REVERSE THE DIRECTION OF THE PORTAL.
JUST A FLARE, THAT'S ALL HE HAD. THE CHURCHERS HAD MISSED IT ON THE WAY IN.
JOHNNY!
ME AND FISH WILSON GOT HIM THROUGH THE PORTAL JUST IN TIME--TOOK HIM TO ONE OF THE CHURCHERS' CARAVANS, TRIED TO REVIVE HIM. IT WAS NO GOOD. HE WASN'T BREATHING.
IT WAS WEIRD. I'VE SEEN A LOT OF DEAD MEN, BUT... THERE WAS SOMETHING DIFFERENT ABOUT HIM. ALL THE LIFE HAD BEEN DRAINED OUT OF HIM AND YET...YET IT WAS LIKE THERE WAS STILL SOME LITTLE EMBER BURNING INSIDE.
HE NEVER WENT COLD, SEE. IN ALL THE TIME I HAD HIM HE STAYED WARM TO THE TOUCH. YOU EVER HEAR OF ANYTHING LIKE THAT?
IT'S ODD, CERTAINLY.
SO WHERE DID YOU TAKE HIM?
FAR AS I KNEW SAGAN WAS STILL IN CONTROL. IF THEY GOT HOLD OF HIM THEY'D USE HIM AS A TROPHY, PARADE HIS HEAD AROUND THE COUNTRY ON A POLE. I COULDN'T LET THAT HAPPEN.
THERE WAS THIS HERMIT, LIVED IN THE BADLANDS OUTSIDE MK. A HEALER. I THOUGHT IF THERE WAS ANY CHANCE THAT'S WHERE I SHOULD TAKE HIM.
YE SURE YE DIDNAE STOP AFF ALANG THE WAY TAE NIBBLE A WEE BIT O' HIS HAIRT?
WHAT--?
OOR INFORMATION IS YE WERE GAUNY EAT HIS HAIRT! NAE MAIR O' YER LYIN', FERAL, I WANT THE TRUTH!

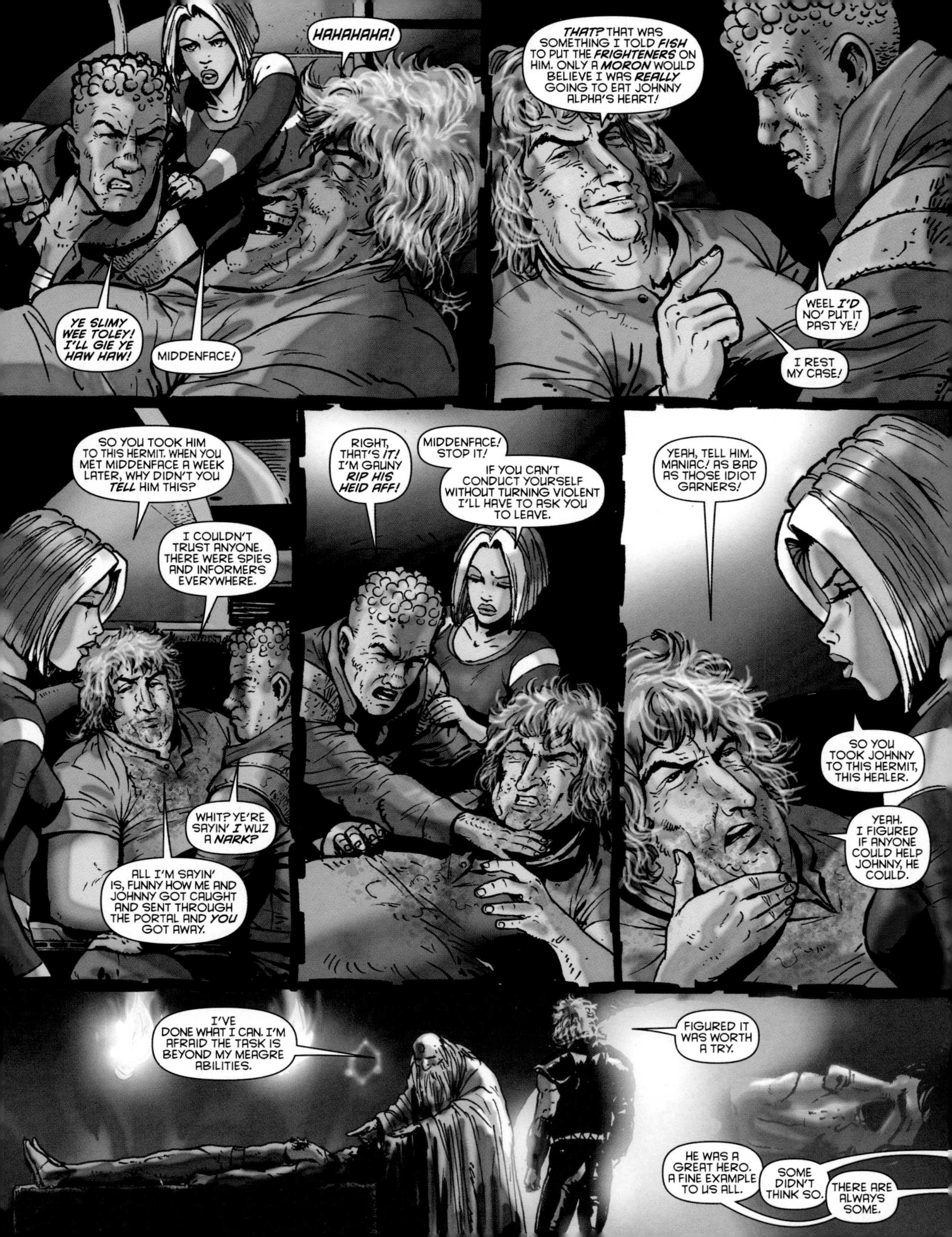
HAHAHAHA!
YE SLIMY WEE TOLEY! I'LL GIE YE HAW HAW!
MIDDENFACE!
THAT? THAT WAS SOMETHING I TOLD FISH TO PUT THE FRIGHTENERS ON HIM. ONLY A MORON WOULD BELIEVE I WAS REALLY GOING TO EAT JOHNNY ALPHA'S HEART!
WEEL I'D NO' PUT IT PAST YE!
I REST MY CASE!
SO YOU TOOK HIM TO THIS HERMIT. WHEN YOU MET MIDDENFACE A WEEK LATER, WHY DIDN'T YOU TELL HIM THIS?
I COULDN'T TRUST ANYONE. THERE WERE SPIES AND INFORMERS EVERYWHERE.
WHIT? YE'RE SAYIN' I WUZ A NARK?
ALL I'M SAYIN' IS, FUNNY HOW ME AND JOHNNY GOT CAUGHT AND SENT THROUGH THE PORTAL AND YOU GOT AWAY.
RIGHT, THAT'S IT! I'M GAUNY RIP HIS HEID AFF!
MIDDENFACE! STOP IT!
IF YOU CAN'T CONDUCT YOURSELF WITHOUT TURNING VIOLENT I'LL HAVE TO ASK YOU TO LEAVE.
YEAH, TELL HIM. MANIAC! AS BAD AS THOSE IDIOT GARNERS!
SO YOU TOOK JOHNNY TO THIS HERMIT, THIS HEALER.
YEAH. I FIGURED IF ANYONE COULD HELP JOHNNY, HE COULD.
I'VE DONE WHAT I CAN. I'M AFRAID THE TASK IS BEYOND MY MEAGRE ABILITIES.
FIGURED IT WAS WORTH A TRY.
HE WAS A GREAT HERO. A FINE EXAMPLE TO US ALL.
SOME DIDN'T THINK SO.
THERE ARE ALWAYS SOME.

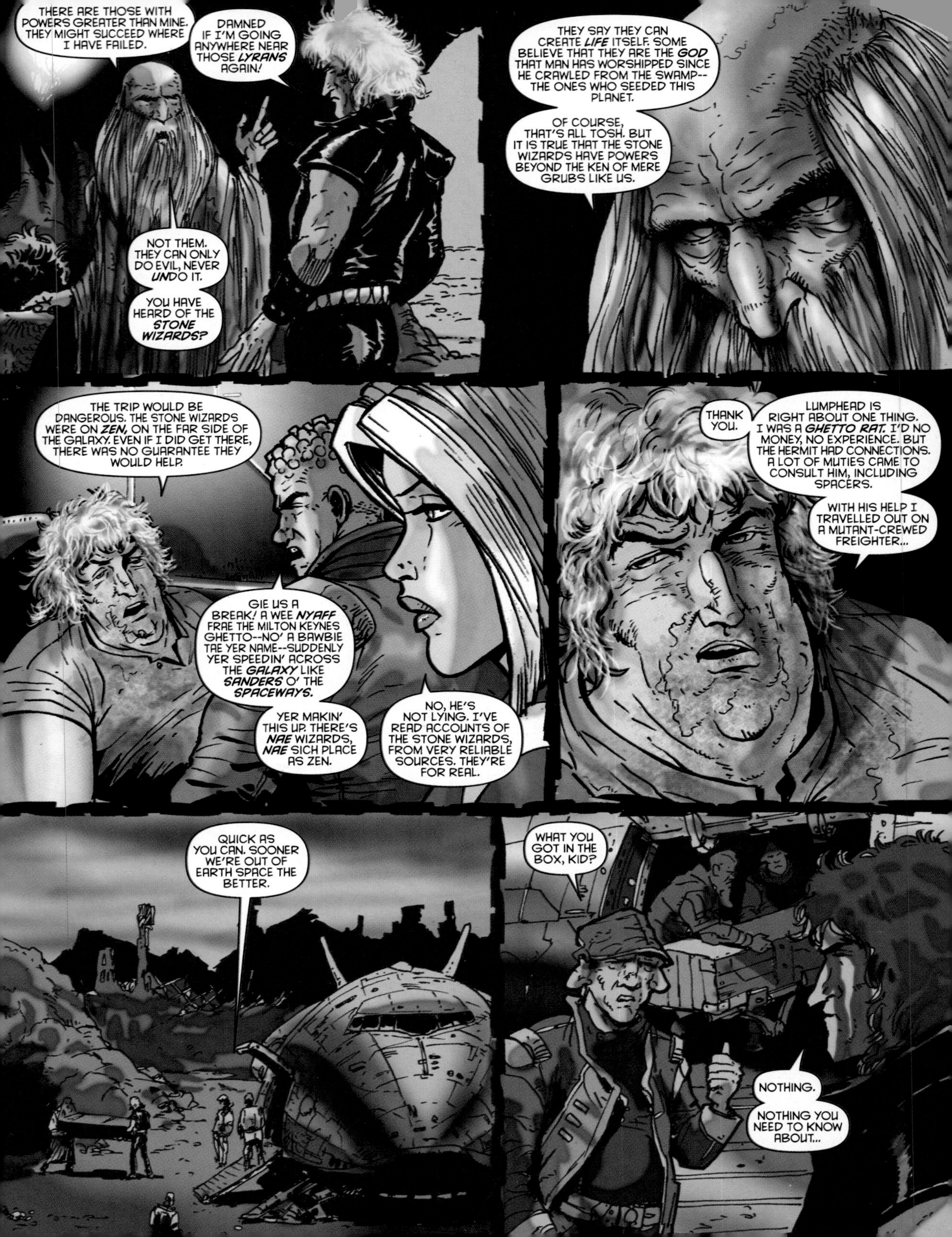
THERE ARE THOSE WITH POWERS GREATER THAN MINE. THEY MIGHT SUCCEED WHERE I HAVE FAILED.
DAMNED IF I'M GOING ANYWHERE NEAR THOSE LYRANS AGAIN!
NOT THEM. THEY CAN ONLY DO EVIL, NEVER UNDO IT.
YOU HAVE HEARD OF THE STONE WIZARDS?
THEY SAY THEY CAN CREATE LIFE ITSELF. SOME BELIEVE THAT THEY ARE THE GOD THAT MAN HAS WORSHIPPED SINCE HE CRAWLED FROM THE SWAMP-- THE ONES WHO SEEDED THIS PLANET.
OF COURSE, THAT'S ALL TOSH. BUT IT IS TRUE THAT THE STONE WIZARDS HAVE POWERS BEYOND THE KEN OF MERE GRUBS LIKE US.
THE TRIP WOULD BE DANGEROUS. THE STONE WIZARDS WERE ON ZEN, ON THE FAR SIDE OF THE GALAXY. EVEN IF I DID GET THERE, THERE WAS NO GUARANTEE THEY WOULD HELP.
GIE US A BREAK! A WEE NYAFF FRAE THE MILTON KEYNES GHETTO--NO' A BAWBIE TAE YER NAME--SUDDENLY YER SPEEDIN' ACROSS THE GALAXY LIKE SANDERS O' THE SPACEWAYS.
YER MAKIN' THIS UP. THERE'S NAE WIZARDS, NAE SICH PLACE AS ZEN.
NO, HE'S NOT LYING. I'VE READ ACCOUNTS OF THE STONE WIZARDS, FROM VERY RELIABLE SOURCES. THEY'RE FOR REAL.
THANK YOU.
LUMPHEAD IS RIGHT ABOUT ONE THING. I WAS A GHETTO RAT. I'D NO MONEY, NO EXPERIENCE. BUT THE HERMIT HAD CONNECTIONS. A LOT OF MUTIES CAME TO CONSULT HIM, INCLUDING SPACERS.
WITH HIS HELP I TRAVELLED OUT ON A MUTANT-CREWED FREIGHTER...
QUICK AS YOU CAN. SOONER WE'RE OUT OF EARTH SPACE THE BETTER.
WHAT YOU GOT IN THE BOX, KID?
NOTHING.
NOTHING YOU NEED TO KNOW ABOUT...

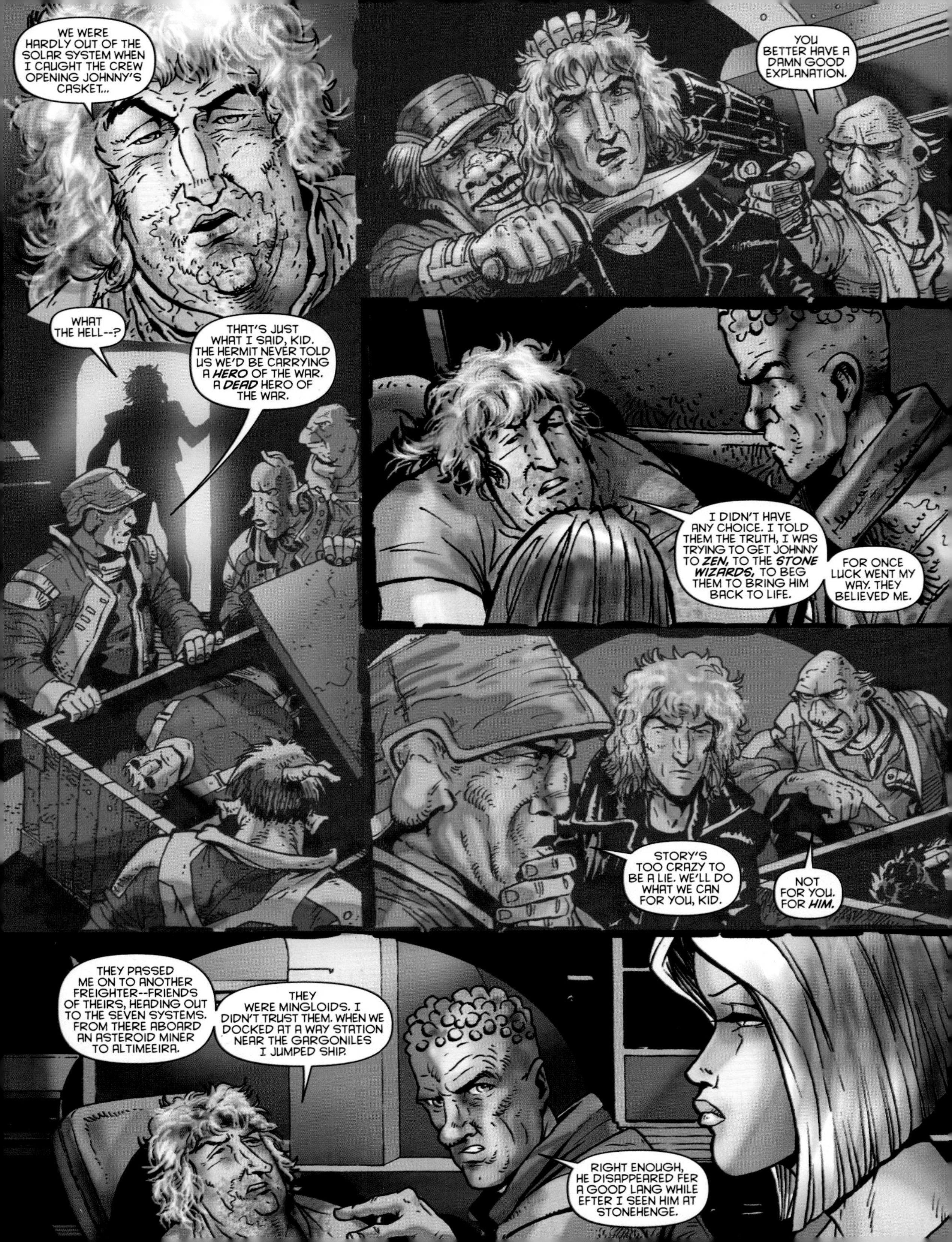
WE WERE HARDLY OUT OF THE SOLAR SYSTEM WHEN I CAUGHT THE CREW OPENING JOHNNY'S CASKET...
YOU BETTER HAVE A DAMN GOOD EXPLANATION.
WHAT THE HELL--?
THAT'S JUST WHAT I SAID, KID. THE HERMIT NEVER TOLD US WE'D BE CARRYING A HERO OF THE WAR. A DEAD HERO OF THE WAR.
I DIDN'T HAVE ANY CHOICE. I TOLD THEM THE TRUTH, I WAS TRYING TO GET JOHNNY TO ZEN, TO THE STONE WIZARDS, TO BEG THEM TO BRING HIM BACK TO LIFE.
FOR ONCE LUCK WENT MY WAY. THEY BELIEVED ME.
STORY'S TOO CRAZY TO BE A LIE. WE'LL DO WHAT WE CAN FOR YOU, KID.
NOT FOR YOU. FOR HIM.
THEY PASSED ME ON TO ANOTHER FREIGHTER--FRIENDS OF THEIRS, HEADING OUT TO THE SEVEN SYSTEMS. FROM THERE ABOARD AN ASTEROID MINER TO ALTIMEEIRA.
THEY WERE MINGLOIDS. I DIDN'T TRUST THEM. WHEN WE DOCKED AT A WAY STATION NEAR THE GARGONILES I JUMPED SHIP.
RIGHT ENOUGH, HE DISAPPEARED FER A GOOD LANG WHILE EFTER I SEEN HIM AT STONEHENGE.

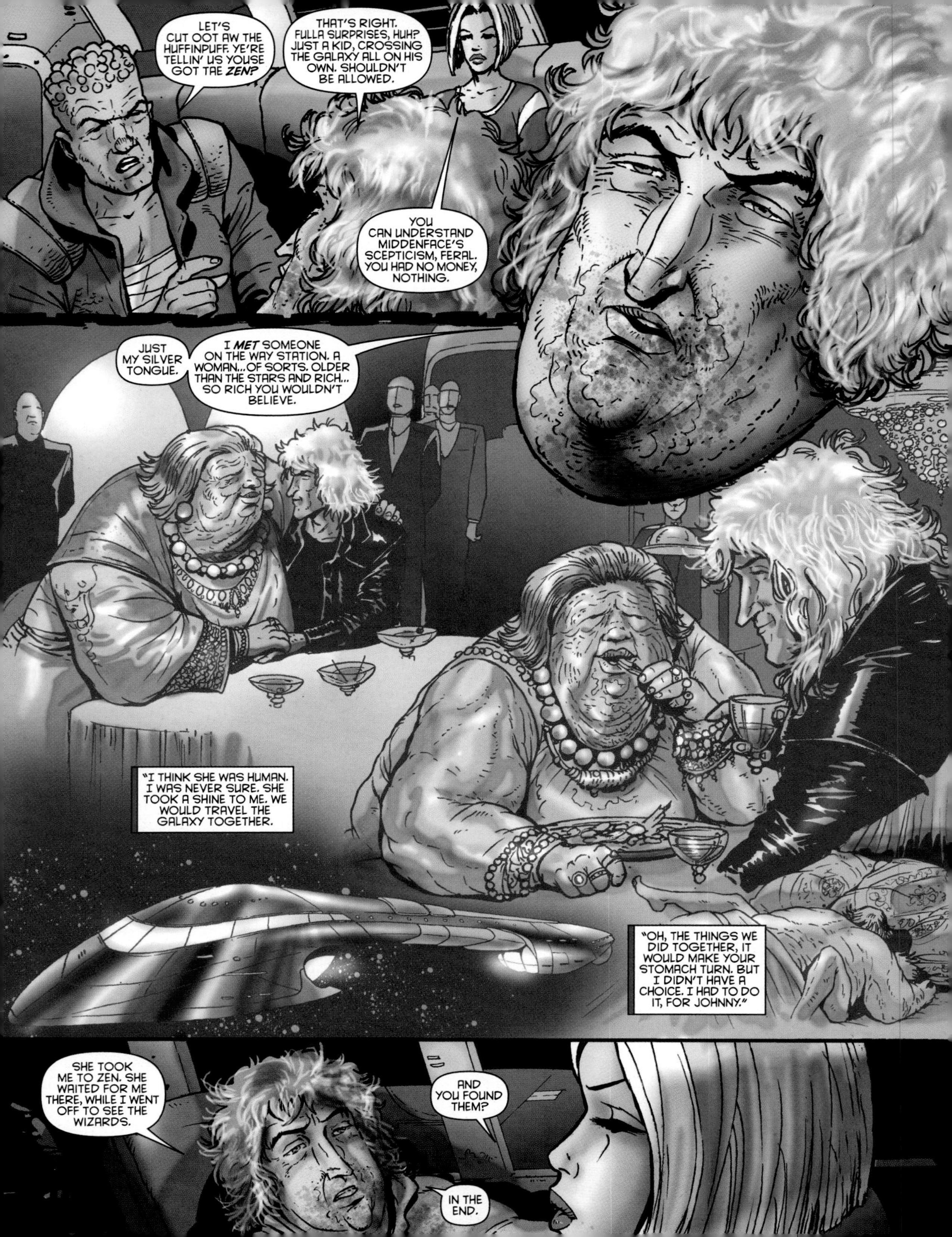

LET'S CUT OOT AW THE HUFFINPUFF. YE'RE TELLIN' US YOUSE GOT TAE ZEN?
THAT'S RIGHT. FULLA SURPRISES, HUH? JUST A KID, CROSSING THE GALAXY ALL ON HIS OWN. SHOULDN'T BE ALLOWED.
YOU CAN UNDERSTAND MIDDENFACE'S SCEPTICISM, FERAL. YOU HAD NO MONEY, NOTHING.
JUST MY SILVER TONGUE.
I MET SOMEONE ON THE WAY STATION. A WOMAN... OF SORTS. OLDER THAN THE STARS AND RICH... SO RICH YOU WOULDN'T BELIEVE.
"I THINK SHE WAS HUMAN. I WAS NEVER SURE. SHE TOOK A SHINE TO ME. WE WOULD TRAVEL THE GALAXY TOGETHER.
"OH, THE THINGS WE DID TOGETHER, IT WOULD MAKE YOUR STOMACH TURN. BUT I DIDN'T HAVE A CHOICE. I HAD TO DO IT, FOR JOHNNY."
SHE TOOK ME TO ZEN. SHE WAITED FOR ME THERE, WHILE I WENT OFF TO SEE THE WIZARDS.
AND YOU FOUND THEM?
IN THE END.

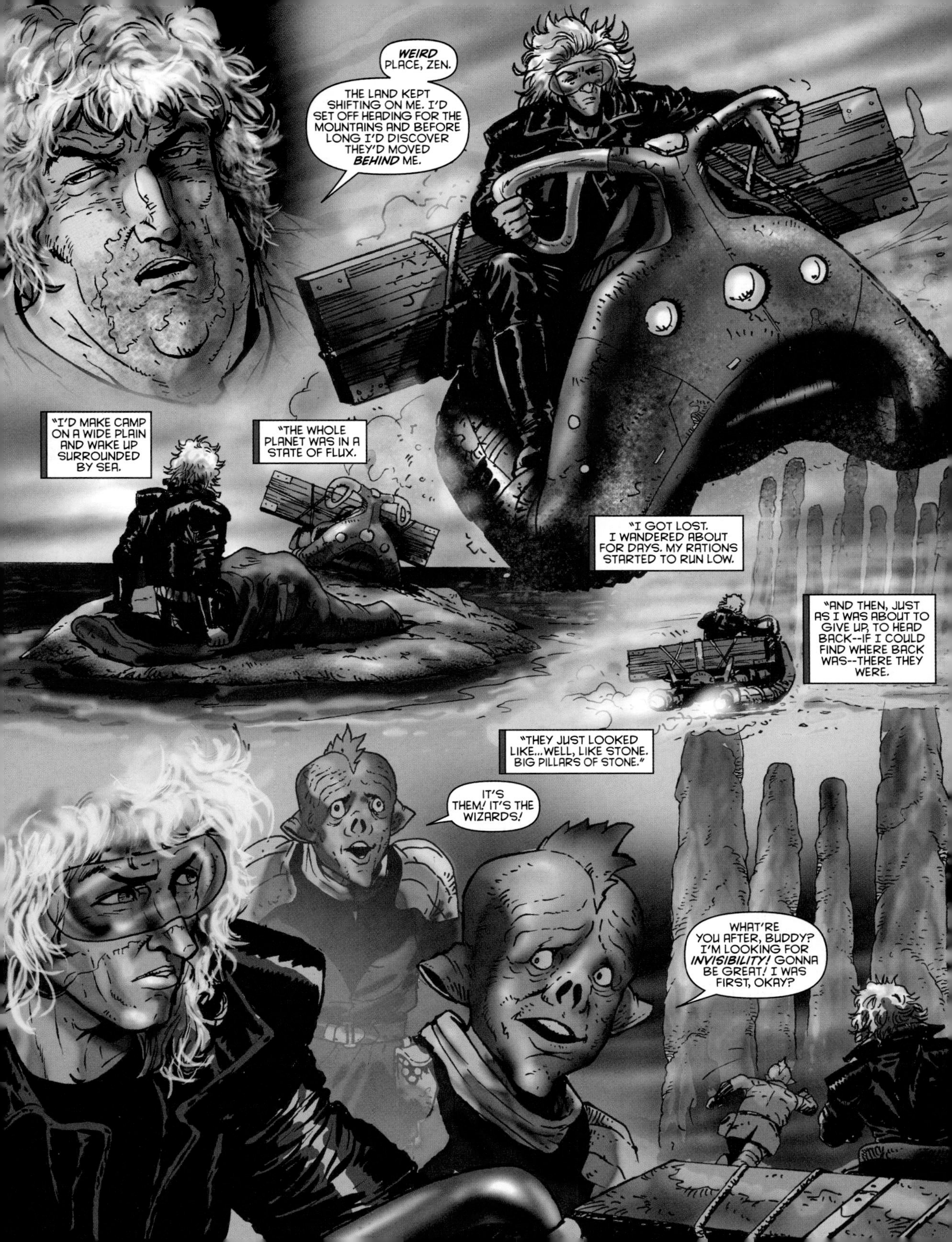

WEIRD PLACE, ZEN.
THE LAND KEPT SHIFTING ON ME. I'D SET OFF HEADING FOR THE MOUNTAINS AND BEFORE LONG I'D DISCOVER THEY'D MOVED BEHIND ME.
"I'D MAKE CAMP ON A WIDE PLAIN AND WAKE UP SURROUNDED BY SEA.
"THE WHOLE PLANET WAS IN A STATE OF FLUX.
"I GOT LOST. I WANDERED ABOUT FOR DAYS. MY RATIONS STARTED TO RUN LOW.
"AND THEN, JUST AS I WAS ABOUT TO GIVE UP, TO HEAD BACK--IF I COULD FIND WHERE BACK WAS--THERE THEY WERE.
"THEY JUST LOOKED LIKE...WELL, LIKE STONE. BIG PILLARS OF STONE."
IT'S THEM! IT'S THE WIZARDS!
WHAT'RE YOU AFTER, BUDDY? I'M LOOKING FOR INVISIBILITY! GONNA BE GREAT! I WAS FIRST, OKAY?

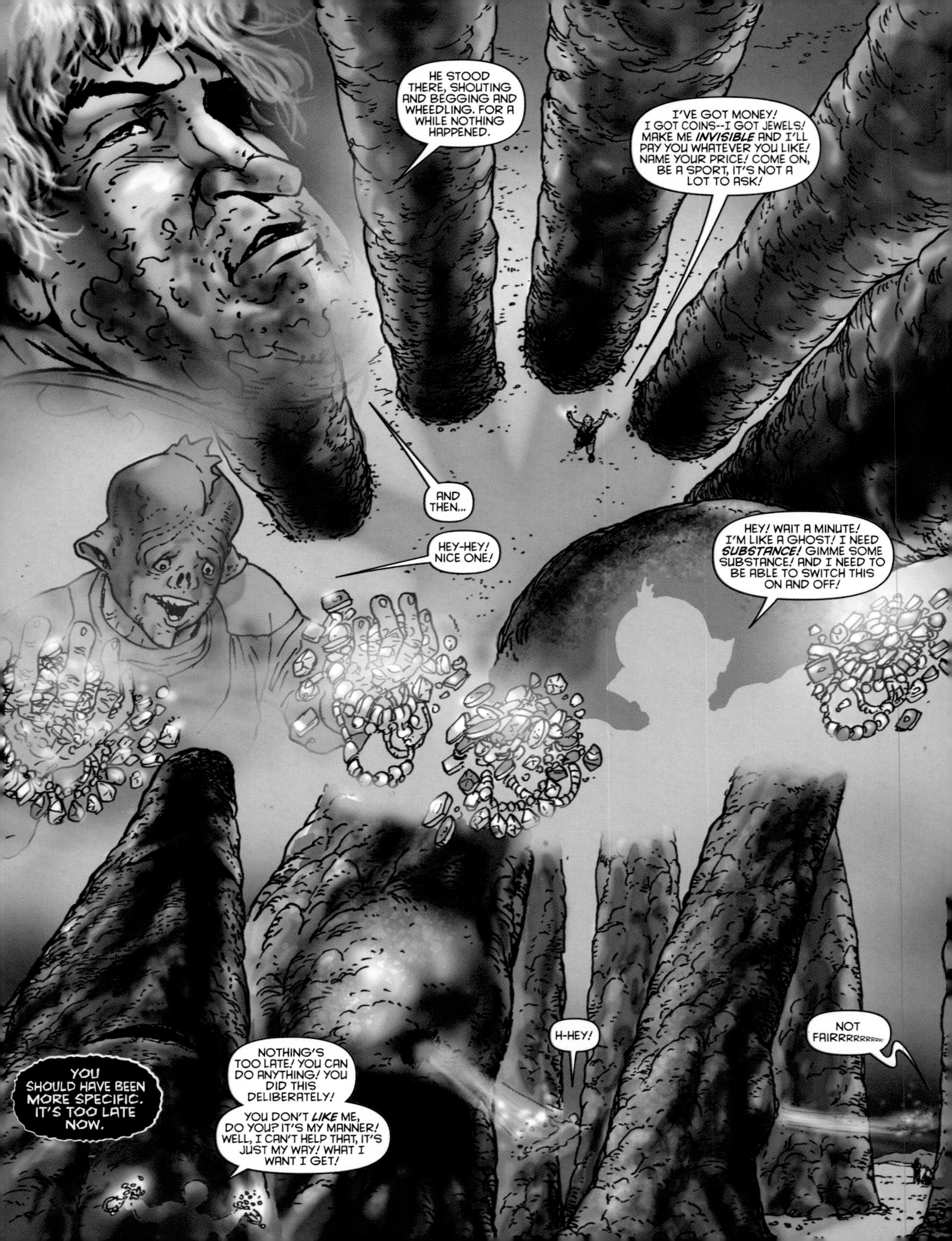
HE STOOD THERE, SHOUTING AND BEGGING AND WHEEDLING. FOR A WHILE NOTHING HAPPENED.
I'VE GOT MONEY! I GOT COINS--I GOT JEWELS! MAKE ME *INVISIBLE* AND I'LL PAY YOU WHATEVER YOU LIKE! NAME YOUR PRICE! COME ON, BE A SPORT, IT'S NOT A LOT TO ASK!
AND THEN...
HEY-HEY! NICE ONE!
HEY! WAIT A MINUTE! I'M LIKE A GHOST! I NEED *SUBSTANCE!* GIMME SOME SUBSTANCE! AND I NEED TO BE ABLE TO SWITCH THIS ON AND OFF!
YOU SHOULD HAVE BEEN MORE SPECIFIC. IT'S TOO LATE NOW.
NOTHING'S TOO LATE! YOU CAN DO ANYTHING! YOU DID THIS DELIBERATELY!
YOU DON'T *LIKE* ME, DO YOU? IT'S MY MANNER! WELL, I CAN'T HELP THAT, IT'S JUST MY WAY! WHAT I WANT I GET!
H-HEY!
NOT FAIRRRRRRRRR!

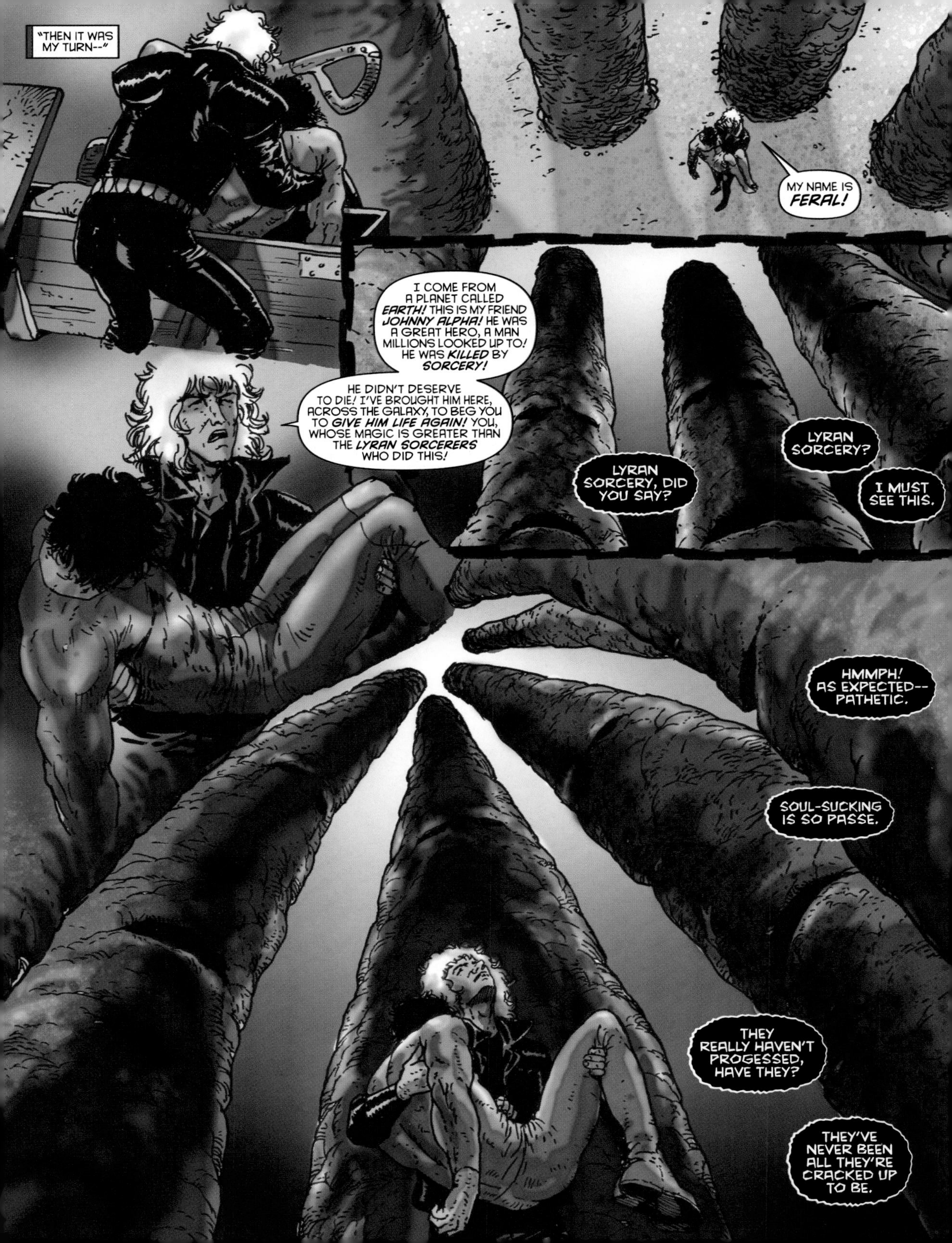

"THEN IT WAS MY TURN--"
MY NAME IS FERAL!
I COME FROM A PLANET CALLED EARTH! THIS IS MY FRIEND JOHNNY ALPHA! HE WAS A GREAT HERO, A MAN MILLIONS LOOKED UP TO! HE WAS KILLED BY SORCERY!
HE DIDN'T DESERVE TO DIE! I'VE BROUGHT HIM HERE, ACROSS THE GALAXY, TO BEG YOU TO GIVE HIM LIFE AGAIN! YOU, WHOSE MAGIC IS GREATER THAN THE LYRAN SORCERERS WHO DID THIS!
LYRAN SORCERY, DID YOU SAY?
LYRAN SORCERY?
I MUST SEE THIS.
HMMPH! AS EXPECTED-- PATHETIC.
SOUL-SUCKING IS SO PASSE.
THEY REALLY HAVEN'T PROGESSED, HAVE THEY?
THEY'VE NEVER BEEN ALL THEY'RE CRACKED UP TO BE.

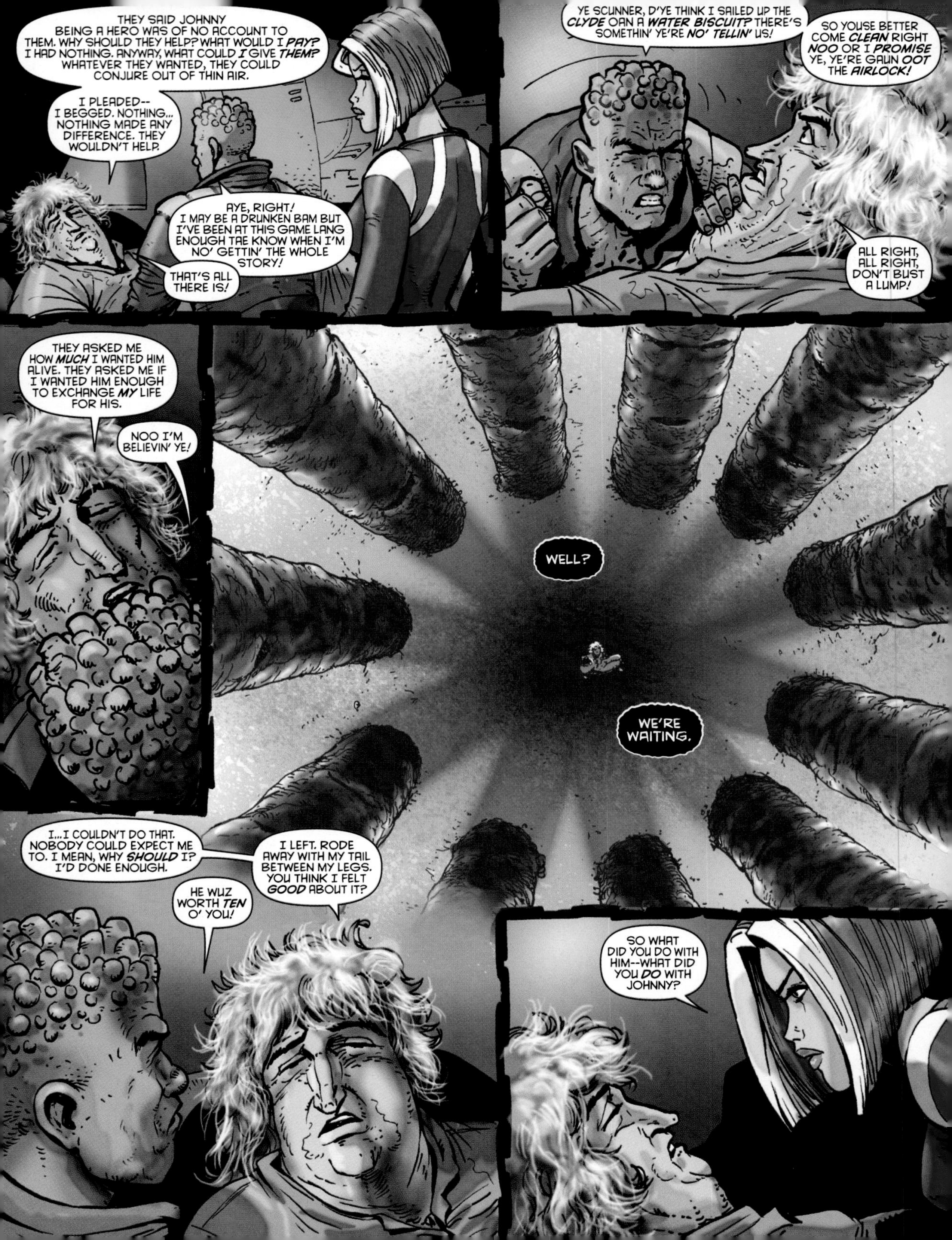
THEY SAID JOHNNY BEING A HERO WAS OF NO ACCOUNT TO THEM. WHY SHOULD THEY HELP? WHAT WOULD I PAY? I HAD NOTHING. ANYWAY, WHAT COULD I GIVE THEM? WHATEVER THEY WANTED, THEY COULD CONJURE OUT OF THIN AIR.
I PLEADED-- I BEGGED. NOTHING... NOTHING MADE ANY DIFFERENCE. THEY WOULDN'T HELP.
AYE, RIGHT! I MAY BE A DRUNKEN BAM BUT I'VE BEEN AT THIS GAME LANG ENOUGH TAE KNOW WHEN I'M NO' GETTIN' THE WHOLE STORY!
THAT'S ALL THERE IS!
YE SCUNNER, D'YE THINK I SAILED UP THE CLYDE OAN A WATER BISCUIT? THERE'S SOMETHIN' YE'RE NO' TELLIN' US!
SO YOUSE BETTER COME CLEAN RIGHT NOO OR I PROMISE YE, YE'RE GAUN OOT THE AIRLOCK!
ALL RIGHT, ALL RIGHT, DON'T BUST A LUMP!
THEY ASKED ME HOW MUCH I WANTED HIM ALIVE. THEY ASKED ME IF I WANTED HIM ENOUGH TO EXCHANGE MY LIFE FOR HIS.
NOO I'M BELIEVIN' YE!
WELL?
WE'RE WAITING.
I...I COULDN'T DO THAT. NOBODY COULD EXPECT ME TO. I MEAN, WHY SHOULD I? I'D DONE ENOUGH.
I LEFT. RODE AWAY WITH MY TAIL BETWEEN MY LEGS. YOU THINK I FELT GOOD ABOUT IT?
HE WUZ WORTH TEN O' YOU!
SO WHAT DID YOU DO WITH HIM--WHAT DID YOU DO WITH JOHNNY?

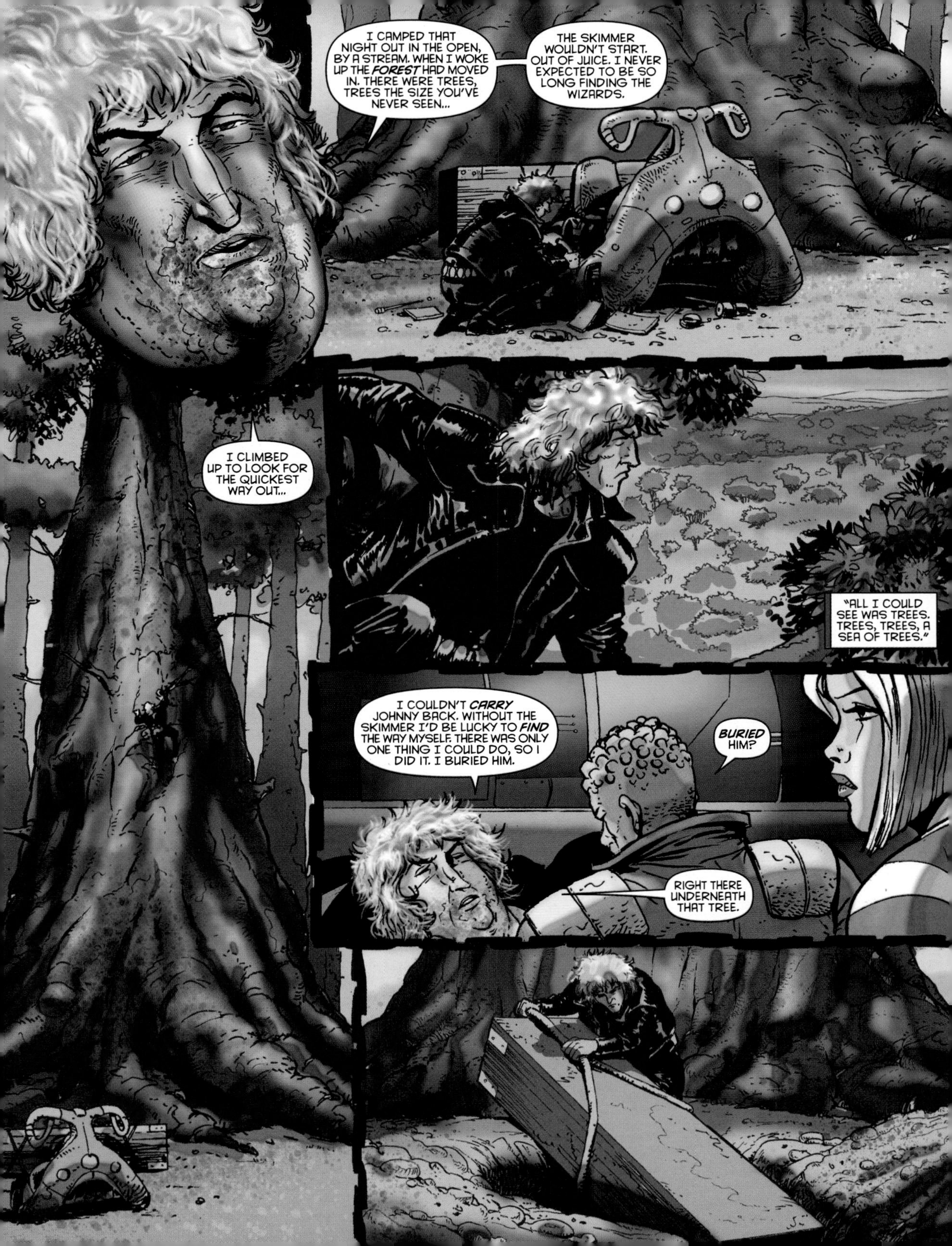

I CAMPED THAT NIGHT OUT IN THE OPEN, BY A STREAM. WHEN I WOKE UP THE FOREST HAD MOVED IN. THERE WERE TREES, TREES THE SIZE YOU'VE NEVER SEEN...
THE SKIMMER WOULDN'T START. OUT OF JUICE. I NEVER EXPECTED TO BE SO LONG FINDING THE WIZARDS.
I CLIMBED UP TO LOOK FOR THE QUICKEST WAY OUT...
"ALL I COULD SEE WAS TREES. TREES, TREES, A SEA OF TREES."
I COULDN'T CARRY JOHNNY BACK. WITHOUT THE SKIMMER I'D BE LUCKY TO FIND THE WAY MYSELF. THERE WAS ONLY ONE THING I COULD DO, SO I DID IT. I BURIED HIM.
BURIED HIM?
RIGHT THERE UNDERNEATH THAT TREE.

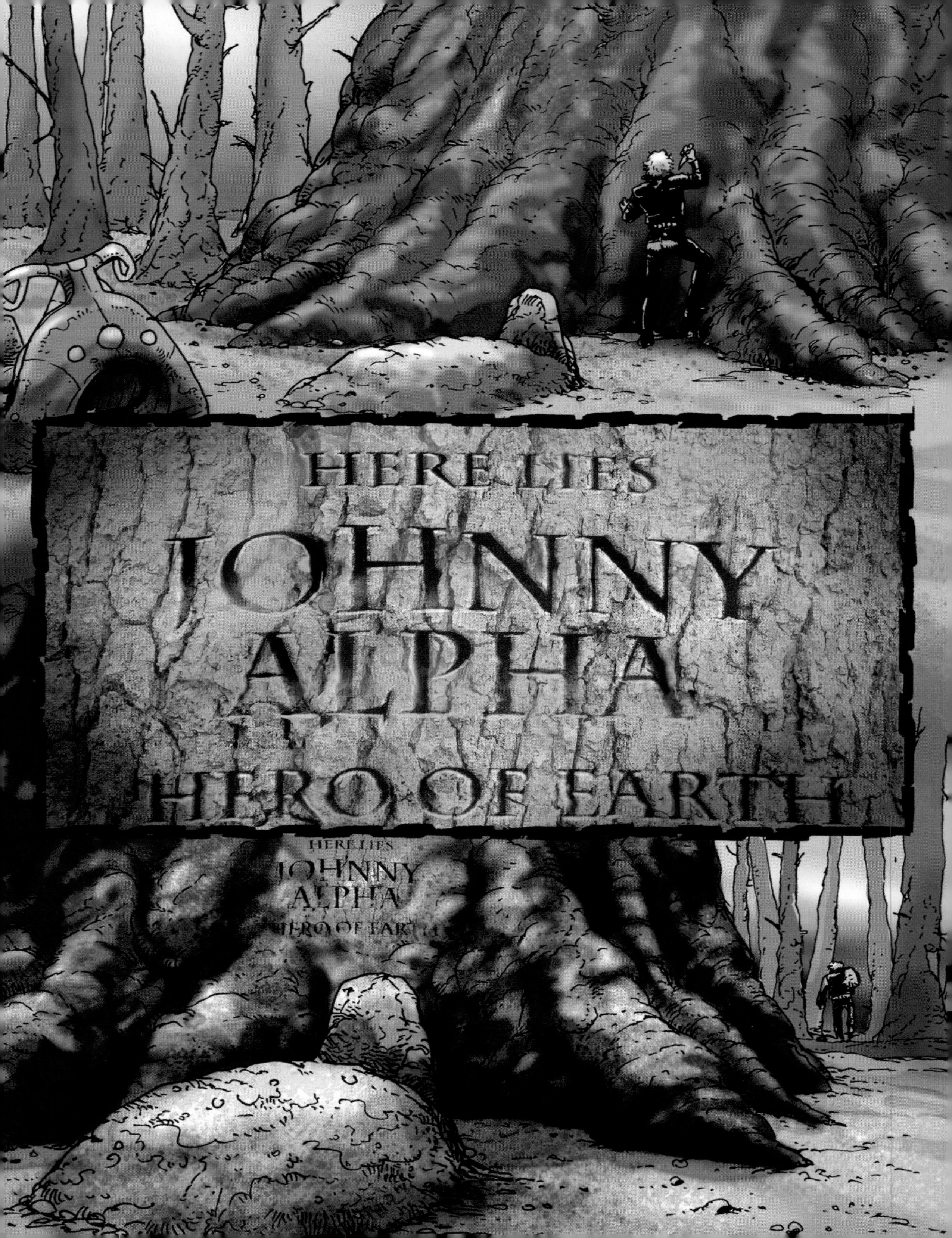
HERE LIES
JOHNNY
ALPHA
HERO OF EARTH
HERE LIES
JOHNNY
ALPHA
HERO OF EARTH

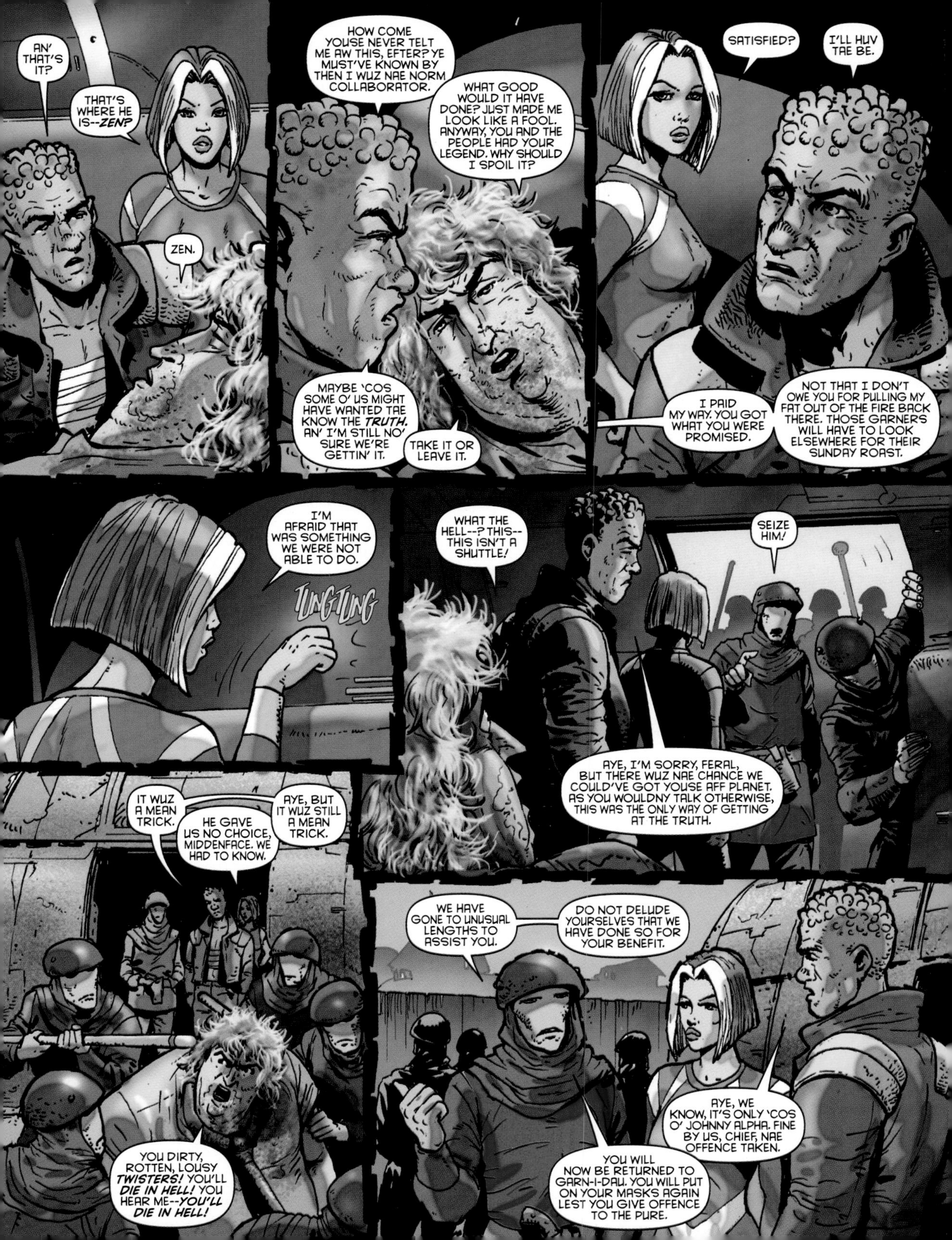

AN' THAT'S IT?
THAT'S WHERE HE IS--*ZEN?*
ZEN.
HOW COME YOUSE NEVER TELT ME AW THIS, EFTER? YE MUST'VE KNOWN BY THEN I WUZ NAE NORM COLLABORATOR.
WHAT GOOD WOULD IT HAVE DONE? JUST MADE ME LOOK LIKE A FOOL. ANYWAY, YOU AND THE PEOPLE HAD YOUR LEGEND. WHY SHOULD I SPOIL IT?
MAYBE 'COS SOME O' US MIGHT HAVE WANTED TAE KNOW THE *TRUTH.* AN' I'M STILL NO' SURE WE'RE GETTIN' IT.
TAKE IT OR LEAVE IT.
SATISFIED?
I'LL HUV TAE BE.
I PAID MY WAY. YOU GOT WHAT YOU WERE PROMISED.
NOT THAT I DON'T OWE YOU FOR PULLING MY FAT OUT OF THE FIRE BACK THERE. THOSE GARNERS WILL HAVE TO LOOK ELSEWHERE FOR THEIR SUNDAY ROAST.
I'M AFRAID THAT WAS SOMETHING WE WERE NOT ABLE TO DO.
TUNG TUNG
WHAT THE HELL--? THIS--THIS ISN'T A SHUTTLE!
SEIZE HIM!
AYE, I'M SORRY, FERAL, BUT THERE WUZ NAE CHANCE WE COULD'VE GOT YOUSE AFF PLANET. AS YOU WOULDNY TALK OTHERWISE, THIS WAS THE ONLY WAY OF GETTING AT THE TRUTH.
IT WUZ A MEAN TRICK.
HE GAVE US NO CHOICE, MIDDENFACE. WE HAD TO KNOW.
AYE, BUT IT WUZ STILL A MEAN TRICK.
YOU DIRTY, ROTTEN, LOUSY *TWISTERS!* YOU'LL *DIE IN HELL!* YOU HEAR ME--*YOU'LL DIE IN HELL!*
WE HAVE GONE TO UNUSUAL LENGTHS TO ASSIST YOU.
DO NOT DELUDE YOURSELVES THAT WE HAVE DONE SO FOR YOUR BENEFIT.
AYE, WE KNOW, IT'S ONLY 'COS O' JOHNNY ALPHA. FINE BY US, CHIEF, NAE OFFENCE TAKEN.
YOU WILL NOW BE RETURNED TO GARN-I-DAU. YOU WILL PUT ON YOUR MASKS AGAIN LEST YOU GIVE OFFENCE TO THE PURE.

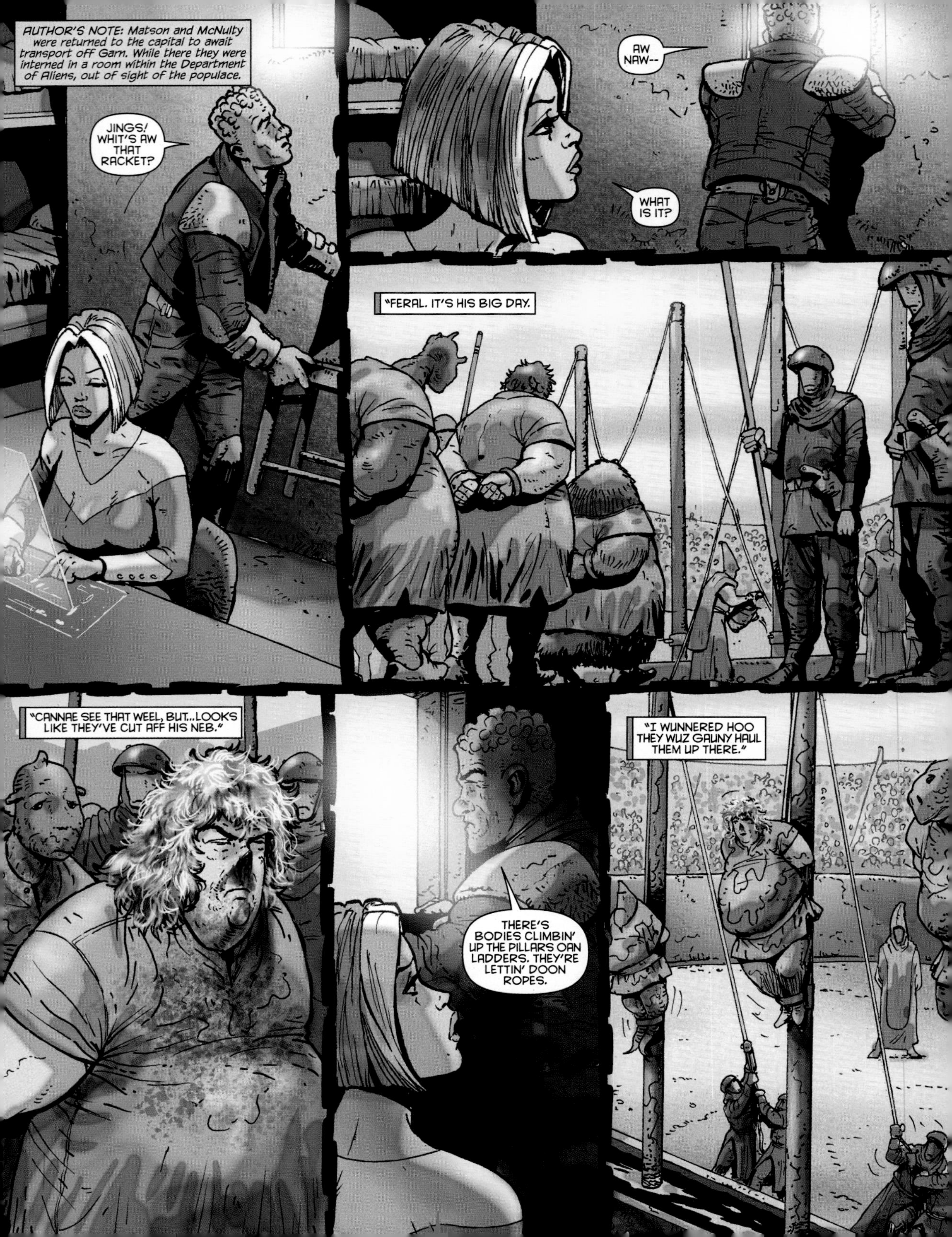
AUTHOR'S NOTE: Matson and McNulty were returned to the capital to await transport off Garn. While there they were interned in a room within the Department of Aliens, out of sight of the populace.
JINGS! WHIT'S AW THAT RACKET?
AW NAW--
WHAT IS IT?
"FERAL. IT'S HIS BIG DAY.
"CANNAE SEE THAT WEEL, BUT...LOOKS LIKE THEY'VE CUT AFF HIS NEB."
THERE'S BODIES CLIMBIN' UP THE PILLARS OAN LADDERS. THEY'RE LETTIN' DOON ROPES.
"I WUNNERED HOO THEY WUZ GAUNY HAUL THEM UP THERE."

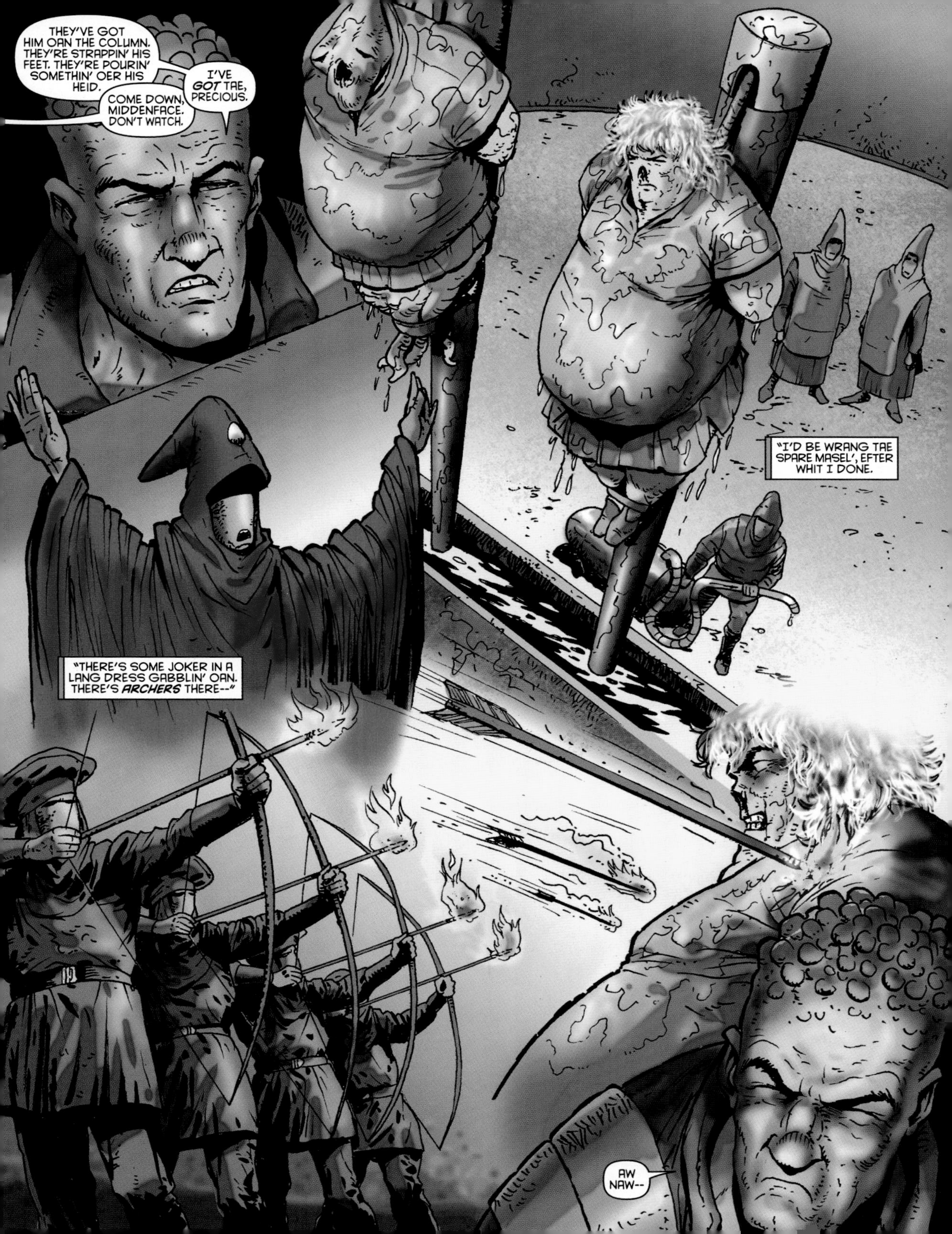
THEY'VE GOT HIM OAN THE COLUMN. THEY'RE STRAPPIN' HIS FEET. THEY'RE POURIN' SOMETHIN' OER HIS HEID.
I'VE GOT TAE, PRECIOUS.
COME DOWN, MIDDENFACE. DON'T WATCH.
"I'D BE WRANG TAE SPARE MASEL', EFTER WHIT I DONE.
"THERE'S SOME JOKER IN A LANG DRESS GABBLIN' OAN. THERE'S ARCHERS THERE--"
AW NAW--

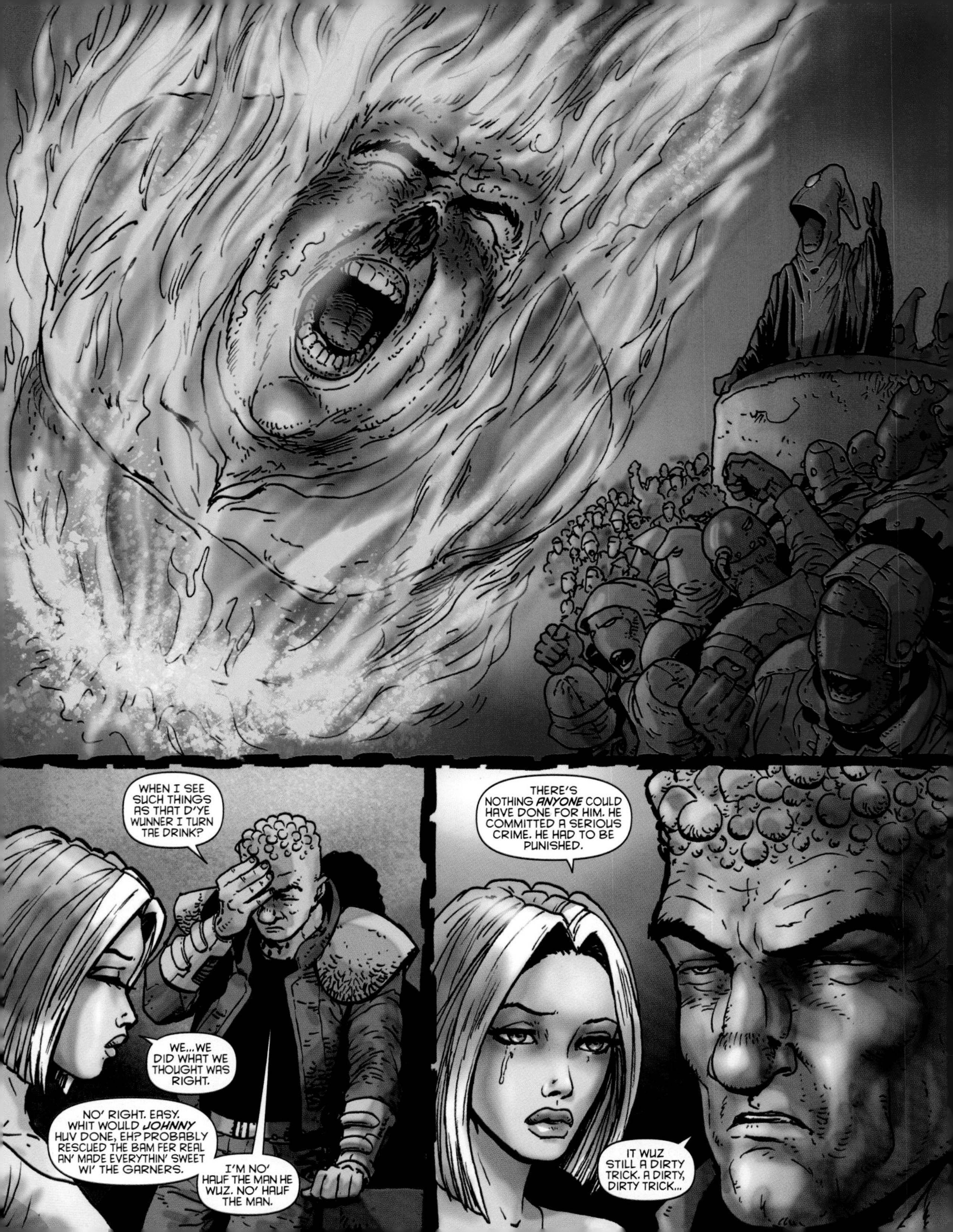
WHEN I SEE SUCH THINGS AS THAT D'YE WUNNER I TURN TAE DRINK?
WE... WE DID WHAT WE THOUGHT WAS RIGHT.
NO' RIGHT. EASY. WHIT WOULD *JOHNNY* HUV DONE, EH? PROBABLY RESCUED THE BAM FER REAL AN' MADE EVERYTHIN' SWEET WI' THE GARNERS.
I'M NO' HAUF THE MAN HE WUZ. NO' HAUF THE MAN.
THERE'S NOTHING *ANYONE* COULD HAVE DONE FOR HIM. HE COMMITTED A SERIOUS CRIME. HE HAD TO BE PUNISHED.
IT WUZ STILL A DIRTY TRICK. A DIRTY, DIRTY TRICK...

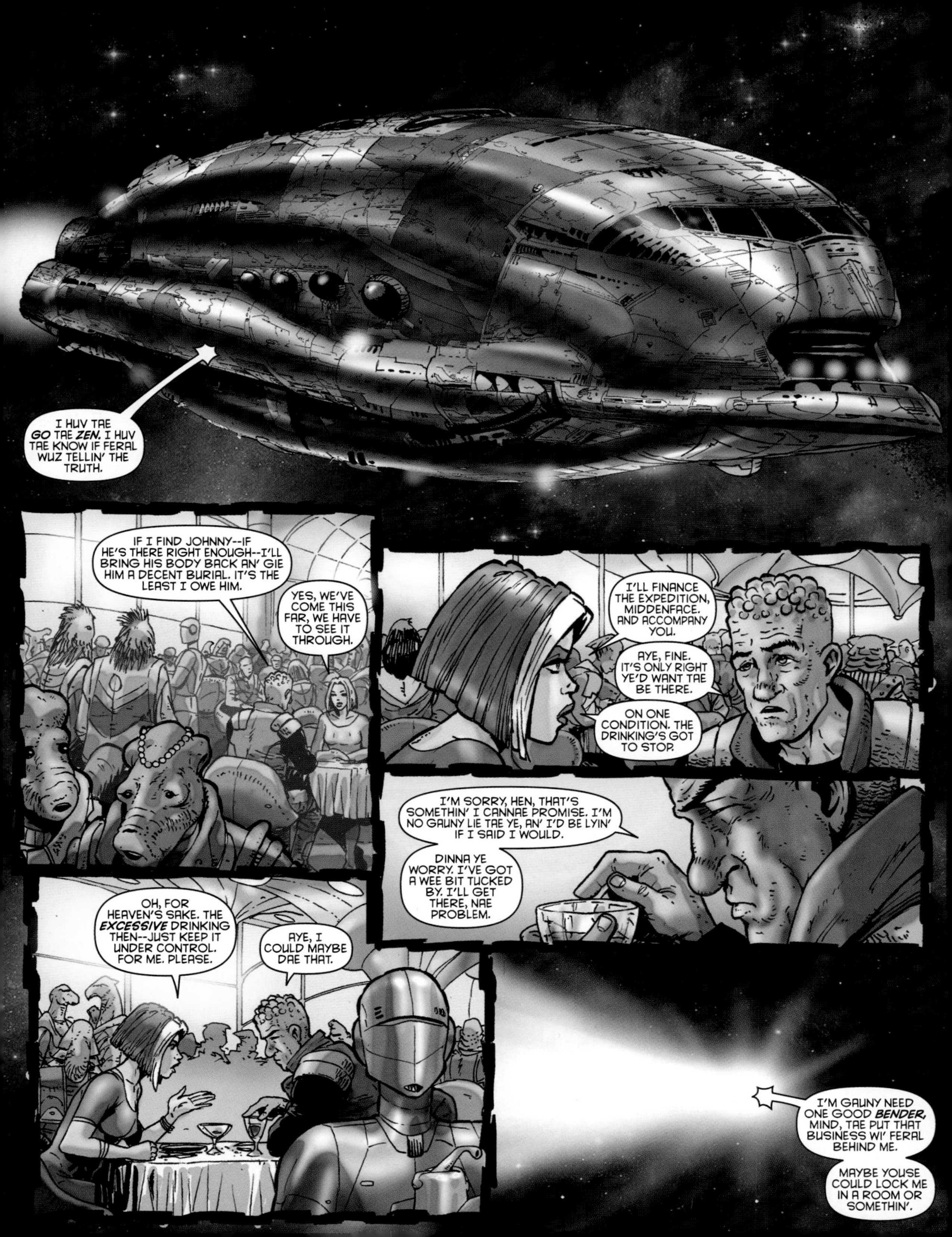
I HUV TAE GO TAE ZEN. I HUV TAE KNOW IF FERAL WUZ TELLIN' THE TRUTH.
IF I FIND JOHNNY--IF HE'S THERE RIGHT ENOUGH--I'LL BRING HIS BODY BACK AN' GIE HIM A DECENT BURIAL. IT'S THE LEAST I OWE HIM.
YES, WE'VE COME THIS FAR, WE HAVE TO SEE IT THROUGH.
I'LL FINANCE THE EXPEDITION, MIDDENFACE. AND ACCOMPANY YOU.
AYE, FINE. IT'S ONLY RIGHT YE'D WANT TAE BE THERE.
ON ONE CONDITION. THE DRINKING'S GOT TO STOP.
I'M SORRY, HEN, THAT'S SOMETHIN' I CANNAE PROMISE. I'M NO GAUNY LIE TAE YE, AN' I'D BE LYIN' IF I SAID I WOULD.
DINNA YE WORRY. I'VE GOT A WEE BIT TUCKED BY. I'LL GET THERE, NAE PROBLEM.
OH, FOR HEAVEN'S SAKE. THE EXCESSIVE DRINKING THEN--JUST KEEP IT UNDER CONTROL. FOR ME. PLEASE.
AYE, I COULD MAYBE DAE THAT.
I'M GAUNY NEED ONE GOOD BENDER, MIND, TAE PUT THAT BUSINESS WI' FERAL BEHIND ME.
MAYBE YOUSE COULD LOCK ME IN A ROOM OR SOMETHIN'.

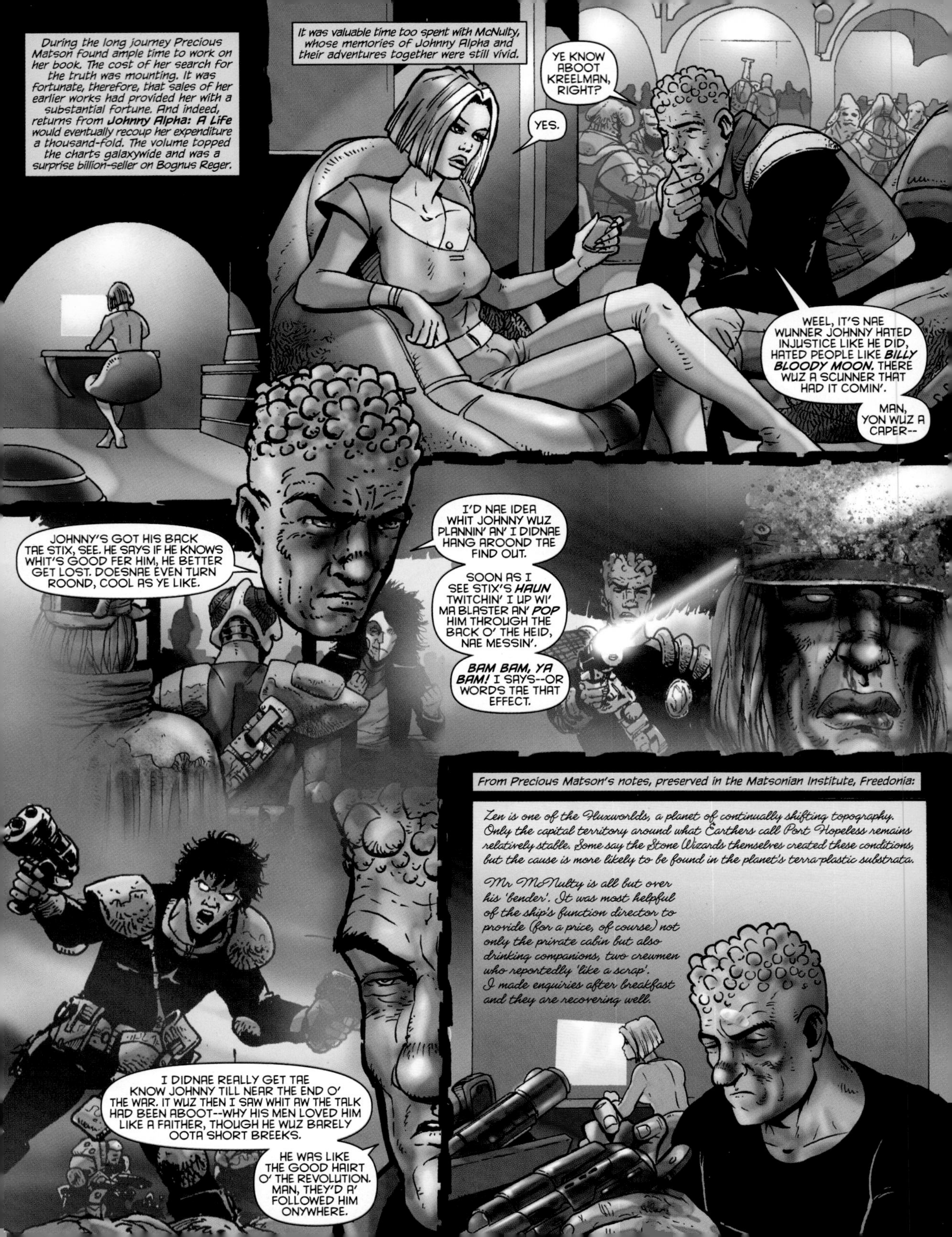
During the long journey Precious Matson found ample time to work on her book. The cost of her search for the truth was mounting. It was fortunate, therefore, that sales of her earlier works had provided her with a substantial fortune. And indeed, returns from **Johnny Alpha: A Life** would eventually recoup her expenditure a thousand-fold. The volume topped the charts galaxywide and was a surprise billion-seller on Bognus Reger.
It was valuable time too spent with McNulty, whose memories of Johnny Alpha and their adventures together were still vivid.
YE KNOW ABOOT KREELMAN, RIGHT?
YES.
WEEL, IT'S NAE WUNNER JOHNNY HATED INJUSTICE LIKE HE DID, HATED PEOPLE LIKE **BILLY BLOODY MOON.** THERE WUZ A SCUNNER THAT HAD IT COMIN'.
MAN, YON WUZ A CAPER--
JOHNNY'S GOT HIS BACK TAE STIX, SEE. HE SAYS IF HE KNOWS WHIT'S GOOD FER HIM, HE BETTER GET LOST. DOESNAE EVEN TURN ROOND, COOL AS YE LIKE.
I'D NAE IDEA WHIT JOHNNY WUZ PLANNIN' AN' I DIDNAE HANG AROOND TAE FIND OUT.
SOON AS I SEE STIX'S ***HAUN*** TWITCHIN' I UP WI' MA BLASTER AN' ***POP*** HIM THROUGH THE BACK O' THE HEID, NAE MESSIN'.
BAM BAM, YA BAM! I SAYS--OR WORDS TAE THAT EFFECT.
From Precious Matson's notes, preserved in the Matsonian Institute, Freedonia:
Zen is one of the Fluxworlds, a planet of continually shifting topography. Only the capital territory around what Earthers call Port Hopeless remains relatively stable. Some say the Stone Wizards themselves created these conditions, but the cause is more likely to be found in the planet's terra-plastic substrata.
Mr McNulty is all but over his 'bender'. It was most helpful of the ship's function director to provide (for a price, of course) not only the private cabin but also drinking companions, two crewmen who reportedly 'like a scrap'. I made enquiries after breakfast and they are recovering well.
I DIDNAE REALLY GET TAE KNOW JOHNNY TILL NEAR THE END O' THE WAR. IT WUZ THEN I SAW WHIT AW THE TALK HAD BEEN ABOOT--WHY HIS MEN LOVED HIM LIKE A FAITHER, THOUGH HE WUZ BARELY OOTA SHORT BREEKS.
HE WAS LIKE THE GOOD HAIRT O' THE REVOLUTION. MAN, THEY'D A' FOLLOWED HIM ONYWHERE.

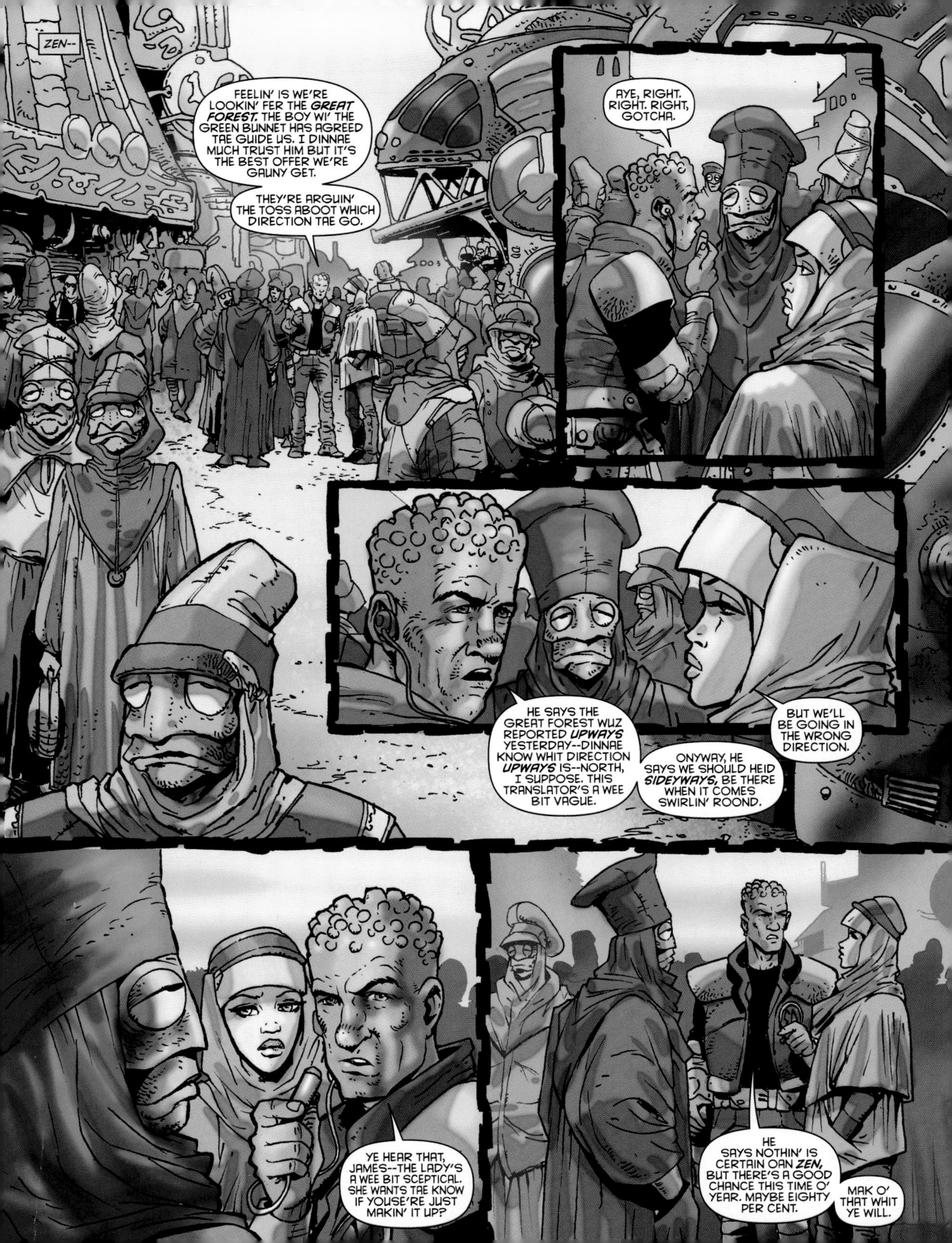

ZEN--
FEELIN' IS WE'RE LOOKIN' FER THE GREAT FOREST. THE BOY WI' THE GREEN BUNNET HAS AGREED TAE GUIDE US. I DINNAE MUCH TRUST HIM BUT IT'S THE BEST OFFER WE'RE GAUNY GET.
THEY'RE ARGUIN' THE TOSS ABOOT WHICH DIRECTION TAE GO.
AYE, RIGHT. RIGHT. RIGHT, GOTCHA.
HE SAYS THE GREAT FOREST WUZ REPORTED UPWAYS YESTERDAY--DINNAE KNOW WHIT DIRECTION UPWAYS IS--NORTH, I SUPPOSE. THIS TRANSLATOR'S A WEE BIT VAGUE.
ONYWAY, HE SAYS WE SHOULD HEID SIDEYWAYS, BE THERE WHEN IT COMES SWIRLIN' ROOND.
BUT WE'LL BE GOING IN THE WRONG DIRECTION.
YE HEAR THAT, JAMES--THE LADY'S A WEE BIT SCEPTICAL. SHE WANTS TAE KNOW IF YOUSE'RE JUST MAKIN' IT UP?
HE SAYS NOTHIN' IS CERTAIN OAN ZEN, BUT THERE'S A GOOD CHANCE THIS TIME O' YEAR. MAYBE EIGHTY PER CENT.
MAK O' THAT WHIT YE WILL.

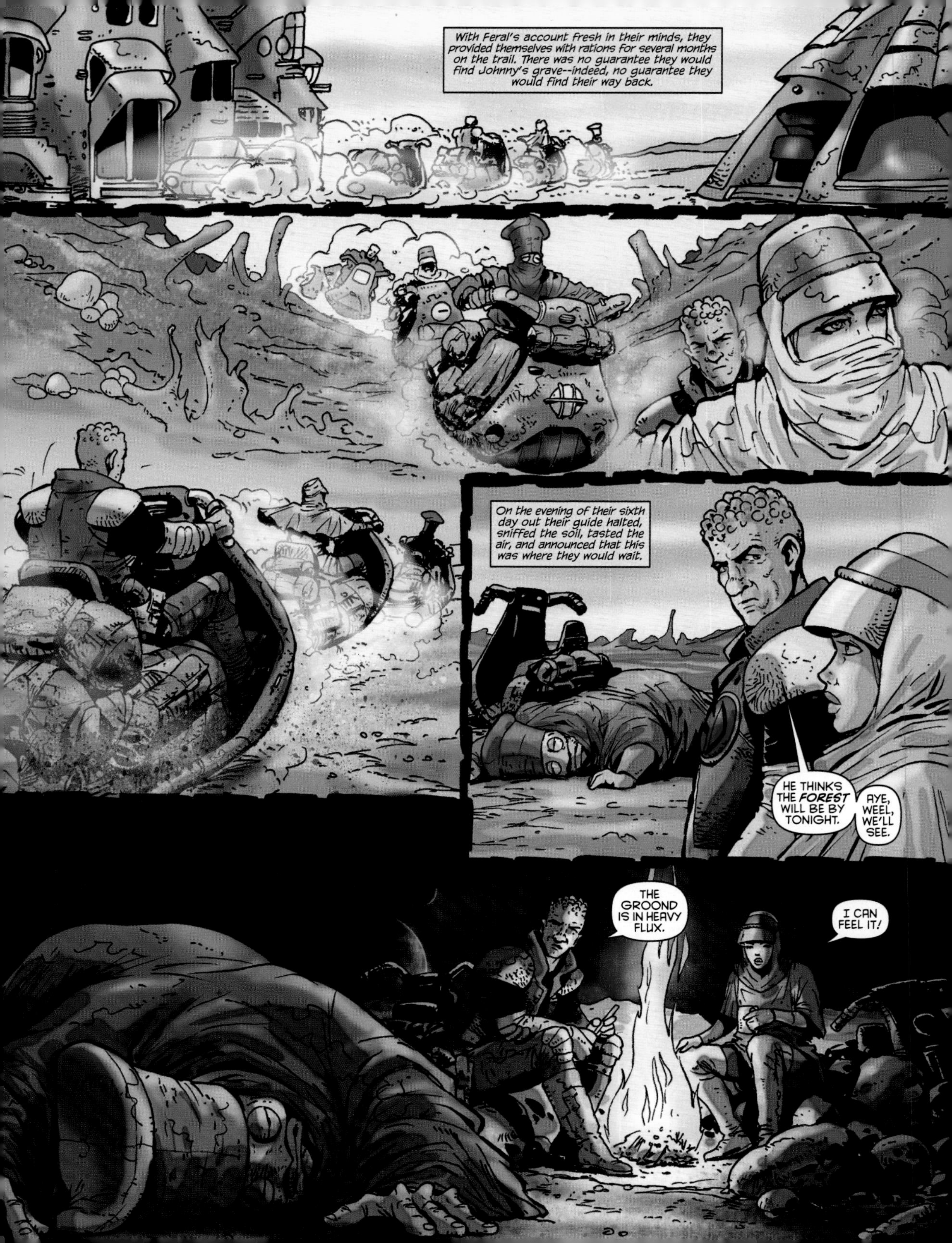

With Feral's account fresh in their minds, they provided themselves with rations for several months on the trail. There was no guarantee they would find Johnny's grave--indeed, no guarantee they would find their way back.
On the evening of their sixth day out their guide halted, sniffed the soil, tasted the air, and announced that this was where they would wait.
HE THINKS THE FOREST WILL BE BY TONIGHT.
AYE, WEEL, WE'LL SEE.
THE GROOND IS IN HEAVY FLUX.
I CAN FEEL IT!

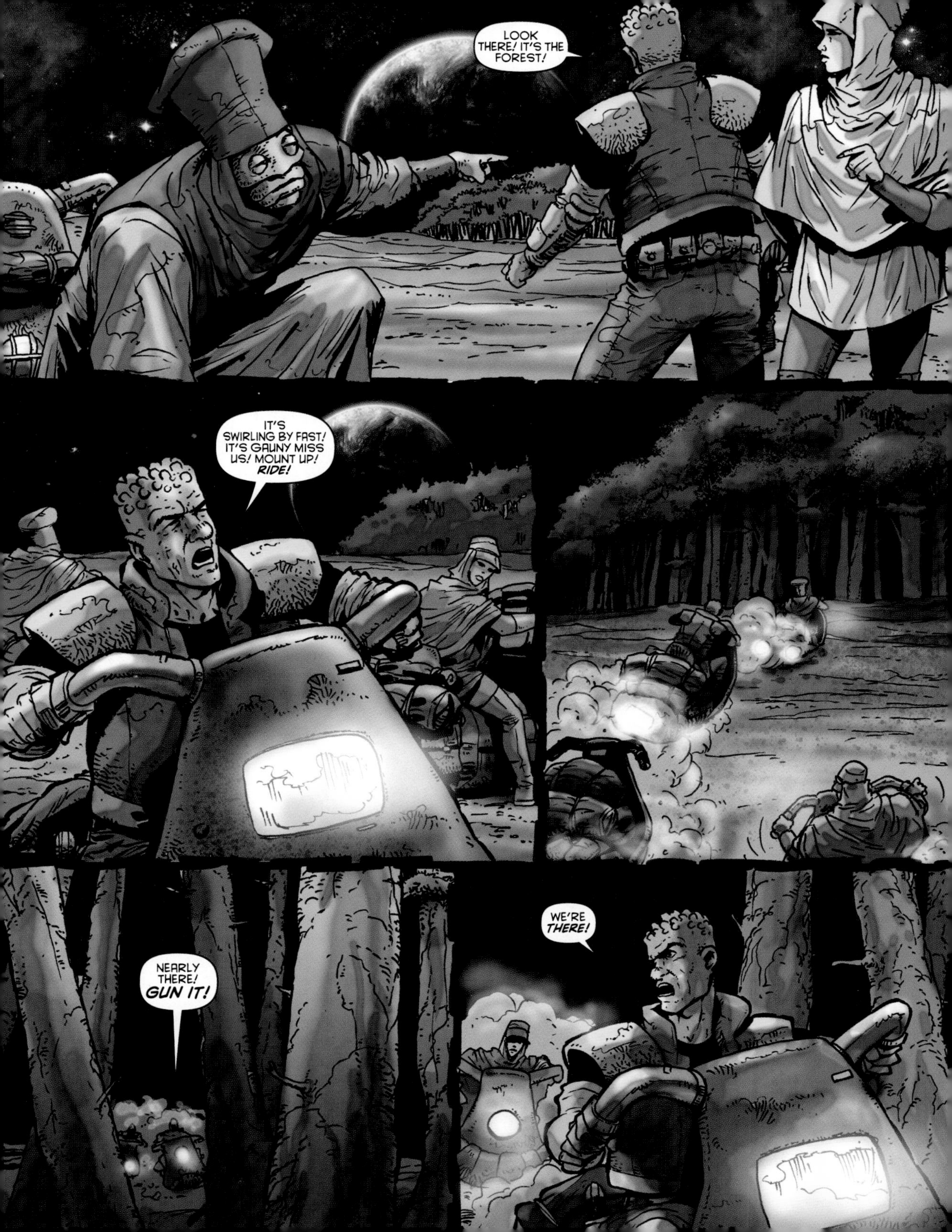
LOOK THERE! IT'S THE FOREST!
IT'S SWIRLING BY FAST! IT'S GAUNY MISS US! MOUNT UP! RIDE!
NEARLY THERE! GUN IT!
WE'RE THERE!

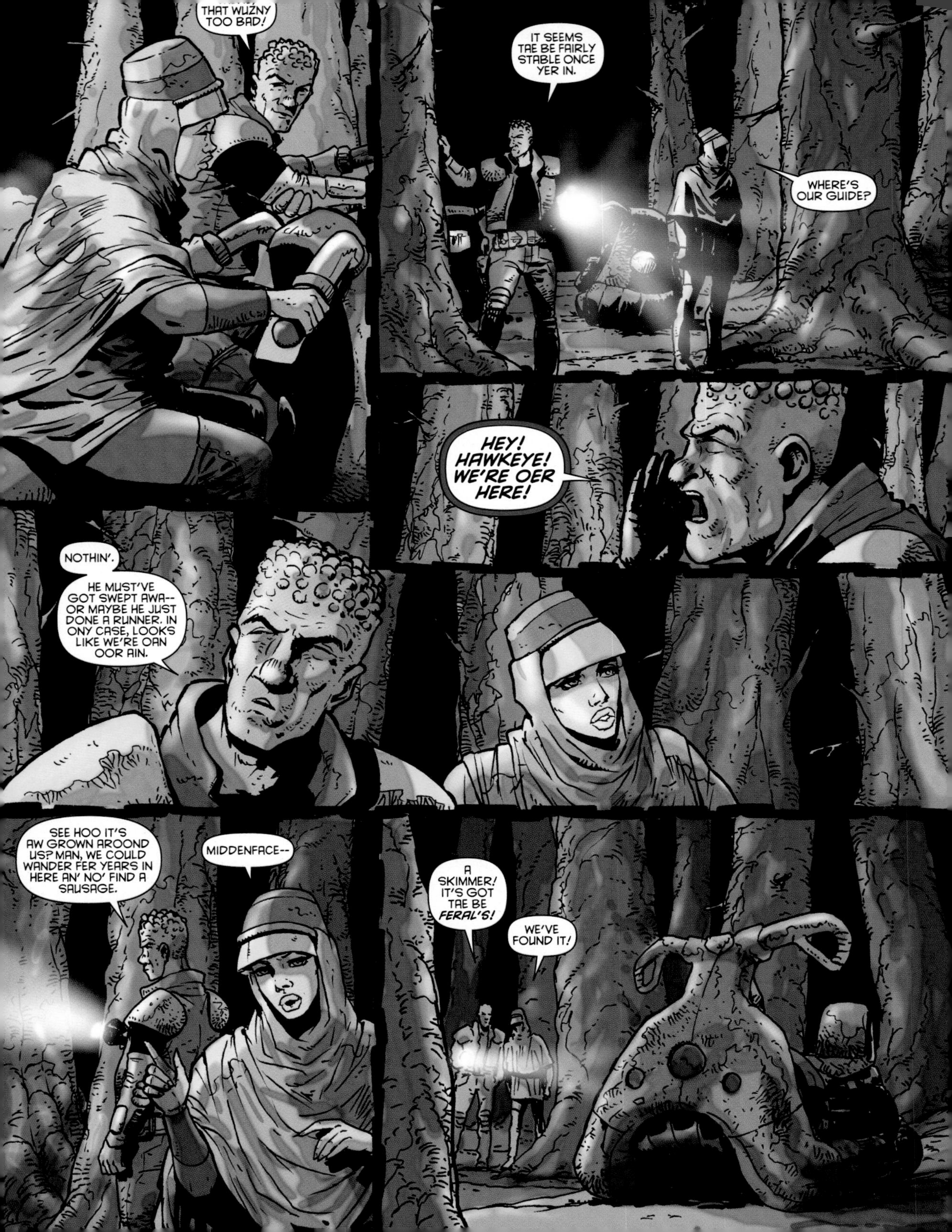
THAT WUZNY TOO BAD!
IT SEEMS TAE BE FAIRLY STABLE ONCE YER IN.
WHERE'S OUR GUIDE?
HEY! HAWKEYE! WE'RE OER HERE!
NOTHIN'.
HE MUST'VE GOT SWEPT AWA-- OR MAYBE HE JUST DONE A RUNNER. IN ONY CASE, LOOKS LIKE WE'RE OAN OOR AIN.
SEE HOO IT'S AW GROWN AROOND US? MAN, WE COULD WANDER FER YEARS IN HERE AN' NO' FIND A SAUSAGE.
MIDDENFACE--
A SKIMMER! IT'S GOT TAE BE FERAL'S!
WE'VE FOUND IT!

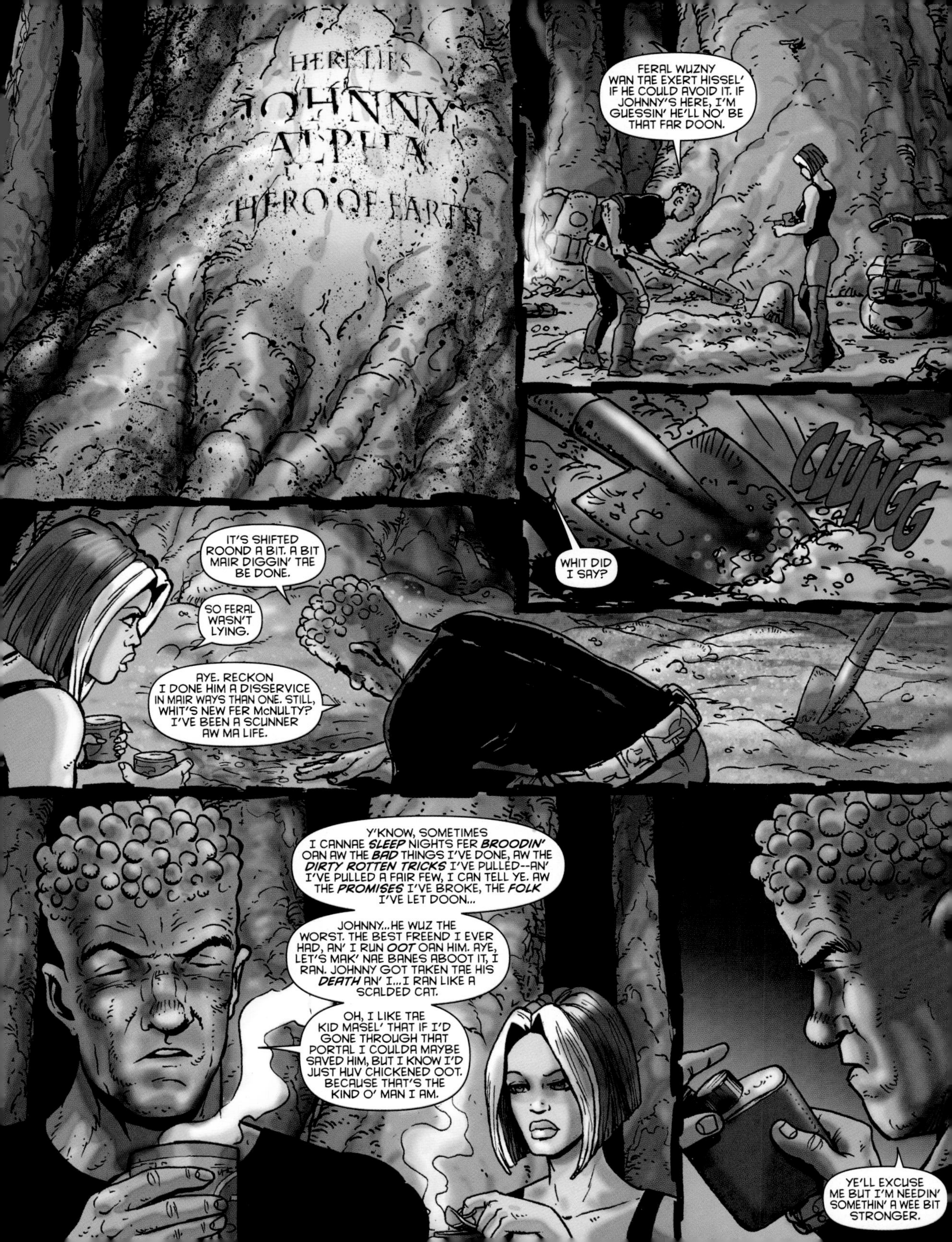
HERE LIES
JOHNNY ALPHA
HERO OF EARTH
FERAL WUZNY WAN TAE EXERT HISSEL' IF HE COULD AVOID IT. IF JOHNNY'S HERE, I'M GUESSIN' HE'LL NO' BE THAT FAR DOON.
CLUNGG
WHIT DID I SAY?
IT'S SHIFTED ROOND A BIT. A BIT MAIR DIGGIN' TAE BE DONE.
SO FERAL WASN'T LYING.
AYE. RECKON I DONE HIM A DISSERVICE IN MAIR WAYS THAN ONE. STILL, WHIT'S NEW FER McNULTY? I'VE BEEN A SCUNNER AW MA LIFE.
Y'KNOW, SOMETIMES I CANNAE SLEEP NIGHTS FER BROODIN' OAN AW THE BAD THINGS I'VE DONE, AW THE DIRTY ROTTEN TRICKS I'VE PULLED--AN' I'VE PULLED A FAIR FEW, I CAN TELL YE. AW THE PROMISES I'VE BROKE, THE FOLK I'VE LET DOON...
JOHNNY...HE WUZ THE WORST. THE BEST FREEND I EVER HAD, AN' I RUN OOT OAN HIM. AYE, LET'S MAK' NAE BANES ABOOT IT, I RAN. JOHNNY GOT TAKEN TAE HIS DEATH AN' I...I RAN LIKE A SCALDED CAT.
OH, I LIKE TAE KID MASEL' THAT IF I'D GONE THROUGH THAT PORTAL I COULDA MAYBE SAVED HIM, BUT I KNOW I'D JUST HUV CHICKENED OOT. BECAUSE THAT'S THE KIND O' MAN I AM.
YE'LL EXCUSE ME BUT I'M NEEDIN' SOMETHIN' A WEE BIT STRONGER.

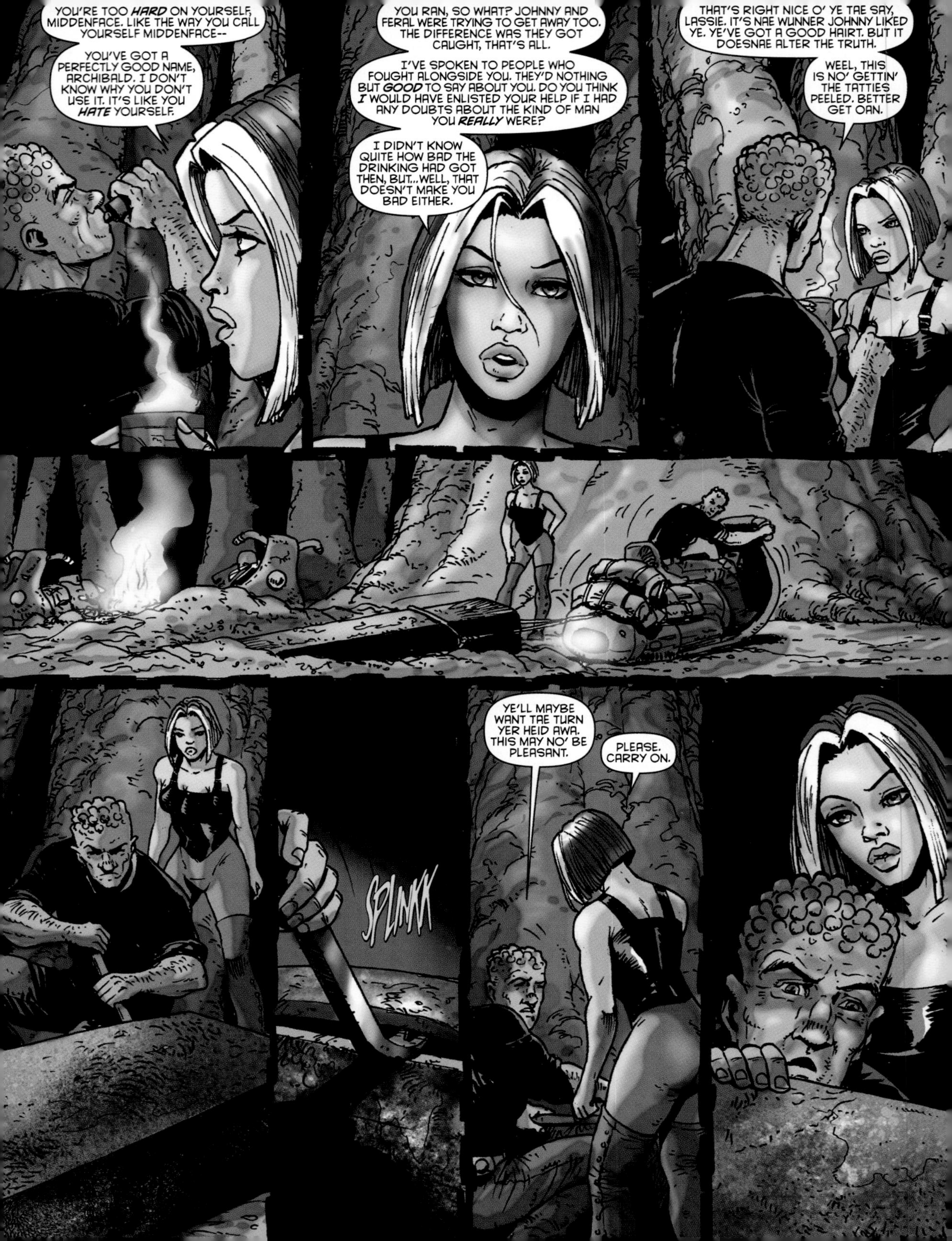
YOU'RE TOO HARD ON YOURSELF, MIDDENFACE. LIKE THE WAY YOU CALL YOURSELF MIDDENFACE--
YOU'VE GOT A PERFECTLY GOOD NAME, ARCHIBALD. I DON'T KNOW WHY YOU DON'T USE IT. IT'S LIKE YOU HATE YOURSELF.
YOU RAN, SO WHAT? JOHNNY AND FERAL WERE TRYING TO GET AWAY TOO. THE DIFFERENCE WAS THEY GOT CAUGHT, THAT'S ALL.
I'VE SPOKEN TO PEOPLE WHO FOUGHT ALONGSIDE YOU. THEY'D NOTHING BUT GOOD TO SAY ABOUT YOU. DO YOU THINK I WOULD HAVE ENLISTED YOUR HELP IF I HAD ANY DOUBTS ABOUT THE KIND OF MAN YOU REALLY WERE?
I DIDN'T KNOW QUITE HOW BAD THE DRINKING HAD GOT THEN, BUT... WELL, THAT DOESN'T MAKE YOU BAD EITHER.
THAT'S RIGHT NICE O' YE TAE SAY, LASSIE. IT'S NAE WUNNER JOHNNY LIKED YE. YE'VE GOT A GOOD HAIRT. BUT IT DOESNAE ALTER THE TRUTH.
WEEL, THIS IS NO' GETTIN' THE TATTIES PEELED. BETTER GET OAN.
SPLINKK
YE'LL MAYBE WANT TAE TURN YER HEID AWA. THIS MAY NO' BE PLEASANT.
PLEASE. CARRY ON.

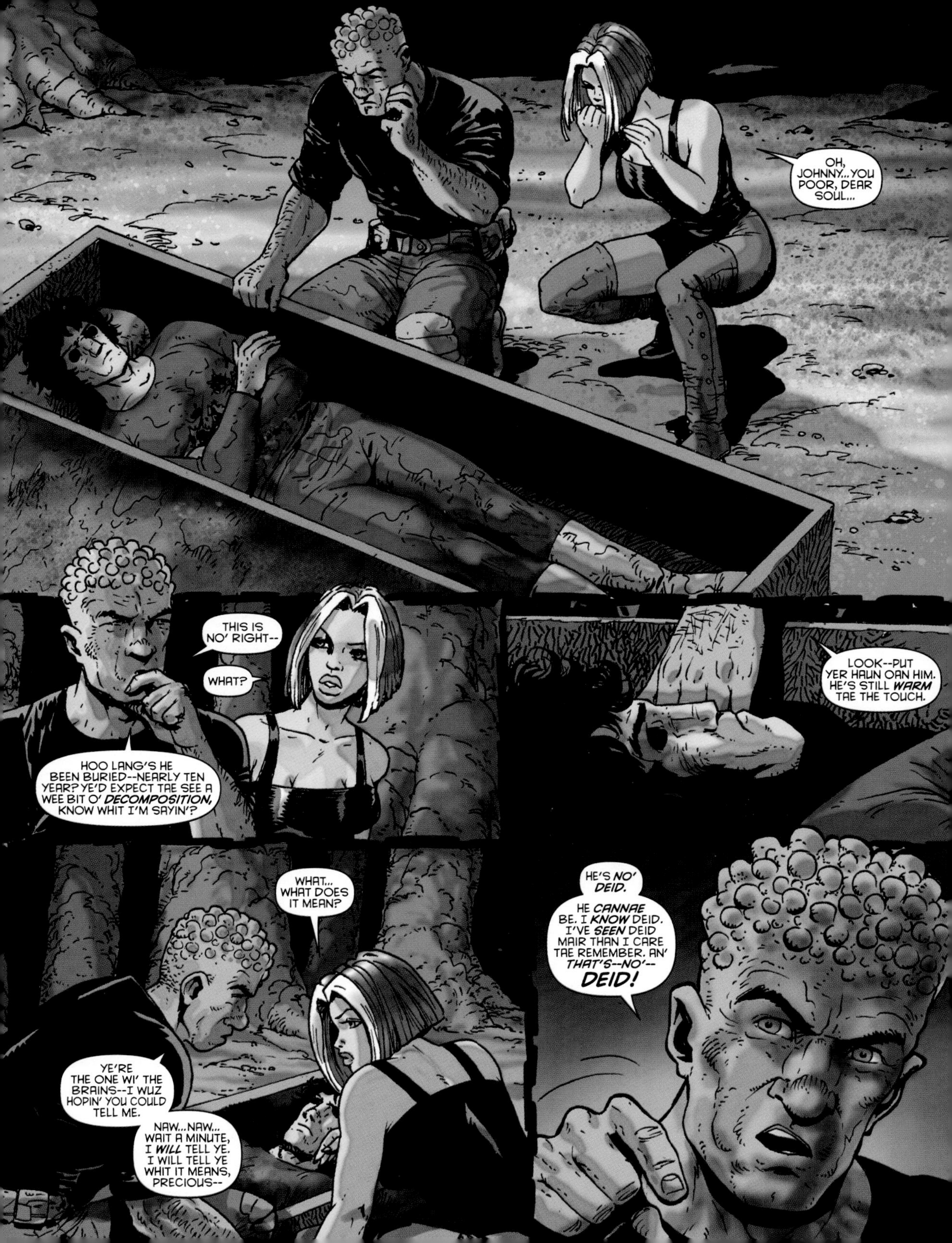
OH, JOHNNY... YOU POOR, DEAR SOUL...
THIS IS NO' RIGHT--
WHAT?
HOO LANG'S HE BEEN BURIED--NEARLY TEN YEAR? YE'D EXPECT TAE SEE A WEE BIT O' *DECOMPOSITION,* KNOW WHIT I'M SAYIN'?
LOOK--PUT YER HAUN OAN HIM. HE'S STILL *WARM* TAE THE TOUCH.
WHAT... WHAT DOES IT MEAN?
YE'RE THE ONE WI' THE BRAINS--I WUZ HOPIN' YOU COULD TELL ME.
NAW...NAW... WAIT A MINUTE, I *WILL* TELL YE. I WILL TELL YE WHIT IT MEANS, PRECIOUS--
HE'S *NO' DEID.*
HE *CANNAE* BE. I *KNOW* DEID. I'VE *SEEN* DEID MAIR THAN I CARE TAE REMEMBER. AN' *THAT'S--NO'--* ***DEID!***

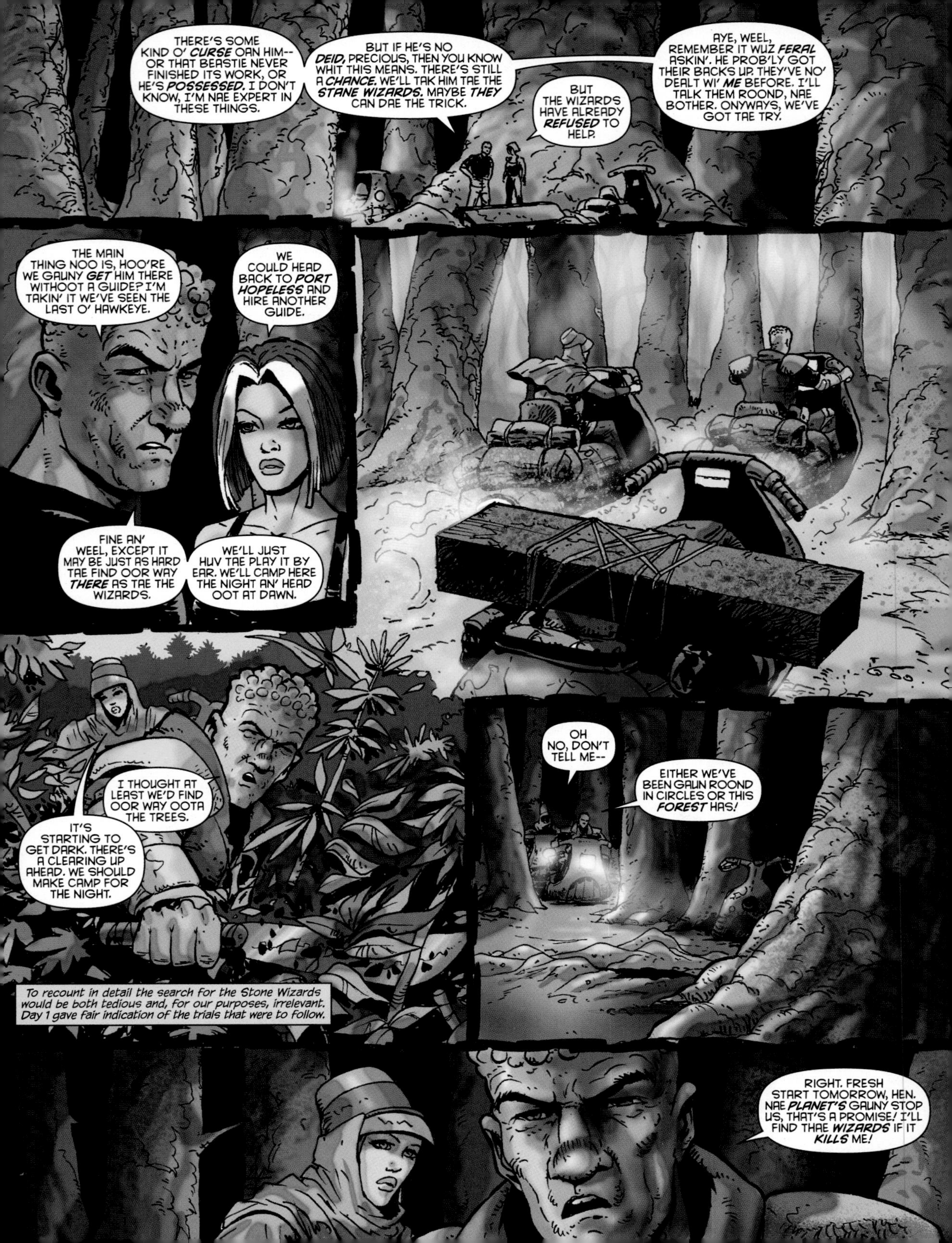

THERE'S SOME KIND O' CURSE OAN HIM-- OR THAT BEASTIE NEVER FINISHED ITS WORK, OR HE'S POSSESSED. I DON'T KNOW, I'M NAE EXPERT IN THESE THINGS.
BUT IF HE'S NO DEID, PRECIOUS, THEN YOU KNOW WHIT THIS MEANS. THERE'S STILL A CHANCE. WE'LL TAK HIM TAE THE STANE WIZARDS. MAYBE THEY CAN DAE THE TRICK.
BUT THE WIZARDS HAVE ALREADY REFUSED TO HELP.
AYE, WEEL, REMEMBER IT WUZ FERAL ASKIN'. HE PROB'LY GOT THEIR BACKS UP. THEY'VE NO' DEALT WI' ME BEFORE. I'LL TALK THEM ROOND, NAE BOTHER. ONYWAYS, WE'VE GOT TAE TRY.
THE MAIN THING NOO IS, HOO'RE WE GAUNY GET HIM THERE WITHOOT A GUIDE? I'M TAKIN' IT WE'VE SEEN THE LAST O' HAWKEYE.
WE COULD HEAD BACK TO PORT HOPELESS AND HIRE ANOTHER GUIDE.
FINE AN' WEEL, EXCEPT IT MAY BE JUST AS HARD TAE FIND OOR WAY THERE AS TAE THE WIZARDS.
WE'LL JUST HUV TAE PLAY IT BY EAR. WE'LL CAMP HERE THE NIGHT AN' HEAD OOT AT DAWN.
I THOUGHT AT LEAST WE'D FIND OOR WAY OOTA THE TREES.
IT'S STARTING TO GET DARK. THERE'S A CLEARING UP AHEAD. WE SHOULD MAKE CAMP FOR THE NIGHT.
To recount in detail the search for the Stone Wizards would be both tedious and, for our purposes, irrelevant. Day 1 gave fair indication of the trials that were to follow.
OH NO, DON'T TELL ME--
EITHER WE'VE BEEN GAUN ROOND IN CIRCLES OR THIS FOREST HAS!
RIGHT. FRESH START TOMORROW, HEN. NAE PLANET'S GAUNY STOP US, THAT'S A PROMISE! I'LL FIND THAE WIZARDS IF IT KILLS ME!

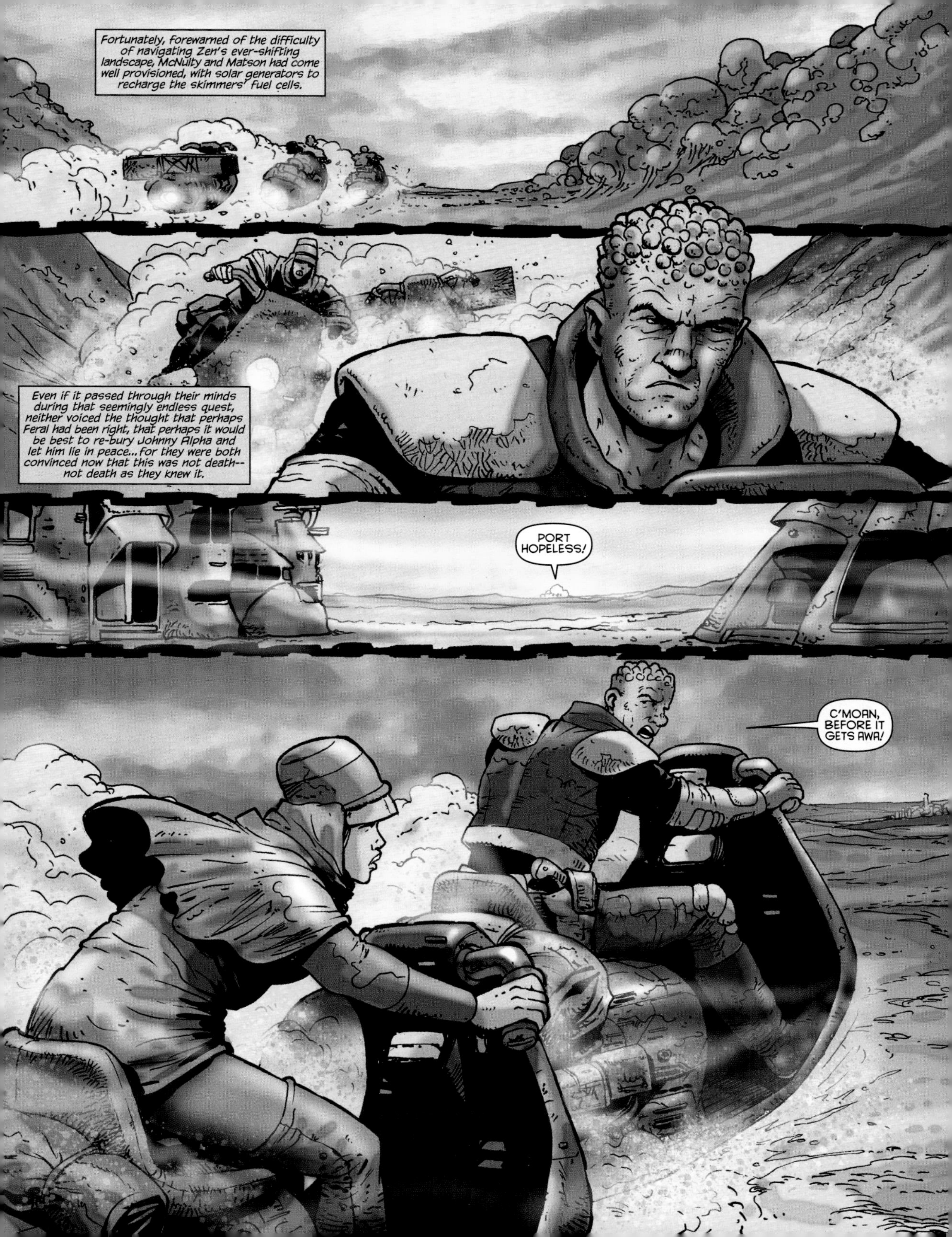
Fortunately, forewarned of the difficulty of navigating Zen's ever-shifting landscape, McNulty and Matson had come well provisioned, with solar generators to recharge the skimmers' fuel cells.
Even if it passed through their minds during that seemingly endless quest, neither voiced the thought that perhaps Feral had been right, that perhaps it would be best to re-bury Johnny Alpha and let him lie in peace... for they were both convinced now that this was not death-- not death as they knew it.
PORT HOPELESS!
C'MOAN, BEFORE IT GETS AWA!

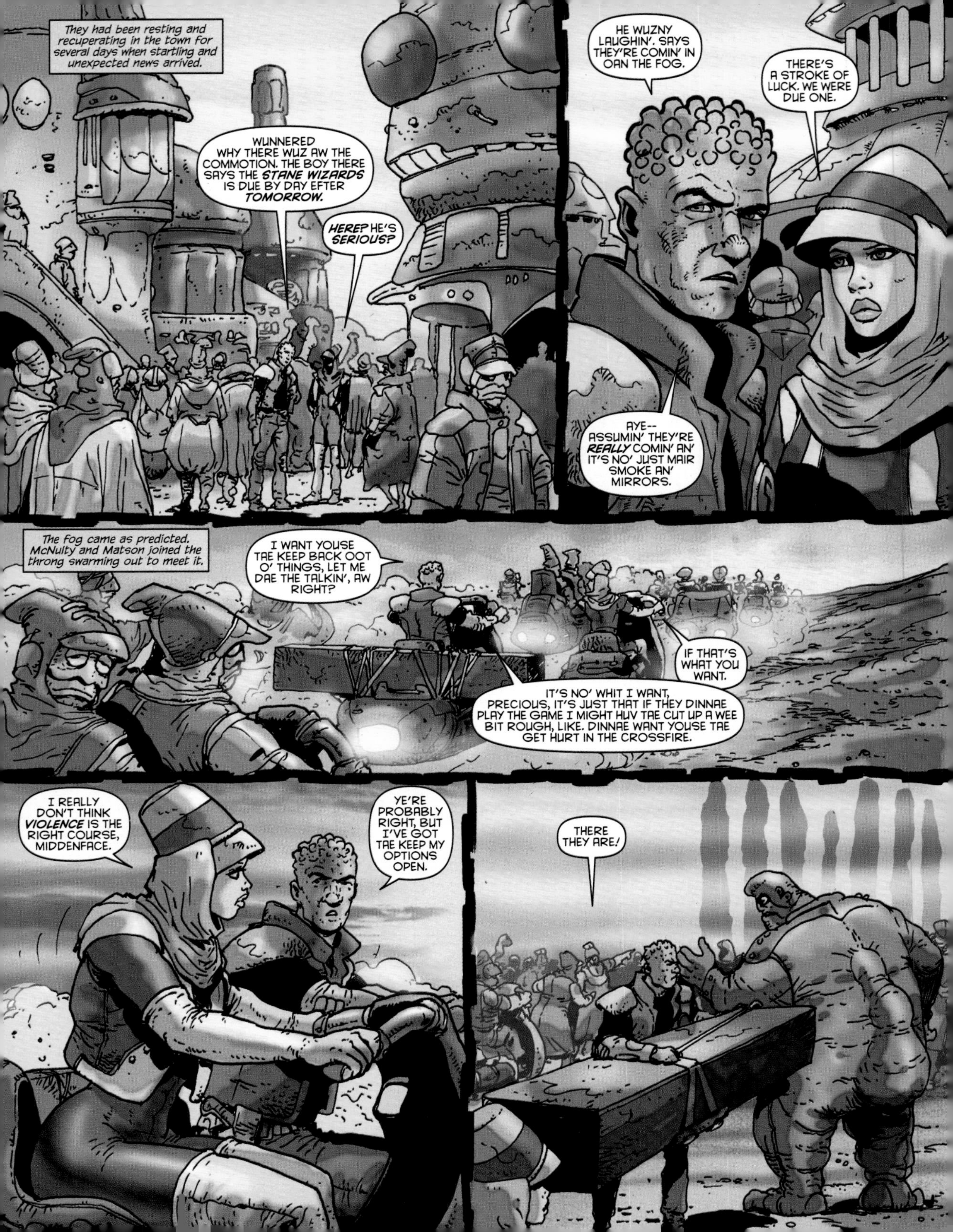
They had been resting and recuperating in the town for several days when startling and unexpected news arrived.
WUNNERED WHY THERE WUZ AW THE COMMOTION. THE BOY THERE SAYS THE STANE WIZARDS IS DUE BY DAY EFTER TOMORROW.
HERE? HE'S SERIOUS?
HE WUZNY LAUGHIN'. SAYS THEY'RE COMIN' IN OAN THE FOG.
THERE'S A STROKE OF LUCK. WE WERE DUE ONE.
AYE-- ASSUMIN' THEY'RE REALLY COMIN' AN' IT'S NO' JUST MAIR SMOKE AN' MIRRORS.
The fog came as predicted. McNulty and Matson joined the throng swarming out to meet it.
I WANT YOUSE TAE KEEP BACK OOT O' THINGS, LET ME DAE THE TALKIN', AW RIGHT?
IF THAT'S WHAT YOU WANT.
IT'S NO' WHIT I WANT, PRECIOUS, IT'S JUST THAT IF THEY DINNAE PLAY THE GAME I MIGHT HUV TAE CUT UP A WEE BIT ROUGH, LIKE. DINNAE WANT YOUSE TAE GET HURT IN THE CROSSFIRE.
I REALLY DON'T THINK VIOLENCE IS THE RIGHT COURSE, MIDDENFACE.
YE'RE PROBABLY RIGHT, BUT I'VE GOT TAE KEEP MY OPTIONS OPEN.
THERE THEY ARE!

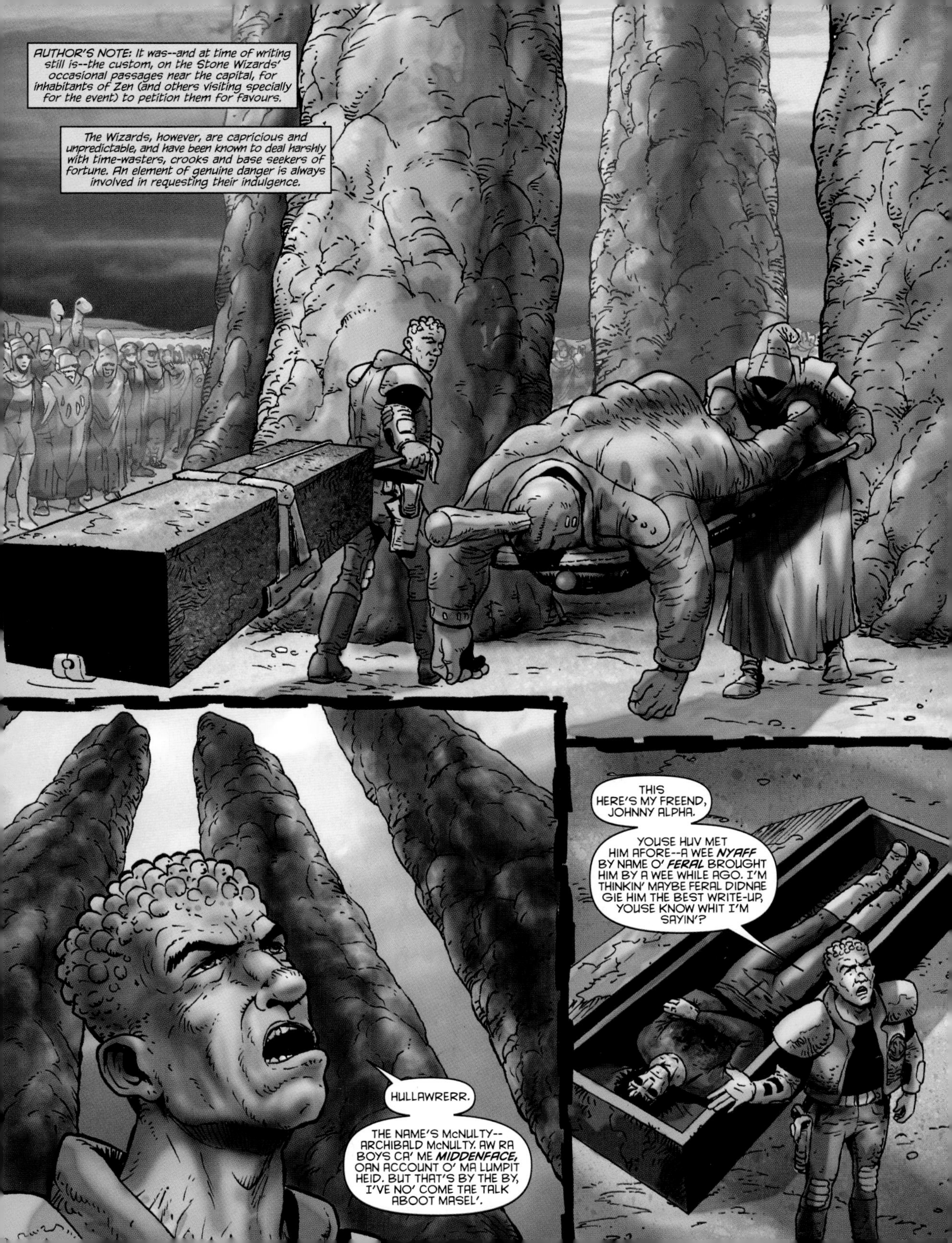
AUTHOR'S NOTE: It was--and at time of writing still is--the custom, on the Stone Wizards' occasional passages near the capital, for inhabitants of Zen (and others visiting specially for the event) to petition them for favours.
The Wizards, however, are capricious and unpredictable, and have been known to deal harshly with time-wasters, crooks and base seekers of fortune. An element of genuine danger is always involved in requesting their indulgence.
HULLAWRERR.
THE NAME'S McNULTY--ARCHIBALD McNULTY. AW RA BOYS CA' ME MIDDENFACE, OAN ACCOUNT O' MA LUMPIT HEID. BUT THAT'S BY THE BY, I'VE NO' COME TAE TALK ABOOT MASEL'.
THIS HERE'S MY FREEND, JOHNNY ALPHA.
YOUSE HUV MET HIM AFORE--A WEE NYAFF BY NAME O' FERAL BROUGHT HIM BY A WEE WHILE AGO. I'M THINKIN' MAYBE FERAL DIDNAE GIE HIM THE BEST WRITE-UP, YOUSE KNOW WHIT I'M SAYIN'?

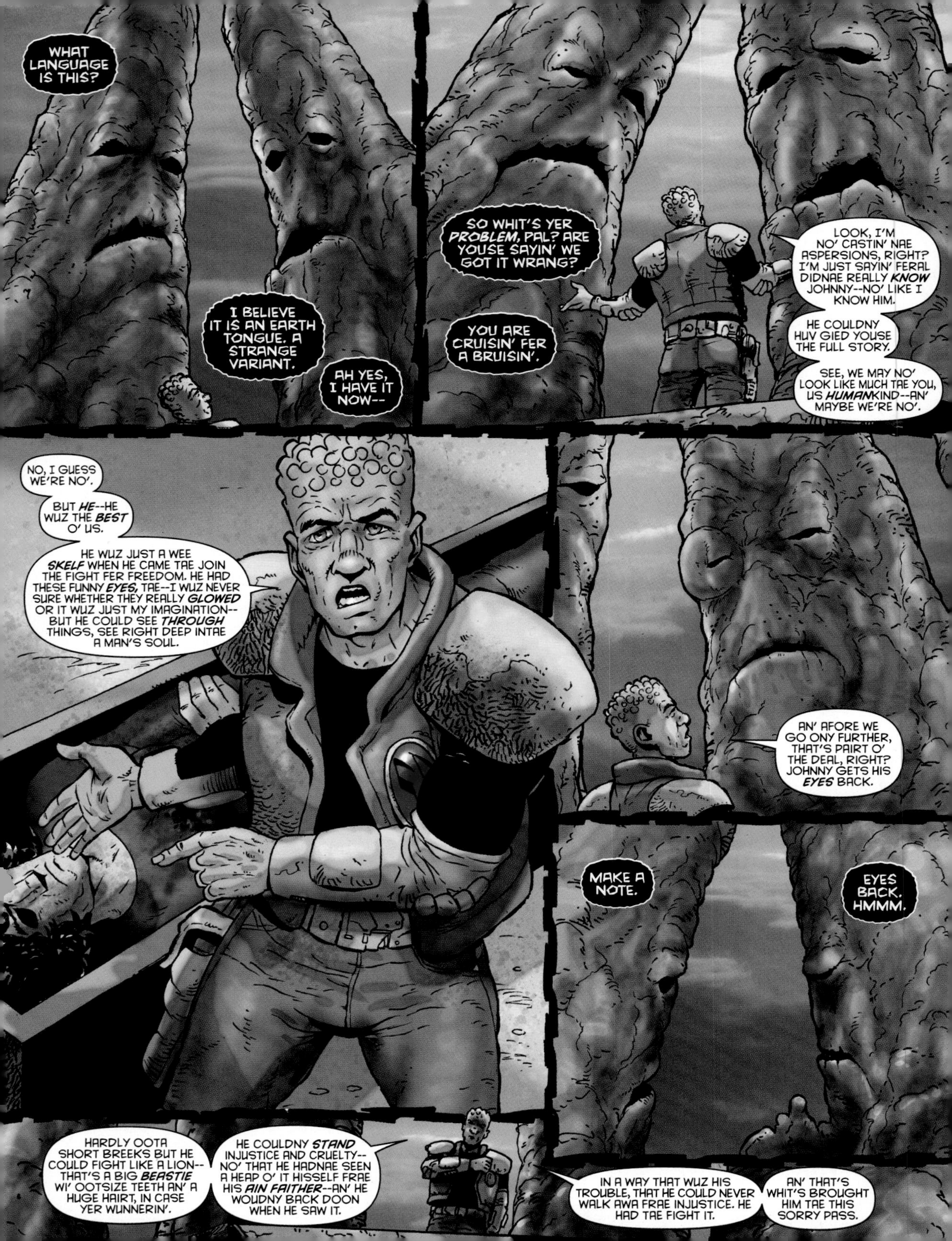
WHAT LANGUAGE IS THIS?
I BELIEVE IT IS AN EARTH TONGUE. A STRANGE VARIANT.
AH YES, I HAVE IT NOW--
SO WHIT'S YER PROBLEM, PAL? ARE YOUSE SAYIN' WE GOT IT WRANG?
YOU ARE CRUISIN' FER A BRUISIN'.
LOOK, I'M NO' CASTIN' NAE ASPERSIONS, RIGHT? I'M JUST SAYIN' FERAL DIDNAE REALLY KNOW JOHNNY--NO' LIKE I KNOW HIM.
HE COULDNY HUV GIED YOUSE THE FULL STORY.
SEE, WE MAY NO' LOOK LIKE MUCH TAE YOU, US HUMANKIND--AN' MAYBE WE'RE NO'.
NO, I GUESS WE'RE NO'.
BUT HE--HE WUZ THE BEST O' US.
HE WUZ JUST A WEE SKELF WHEN HE CAME TAE JOIN THE FIGHT FER FREEDOM. HE HAD THESE FUNNY EYES, TAE--I WUZ NEVER SURE WHETHER THEY REALLY GLOWED OR IT WUZ JUST MY IMAGINATION--BUT HE COULD SEE THROUGH THINGS, SEE RIGHT DEEP INTAE A MAN'S SOUL.
AN' AFORE WE GO ONY FURTHER, THAT'S PAIRT O' THE DEAL, RIGHT? JOHNNY GETS HIS EYES BACK.
MAKE A NOTE.
EYES BACK. HMMM.
HARDLY OOTA SHORT BREEKS BUT HE COULD FIGHT LIKE A LION--THAT'S A BIG BEASTIE WI' OOTSIZE TEETH AN' A HUGE HAIRT, IN CASE YER WUNNERIN'.
HE COULDNY STAND INJUSTICE AND CRUELTY--NO' THAT HE HADNAE SEEN A HEAP O' IT HISSELF FRAE HIS AIN FAITHER--AN' HE WOUDNY BACK DOON WHEN HE SAW IT.
IN A WAY THAT WUZ HIS TROUBLE, THAT HE COULD NEVER WALK AWA FRAE INJUSTICE. HE HAD TAE FIGHT IT.
AN' THAT'S WHIT'S BROUGHT HIM TAE THIS SORRY PASS.

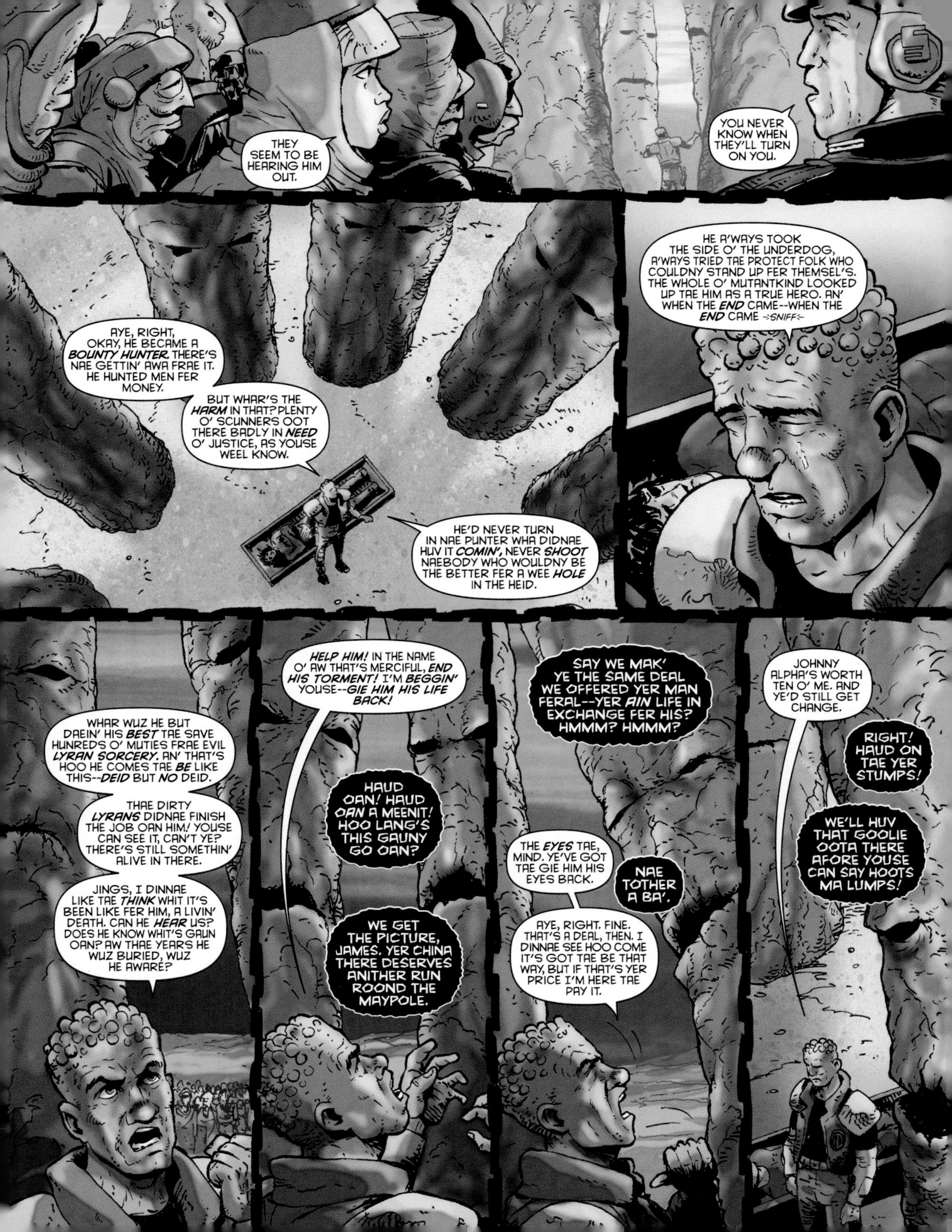
THEY SEEM TO BE HEARING HIM OUT.
YOU NEVER KNOW WHEN THEY'LL TURN ON YOU.
AYE, RIGHT, OKAY, HE BECAME A BOUNTY HUNTER. THERE'S NAE GETTIN' AWA FRAE IT. HE HUNTED MEN FER MONEY.
BUT WHAR'S THE HARM IN THAT? PLENTY O' SCUNNERS OOT THERE BADLY IN NEED O' JUSTICE, AS YOUSE WEEL KNOW.
HE'D NEVER TURN IN NAE PUNTER WHA DIDNAE HUV IT COMIN', NEVER SHOOT NAEBODY WHO WOULDNY BE THE BETTER FER A WEE HOLE IN THE HEID.
HE A'WAYS TOOK THE SIDE O' THE UNDERDOG, A'WAYS TRIED TAE PROTECT FOLK WHO COULDNY STAND UP FER THEMSEL'S. THE WHOLE O' MUTANTKIND LOOKED UP TAE HIM AS A TRUE HERO. AN' WHEN THE END CAME--WHEN THE END CAME >SNIFF<
WHAR WUZ HE BUT DAEIN' HIS BEST TAE SAVE HUNREDS O' MUTIES FRAE EVIL LYRAN SORCERY. AN' THAT'S HOO HE COMES TAE BE LIKE THIS--DEID BUT NO DEID.
THAE DIRTY LYRANS DIDNAE FINISH THE JOB OAN HIM! YOUSE CAN SEE IT, CAN'T YE? THERE'S STILL SOMETHIN' ALIVE IN THERE.
JINGS, I DINNAE LIKE TAE THINK WHIT IT'S BEEN LIKE FER HIM, A LIVIN' DEATH. CAN HE HEAR US? DOES HE KNOW WHIT'S GAUN OAN? AW THAE YEARS HE WUZ BURIED, WUZ HE AWARE?
HELP HIM! IN THE NAME O' AW THAT'S MERCIFUL, END HIS TORMENT! I'M BEGGIN' YOUSE--GIE HIM HIS LIFE BACK!
HAUD OAN! HAUD OAN A MEENIT! HOO LANG'S THIS GAUNY GO OAN?
WE GET THE PICTURE, JAMES. YER CHINA THERE DESERVES ANITHER RUN ROOND THE MAYPOLE.
SAY WE MAK' YE THE SAME DEAL WE OFFERED YER MAN FERAL--YER AIN LIFE IN EXCHANGE FER HIS? HMMM? HMMM?
THE EYES TAE, MIND. YE'VE GOT TAE GIE HIM HIS EYES BACK.
NAE TOTHER A BA'.
AYE, RIGHT. FINE. THAT'S A DEAL, THEN. I DINNAE SEE HOO COME IT'S GOT TAE BE THAT WAY, BUT IF THAT'S YER PRICE I'M HERE TAE PAY IT.
JOHNNY ALPHA'S WORTH TEN O' ME. AND YE'D STILL GET CHANGE.
RIGHT! HAUD ON TAE YER STUMPS!
WE'LL HUV THAT GOOLIE OOTA THERE AFORE YOUSE CAN SAY HOOTS MA LUMPS!

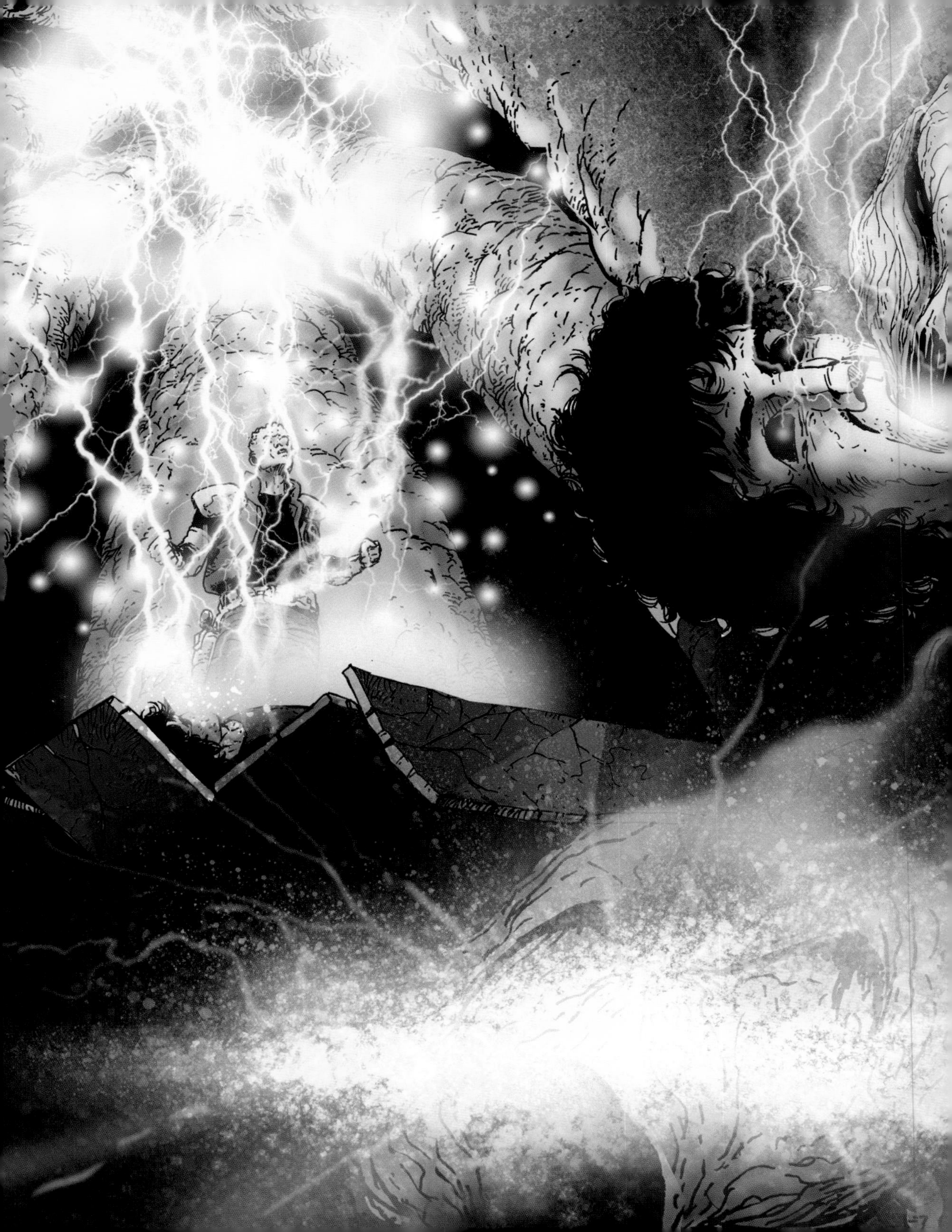

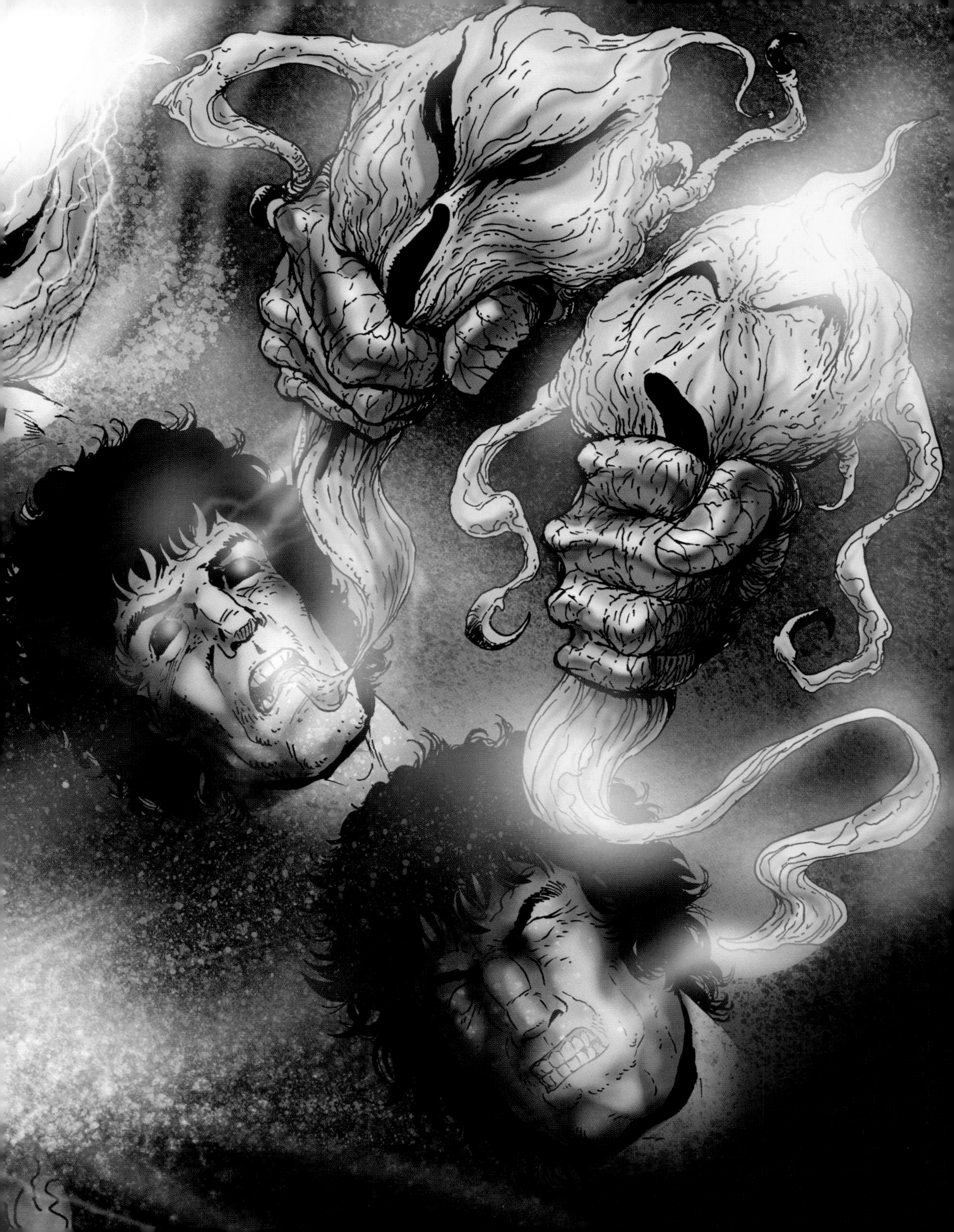

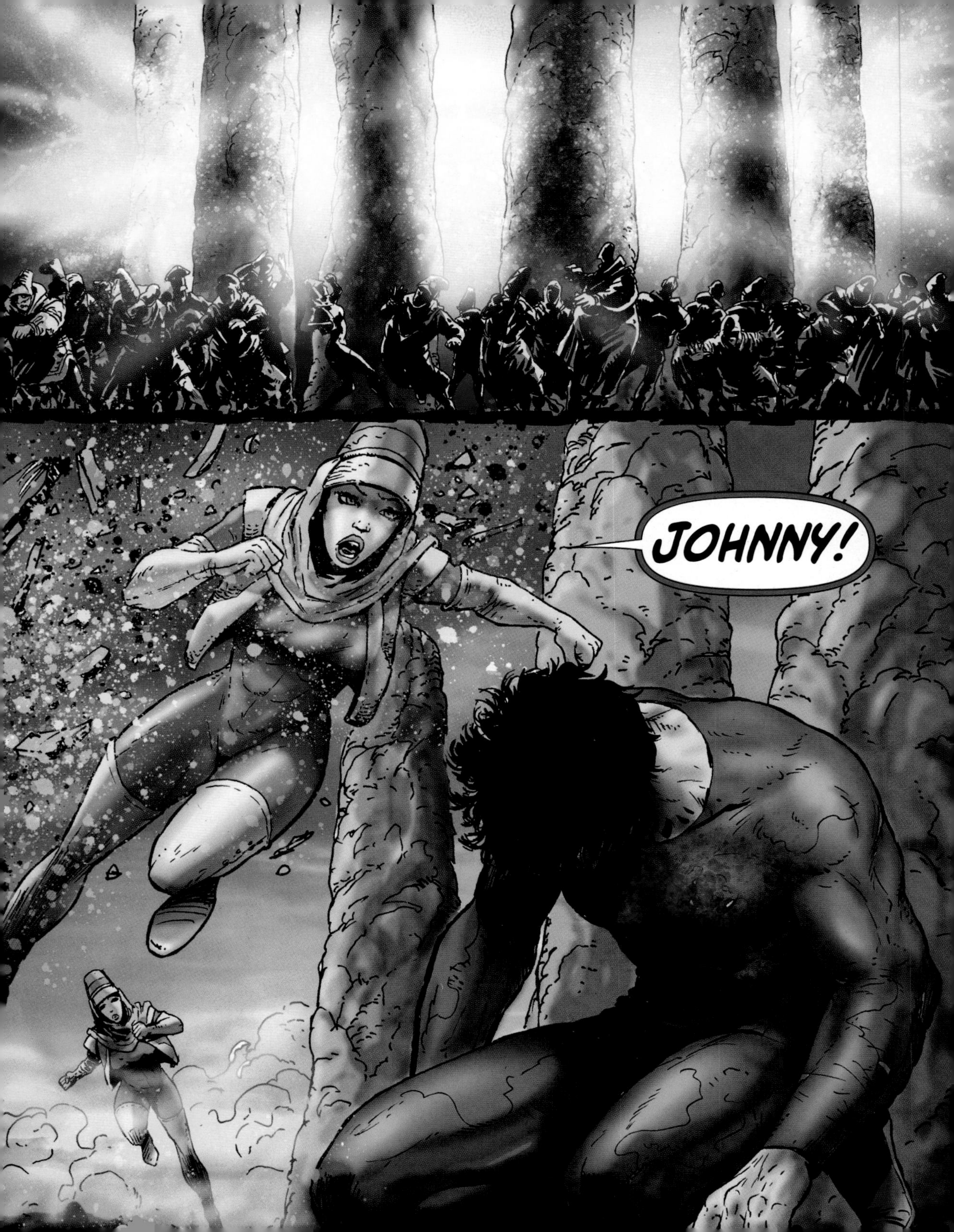
JOHNNY!

THE LIFE AND DEATH OF JOHNNY ALPHA
CHAPTER TWO: THE PROJECT

Writer: John Wagner
Artist: Carlos Ezquerra
Colours: Hector Ezquerra
Letters: Simon Bowland

Originally published in *2000 AD* Prog 2012 & Progs 1764-1771

THE AWAKENING OF JOHNNY ALPHA BY THE WIZARDS OF ZEN IS WELL DOCUMENTED IN PRECIOUS MATSON'S EYE-WITNESS ACCOUNT. THERE WERE, HOWEVER, STILL THOSE WHO DISPUTED THE FACTS--NOTABLY PROFESSOR ALDOUS SKROATE OF KREELMAN COLLEGE, OXFORD, WHOSE EPISTLE TO THE MUTANTS, ***THE ALPHA IMPOSTOR,*** ATTEMPTED TO "DEBUNK THE MYTH". SUFFICE TO SAY THAT SKROATE IS TODAY A GENERAL TERM OF ABUSE WHILE MATSON'S ***JOHNNY ALPHA: A LIFE*** IS REGARDED AS THE ONLY ACCURATE ACCOUNT OF THE BOUNTY HUNTER'S RESURRECTION AND THE SHOCKING AND VIOLENT EVENTS THAT WERE TO FOLLOW.

ARCHIVE COMPUTER 3/301B - EARTHCOM INFORMATION OFFICE - DECEMBER 2401

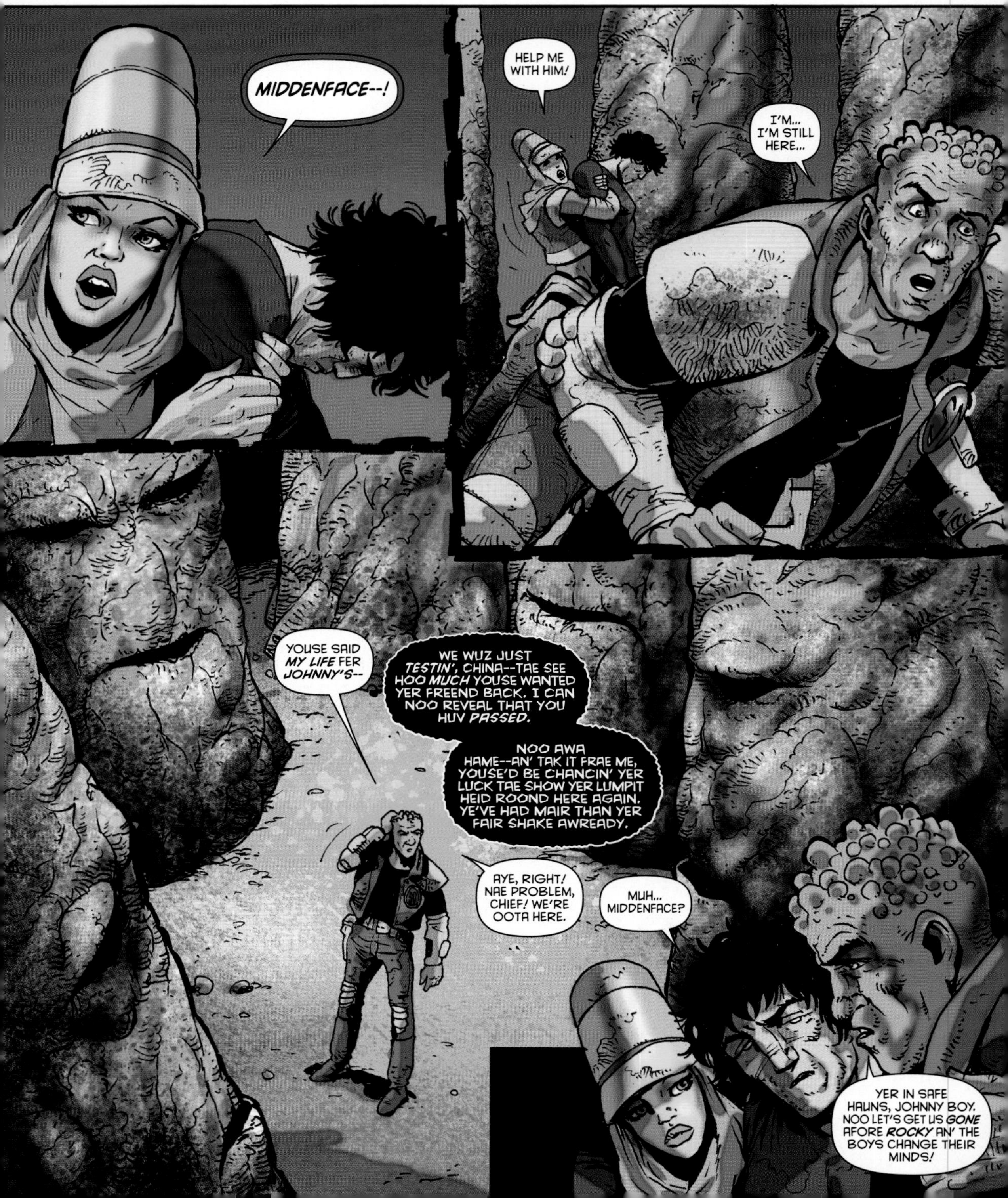
MIDDENFACE--!
HELP ME WITH HIM!
I'M... I'M STILL HERE...
YOUSE SAID MY LIFE FER JOHNNY'S--
WE WUZ JUST TESTIN', CHINA--TAE SEE HOO MUCH YOUSE WANTED YER FREEND BACK. I CAN NOO REVEAL THAT YOU HUV PASSED.
NOO AWA HAME--AN' TAK IT FRAE ME, YOUSE'D BE CHANCIN' YER LUCK TAE SHOW YER LUMPIT HEID ROOND HERE AGAIN. YE'VE HAD MAIR THAN YER FAIR SHAKE AWREADY.
AYE, RIGHT! NAE PROBLEM, CHIEF! WE'RE OOTA HERE.
MUH... MIDDENFACE?
YER IN SAFE HAUNS, JOHNNY BOY. NOO LET'S GET US GONE AFORE ROCKY AN' THE BOYS CHANGE THEIR MINDS!

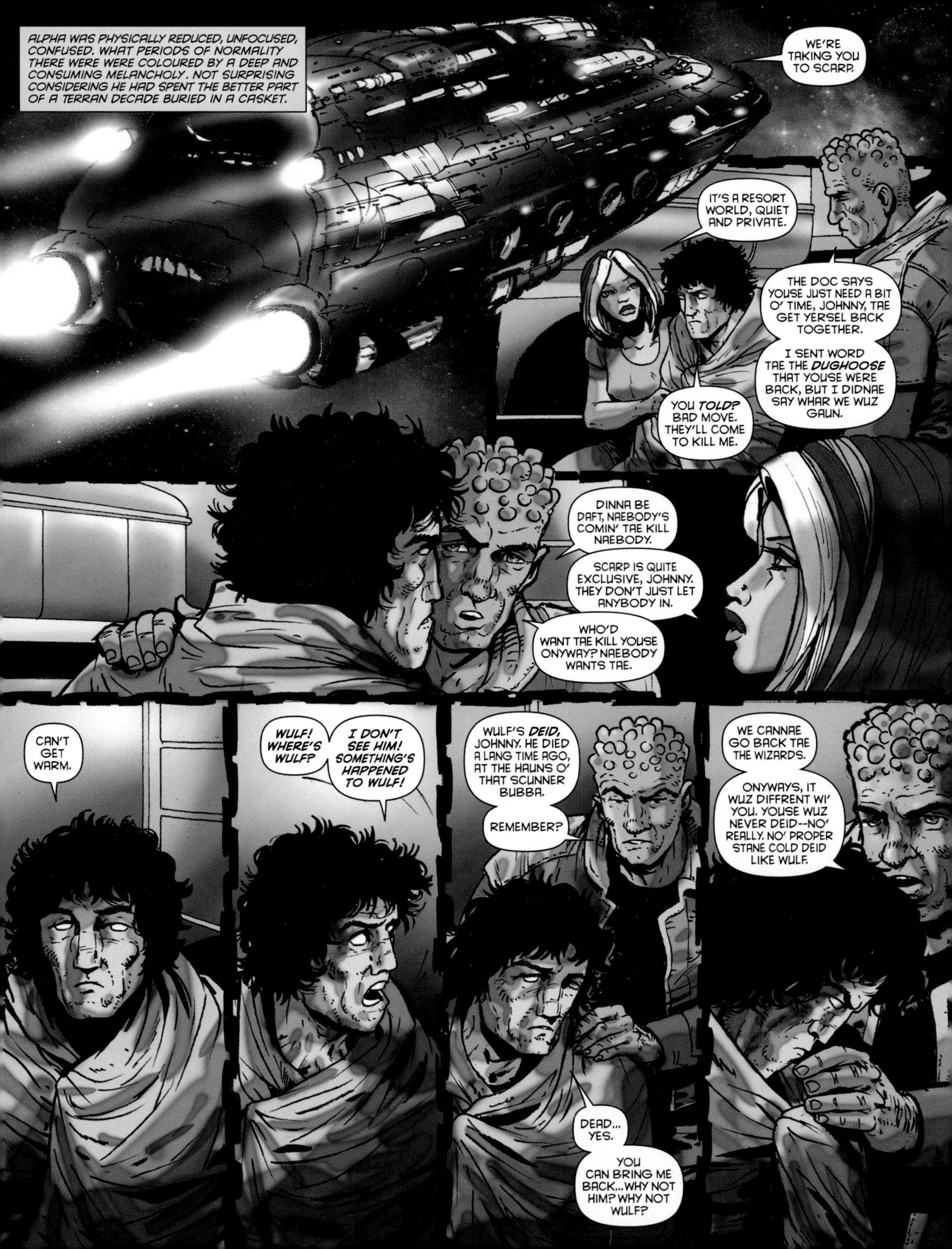

ALPHA WAS PHYSICALLY REDUCED, UNFOCUSED, CONFUSED. WHAT PERIODS OF NORMALITY THERE WERE WERE COLOURED BY A DEEP AND CONSUMING MELANCHOLY. NOT SURPRISING CONSIDERING HE HAD SPENT THE BETTER PART OF A TERRAN DECADE BURIED IN A CASKET.
WE'RE TAKING YOU TO SCARP.
IT'S A RESORT WORLD, QUIET AND PRIVATE.
THE DOC SAYS YOUSE JUST NEED A BIT O' TIME, JOHNNY, TAE GET YERSEL BACK TOGETHER.
I SENT WORD TAE THE DUGHOOSE THAT YOUSE WERE BACK, BUT I DIDNAE SAY WHAR WE WUZ GAUN.
YOU TOLD? BAD MOVE. THEY'LL COME TO KILL ME.
DINNA BE DAFT, NAEBODY'S COMIN' TAE KILL NAEBODY.
SCARP IS QUITE EXCLUSIVE, JOHNNY. THEY DON'T JUST LET ANYBODY IN.
WHO'D WANT TAE KILL YOUSE ONYWAY? NAEBODY WANTS TAE.
CAN'T GET WARM.
WULF! WHERE'S WULF?
I DON'T SEE HIM! SOMETHING'S HAPPENED TO WULF!
WULF'S DEID, JOHNNY. HE DIED A LANG TIME AGO, AT THE HAUNS O' THAT SCUNNER BUBBA.
REMEMBER?
DEAD... YES.
YOU CAN BRING ME BACK...WHY NOT HIM? WHY NOT WULF?
WE CANNAE GO BACK TAE THE WIZARDS.
ONYWAYS, IT WUZ DIFFRENT WI' YOU. YOUSE WUZ NEVER DEID--NO' REALLY. NO' PROPER STANE COLD DEID LIKE WULF.

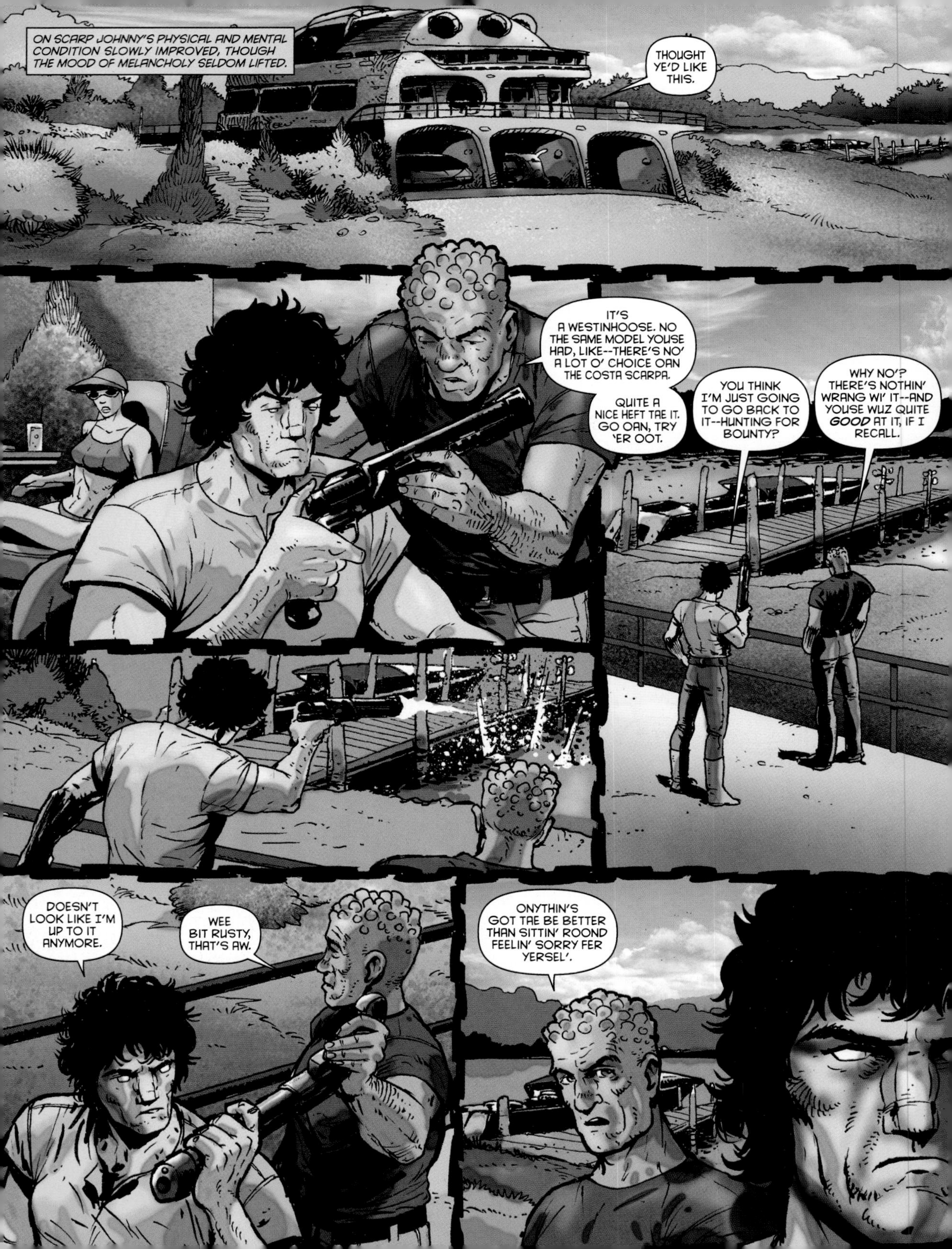

ON SCARP JOHNNY'S PHYSICAL AND MENTAL CONDITION SLOWLY IMPROVED, THOUGH THE MOOD OF MELANCHOLY SELDOM LIFTED.
THOUGHT YE'D LIKE THIS.
IT'S A WESTINHOOSE. NO THE SAME MODEL YOUSE HAD, LIKE--THERE'S NO' A LOT O' CHOICE OAN THE COSTA SCARPA.
QUITE A NICE HEFT TAE IT. GO OAN, TRY 'ER OOT.
YOU THINK I'M JUST GOING TO GO BACK TO IT--HUNTING FOR BOUNTY?
WHY NO'? THERE'S NOTHIN' WRANG WI' IT--AND YOUSE WUZ QUITE GOOD AT IT, IF I RECALL.
DOESN'T LOOK LIKE I'M UP TO IT ANYMORE.
WEE BIT RUSTY, THAT'S AW.
ONYTHIN'S GOT TAE BE BETTER THAN SITTIN' ROOND FEELIN' SORRY FER YERSEL'.

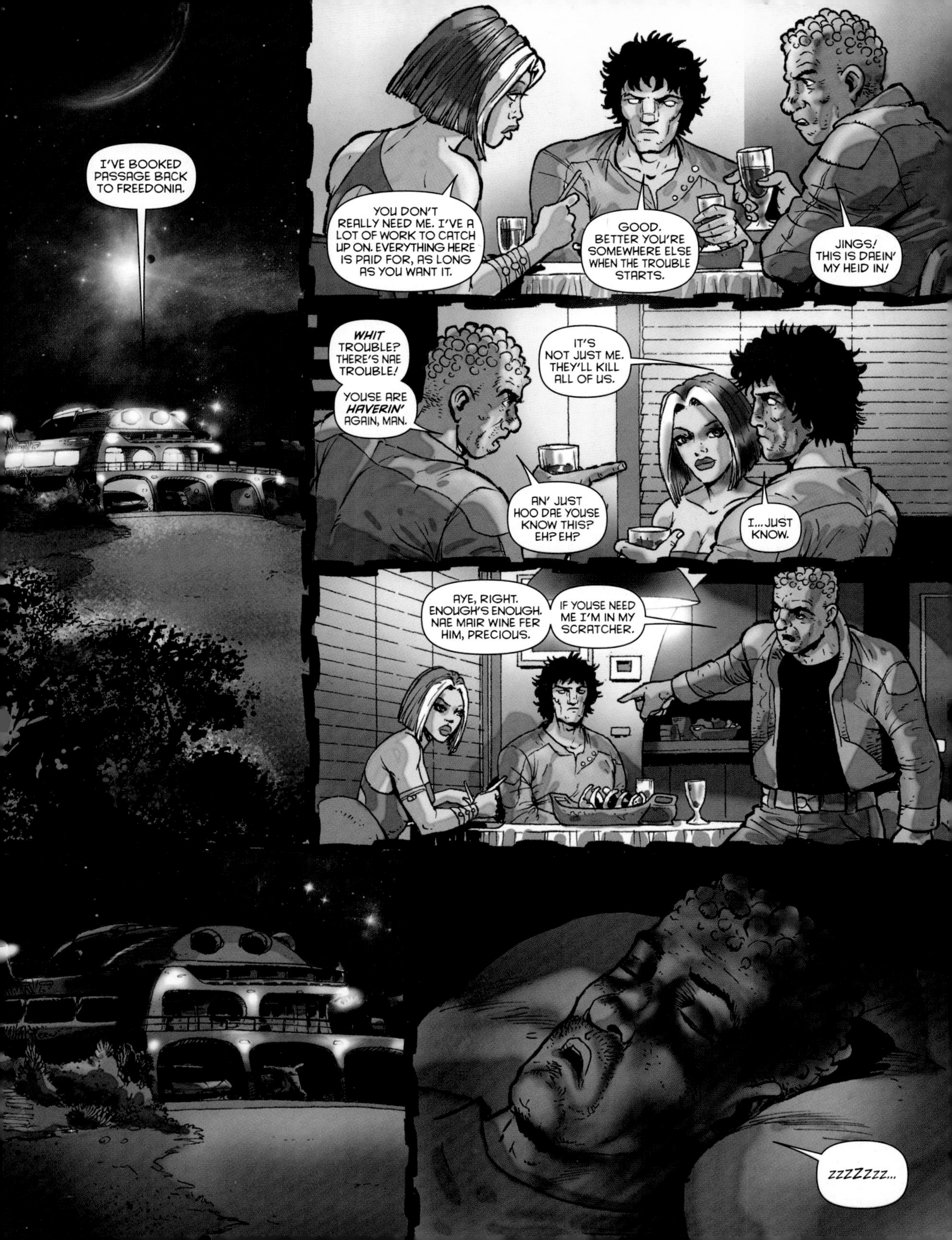

I'VE BOOKED PASSAGE BACK TO FREEDONIA.
YOU DON'T REALLY NEED ME. I'VE A LOT OF WORK TO CATCH UP ON. EVERYTHING HERE IS PAID FOR, AS LONG AS YOU WANT IT.
GOOD. BETTER YOU'RE SOMEWHERE ELSE WHEN THE TROUBLE STARTS.
JINGS! THIS IS DAEIN' MY HEID IN!
WHIT TROUBLE? THERE'S NAE TROUBLE!
YOUSE ARE HAVERIN' AGAIN, MAN.
IT'S NOT JUST ME. THEY'LL KILL ALL OF US.
AN' JUST HOO DAE YOUSE KNOW THIS? EH? EH?
I... JUST KNOW.
AYE, RIGHT. ENOUGH'S ENOUGH. NAE MAIR WINE FER HIM, PRECIOUS.
IF YOUSE NEED ME I'M IN MY SCRATCHER.
zzzZZzz...

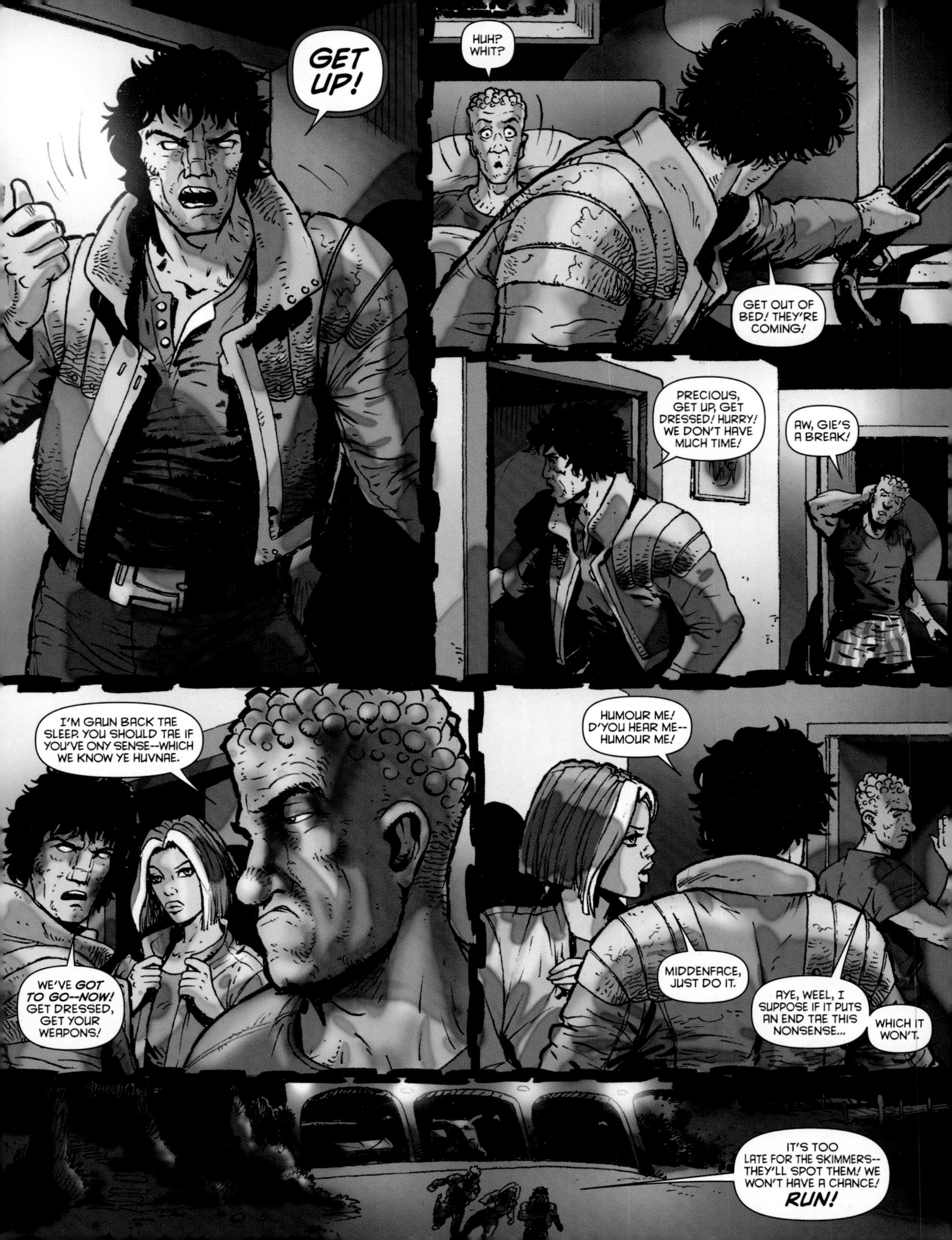
GET UP!
HUH? WHIT?
GET OUT OF BED! THEY'RE COMING!
PRECIOUS, GET UP, GET DRESSED! HURRY! WE DON'T HAVE MUCH TIME!
AW, GIE'S A BREAK!
I'M GAUN BACK TAE SLEEP. YOU SHOULD TAE IF YOU'VE ONY SENSE--WHICH WE KNOW YE HUVNAE.
WE'VE GOT TO GO--NOW! GET DRESSED, GET YOUR WEAPONS!
HUMOUR ME! D'YOU HEAR ME--HUMOUR ME!
MIDDENFACE, JUST DO IT.
AYE, WEEL, I SUPPOSE IF IT PUTS AN END TAE THIS NONSENSE...
WHICH IT WON'T.
IT'S TOO LATE FOR THE SKIMMERS--THEY'LL SPOT THEM! WE WON'T HAVE A CHANCE! RUN!

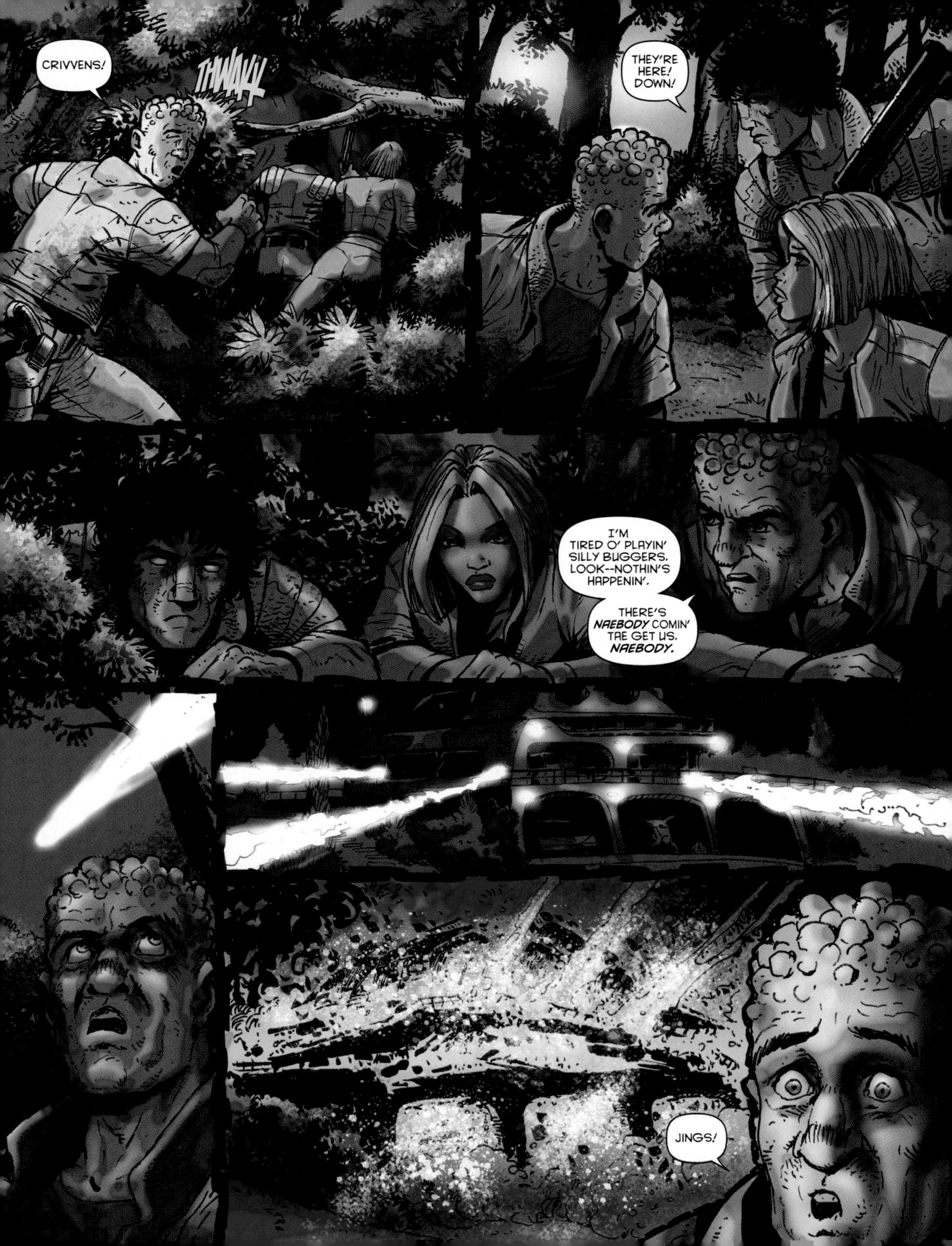
CRIVVENS!
THWAKK
THEY'RE HERE! DOWN!
I'M TIRED O' PLAYIN' SILLY BUGGERS. LOOK--NOTHIN'S HAPPENIN'.
THERE'S NAEBODY COMIN' TAE GET US. NAEBODY.
JINGS!

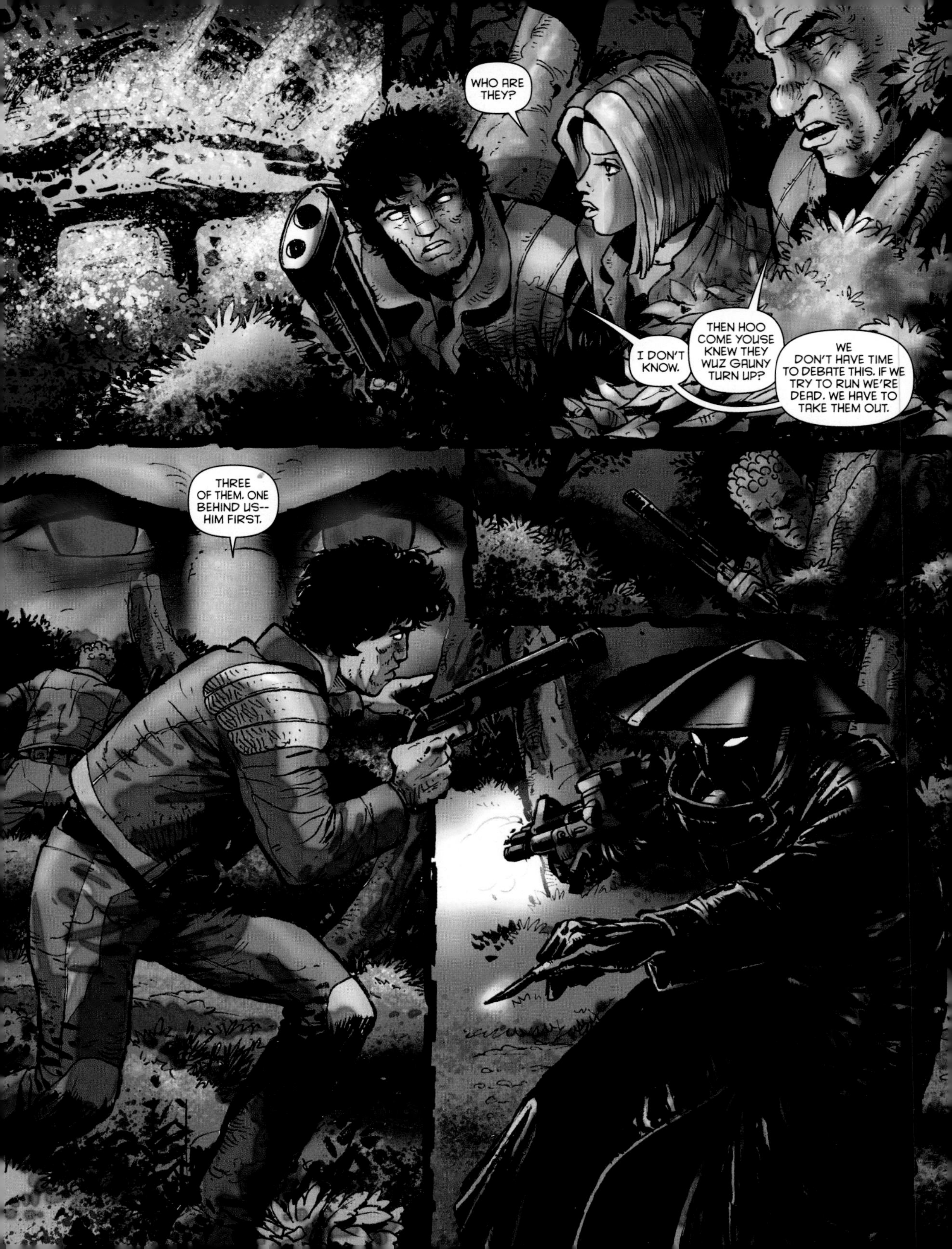
WHO ARE THEY?
I DON'T KNOW.
THEN HOO COME YOUSE KNEW THEY WUZ GAUNY TURN UP?
WE DON'T HAVE TIME TO DEBATE THIS. IF WE TRY TO RUN WE'RE DEAD. WE HAVE TO TAKE THEM OUT.
THREE OF THEM. ONE BEHIND US-- HIM FIRST.

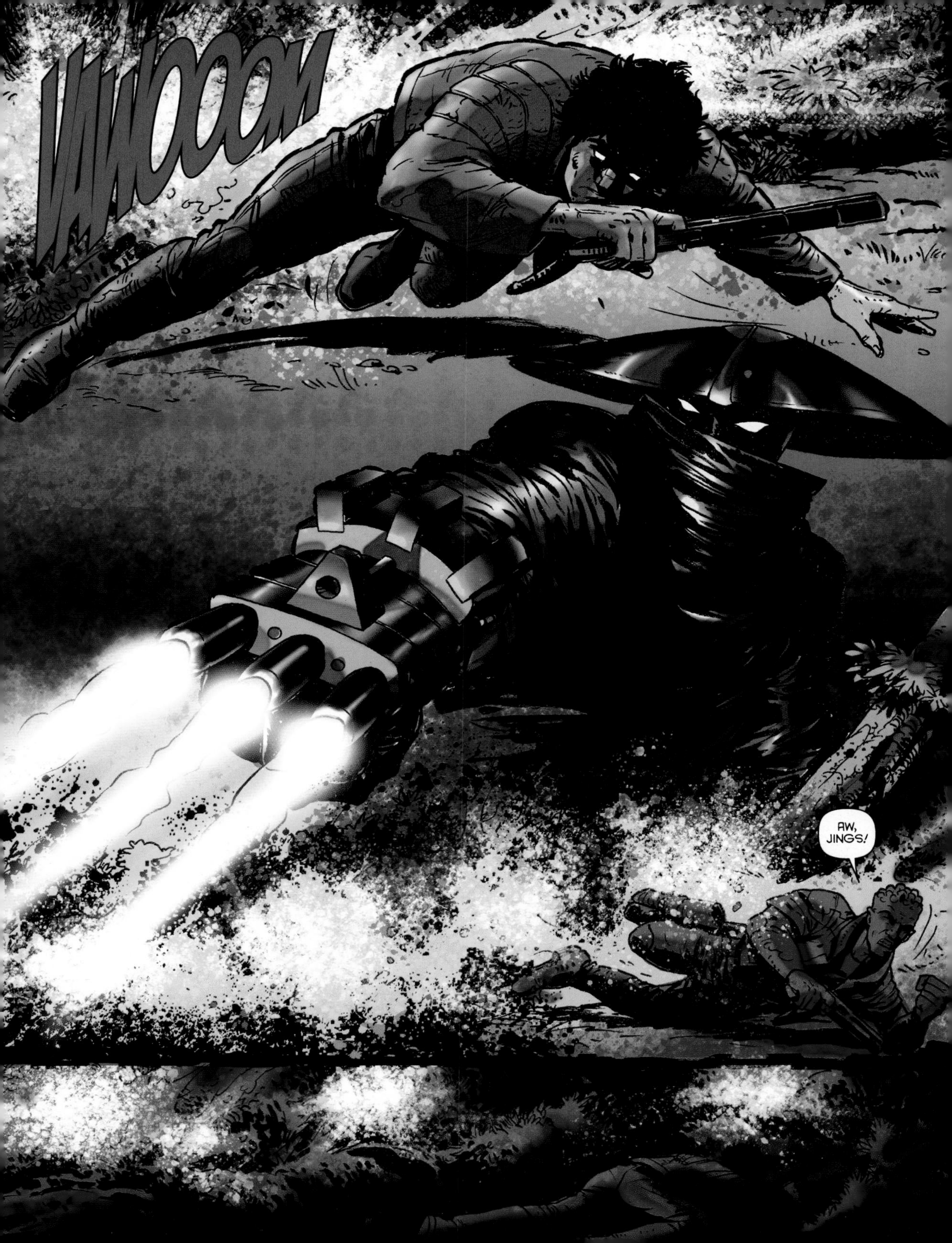
VAWOOOM
AW, JINGS!

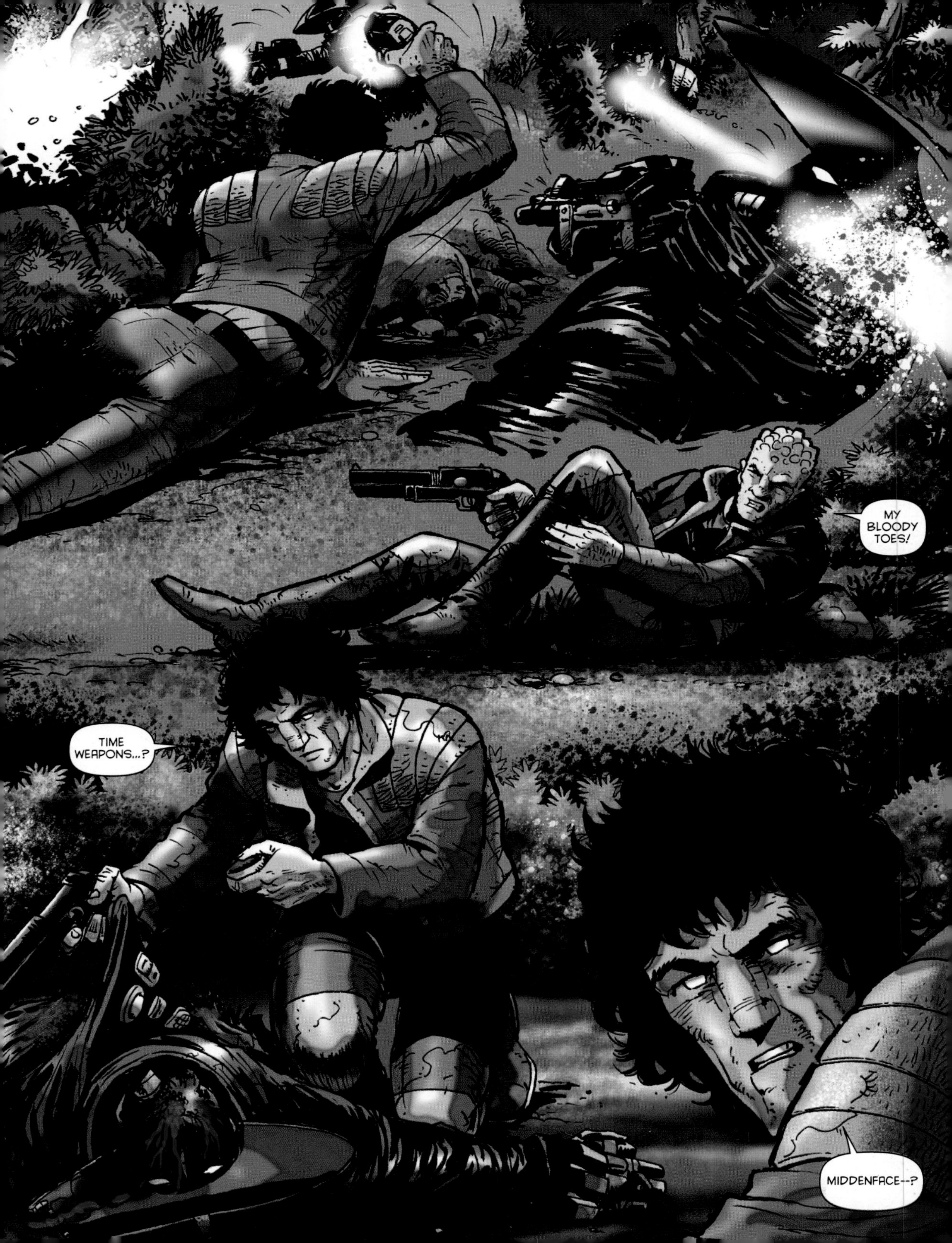
MY BLOODY TOES!
TIME WEAPONS...?
MIDDENFACE--?

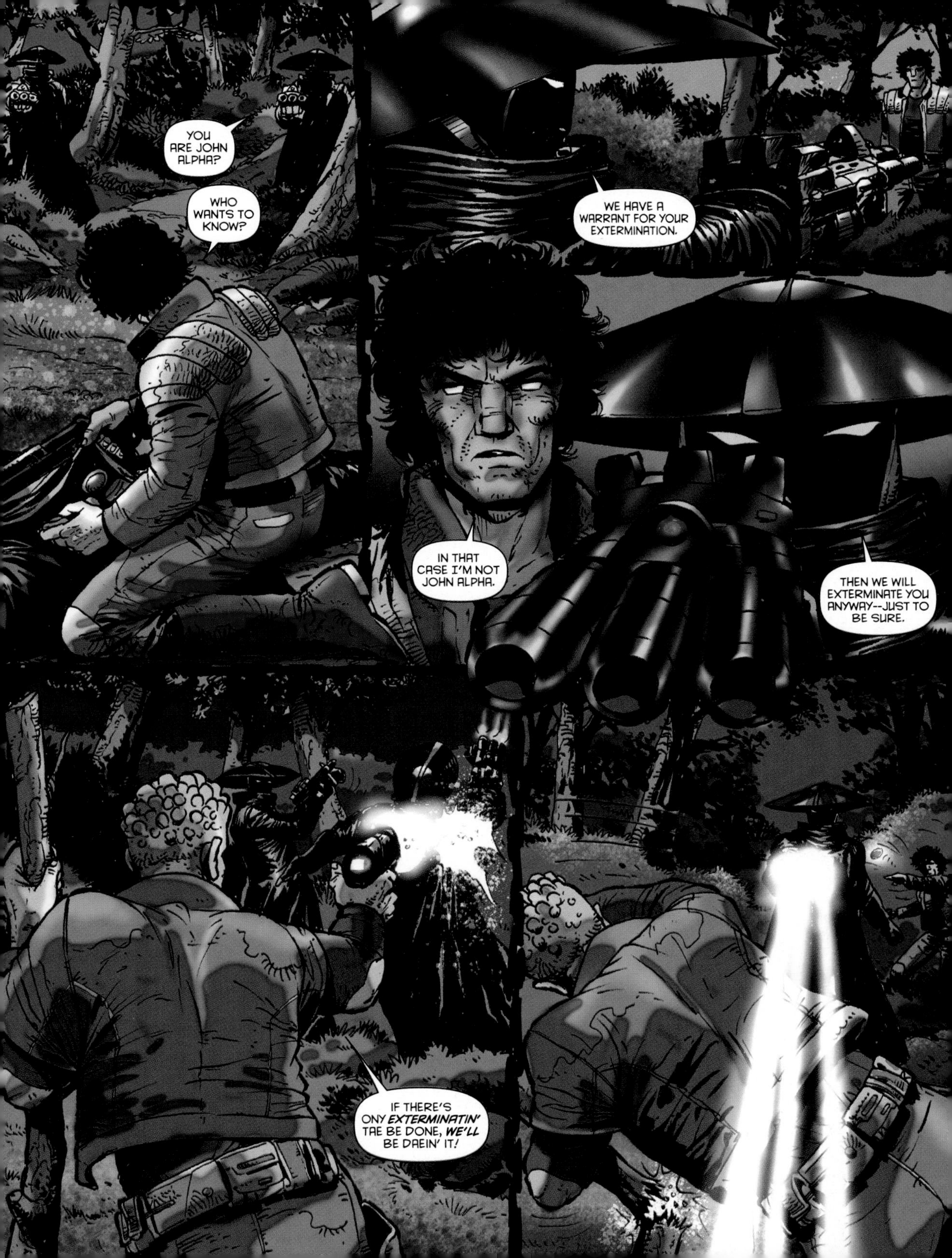

YOU ARE JOHN ALPHA?
WHO WANTS TO KNOW?
WE HAVE A WARRANT FOR YOUR EXTERMINATION.
IN THAT CASE I'M NOT JOHN ALPHA.
THEN WE WILL EXTERMINATE YOU ANYWAY--JUST TO BE SURE.
IF THERE'S ONY EXTERMINATIN' TAE BE DONE, WE'LL BE DAEIN' IT!

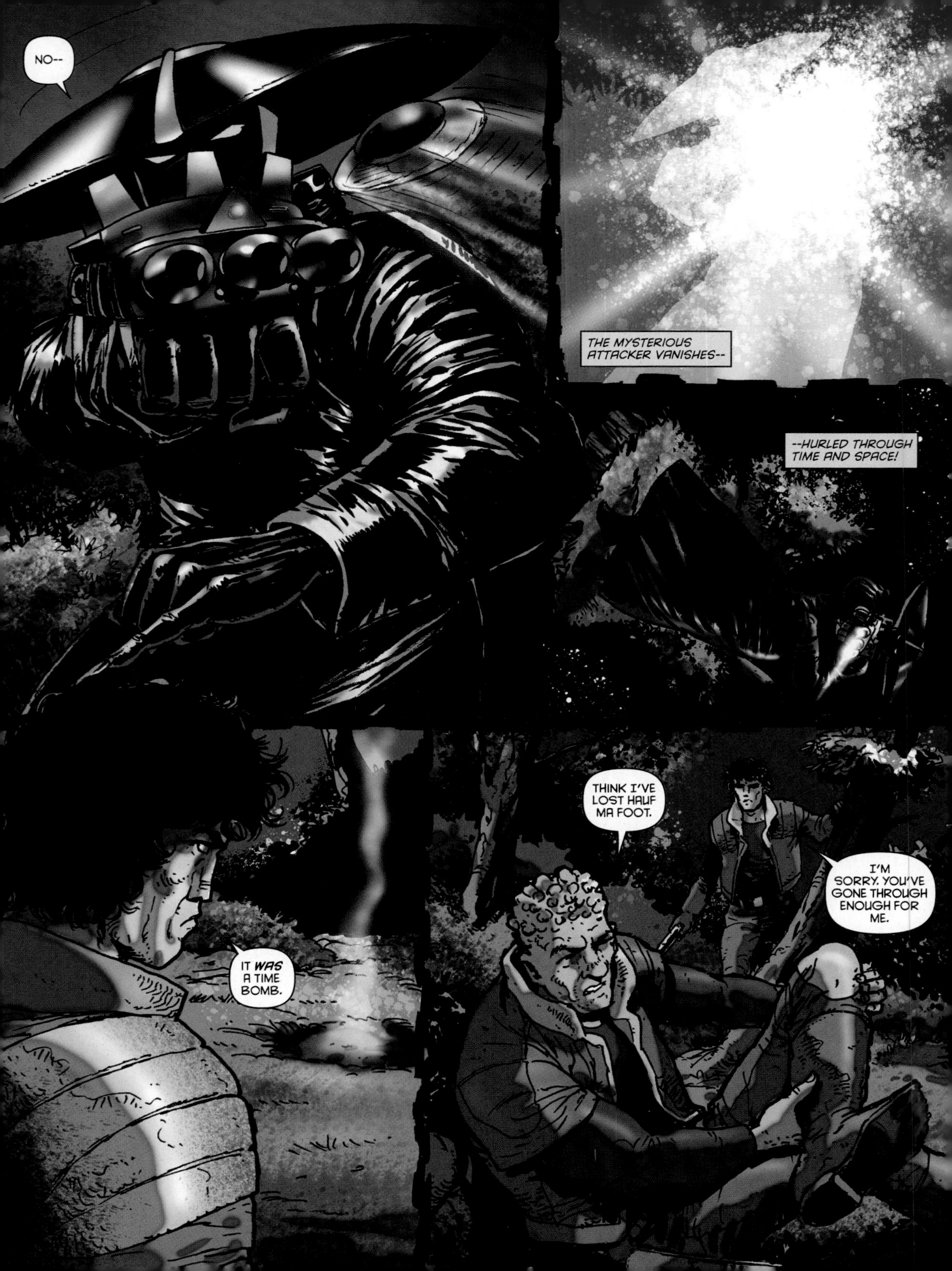
NO--
THE MYSTERIOUS ATTACKER VANISHES--
--HURLED THROUGH TIME AND SPACE!
IT *WAS* A TIME BOMB.
THINK I'VE LOST HALF MA FOOT.
I'M SORRY. YOU'VE GONE THROUGH ENOUGH FOR ME.

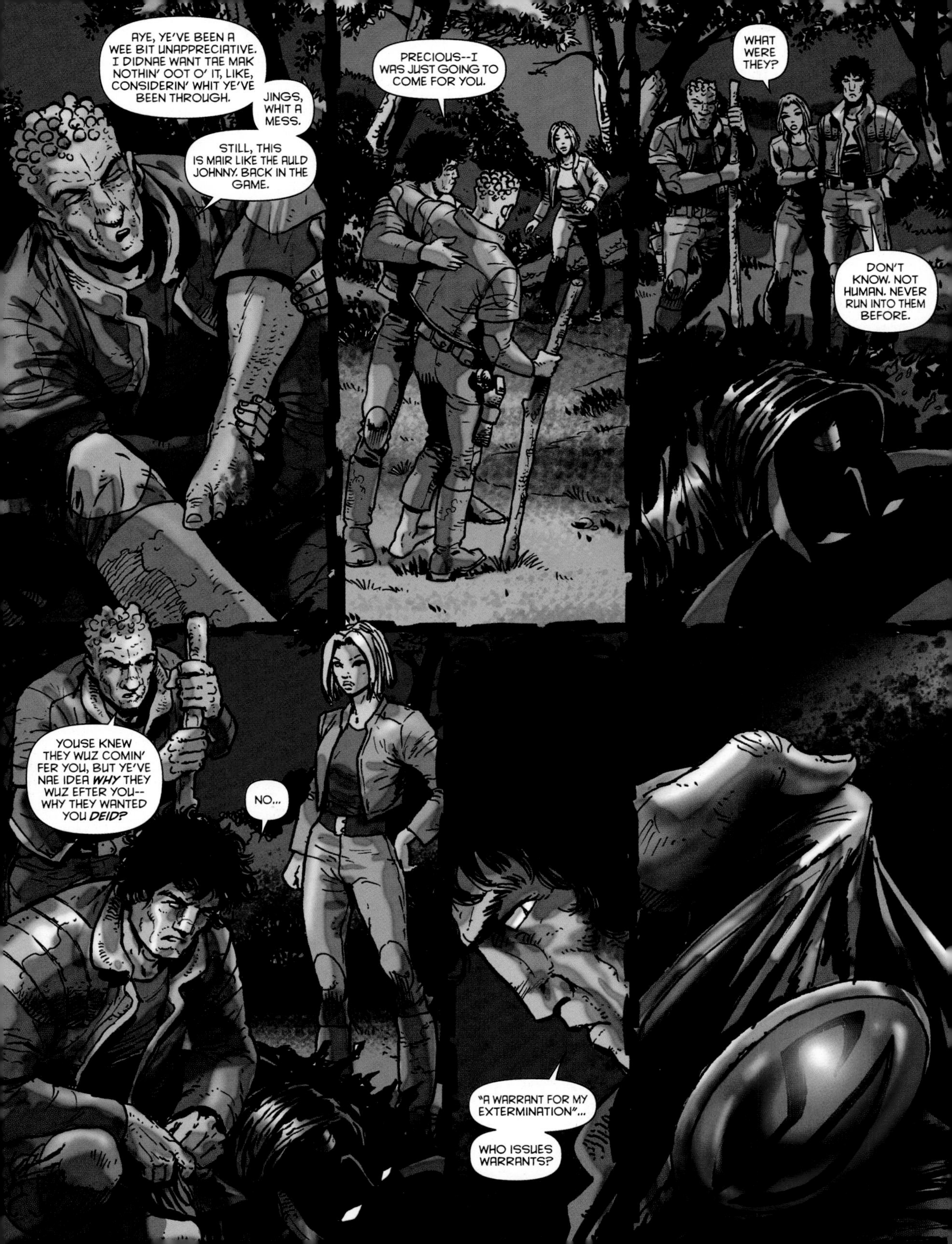
AYE, YE'VE BEEN A WEE BIT UNAPPRECIATIVE. I DIDNAE WANT TAE MAK NOTHIN' OOT O' IT, LIKE, CONSIDERIN' WHIT YE'VE BEEN THROUGH.
JINGS, WHIT A MESS.
STILL, THIS IS MAIR LIKE THE AULD JOHNNY. BACK IN THE GAME.
PRECIOUS--I WAS JUST GOING TO COME FOR YOU.
WHAT WERE THEY?
DON'T KNOW. NOT HUMAN. NEVER RUN INTO THEM BEFORE.
YOUSE KNEW THEY WUZ COMIN' FER YOU, BUT YE'VE NAE IDEA *WHY* THEY WUZ EFTER YOU-- WHY THEY WANTED YOU *DEID?*
NO...
"A WARRANT FOR MY EXTERMINATION"...
WHO ISSUES WARRANTS?

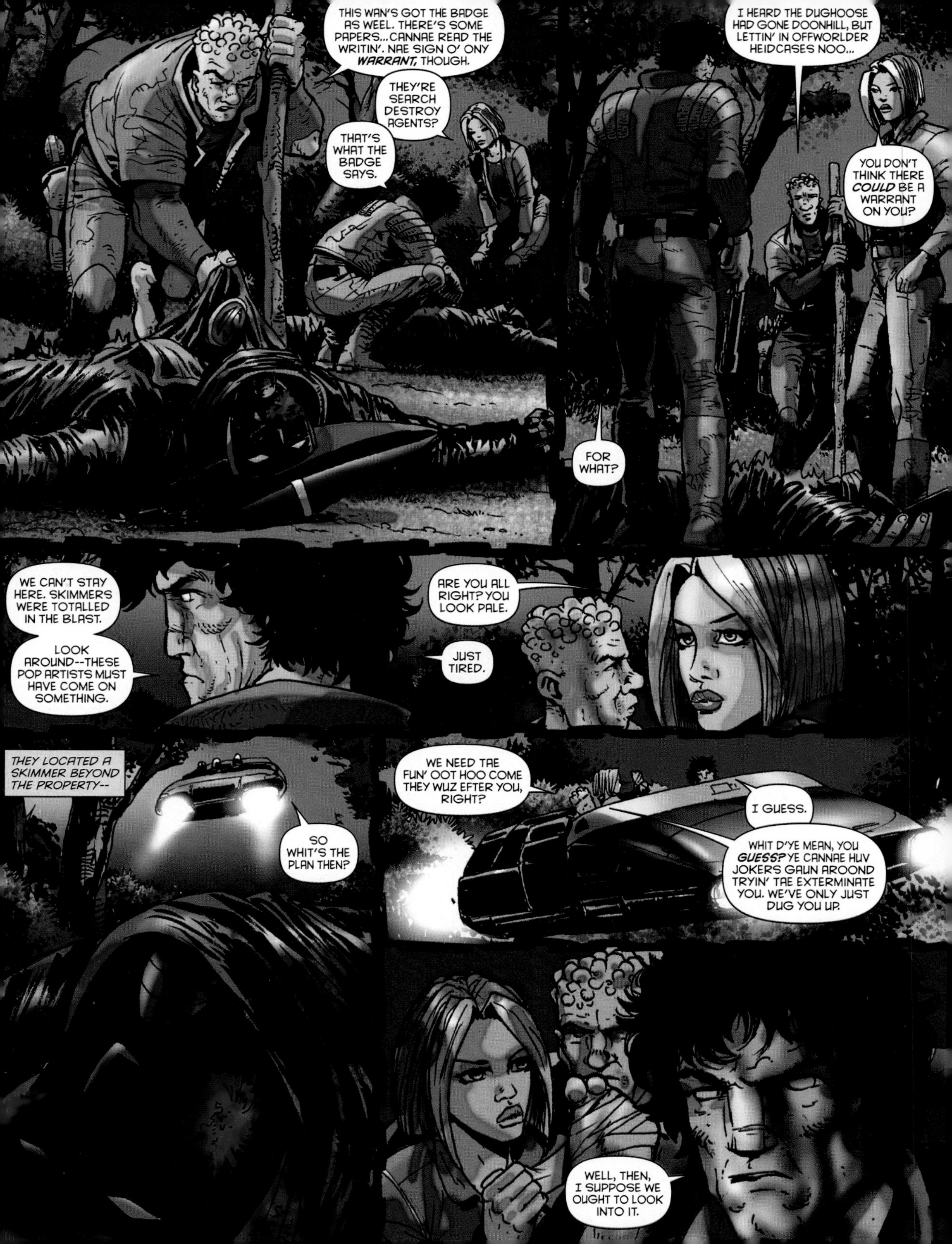

THIS WAN'S GOT THE BADGE AS WEEL. THERE'S SOME PAPERS...CANNAE READ THE WRITIN'. NAE SIGN O' ONY *WARRANT,* THOUGH.
THEY'RE SEARCH DESTROY AGENTS?
THAT'S WHAT THE BADGE SAYS.
I HEARD THE DUGHOOSE HAD GONE DOONHILL, BUT LETTIN' IN OFFWORLDER HEIDCASES NOO...
YOU DON'T THINK THERE *COULD* BE A WARRANT ON YOU?
FOR WHAT?
WE CAN'T STAY HERE. SKIMMERS WERE TOTALLED IN THE BLAST.
LOOK AROUND--THESE POP ARTISTS MUST HAVE COME ON SOMETHING.
ARE YOU ALL RIGHT? YOU LOOK PALE.
JUST TIRED.
THEY LOCATED A SKIMMER BEYOND THE PROPERTY--
SO WHIT'S THE PLAN THEN?
WE NEED TAE FUN' OOT HOO COME THEY WUZ EFTER YOU, RIGHT?
I GUESS.
WHIT D'YE MEAN, YOU *GUESS?* YE CANNAE HUV JOKERS GAUN AROOND TRYIN' TAE EXTERMINATE YOU. WE'VE ONLY JUST DUG YOU UP.
WELL, THEN, I SUPPOSE WE OUGHT TO LOOK INTO IT.

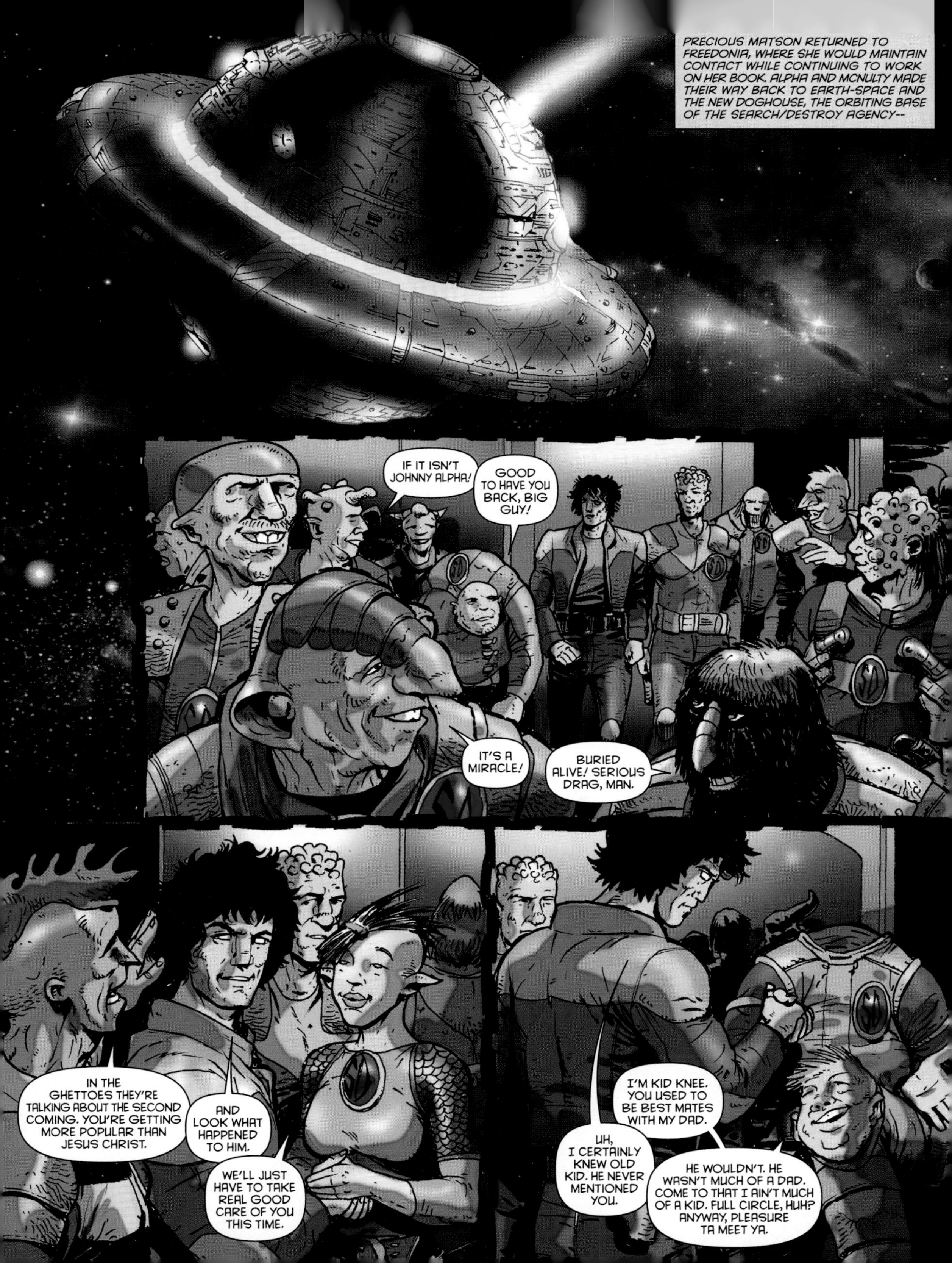
PRECIOUS MATSON RETURNED TO FREEDONIA, WHERE SHE WOULD MAINTAIN CONTACT WHILE CONTINUING TO WORK ON HER BOOK. ALPHA AND MCNULTY MADE THEIR WAY BACK TO EARTH-SPACE AND THE NEW DOGHOUSE, THE ORBITING BASE OF THE SEARCH/DESTROY AGENCY--
IF IT ISN'T JOHNNY ALPHA!
GOOD TO HAVE YOU BACK, BIG GUY!
IT'S A MIRACLE!
BURIED ALIVE! SERIOUS DRAG, MAN.
IN THE GHETTOES THEY'RE TALKING ABOUT THE SECOND COMING. YOU'RE GETTING MORE POPULAR THAN JESUS CHRIST.
AND LOOK WHAT HAPPENED TO HIM.
WE'LL JUST HAVE TO TAKE REAL GOOD CARE OF YOU THIS TIME.
I'M KID KNEE. YOU USED TO BE BEST MATES WITH MY DAD.
UH, I CERTAINLY KNEW OLD KID. HE NEVER MENTIONED YOU.
HE WOULDN'T. HE WASN'T MUCH OF A DAD. COME TO THAT I AIN'T MUCH OF A KID. FULL CIRCLE, HUH? ANYWAY, PLEASURE TA MEET YA.

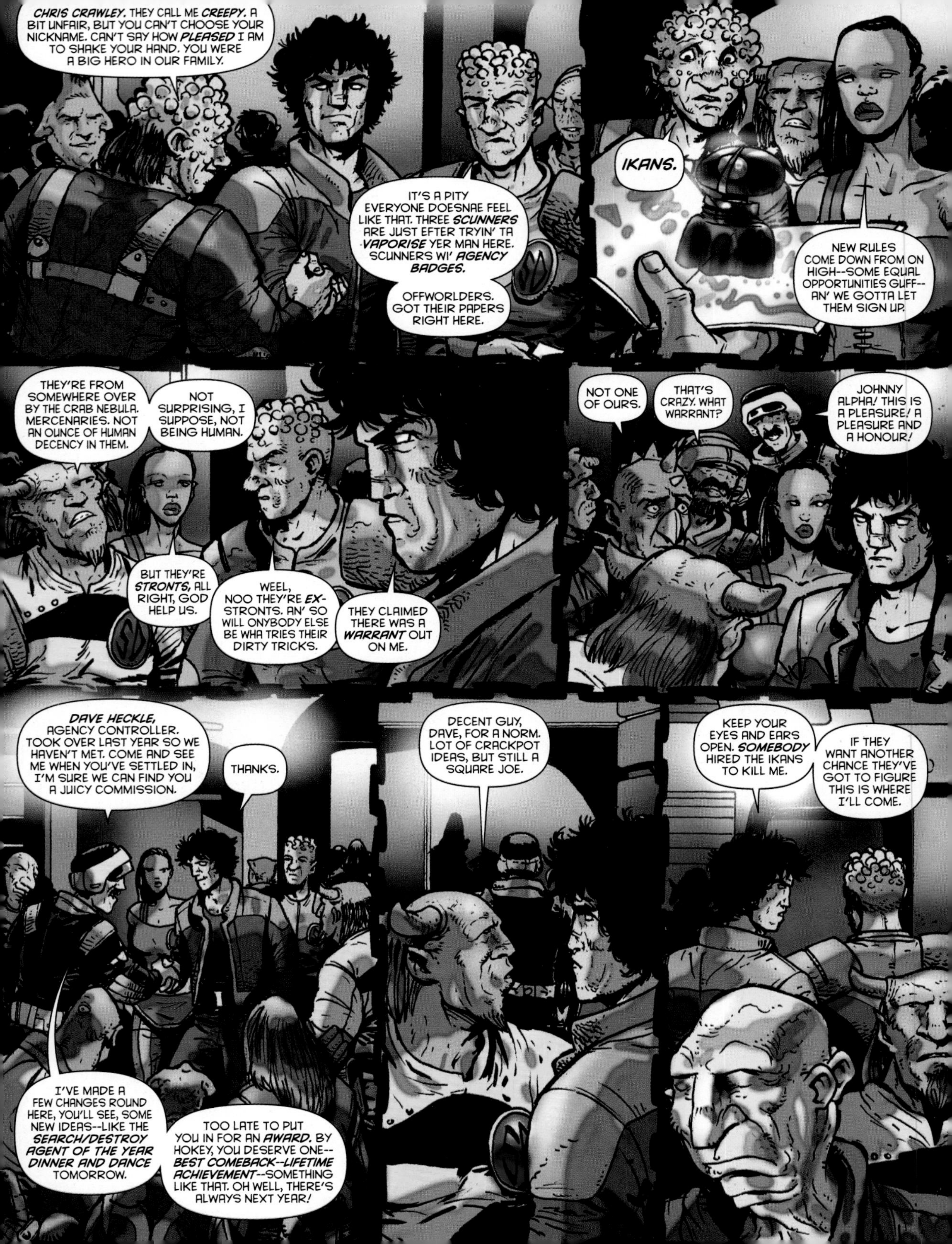

CHRIS CRAWLEY. THEY CALL ME CREEPY. A BIT UNFAIR, BUT YOU CAN'T CHOOSE YOUR NICKNAME. CAN'T SAY HOW PLEASED I AM TO SHAKE YOUR HAND. YOU WERE A BIG HERO IN OUR FAMILY.
IT'S A PITY EVERYONE DOESNAE FEEL LIKE THAT. THREE SCUNNERS ARE JUST EFTER TRYIN' TA VAPORISE YER MAN HERE. SCUNNERS WI' AGENCY BADGES.
OFFWORLDERS. GOT THEIR PAPERS RIGHT HERE.
IKANS.
NEW RULES COME DOWN FROM ON HIGH--SOME EQUAL OPPORTUNITIES GUFF--AN' WE GOTTA LET THEM SIGN UP.
THEY'RE FROM SOMEWHERE OVER BY THE CRAB NEBULA. MERCENARIES. NOT AN OUNCE OF HUMAN DECENCY IN THEM.
NOT SURPRISING, I SUPPOSE, NOT BEING HUMAN.
BUT THEY'RE STRONTS, ALL RIGHT, GOD HELP US.
WEEL, NOO THEY'RE EX-STRONTS. AN' SO WILL ONYBODY ELSE BE WHA TRIES THEIR DIRTY TRICKS.
THEY CLAIMED THERE WAS A WARRANT OUT ON ME.
NOT ONE OF OURS.
THAT'S CRAZY. WHAT WARRANT?
JOHNNY ALPHA! THIS IS A PLEASURE! A PLEASURE AND A HONOUR!
DAVE HECKLE, AGENCY CONTROLLER. TOOK OVER LAST YEAR SO WE HAVEN'T MET. COME AND SEE ME WHEN YOU'VE SETTLED IN, I'M SURE WE CAN FIND YOU A JUICY COMMISSION.
THANKS.
I'VE MADE A FEW CHANGES ROUND HERE, YOU'LL SEE, SOME NEW IDEAS--LIKE THE SEARCH/DESTROY AGENT OF THE YEAR DINNER AND DANCE TOMORROW.
TOO LATE TO PUT YOU IN FOR AN AWARD. BY HOKEY, YOU DESERVE ONE--BEST COMEBACK--LIFETIME ACHIEVEMENT--SOMETHING LIKE THAT. OH WELL, THERE'S ALWAYS NEXT YEAR!
DECENT GUY, DAVE, FOR A NORM. LOT OF CRACKPOT IDEAS, BUT STILL A SQUARE JOE.
KEEP YOUR EYES AND EARS OPEN. SOMEBODY HIRED THE IKANS TO KILL ME.
IF THEY WANT ANOTHER CHANCE THEY'VE GOT TO FIGURE THIS IS WHERE I'LL COME.

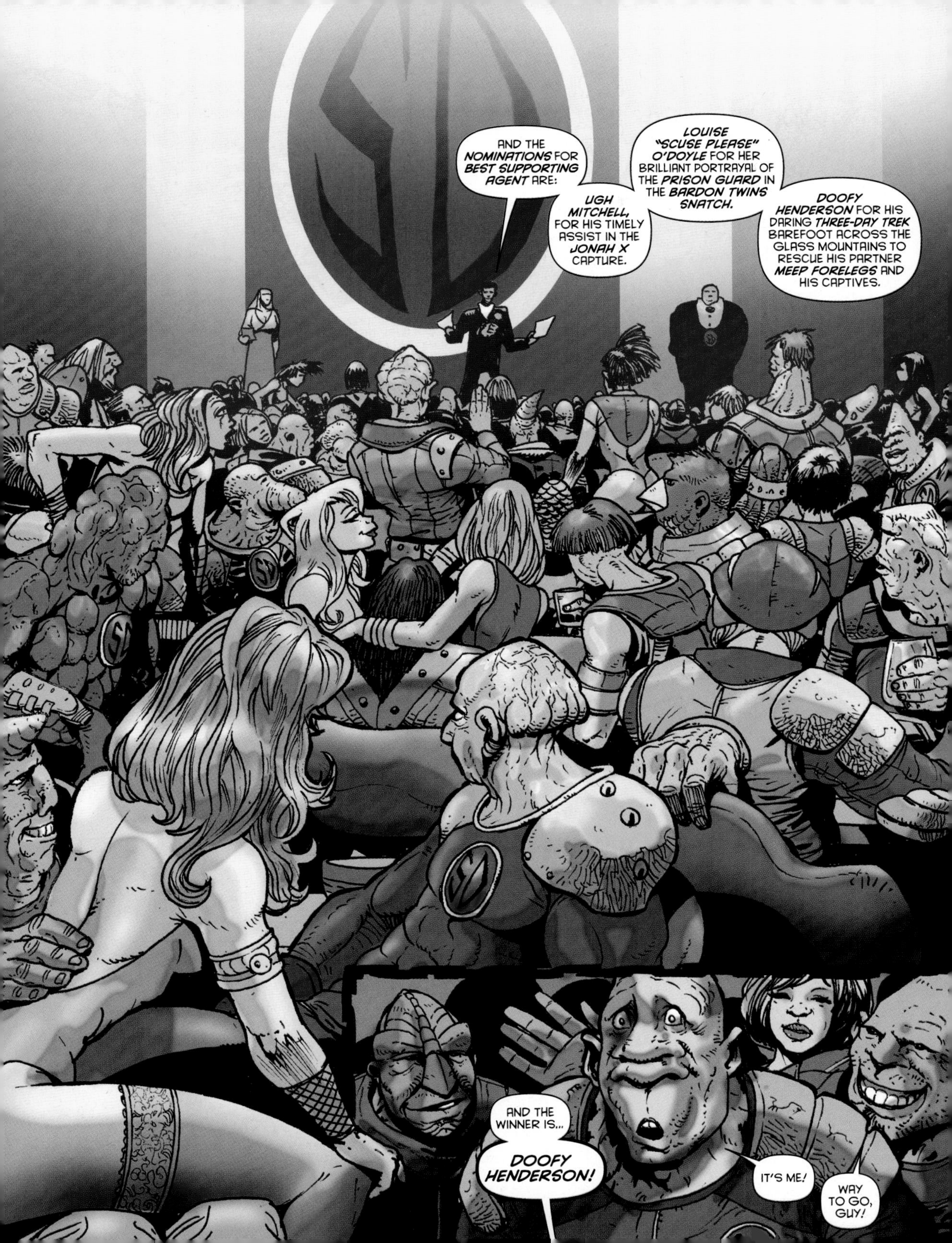
AND THE NOMINATIONS FOR BEST SUPPORTING AGENT ARE:
UGH MITCHELL, FOR HIS TIMELY ASSIST IN THE JONAH X CAPTURE.
LOUISE "SCUSE PLEASE" O'DOYLE FOR HER BRILLIANT PORTRAYAL OF THE PRISON GUARD IN THE BARDON TWINS SNATCH.
DOOFY HENDERSON FOR HIS DARING THREE-DAY TREK BAREFOOT ACROSS THE GLASS MOUNTAINS TO RESCUE HIS PARTNER MEEP FORELEGS AND HIS CAPTIVES.
AND THE WINNER IS...
DOOFY HENDERSON!
IT'S ME!
WAY TO GO, GUY!

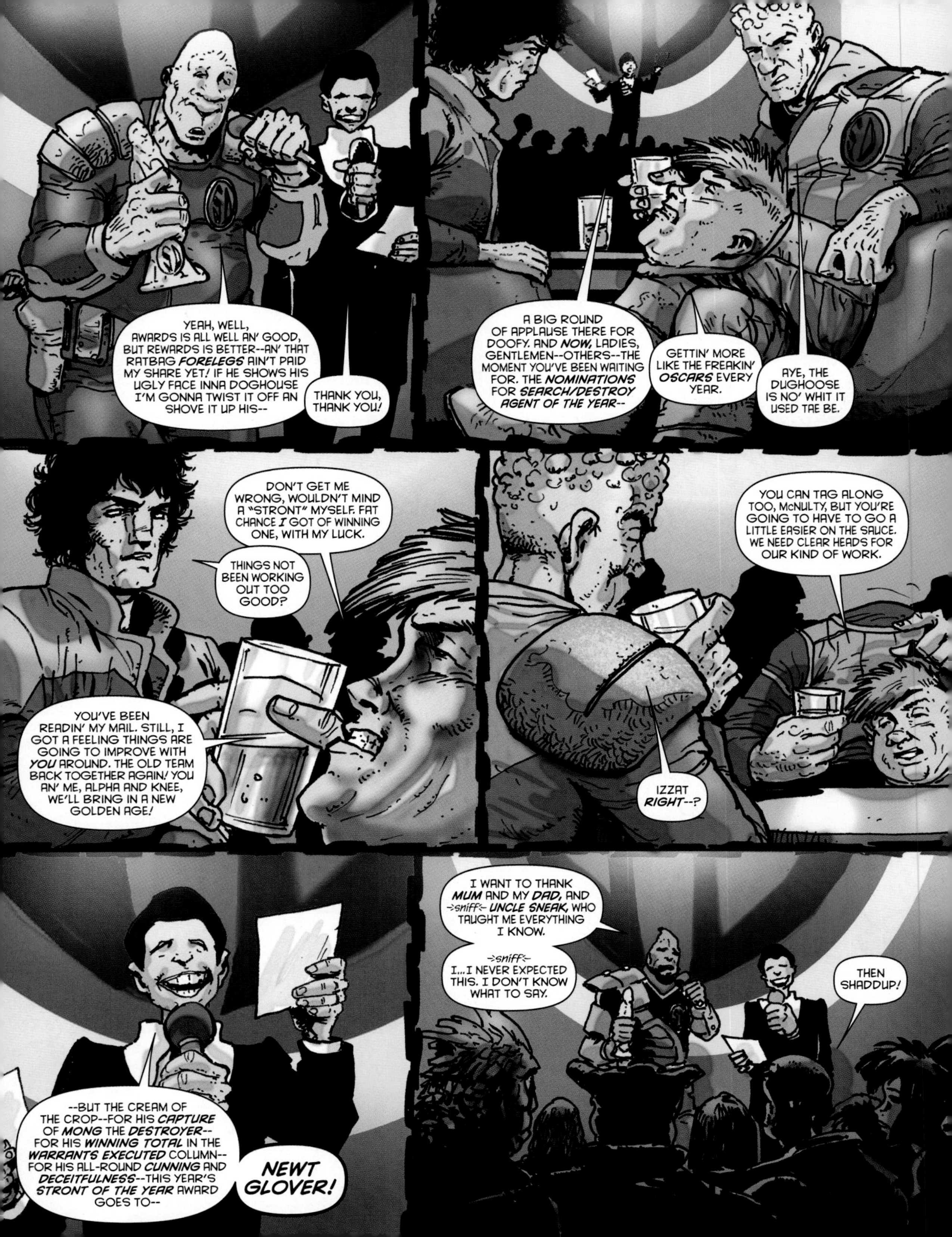

YEAH, WELL, AWARDS IS ALL WELL AN' GOOD, BUT REWARDS IS BETTER--AN' THAT RATBAG *FORELEGS* AIN'T PAID MY SHARE YET! IF HE SHOWS HIS UGLY FACE INNA DOGHOUSE I'M GONNA TWIST IT OFF AN SHOVE IT UP HIS--
THANK YOU, THANK YOU!
A BIG ROUND OF APPLAUSE THERE FOR DOOFY. AND *NOW,* LADIES, GENTLEMEN--OTHERS--THE MOMENT YOU'VE BEEN WAITING FOR. THE *NOMINATIONS* FOR *SEARCH/DESTROY AGENT OF THE YEAR*--
GETTIN' MORE LIKE THE FREAKIN' *OSCARS* EVERY YEAR.
AYE, THE DUGHOOSE IS NO' WHIT IT USED TAE BE.
THINGS NOT BEEN WORKING OUT TOO GOOD?
DON'T GET ME WRONG, WOULDN'T MIND A "STRONT" MYSELF. FAT CHANCE *I* GOT OF WINNING ONE, WITH MY LUCK.
YOU'VE BEEN READIN' MY MAIL. STILL, I GOT A FEELING THINGS ARE GOING TO IMPROVE WITH *YOU* AROUND. THE OLD TEAM BACK TOGETHER AGAIN! YOU AN' ME, ALPHA AND KNEE, WE'LL BRING IN A NEW GOLDEN AGE!
YOU CAN TAG ALONG TOO, McNULTY, BUT YOU'RE GOING TO HAVE TO GO A LITTLE EASIER ON THE SAUCE. WE NEED CLEAR HEADS FOR OUR KIND OF WORK.
IZZAT *RIGHT*--?
--BUT THE CREAM OF THE CROP--FOR HIS *CAPTURE* OF *MONG* THE *DESTROYER*--FOR HIS *WINNING TOTAL* IN THE *WARRANTS EXECUTED* COLUMN--FOR HIS ALL-ROUND *CUNNING* AND *DECEITFULNESS*--THIS YEAR'S *STRONT OF THE YEAR* AWARD GOES TO--
NEWT GLOVER!
I WANT TO THANK *MUM* AND MY *DAD,* AND ~sniff~ *UNCLE SNEAK,* WHO TAUGHT ME EVERYTHING I KNOW.
~sniff~ I... I NEVER EXPECTED THIS. I DON'T KNOW WHAT TO SAY.
THEN SHADDUP!

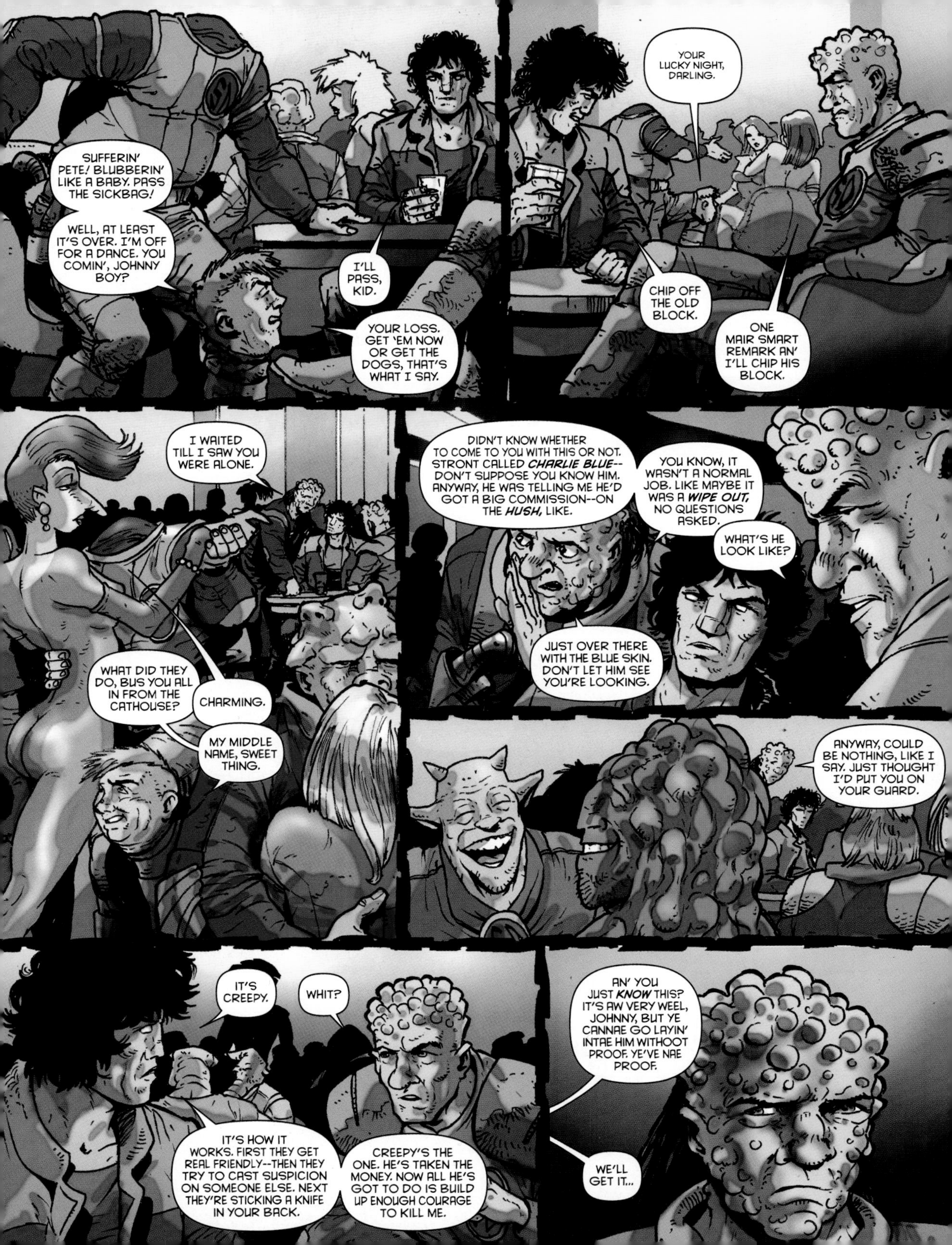
SUFFERIN' PETE! BLUBBERIN' LIKE A BABY. PASS THE SICKBAG!
WELL, AT LEAST IT'S OVER. I'M OFF FOR A DANCE. YOU COMIN', JOHNNY BOY?
I'LL PASS, KID.
YOUR LOSS. GET 'EM NOW OR GET THE DOGS, THAT'S WHAT I SAY.
YOUR LUCKY NIGHT, DARLING.
CHIP OFF THE OLD BLOCK.
ONE MAIR SMART REMARK AN' I'LL CHIP HIS BLOCK.
I WAITED TILL I SAW YOU WERE ALONE.
WHAT DID THEY DO, BUS YOU ALL IN FROM THE CATHOUSE?
CHARMING.
MY MIDDLE NAME, SWEET THING.
DIDN'T KNOW WHETHER TO COME TO YOU WITH THIS OR NOT. STRONT CALLED CHARLIE BLUE-- DON'T SUPPOSE YOU KNOW HIM. ANYWAY, HE WAS TELLING ME HE'D GOT A BIG COMMISSION--ON THE HUSH, LIKE.
YOU KNOW, IT WASN'T A NORMAL JOB. LIKE MAYBE IT WAS A WIPE OUT, NO QUESTIONS ASKED.
WHAT'S HE LOOK LIKE?
JUST OVER THERE WITH THE BLUE SKIN. DON'T LET HIM SEE YOU'RE LOOKING.
ANYWAY, COULD BE NOTHING, LIKE I SAY. JUST THOUGHT I'D PUT YOU ON YOUR GUARD.
IT'S CREEPY.
WHIT?
IT'S HOW IT WORKS. FIRST THEY GET REAL FRIENDLY--THEN THEY TRY TO CAST SUSPICION ON SOMEONE ELSE. NEXT THEY'RE STICKING A KNIFE IN YOUR BACK.
CREEPY'S THE ONE. HE'S TAKEN THE MONEY. NOW ALL HE'S GOT TO DO IS BUILD UP ENOUGH COURAGE TO KILL ME.
AN' YOU JUST KNOW THIS? IT'S AW VERY WEEL, JOHNNY, BUT YE CANNAE GO LAYIN' INTAE HIM WITHOOT PROOF. YE'VE NAE PROOF.
WE'LL GET IT...

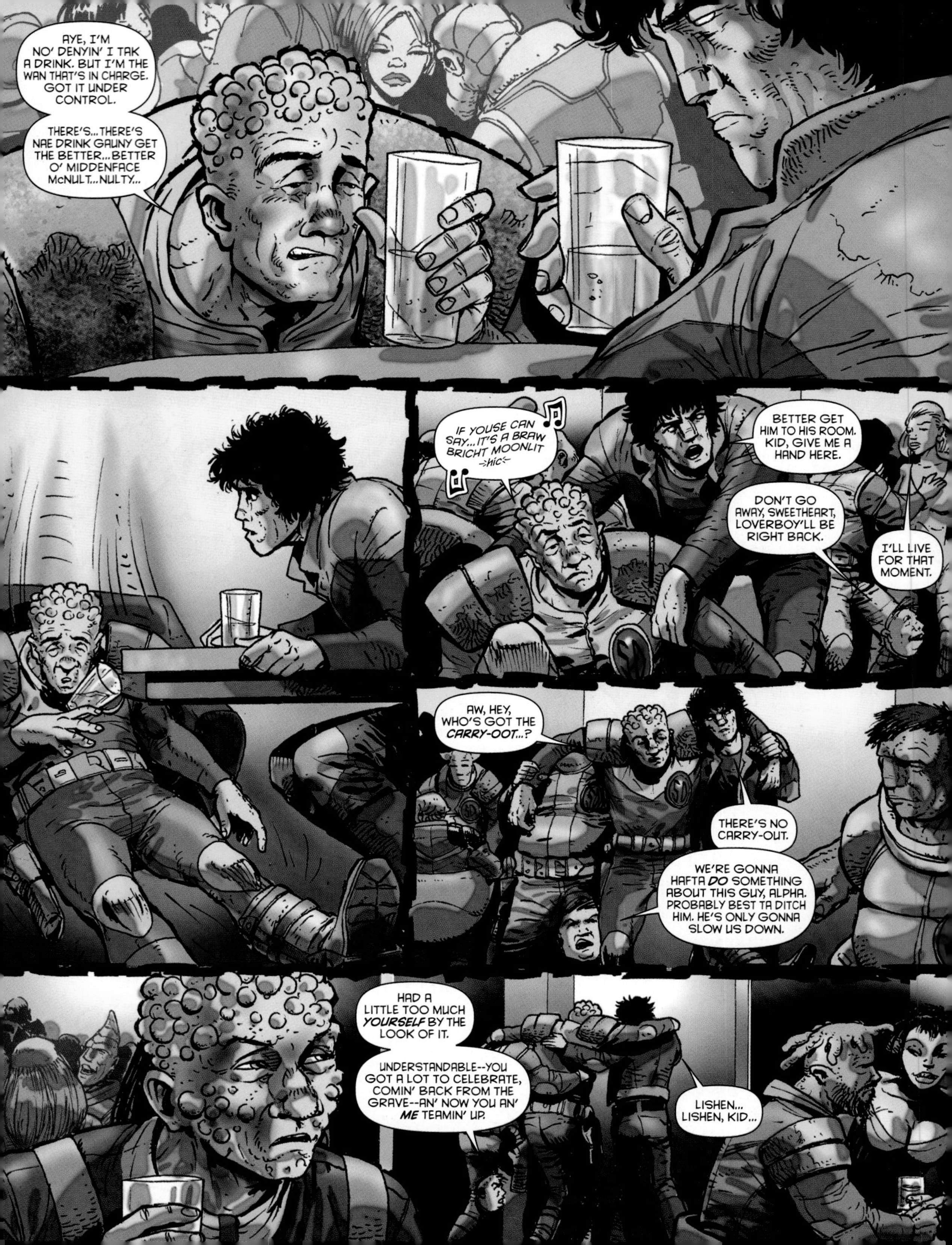
AYE, I'M NO' DENYIN' I TAK A DRINK. BUT I'M THE WAN THAT'S IN CHARGE. GOT IT UNDER CONTROL.
THERE'S... THERE'S NAE DRINK GAUNY GET THE BETTER... BETTER O' MIDDENFACE McNULT... NULTY...
IF YOUSE CAN SAY... IT'S A BRAW BRICHT MOONLIT -hic-
BETTER GET HIM TO HIS ROOM. KID, GIVE ME A HAND HERE.
DON'T GO AWAY, SWEETHEART, LOVERBOY'LL BE RIGHT BACK.
I'LL LIVE FOR THAT MOMENT.
AW, HEY, WHO'S GOT THE CARRY-OOT...?
THERE'S NO CARRY-OUT.
WE'RE GONNA HAFTA DO SOMETHING ABOUT THIS GUY, ALPHA. PROBABLY BEST TA DITCH HIM. HE'S ONLY GONNA SLOW US DOWN.
HAD A LITTLE TOO MUCH YOURSELF BY THE LOOK OF IT.
UNDERSTANDABLE--YOU GOT A LOT TO CELEBRATE, COMIN' BACK FROM THE GRAVE--AN' NOW YOU AN' ME TEAMIN' UP.
LISHEN... LISHEN, KID...

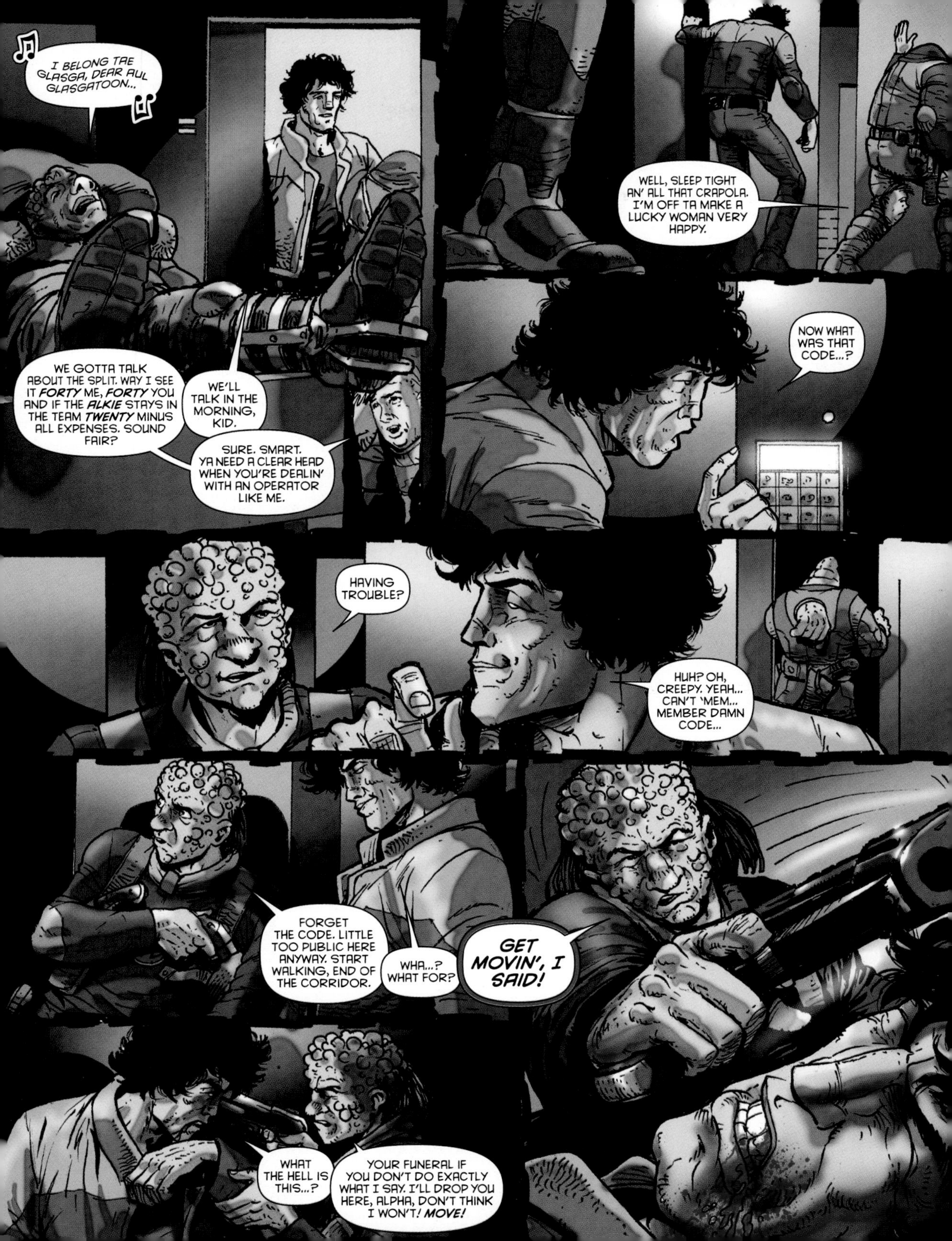

I BELONG TAE GLASGA, DEAR AUL GLASGATOON...
WE GOTTA TALK ABOUT THE SPLIT. WAY I SEE IT FORTY ME, FORTY YOU AND IF THE ALKIE STAYS IN THE TEAM TWENTY MINUS ALL EXPENSES. SOUND FAIR?
WE'LL TALK IN THE MORNING, KID.
SURE. SMART. YA NEED A CLEAR HEAD WHEN YOU'RE DEALIN' WITH AN OPERATOR LIKE ME.
WELL, SLEEP TIGHT AN' ALL THAT CRAPOLA. I'M OFF TA MAKE A LUCKY WOMAN VERY HAPPY.
NOW WHAT WAS THAT CODE...?
HAVING TROUBLE?
HUH? OH, CREEPY. YEAH... CAN'T 'MEM... MEMBER DAMN CODE...
FORGET THE CODE. LITTLE TOO PUBLIC HERE ANYWAY. START WALKING, END OF THE CORRIDOR.
WHA...? WHAT FOR?
GET MOVIN', I SAID!
WHAT THE HELL IS THIS...?
YOUR FUNERAL IF YOU DON'T DO EXACTLY WHAT I SAY. I'LL DROP YOU HERE, ALPHA, DON'T THINK I WON'T! MOVE!

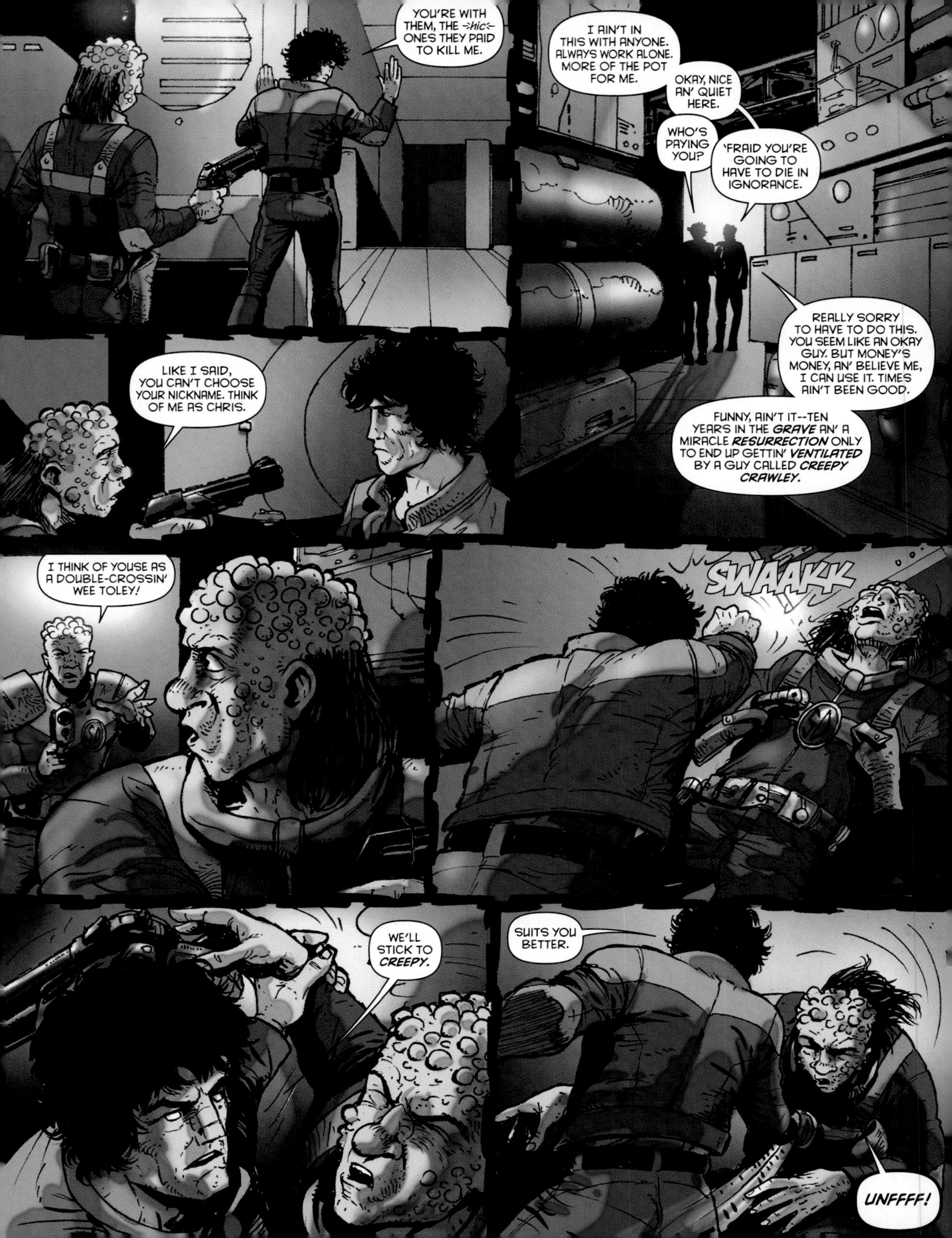

YOU'RE WITH THEM, THE -hic- ONES THEY PAID TO KILL ME.
I AIN'T IN THIS WITH ANYONE. ALWAYS WORK ALONE. MORE OF THE POT FOR ME.
OKAY, NICE AN' QUIET HERE.
WHO'S PAYING YOU?
'FRAID YOU'RE GOING TO HAVE TO DIE IN IGNORANCE.
LIKE I SAID, YOU CAN'T CHOOSE YOUR NICKNAME. THINK OF ME AS CHRIS.
REALLY SORRY TO HAVE TO DO THIS. YOU SEEM LIKE AN OKAY GUY. BUT MONEY'S MONEY, AN' BELIEVE ME, I CAN USE IT. TIMES AIN'T BEEN GOOD.
FUNNY, AIN'T IT--TEN YEARS IN THE GRAVE AN' A MIRACLE RESURRECTION ONLY TO END UP GETTIN' VENTILATED BY A GUY CALLED CREEPY CRAWLEY.
I THINK OF YOUSE AS A DOUBLE-CROSSIN' WEE TOLEY!
SWAAKK
WE'LL STICK TO CREEPY.
SUITS YOU BETTER.
UNFFFF!

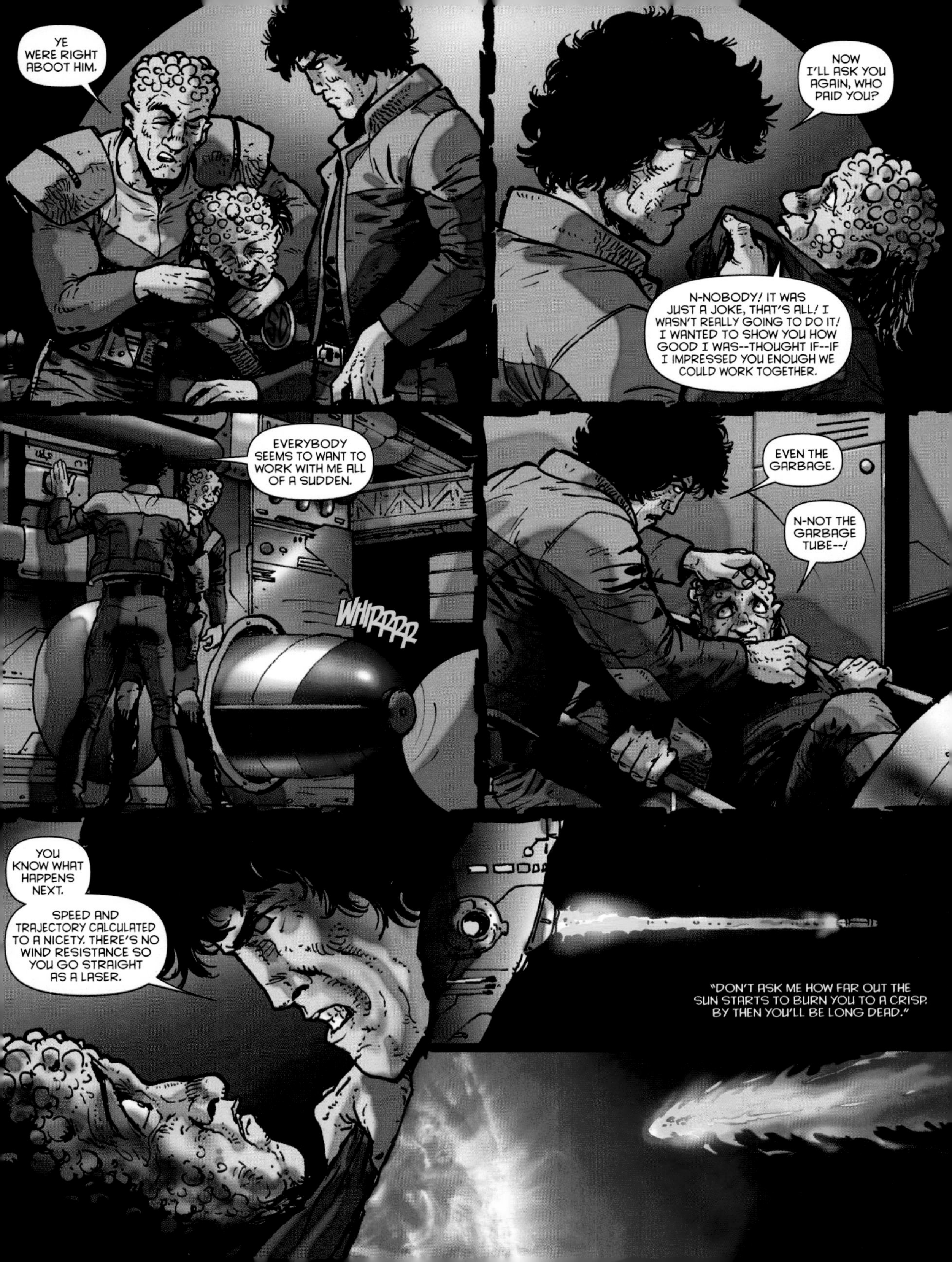
YE WERE RIGHT ABOOT HIM.
NOW I'LL ASK YOU AGAIN, WHO PAID YOU?
N-NOBODY! IT WAS JUST A JOKE, THAT'S ALL! I WASN'T REALLY GOING TO DO IT! I WANTED TO SHOW YOU HOW GOOD I WAS--THOUGHT IF--IF I IMPRESSED YOU ENOUGH WE COULD WORK TOGETHER.
EVERYBODY SEEMS TO WANT TO WORK WITH ME ALL OF A SUDDEN.
WHIRRRR
EVEN THE GARBAGE.
N-NOT THE GARBAGE TUBE--!
YOU KNOW WHAT HAPPENS NEXT.
SPEED AND TRAJECTORY CALCULATED TO A NICETY. THERE'S NO WIND RESISTANCE SO YOU GO STRAIGHT AS A LASER.
"DON'T ASK ME HOW FAR OUT THE SUN STARTS TO BURN YOU TO A CRISP. BY THEN YOU'LL BE LONG DEAD."

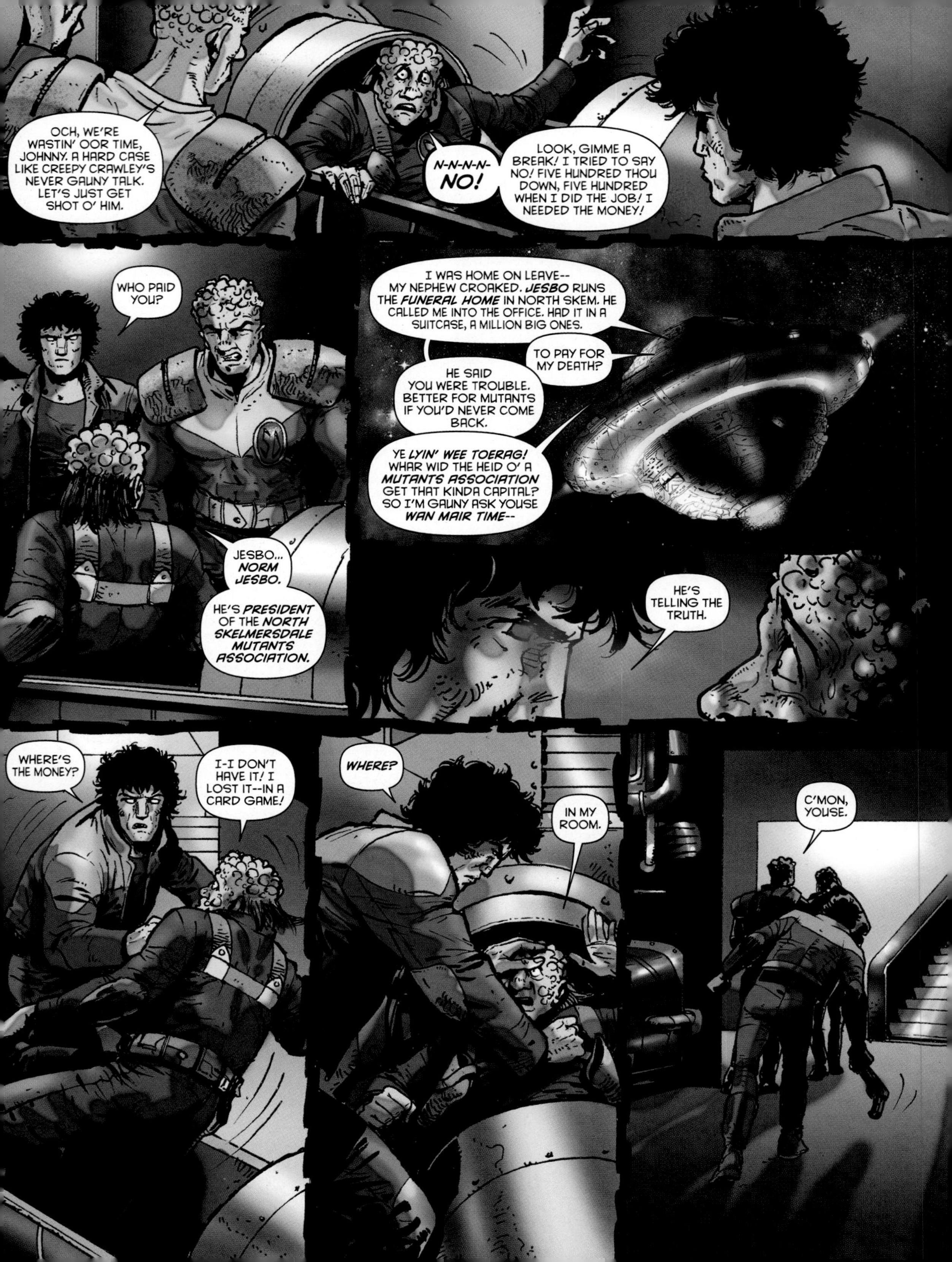
OCH, WE'RE WASTIN' OOR TIME, JOHNNY. A HARD CASE LIKE CREEPY CRAWLEY'S NEVER GAUNY TALK. LET'S JUST GET SHOT O' HIM.
N-N-N-N-NO!
LOOK, GIMME A BREAK! I TRIED TO SAY NO! FIVE HUNDRED THOU DOWN, FIVE HUNDRED WHEN I DID THE JOB! I NEEDED THE MONEY!
WHO PAID YOU?
JESBO... NORM JESBO.
HE'S PRESIDENT OF THE NORTH SKELMERSDALE MUTANTS ASSOCIATION.
I WAS HOME ON LEAVE-- MY NEPHEW CROAKED. JESBO RUNS THE FUNERAL HOME IN NORTH SKEM. HE CALLED ME INTO THE OFFICE. HAD IT IN A SUITCASE, A MILLION BIG ONES.
TO PAY FOR MY DEATH?
HE SAID YOU WERE TROUBLE. BETTER FOR MUTANTS IF YOU'D NEVER COME BACK.
YE LYIN' WEE TOERAG! WHAR WID THE HEID O' A MUTANTS ASSOCIATION GET THAT KINDA CAPITAL? SO I'M GAUNY ASK YOUSE WAN MAIR TIME--
HE'S TELLING THE TRUTH.
WHERE'S THE MONEY?
I-I DON'T HAVE IT! I LOST IT--IN A CARD GAME!
WHERE?
IN MY ROOM.
C'MON, YOUSE.

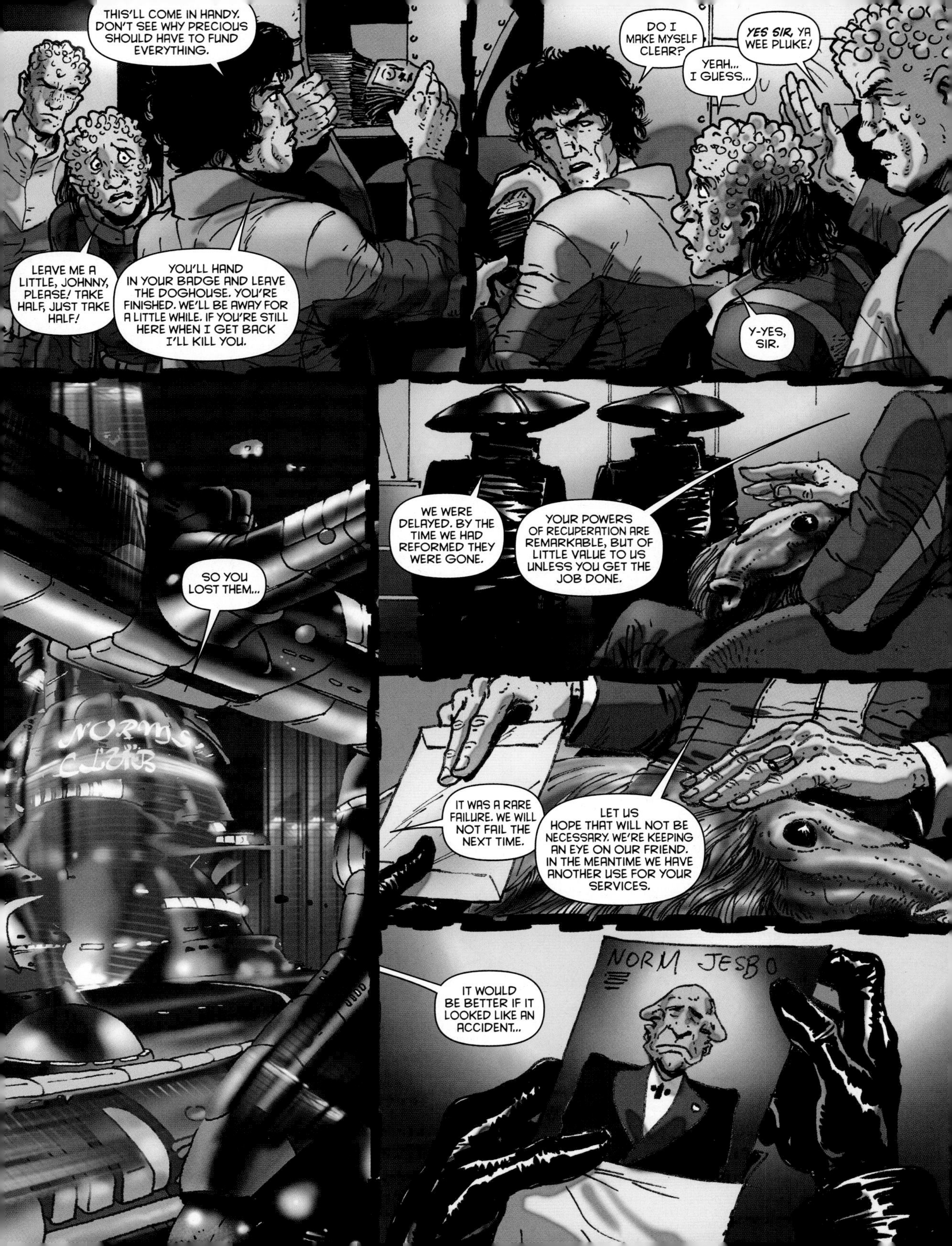
THIS'LL COME IN HANDY. DON'T SEE WHY PRECIOUS SHOULD HAVE TO FUND EVERYTHING.
LEAVE ME A LITTLE, JOHNNY, PLEASE! TAKE HALF, JUST TAKE HALF!
YOU'LL HAND IN YOUR BADGE AND LEAVE THE DOGHOUSE. YOU'RE FINISHED. WE'LL BE AWAY FOR A LITTLE WHILE. IF YOU'RE STILL HERE WHEN I GET BACK I'LL KILL YOU.
DO I MAKE MYSELF CLEAR?
YEAH... I GUESS...
YES SIR, YA WEE PLUKE!
Y-YES, SIR.
NORMS CLUB
SO YOU LOST THEM...
WE WERE DELAYED. BY THE TIME WE HAD REFORMED THEY WERE GONE.
YOUR POWERS OF RECUPERATION ARE REMARKABLE, BUT OF LITTLE VALUE TO US UNLESS YOU GET THE JOB DONE.
IT WAS A RARE FAILURE. WE WILL NOT FAIL THE NEXT TIME.
LET US HOPE THAT WILL NOT BE NECESSARY. WE'RE KEEPING AN EYE ON OUR FRIEND. IN THE MEANTIME WE HAVE ANOTHER USE FOR YOUR SERVICES.
NORM JESBO
IT WOULD BE BETTER IF IT LOOKED LIKE AN ACCIDENT...

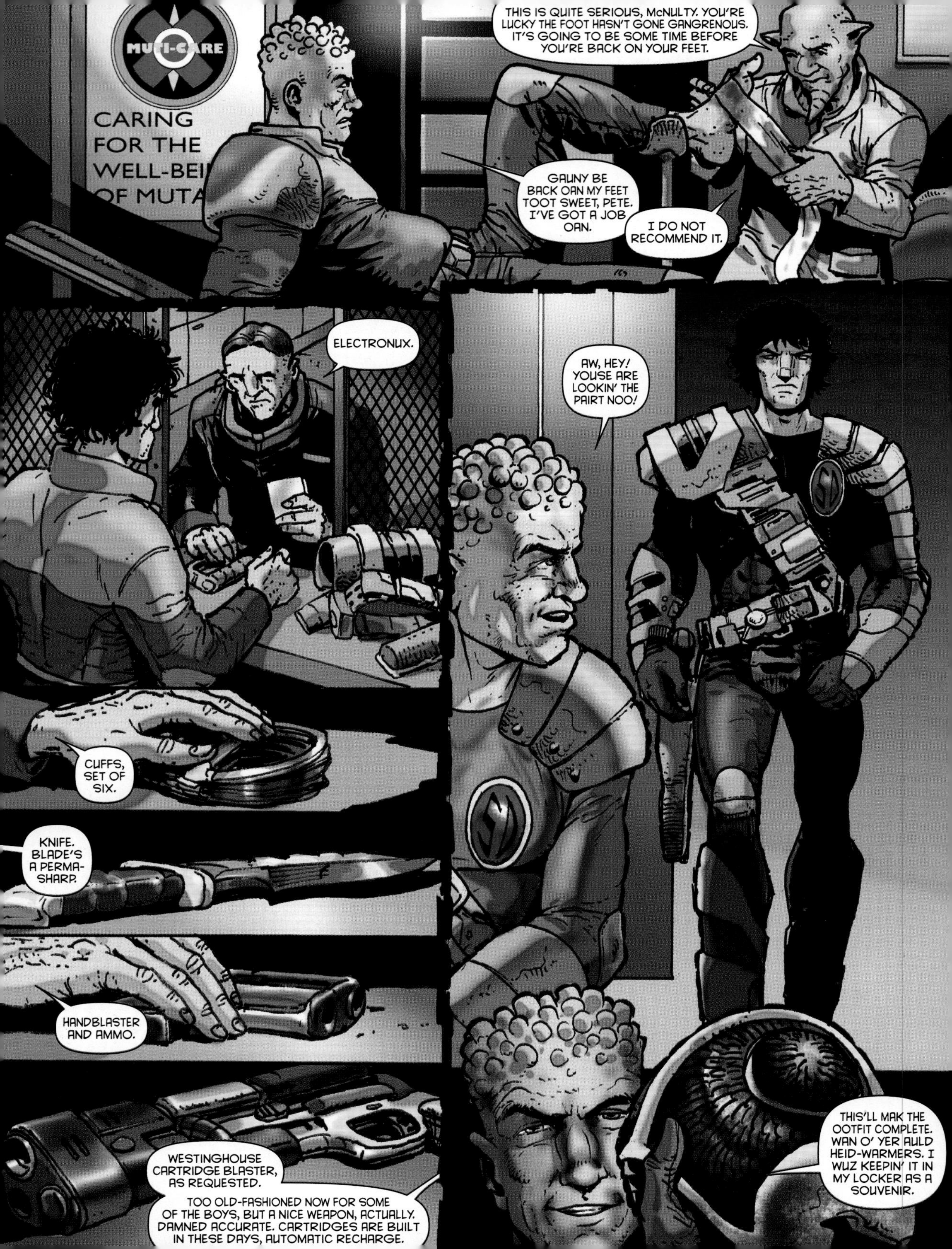
MUTI-CARE
CARING FOR THE WELL-BEI OF MUTA
THIS IS QUITE SERIOUS, McNULTY. YOU'RE LUCKY THE FOOT HASN'T GONE GANGRENOUS. IT'S GOING TO BE SOME TIME BEFORE YOU'RE BACK ON YOUR FEET.
GAUNY BE BACK OAN MY FEET TOOT SWEET, PETE. I'VE GOT A JOB OAN.
I DO NOT RECOMMEND IT.
ELECTRONUX.
CUFFS, SET OF SIX.
KNIFE. BLADE'S A PERMA-SHARP.
HANDBLASTER AND AMMO.
WESTINGHOUSE CARTRIDGE BLASTER, AS REQUESTED.
TOO OLD-FASHIONED NOW FOR SOME OF THE BOYS, BUT A NICE WEAPON, ACTUALLY. DAMNED ACCURATE. CARTRIDGES ARE BUILT IN THESE DAYS, AUTOMATIC RECHARGE.
AW, HEY! YOUSE ARE LOOKIN' THE PAIRT NOO!
THIS'LL MAK THE OOTFIT COMPLETE. WAN O' YER AULD HEID-WARMERS. I WUZ KEEPIN' IT IN MY LOCKER AS A SOUVENIR.

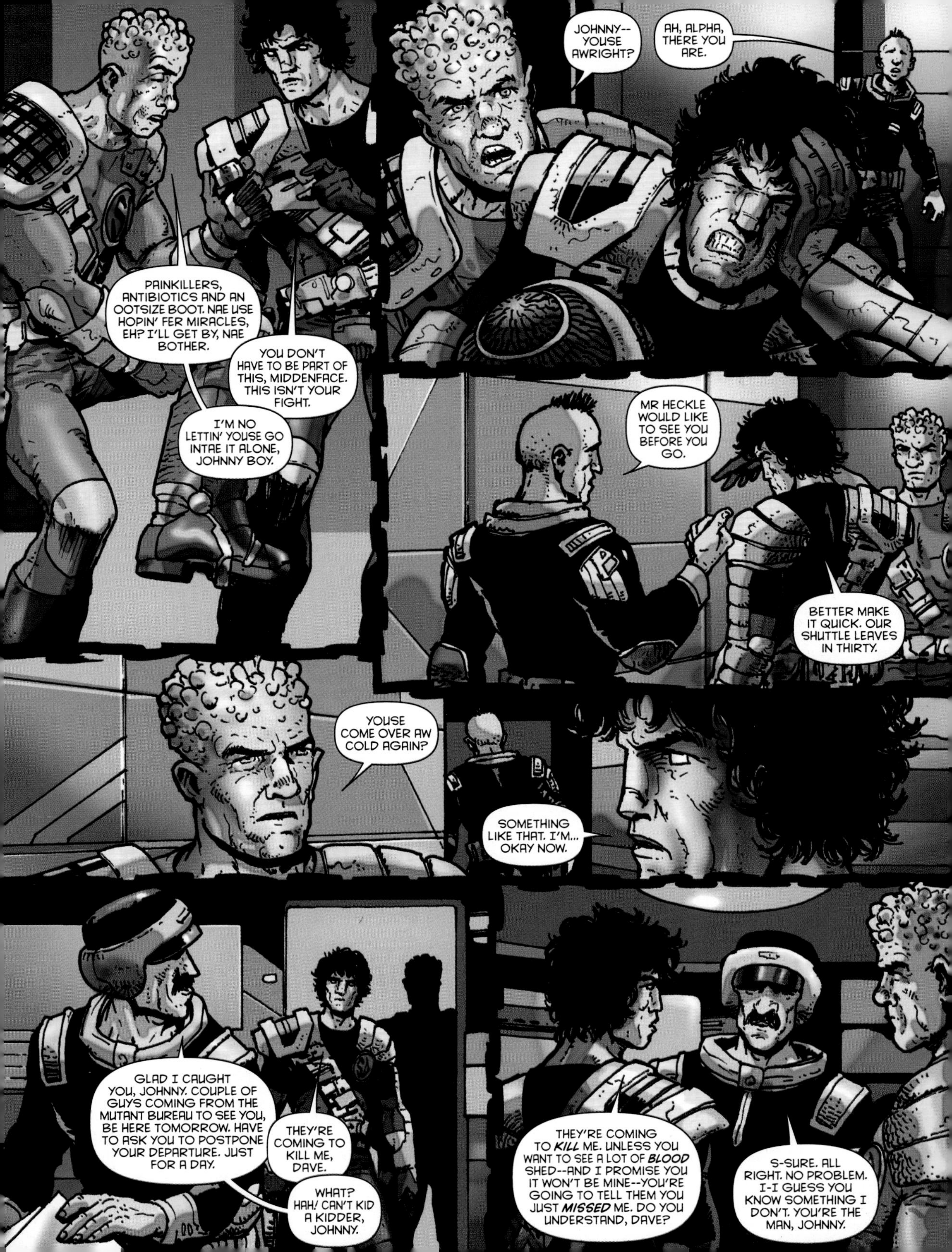
PAINKILLERS, ANTIBIOTICS AND AN OOTSIZE BOOT. NAE USE HOPIN' FER MIRACLES, EH? I'LL GET BY, NAE BOTHER.
YOU DON'T HAVE TO BE PART OF THIS, MIDDENFACE. THIS ISN'T YOUR FIGHT.
I'M NO LETTIN' YOUSE GO INTAE IT ALONE, JOHNNY BOY.
JOHNNY-- YOUSE AWRIGHT?
AH, ALPHA, THERE YOU ARE.
MR HECKLE WOULD LIKE TO SEE YOU BEFORE YOU GO.
BETTER MAKE IT QUICK. OUR SHUTTLE LEAVES IN THIRTY.
YOUSE COME OVER AW COLD AGAIN?
SOMETHING LIKE THAT. I'M... OKAY NOW.
GLAD I CAUGHT YOU, JOHNNY. COUPLE OF GUYS COMING FROM THE MUTANT BUREAU TO SEE YOU, BE HERE TOMORROW. HAVE TO ASK YOU TO POSTPONE YOUR DEPARTURE. JUST FOR A DAY.
THEY'RE COMING TO KILL ME, DAVE.
WHAT? HAH! CAN'T KID A KIDDER, JOHNNY.
THEY'RE COMING TO KILL ME. UNLESS YOU WANT TO SEE A LOT OF BLOOD SHED--AND I PROMISE YOU IT WON'T BE MINE--YOU'RE GOING TO TELL THEM YOU JUST MISSED ME. DO YOU UNDERSTAND, DAVE?
S-SURE. ALL RIGHT. NO PROBLEM. I-I GUESS YOU KNOW SOMETHING I DON'T. YOU'RE THE MAN, JOHNNY.

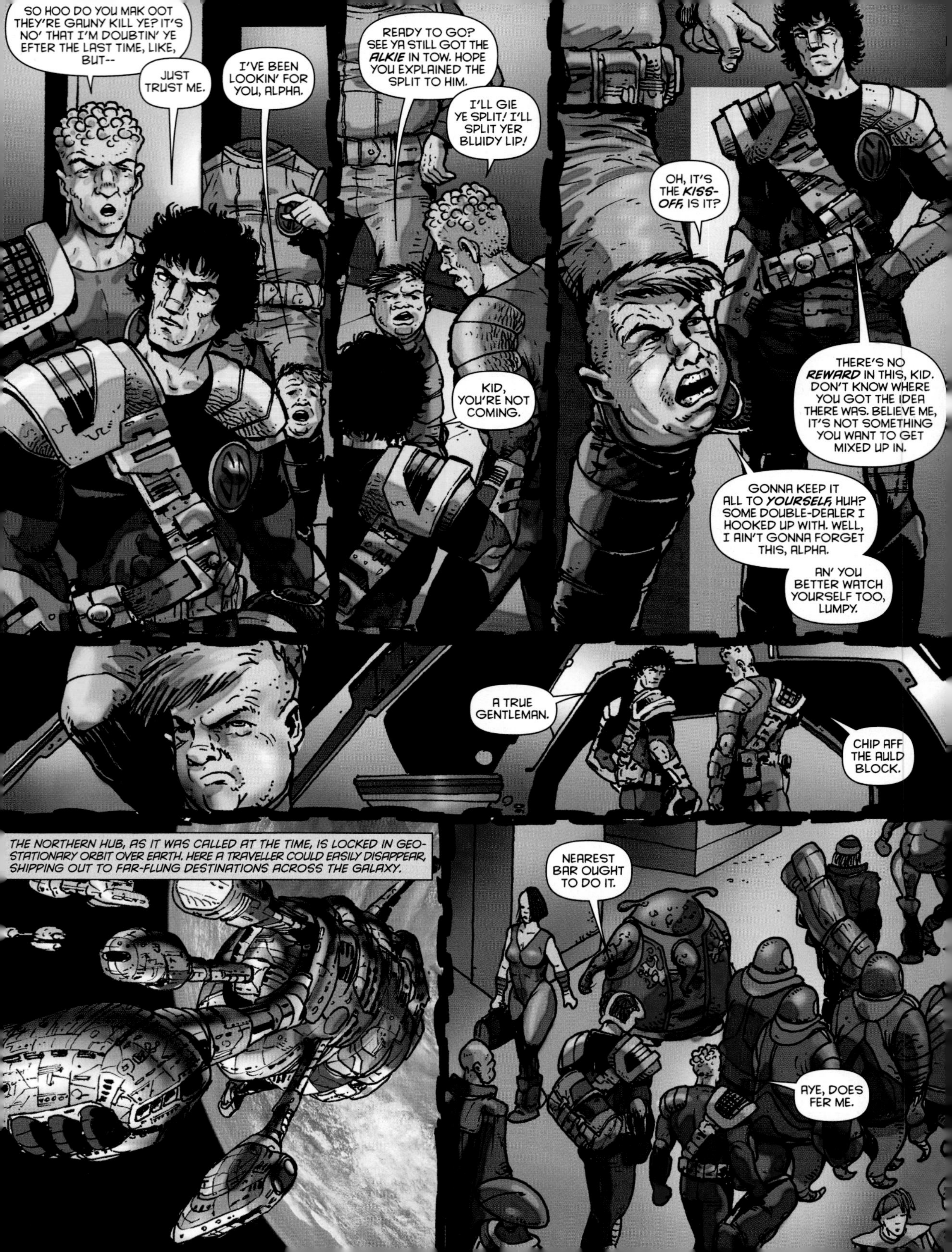
SO HOO DO YOU MAK OOT THEY'RE GAUNY KILL YE? IT'S NO' THAT I'M DOUBTIN' YE EFTER THE LAST TIME, LIKE, BUT--
JUST TRUST ME.
I'VE BEEN LOOKIN' FOR YOU, ALPHA.
READY TO GO? SEE YA STILL GOT THE ALKIE IN TOW. HOPE YOU EXPLAINED THE SPLIT TO HIM.
I'LL GIE YE SPLIT! I'LL SPLIT YER BLUIDY LIP!
KID, YOU'RE NOT COMING.
OH, IT'S THE KISS-OFF, IS IT?
THERE'S NO REWARD IN THIS, KID. DON'T KNOW WHERE YOU GOT THE IDEA THERE WAS. BELIEVE ME, IT'S NOT SOMETHING YOU WANT TO GET MIXED UP IN.
GONNA KEEP IT ALL TO YOURSELF, HUH? SOME DOUBLE-DEALER I HOOKED UP WITH. WELL, I AIN'T GONNA FORGET THIS, ALPHA.
AN' YOU BETTER WATCH YOURSELF TOO, LUMPY.
A TRUE GENTLEMAN.
CHIP AFF THE AULD BLOCK.
THE NORTHERN HUB, AS IT WAS CALLED AT THE TIME, IS LOCKED IN GEO-STATIONARY ORBIT OVER EARTH. HERE A TRAVELLER COULD EASILY DISAPPEAR, SHIPPING OUT TO FAR-FLUNG DESTINATIONS ACROSS THE GALAXY.
NEAREST BAR OUGHT TO DO IT.
AYE, DOES FER ME.

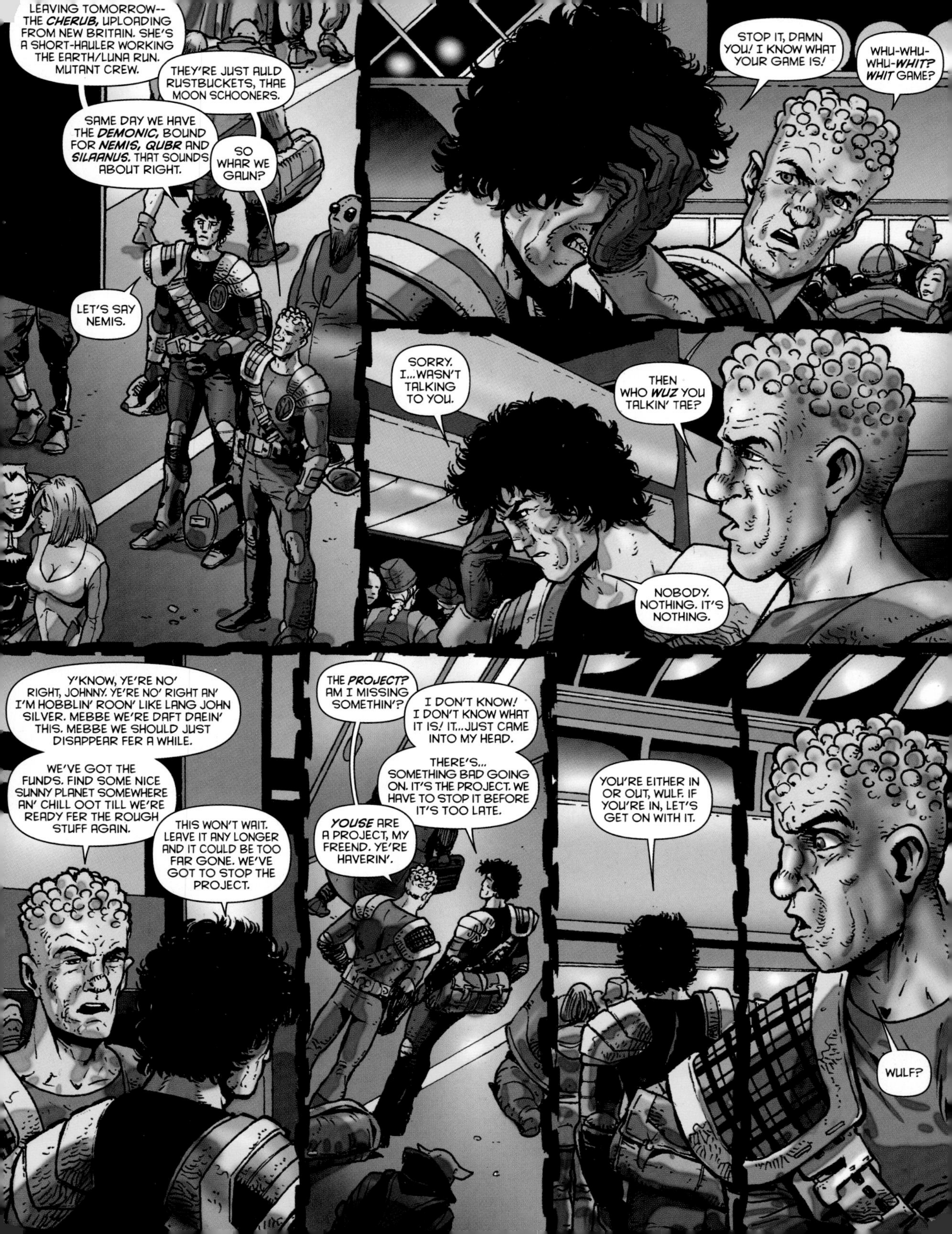
LEAVING TOMORROW-- THE *CHERUB,* UPLOADING FROM NEW BRITAIN. SHE'S A SHORT-HAULER WORKING THE EARTH/LUNA RUN. MUTANT CREW.
THEY'RE JUST AULD RUSTBUCKETS, THAE MOON SCHOONERS.
SAME DAY WE HAVE THE *DEMONIC,* BOUND FOR *NEMIS, QUBR* AND *SILAANUS.* THAT SOUNDS ABOUT RIGHT.
SO WHAR WE GAUN?
LET'S SAY NEMIS.
STOP IT, DAMN YOU! I KNOW WHAT YOUR GAME IS!
WHU-WHU-WHU-*WHIT? WHIT* GAME?
SORRY. I...WASN'T TALKING TO YOU.
THEN WHO *WUZ* YOU TALKIN' TAE?
NOBODY. NOTHING. IT'S NOTHING.
Y'KNOW, YE'RE NO' RIGHT, JOHNNY. YE'RE NO' RIGHT AN' I'M HOBBLIN' ROON' LIKE LANG JOHN SILVER. MEBBE WE'RE DAFT DAEIN' THIS. MEBBE WE SHOULD JUST DISAPPEAR FER A WHILE.
WE'VE GOT THE FUNDS. FIND SOME NICE SUNNY PLANET SOMEWHERE AN' CHILL OOT TILL WE'RE READY FER THE ROUGH STUFF AGAIN.
THIS WON'T WAIT. LEAVE IT ANY LONGER AND IT COULD BE TOO FAR GONE. WE'VE GOT TO STOP THE PROJECT.
THE *PROJECT?* AM I MISSING SOMETHIN'?
I DON'T KNOW! I DON'T KNOW WHAT IT IS! IT...JUST CAME INTO MY HEAD.
THERE'S... SOMETHING BAD GOING ON. IT'S THE PROJECT. WE HAVE TO STOP IT BEFORE IT'S TOO LATE.
YOUSE ARE A PROJECT, MY FREEND. YE'RE HAVERIN'.
YOU'RE EITHER IN OR OUT, WULF. IF YOU'RE IN, LET'S GET ON WITH IT.
WULF?

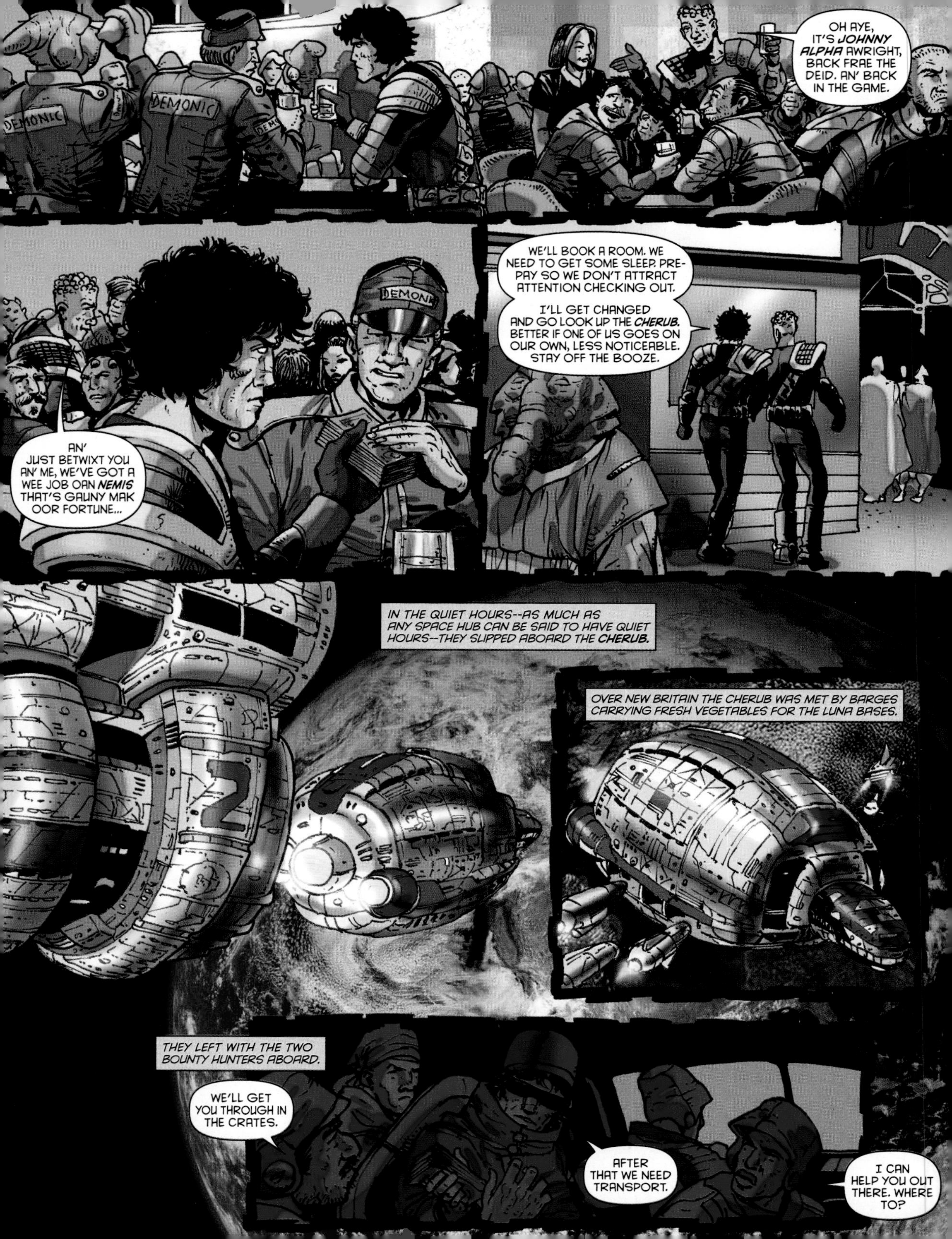
DEMONIC
OH AYE, IT'S JOHNNY ALPHA AWRIGHT, BACK FRAE THE DEID. AN' BACK IN THE GAME.
AN' JUST BETWIXT YOU AN' ME, WE'VE GOT A WEE JOB OAN NEMIS THAT'S GAUNY MAK OOR FORTUNE...
WE'LL BOOK A ROOM. WE NEED TO GET SOME SLEEP. PRE-PAY SO WE DON'T ATTRACT ATTENTION CHECKING OUT.
I'LL GET CHANGED AND GO LOOK UP THE CHERUB. BETTER IF ONE OF US GOES ON OUR OWN, LESS NOTICEABLE. STAY OFF THE BOOZE.
IN THE QUIET HOURS--AS MUCH AS ANY SPACE HUB CAN BE SAID TO HAVE QUIET HOURS--THEY SLIPPED ABOARD THE CHERUB.
OVER NEW BRITAIN THE CHERUB WAS MET BY BARGES CARRYING FRESH VEGETABLES FOR THE LUNA BASES.
THEY LEFT WITH THE TWO BOUNTY HUNTERS ABOARD.
WE'LL GET YOU THROUGH IN THE CRATES.
AFTER THAT WE NEED TRANSPORT.
I CAN HELP YOU OUT THERE. WHERE TO?

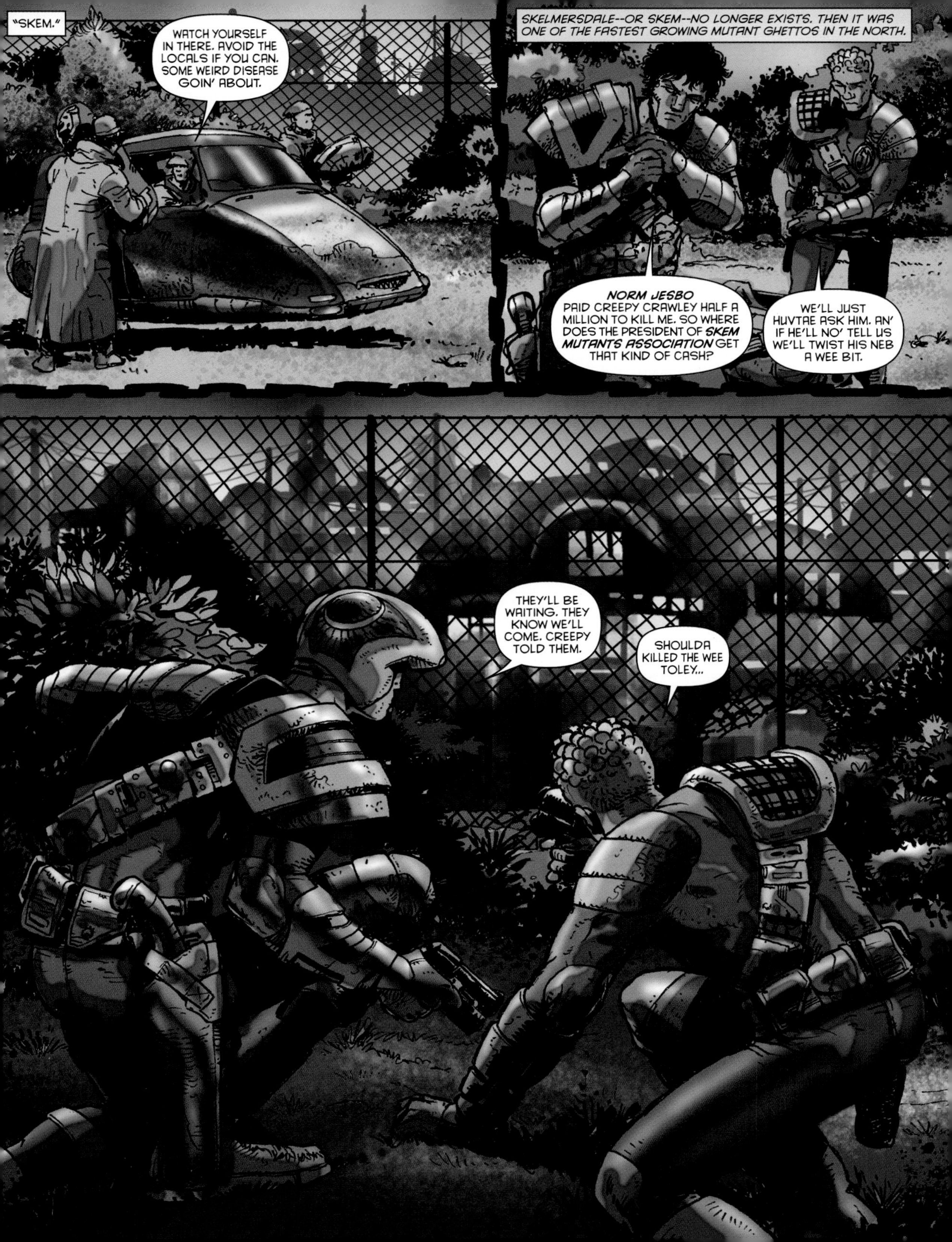
"SKEM."
WATCH YOURSELF IN THERE. AVOID THE LOCALS IF YOU CAN. SOME WEIRD DISEASE GOIN' ABOUT.
SKELMERSDALE--OR SKEM--NO LONGER EXISTS. THEN IT WAS ONE OF THE FASTEST GROWING MUTANT GHETTOS IN THE NORTH.
NORM JESBO PAID CREEPY CRAWLEY HALF A MILLION TO KILL ME. SO WHERE DOES THE PRESIDENT OF SKEM MUTANTS ASSOCIATION GET THAT KIND OF CASH?
WE'LL JUST HUVTAE ASK HIM. AN' IF HE'LL NO' TELL US WE'LL TWIST HIS NEB A WEE BIT.
THEY'LL BE WAITING. THEY KNOW WE'LL COME. CREEPY TOLD THEM.
SHOULDA KILLED THE WEE TOLEY...

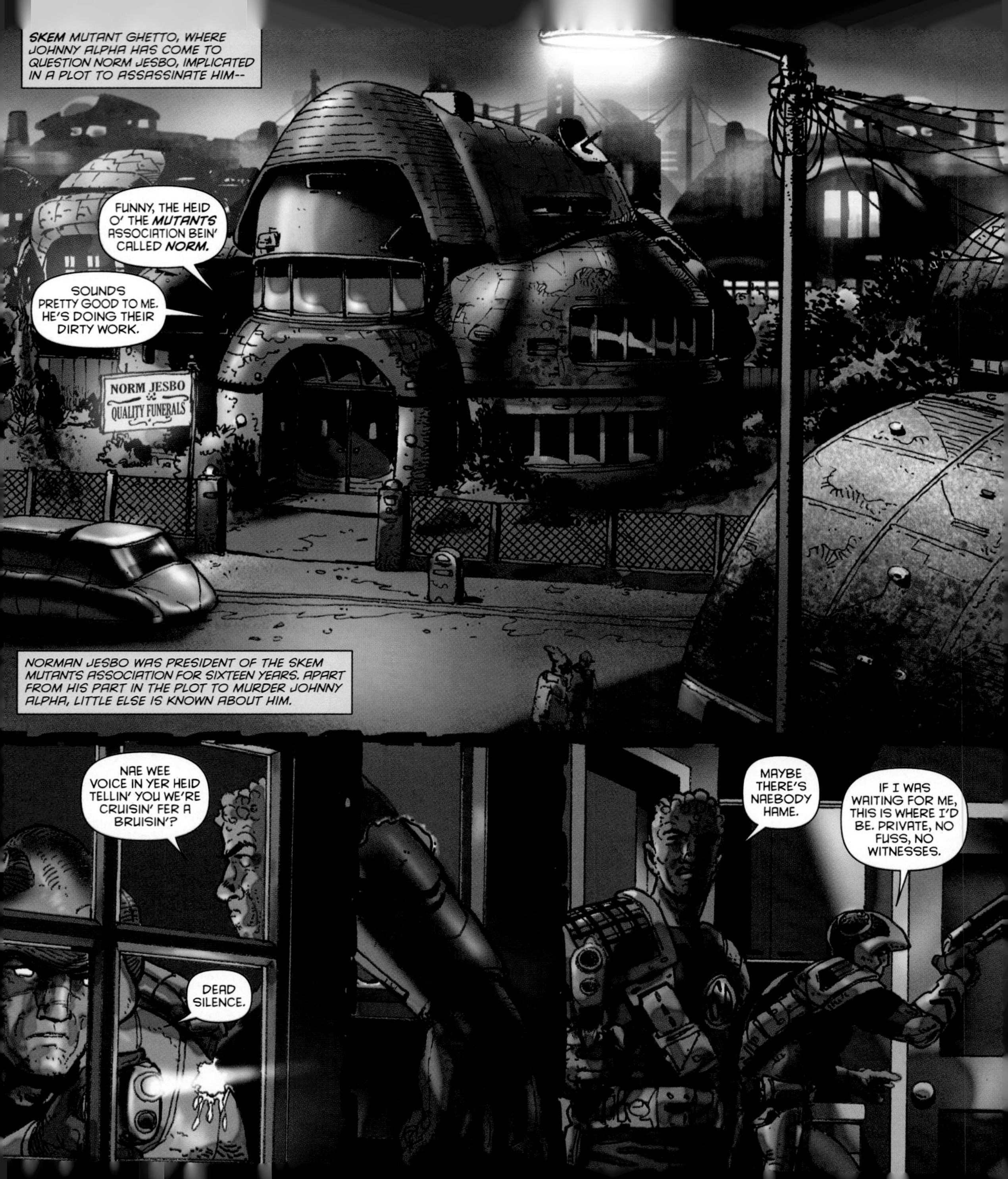
SKEM MUTANT GHETTO, WHERE JOHNNY ALPHA HAS COME TO QUESTION NORM JESBO, IMPLICATED IN A PLOT TO ASSASSINATE HIM--
FUNNY, THE HEID O' THE MUTANTS ASSOCIATION BEIN' CALLED NORM.
SOUNDS PRETTY GOOD TO ME. HE'S DOING THEIR DIRTY WORK.
NORM JESBO
QUALITY FUNERALS
NORMAN JESBO WAS PRESIDENT OF THE SKEM MUTANTS ASSOCIATION FOR SIXTEEN YEARS. APART FROM HIS PART IN THE PLOT TO MURDER JOHNNY ALPHA, LITTLE ELSE IS KNOWN ABOUT HIM.
NAE WEE VOICE IN YER HEID TELLIN' YOU WE'RE CRUISIN' FER A BRUISIN'?
DEAD SILENCE.
MAYBE THERE'S NAEBODY HAME.
IF I WAS WAITING FOR ME, THIS IS WHERE I'D BE. PRIVATE, NO FUSS, NO WITNESSES.

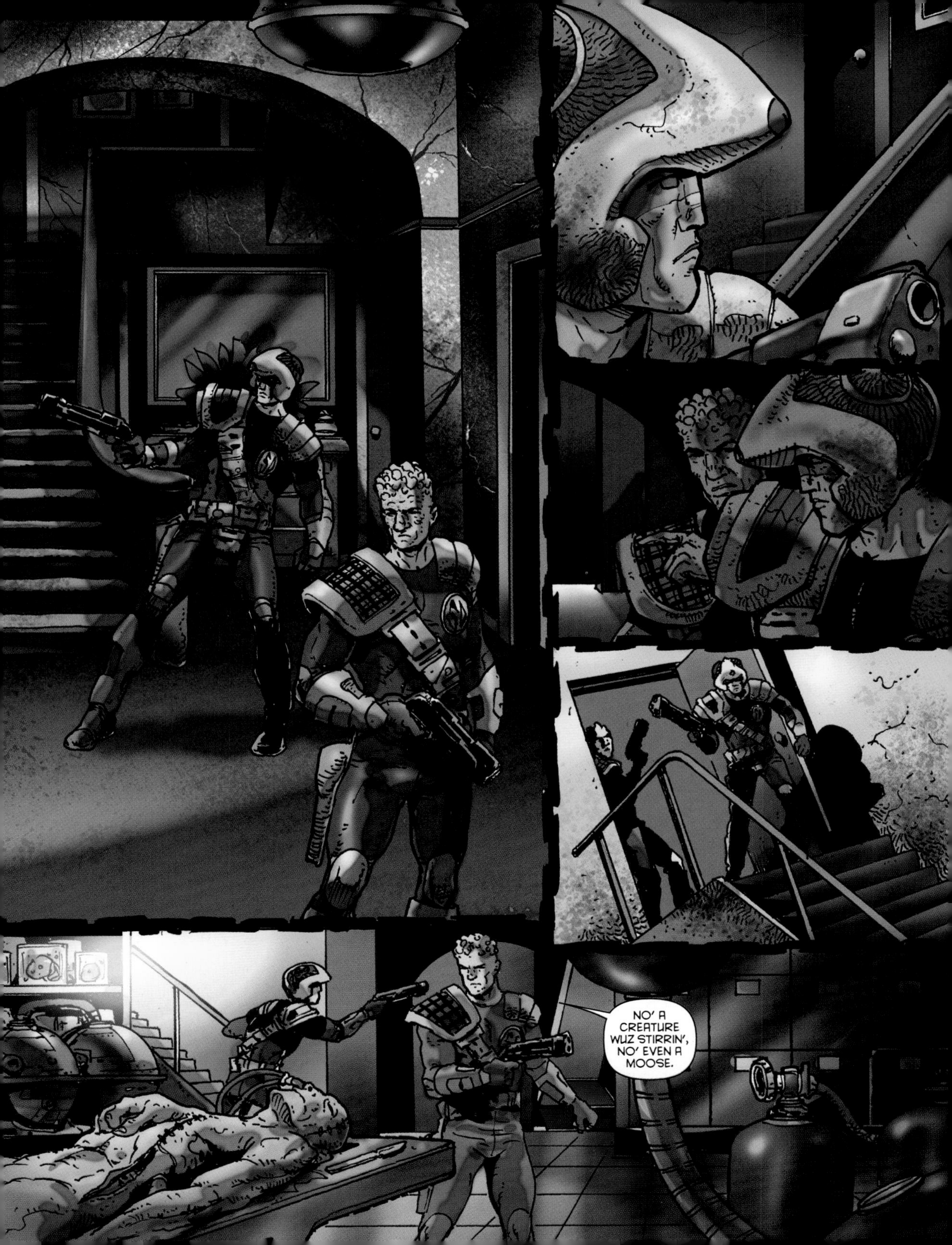
NO' A CREATURE WUZ STIRRIN', NO' EVEN A MOOSE.

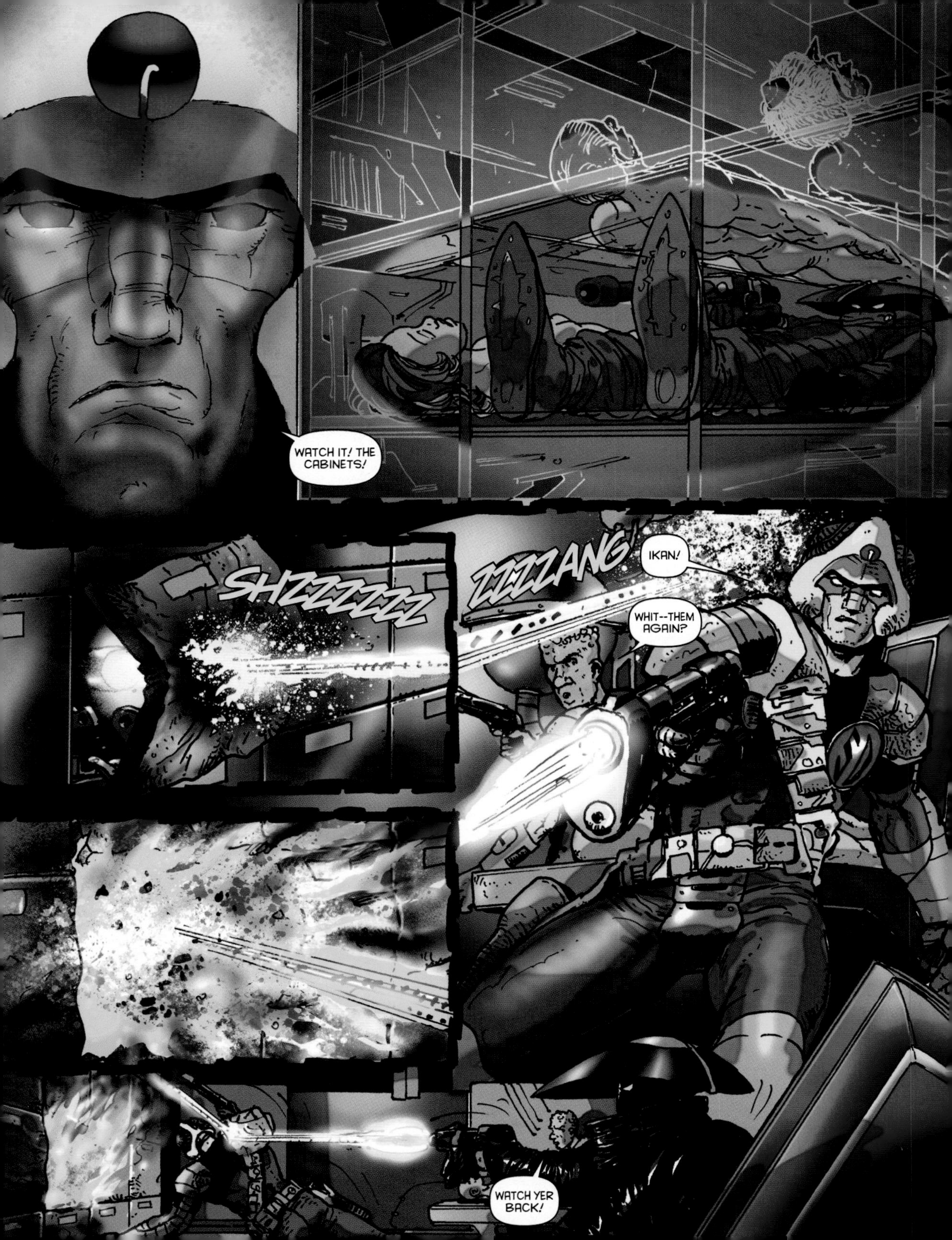
WATCH IT! THE CABINETS!
SHZZZZZZZ
ZZZZANG
IKAN!
WHIT--THEM AGAIN?
WATCH YER BACK!

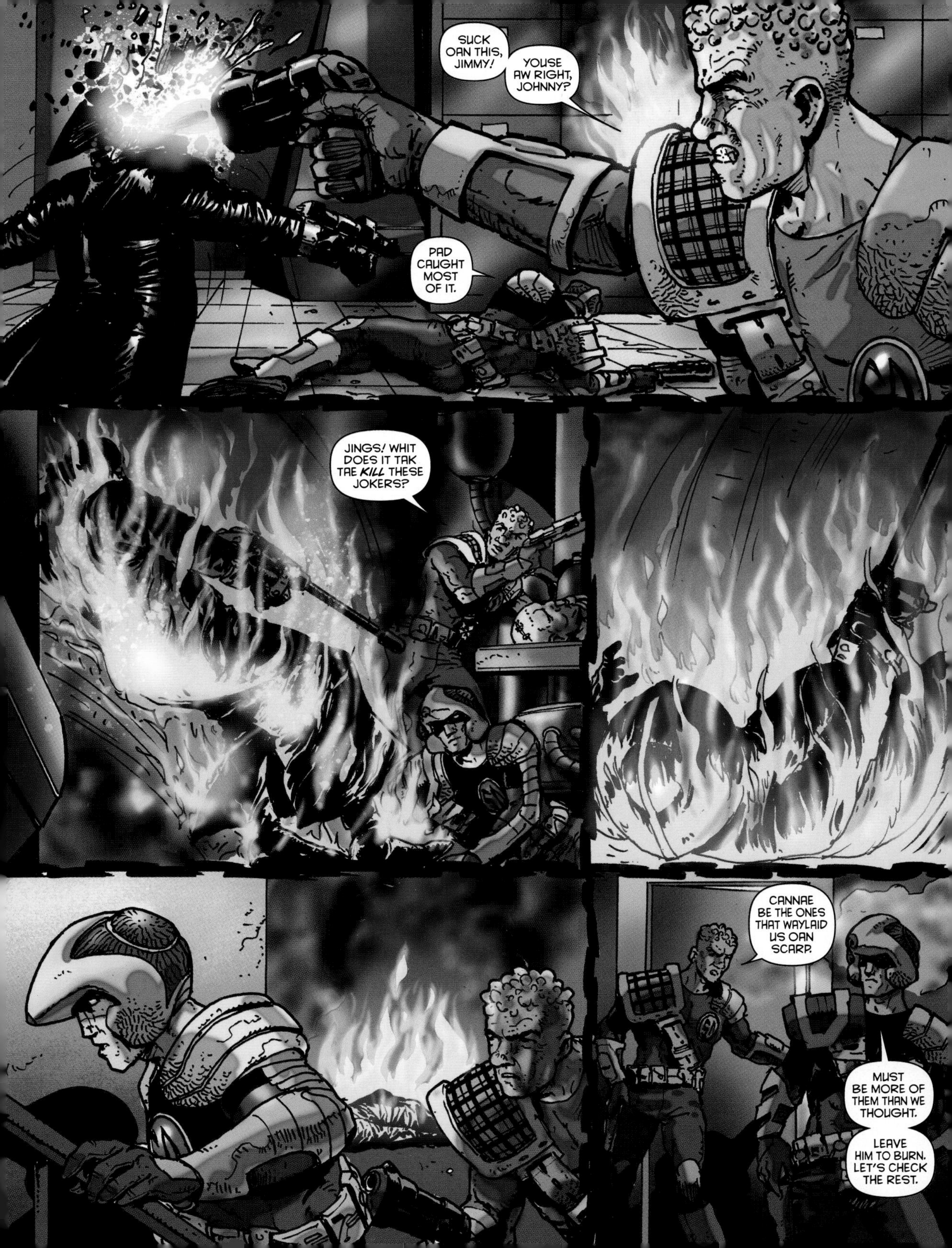
SUCK OAN THIS, JIMMY!
YOUSE AW RIGHT, JOHNNY?
PAD CAUGHT MOST OF IT.
JINGS! WHIT DOES IT TAK TAE *KILL* THESE JOKERS?
CANNAE BE THE ONES THAT WAYLAID US OAN SCARP.
MUST BE MORE OF THEM THAN WE THOUGHT.
LEAVE HIM TO BURN. LET'S CHECK THE REST.

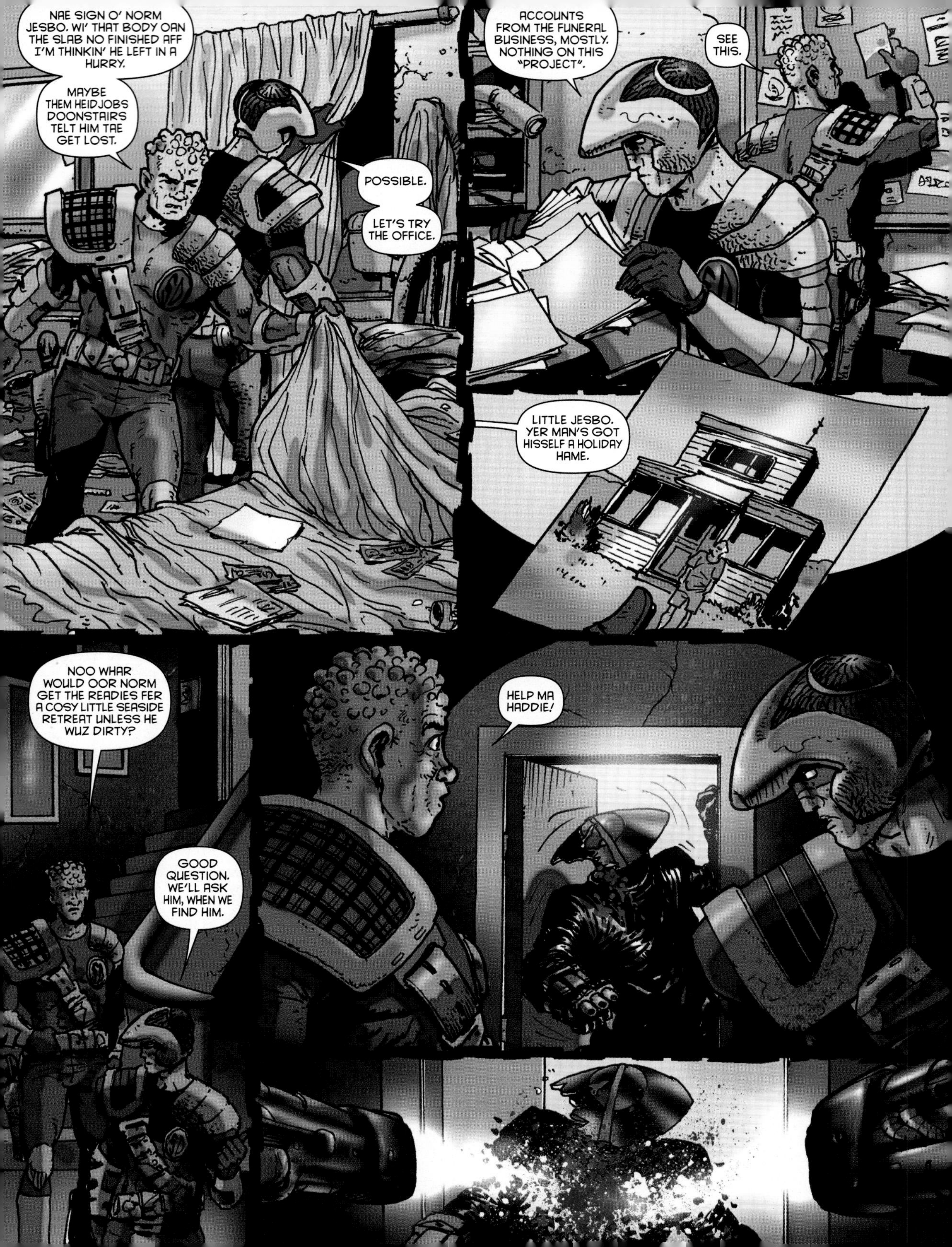
NAE SIGN O' NORM JESBO. WI' THAT BODY OAN THE SLAB NO FINISHED AFF I'M THINKIN' HE LEFT IN A HURRY.
MAYBE THEM HEIDJOBS DOONSTAIRS TELT HIM TAE GET LOST.
POSSIBLE.
LET'S TRY THE OFFICE.
ACCOUNTS FROM THE FUNERAL BUSINESS, MOSTLY. NOTHING ON THIS "PROJECT".
SEE THIS.
LITTLE JESBO. YER MAN'S GOT HISSELF A HOLIDAY HAME.
NOO WHAR WOULD OOR NORM GET THE READIES FER A COSY LITTLE SEASIDE RETREAT UNLESS HE WUZ DIRTY?
GOOD QUESTION. WE'LL ASK HIM, WHEN WE FIND HIM.
HELP MA HADDIE!

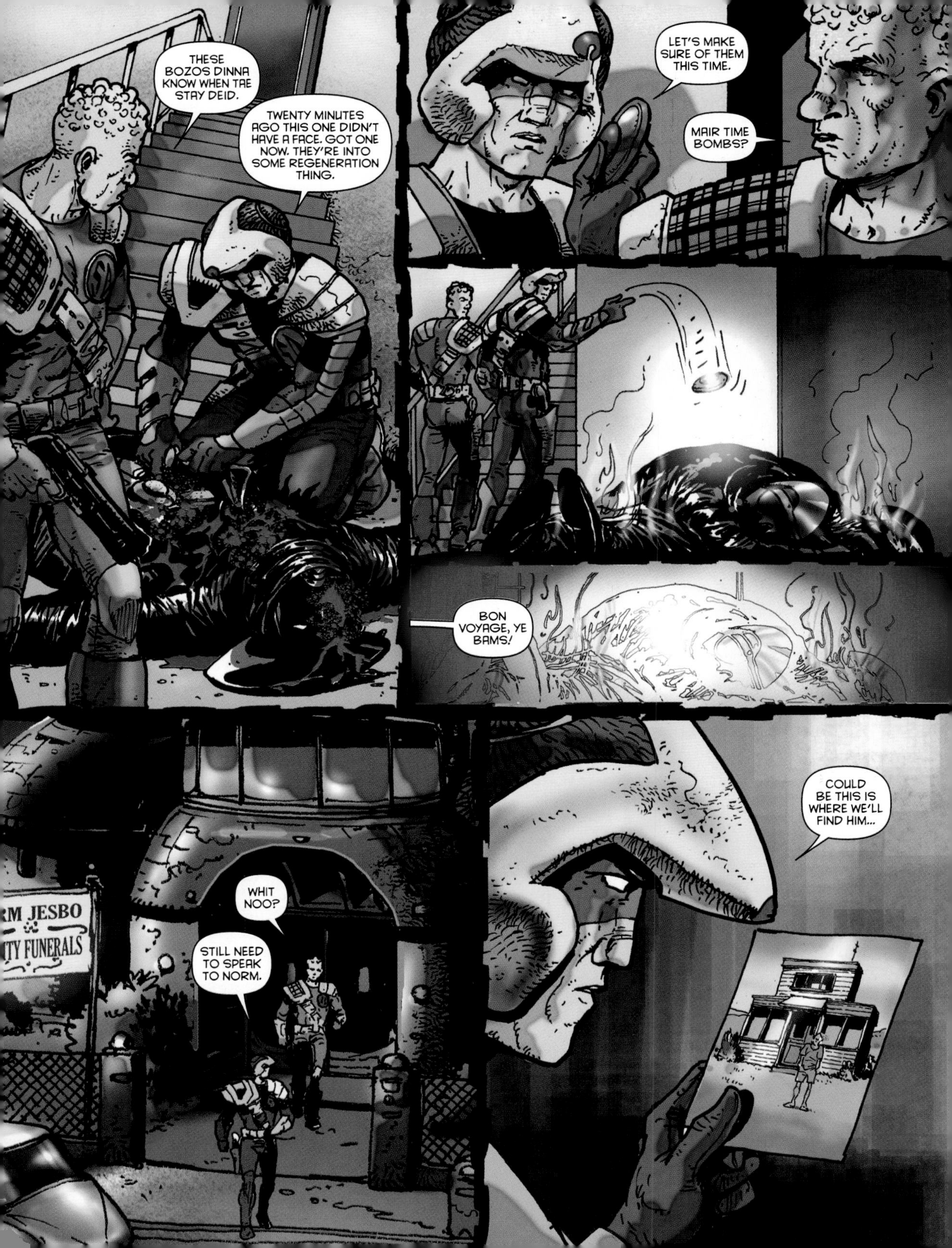
THESE BOZOS DINNA KNOW WHEN TAE STAY DEID.
TWENTY MINUTES AGO THIS ONE DIDN'T HAVE A FACE. GOT ONE NOW. THEY'RE INTO SOME REGENERATION THING.
LET'S MAKE SURE OF THEM THIS TIME.
MAIR TIME BOMBS?
BON VOYAGE, YE BAMS!
RM JESBO
ITY FUNERALS
WHIT NOO?
STILL NEED TO SPEAK TO NORM.
COULD BE THIS IS WHERE WE'LL FIND HIM...

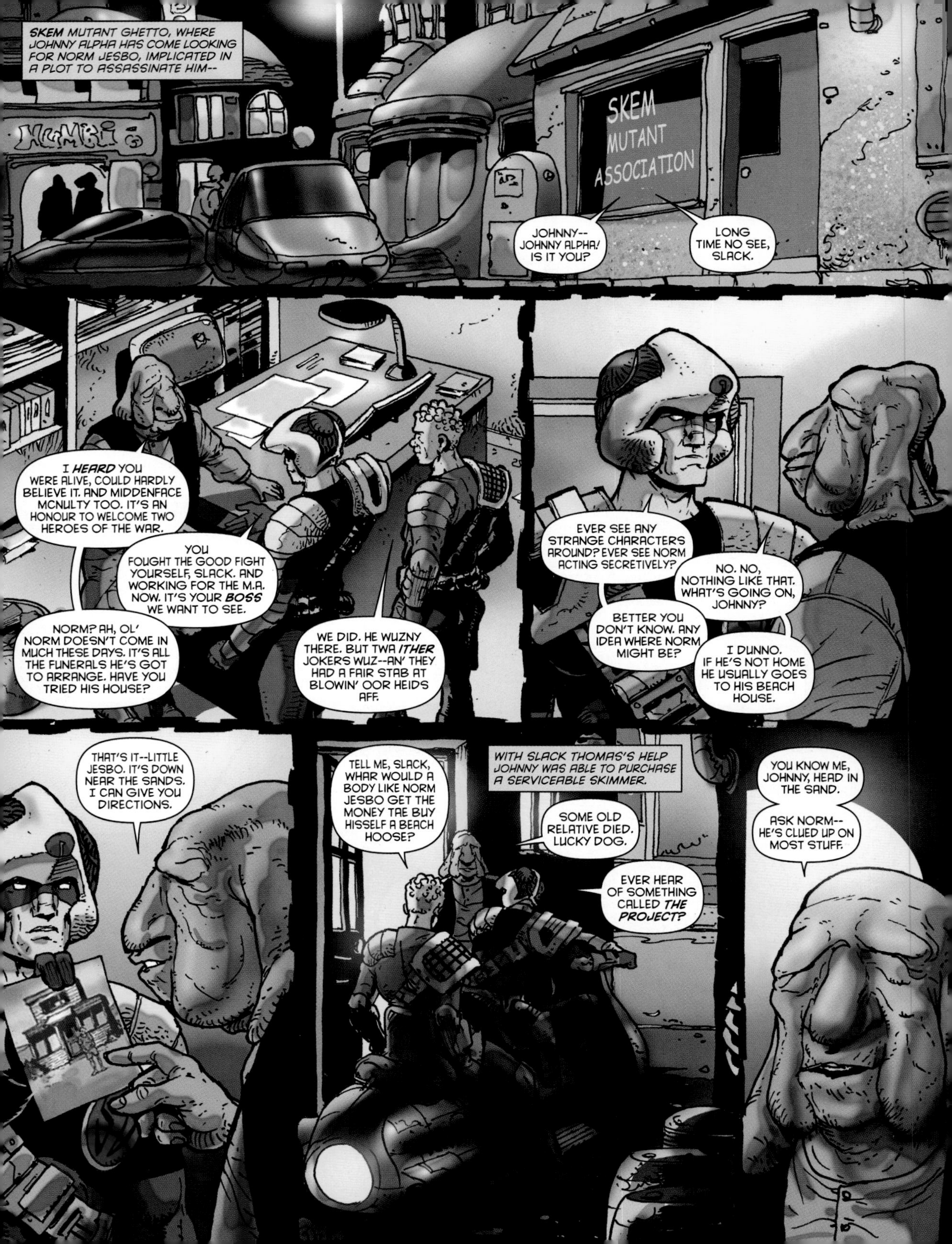
SKEM MUTANT GHETTO, WHERE JOHNNY ALPHA HAS COME LOOKING FOR NORM JESBO, IMPLICATED IN A PLOT TO ASSASSINATE HIM--
SKEM MUTANT ASSOCIATION
JOHNNY-- JOHNNY ALPHA! IS IT YOU?
LONG TIME NO SEE, SLACK.
I HEARD YOU WERE ALIVE, COULD HARDLY BELIEVE IT. AND MIDDENFACE MCNULTY TOO. IT'S AN HONOUR TO WELCOME TWO HEROES OF THE WAR.
YOU FOUGHT THE GOOD FIGHT YOURSELF, SLACK. AND WORKING FOR THE M.A. NOW. IT'S YOUR BOSS WE WANT TO SEE.
NORM? AH, OL' NORM DOESN'T COME IN MUCH THESE DAYS. IT'S ALL THE FUNERALS HE'S GOT TO ARRANGE. HAVE YOU TRIED HIS HOUSE?
WE DID. HE WUZNY THERE. BUT TWA ITHER JOKERS WUZ--AN' THEY HAD A FAIR STAB AT BLOWIN' OOR HEIDS AFF.
EVER SEE ANY STRANGE CHARACTERS AROUND? EVER SEE NORM ACTING SECRETIVELY?
NO. NO, NOTHING LIKE THAT. WHAT'S GOING ON, JOHNNY?
BETTER YOU DON'T KNOW. ANY IDEA WHERE NORM MIGHT BE?
I DUNNO. IF HE'S NOT HOME HE USUALLY GOES TO HIS BEACH HOUSE.
THAT'S IT--LITTLE JESBO. IT'S DOWN NEAR THE SANDS. I CAN GIVE YOU DIRECTIONS.
TELL ME, SLACK, WHAR WOULD A BODY LIKE NORM JESBO GET THE MONEY TAE BUY HISSELF A BEACH HOOSE?
WITH SLACK THOMAS'S HELP JOHNNY WAS ABLE TO PURCHASE A SERVICEABLE SKIMMER.
SOME OLD RELATIVE DIED. LUCKY DOG.
EVER HEAR OF SOMETHING CALLED THE PROJECT?
YOU KNOW ME, JOHNNY, HEAD IN THE SAND.
ASK NORM-- HE'S CLUED UP ON MOST STUFF.

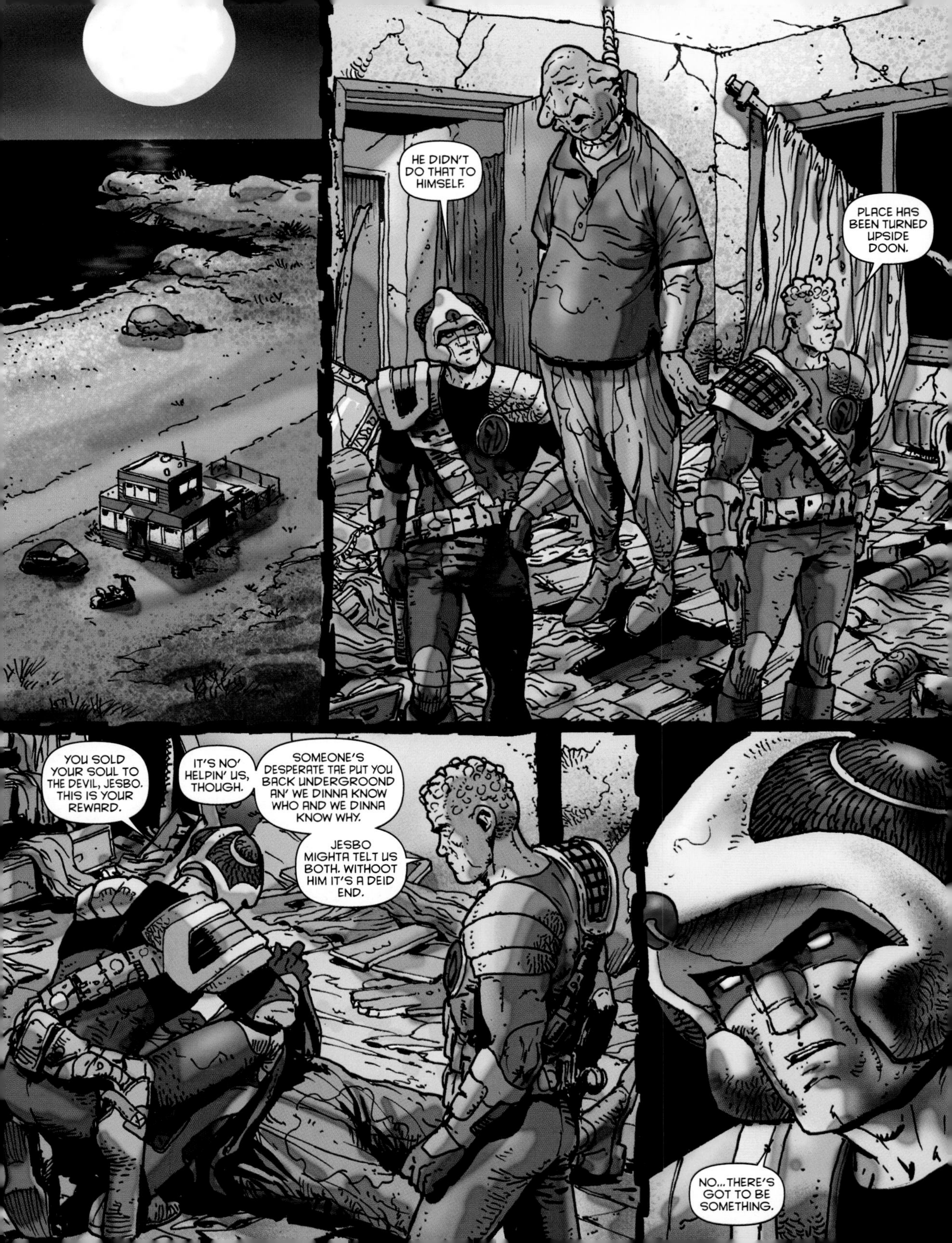
HE DIDN'T DO THAT TO HIMSELF.
PLACE HAS BEEN TURNED UPSIDE DOON.
YOU SOLD YOUR SOUL TO THE DEVIL, JESBO. THIS IS YOUR REWARD.
IT'S NO' HELPIN' US, THOUGH.
SOMEONE'S DESPERATE TAE PUT YOU BACK UNDERGROOND AN' WE DINNA KNOW WHO AND WE DINNA KNOW WHY.
JESBO MIGHTA TELT US BOTH. WITHOOT HIM IT'S A DEID END.
NO... THERE'S GOT TO BE SOMETHING.

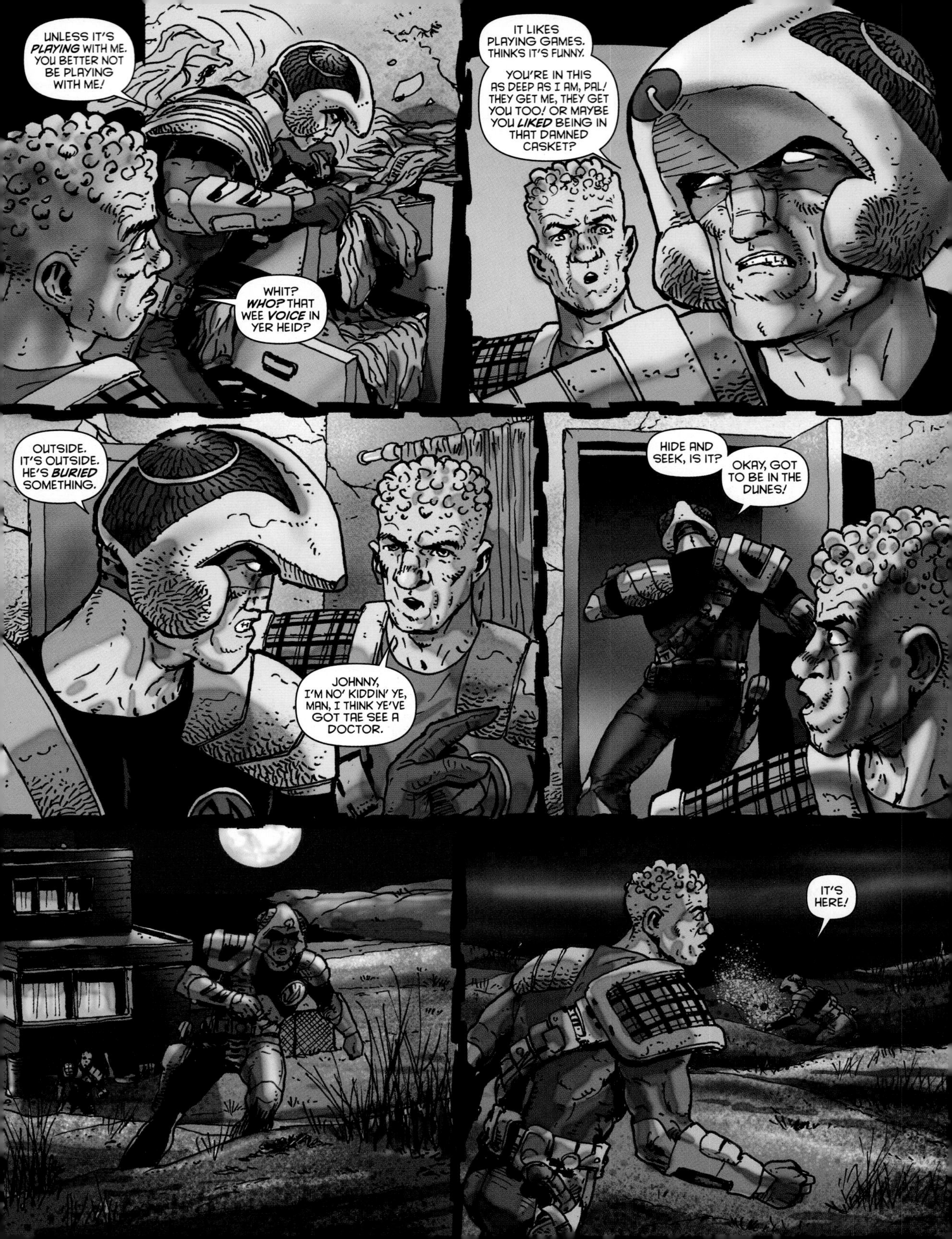

UNLESS IT'S *PLAYING* WITH ME. YOU BETTER NOT BE PLAYING WITH ME!
WHIT? *WHO?* THAT WEE *VOICE* IN YER HEID?
IT LIKES PLAYING GAMES. THINKS IT'S FUNNY.
YOU'RE IN THIS AS DEEP AS I AM, PAL! THEY GET ME, THEY GET YOU TOO! OR MAYBE YOU *LIKED* BEING IN THAT DAMNED CASKET?
OUTSIDE. IT'S OUTSIDE. HE'S *BURIED* SOMETHING.
JOHNNY, I'M NO' KIDDIN' YE, MAN, I THINK YE'VE GOT TAE SEE A DOCTOR.
HIDE AND SEEK, IS IT?
OKAY, GOT TO BE IN THE DUNES!
IT'S HERE!

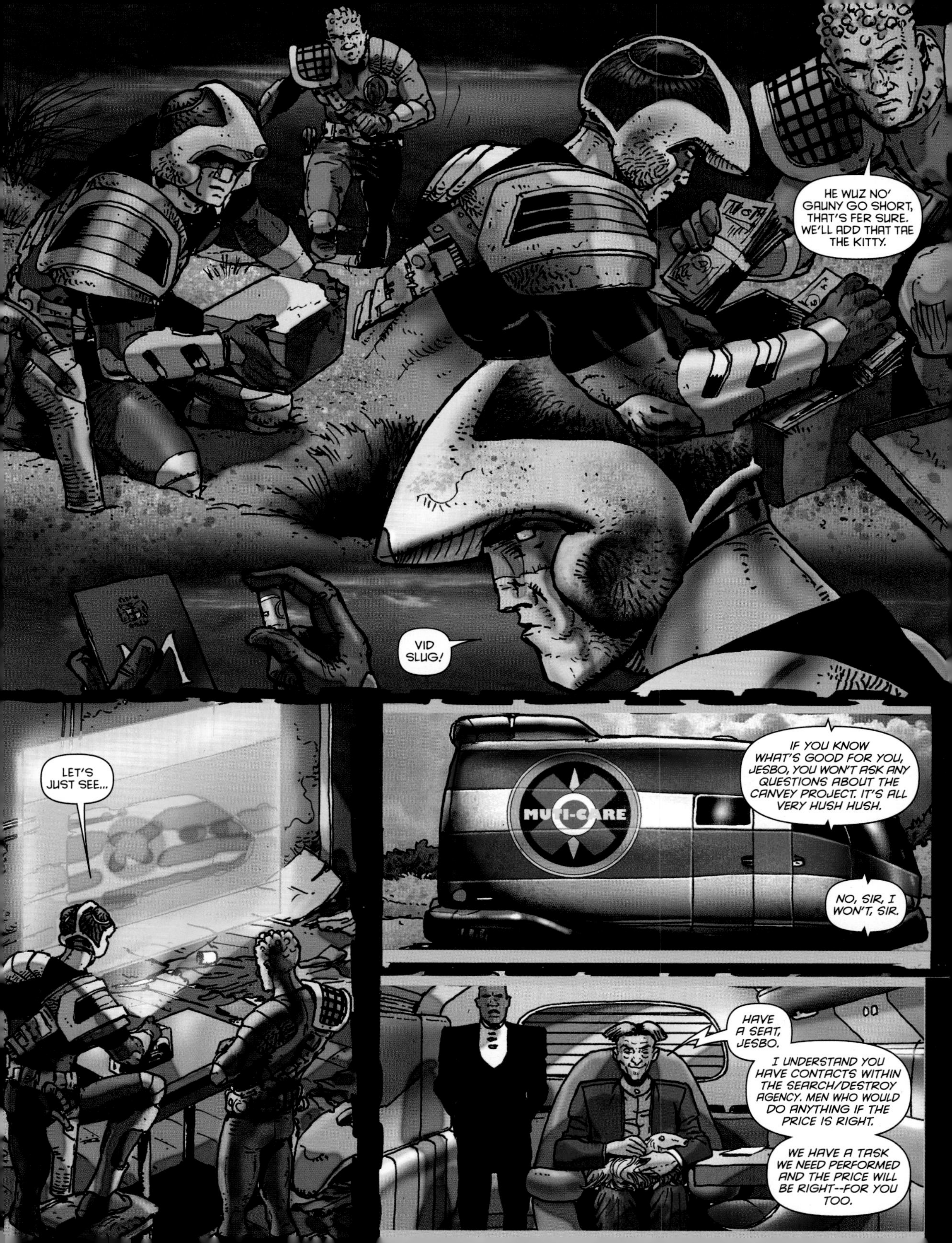
HE WUZ NO' GAUNY GO SHORT, THAT'S FER SURE. WE'LL ADD THAT TAE THE KITTY.
VID SLUG!
LET'S JUST SEE...
IF YOU KNOW WHAT'S GOOD FOR YOU, JESBO, YOU WON'T ASK ANY QUESTIONS ABOUT THE CANVEY PROJECT. IT'S ALL VERY HUSH HUSH.
NO, SIR, I WON'T, SIR.
HAVE A SEAT, JESBO.
I UNDERSTAND YOU HAVE CONTACTS WITHIN THE SEARCH/DESTROY AGENCY. MEN WHO WOULD DO ANYTHING IF THE PRICE IS RIGHT.
WE HAVE A TASK WE NEED PERFORMED AND THE PRICE WILL BE RIGHT--FOR YOU TOO.

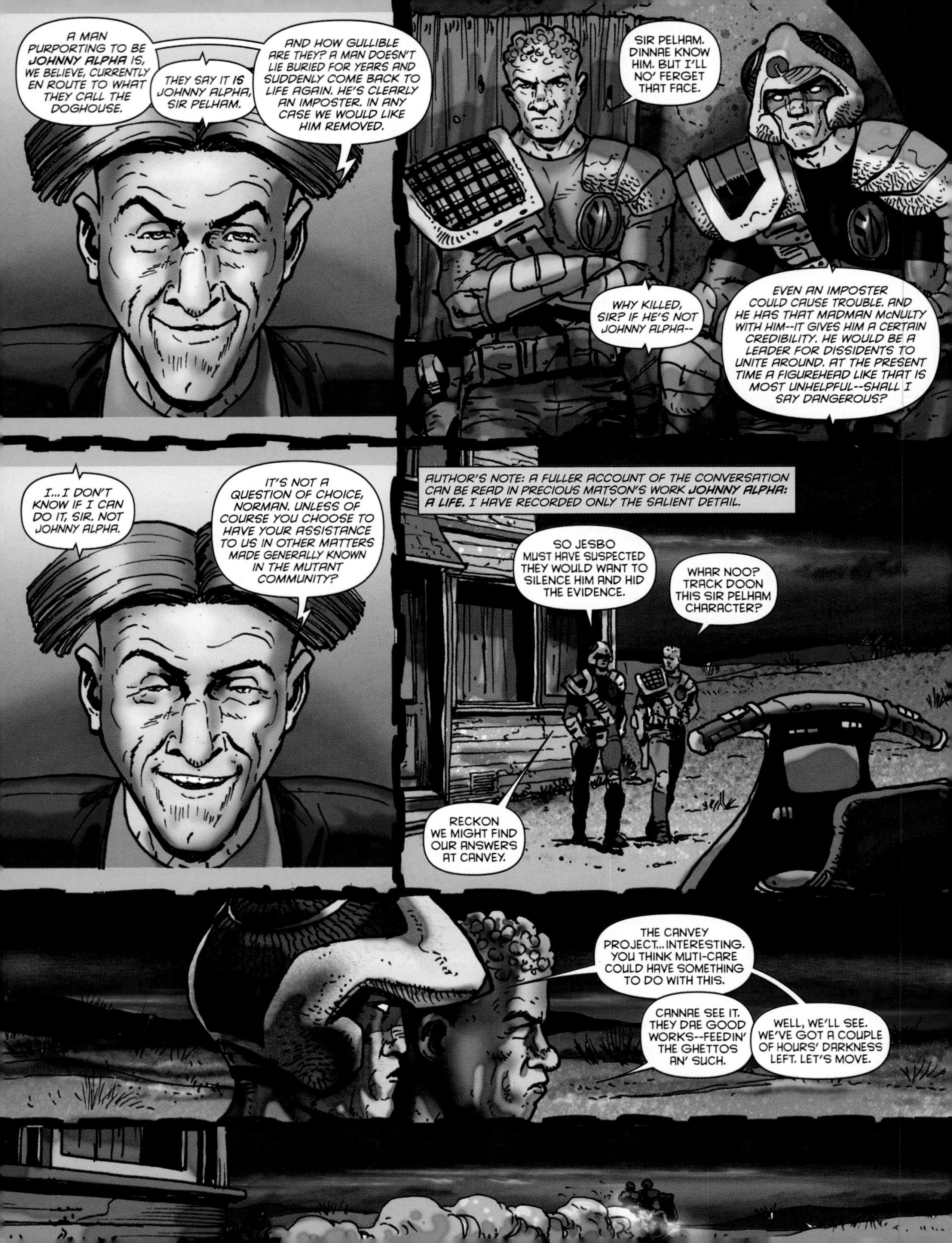
A MAN PURPORTING TO BE **JOHNNY ALPHA** IS, WE BELIEVE, CURRENTLY EN ROUTE TO WHAT THEY CALL THE DOGHOUSE.
THEY SAY IT **IS** JOHNNY ALPHA, SIR PELHAM.
AND HOW GULLIBLE ARE THEY? A MAN DOESN'T LIE BURIED FOR YEARS AND SUDDENLY COME BACK TO LIFE AGAIN. HE'S CLEARLY AN IMPOSTER. IN ANY CASE WE WOULD LIKE HIM REMOVED.
SIR PELHAM. DINNAE KNOW HIM. BUT I'LL NO' FERGET THAT FACE.
WHY KILLED, SIR? IF HE'S NOT JOHNNY ALPHA--
EVEN AN IMPOSTER COULD CAUSE TROUBLE. AND HE HAS THAT MADMAN McNULTY WITH HIM--IT GIVES HIM A CERTAIN CREDIBILITY. HE WOULD BE A LEADER FOR DISSIDENTS TO UNITE AROUND. AT THE PRESENT TIME A FIGUREHEAD LIKE THAT IS MOST UNHELPFUL--SHALL I SAY DANGEROUS?
I...I DON'T KNOW IF I CAN DO IT, SIR. NOT JOHNNY ALPHA.
IT'S NOT A QUESTION OF CHOICE, NORMAN. UNLESS OF COURSE YOU CHOOSE TO HAVE YOUR ASSISTANCE TO US IN OTHER MATTERS MADE GENERALLY KNOWN IN THE MUTANT COMMUNITY?
AUTHOR'S NOTE: A FULLER ACCOUNT OF THE CONVERSATION CAN BE READ IN PRECIOUS MATSON'S WORK **JOHNNY ALPHA: A LIFE.** I HAVE RECORDED ONLY THE SALIENT DETAIL.
SO JESBO MUST HAVE SUSPECTED THEY WOULD WANT TO SILENCE HIM AND HID THE EVIDENCE.
WHAR NOO? TRACK DOON THIS SIR PELHAM CHARACTER?
RECKON WE MIGHT FIND OUR ANSWERS AT CANVEY.
THE CANVEY PROJECT...INTERESTING. YOU THINK MUTI-CARE COULD HAVE SOMETHING TO DO WITH THIS.
CANNAE SEE IT. THEY DAE GOOD WORKS--FEEDIN' THE GHETTOS AN' SUCH.
WELL, WE'LL SEE. WE'VE GOT A COUPLE OF HOURS' DARKNESS LEFT. LET'S MOVE.

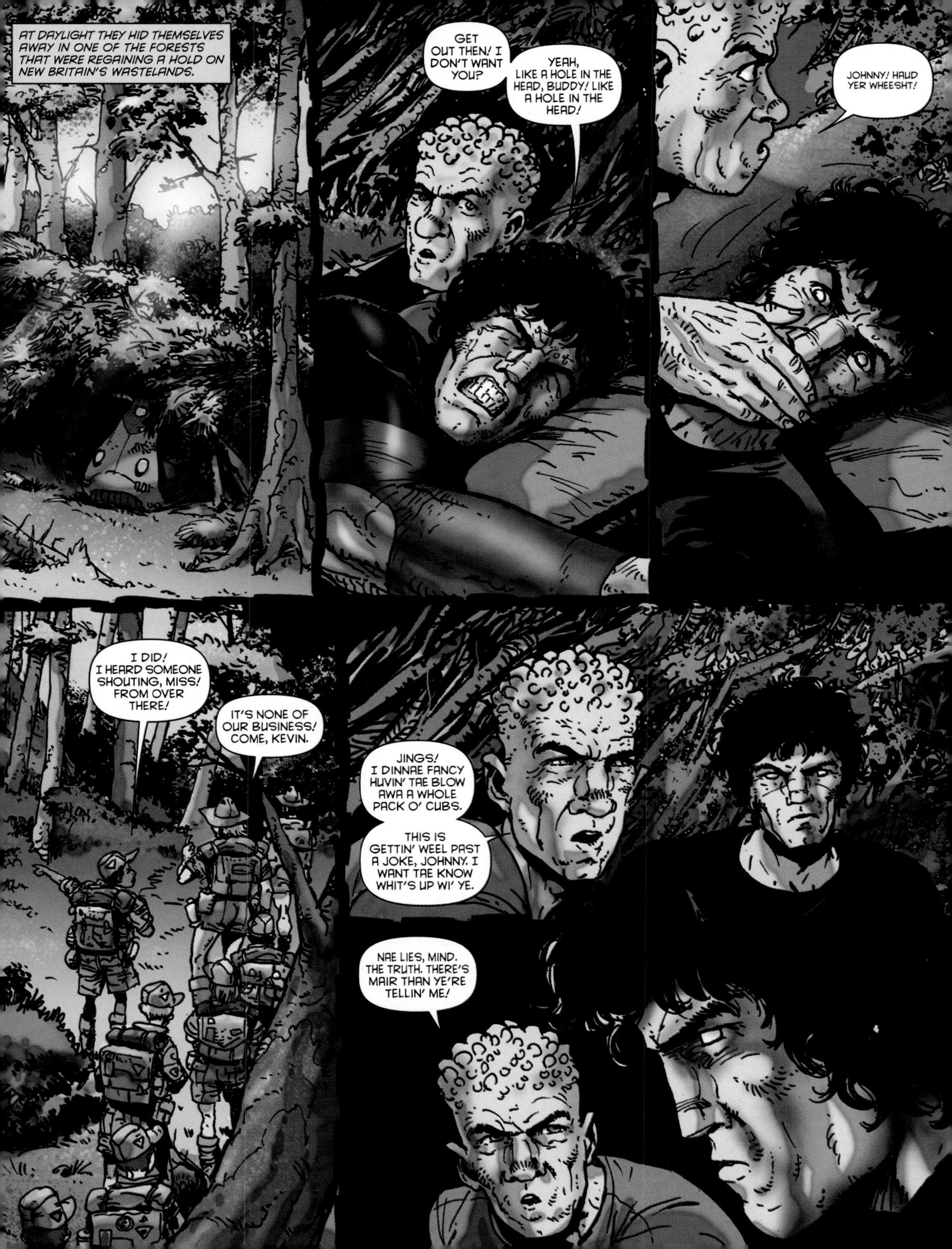

AT DAYLIGHT THEY HID THEMSELVES AWAY IN ONE OF THE FORESTS THAT WERE REGAINING A HOLD ON NEW BRITAIN'S WASTELANDS.
GET OUT THEN! I DON'T WANT YOU?
YEAH, LIKE A HOLE IN THE HEAD, BUDDY! LIKE A HOLE IN THE HEAD!
JOHNNY! HAUD YER WHEESHT!
I DID! I HEARD SOMEONE SHOUTING, MISS! FROM OVER THERE!
IT'S NONE OF OUR BUSINESS! COME, KEVIN.
JINGS! I DINNAE FANCY HUVIN' TAE BLOW AWA A WHOLE PACK O' CUBS.
THIS IS GETTIN' WEEL PAST A JOKE, JOHNNY. I WANT TAE KNOW WHIT'S UP WI' YE.
NAE LIES, MIND. THE TRUTH. THERE'S MAIR THAN YE'RE TELLIN' ME!

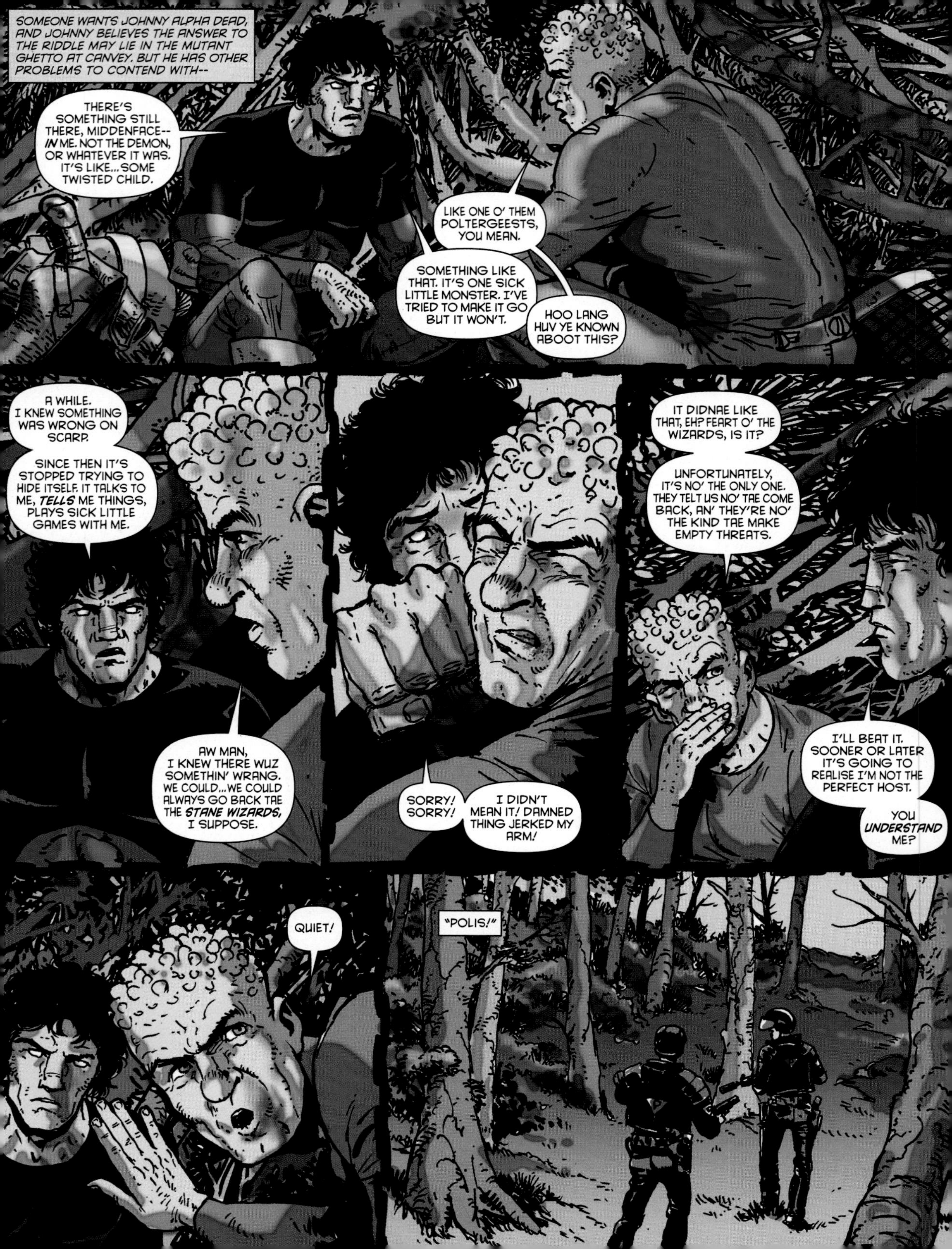
SOMEONE WANTS JOHNNY ALPHA DEAD, AND JOHNNY BELIEVES THE ANSWER TO THE RIDDLE MAY LIE IN THE MUTANT GHETTO AT CANVEY. BUT HE HAS OTHER PROBLEMS TO CONTEND WITH--
THERE'S SOMETHING STILL THERE, MIDDENFACE-- IN ME. NOT THE DEMON, OR WHATEVER IT WAS. IT'S LIKE... SOME TWISTED CHILD.
LIKE ONE O' THEM POLTERGEESTS, YOU MEAN.
SOMETHING LIKE THAT. IT'S ONE SICK LITTLE MONSTER. I'VE TRIED TO MAKE IT GO BUT IT WON'T.
HOO LANG HUV YE KNOWN ABOOT THIS?
A WHILE. I KNEW SOMETHING WAS WRONG ON SCARP.
SINCE THEN IT'S STOPPED TRYING TO HIDE ITSELF. IT TALKS TO ME, TELLS ME THINGS, PLAYS SICK LITTLE GAMES WITH ME.
AW MAN, I KNEW THERE WUZ SOMETHIN' WRANG. WE COULD... WE COULD ALWAYS GO BACK TAE THE STANE WIZARDS, I SUPPOSE.
SORRY! SORRY!
I DIDN'T MEAN IT! DAMNED THING JERKED MY ARM!
IT DIDNAE LIKE THAT, EH? FEART O' THE WIZARDS, IS IT?
UNFORTUNATELY, IT'S NO' THE ONLY ONE. THEY TELT US NO' TAE COME BACK, AN' THEY'RE NO' THE KIND TAE MAKE EMPTY THREATS.
I'LL BEAT IT. SOONER OR LATER IT'S GOING TO REALISE I'M NOT THE PERFECT HOST.
YOU UNDERSTAND ME?
QUIET!
"POLIS!"

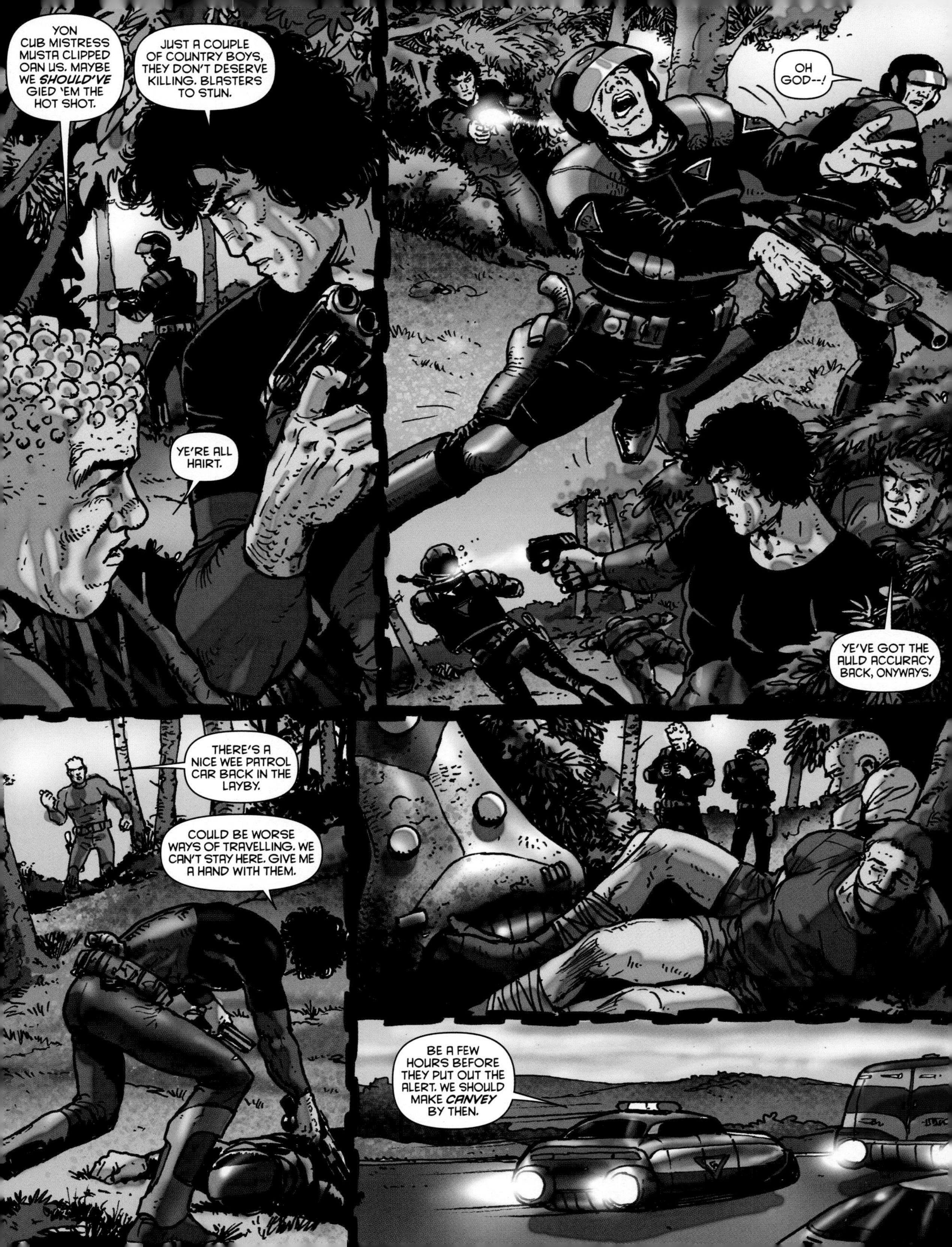

YON CUB MISTRESS MUSTA CLIPPED OAN US. MAYBE WE *SHOULD'VE* GIED 'EM THE HOT SHOT.
JUST A COUPLE OF COUNTRY BOYS, THEY DON'T DESERVE KILLING. BLASTERS TO STUN.
YE'RE ALL HAIRT.
OH GOD--!
YE'VE GOT THE AULD ACCURACY BACK, ONYWAYS.
THERE'S A NICE WEE PATROL CAR BACK IN THE LAYBY.
COULD BE WORSE WAYS OF TRAVELLING. WE CAN'T STAY HERE. GIVE ME A HAND WITH THEM.
BE A FEW HOURS BEFORE THEY PUT OUT THE ALERT. WE SHOULD MAKE *CANVEY* BY THEN.

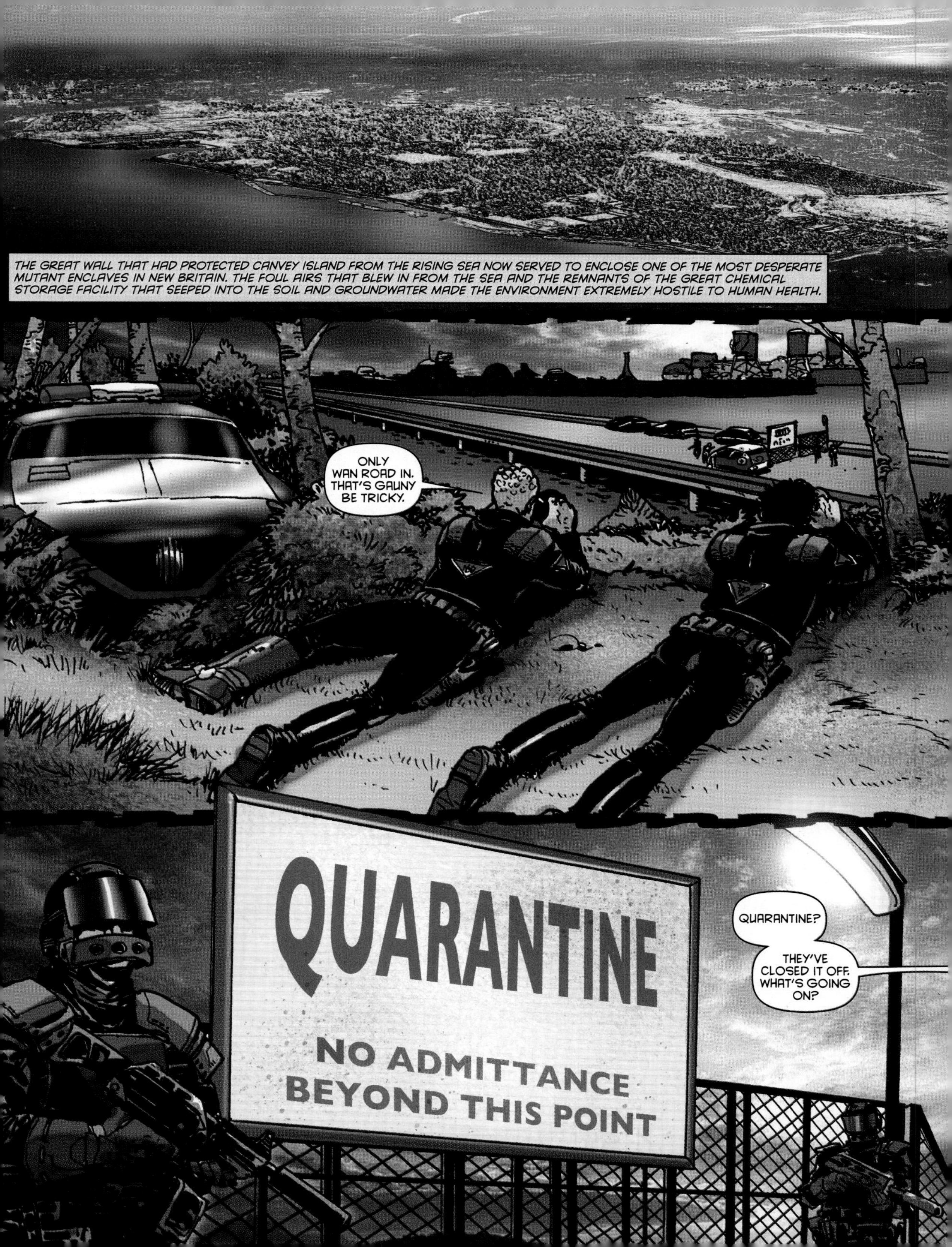
THE GREAT WALL THAT HAD PROTECTED CANVEY ISLAND FROM THE RISING SEA NOW SERVED TO ENCLOSE ONE OF THE MOST DESPERATE MUTANT ENCLAVES IN NEW BRITAIN. THE FOUL AIRS THAT BLEW IN FROM THE SEA AND THE REMNANTS OF THE GREAT CHEMICAL STORAGE FACILITY THAT SEEPED INTO THE SOIL AND GROUNDWATER MADE THE ENVIRONMENT EXTREMELY HOSTILE TO HUMAN HEALTH.
ONLY WAN ROAD IN. THAT'S GAUNY BE TRICKY.
QUARANTINE
NO ADMITTANCE BEYOND THIS POINT
QUARANTINE?
THEY'VE CLOSED IT OFF. WHAT'S GOING ON?

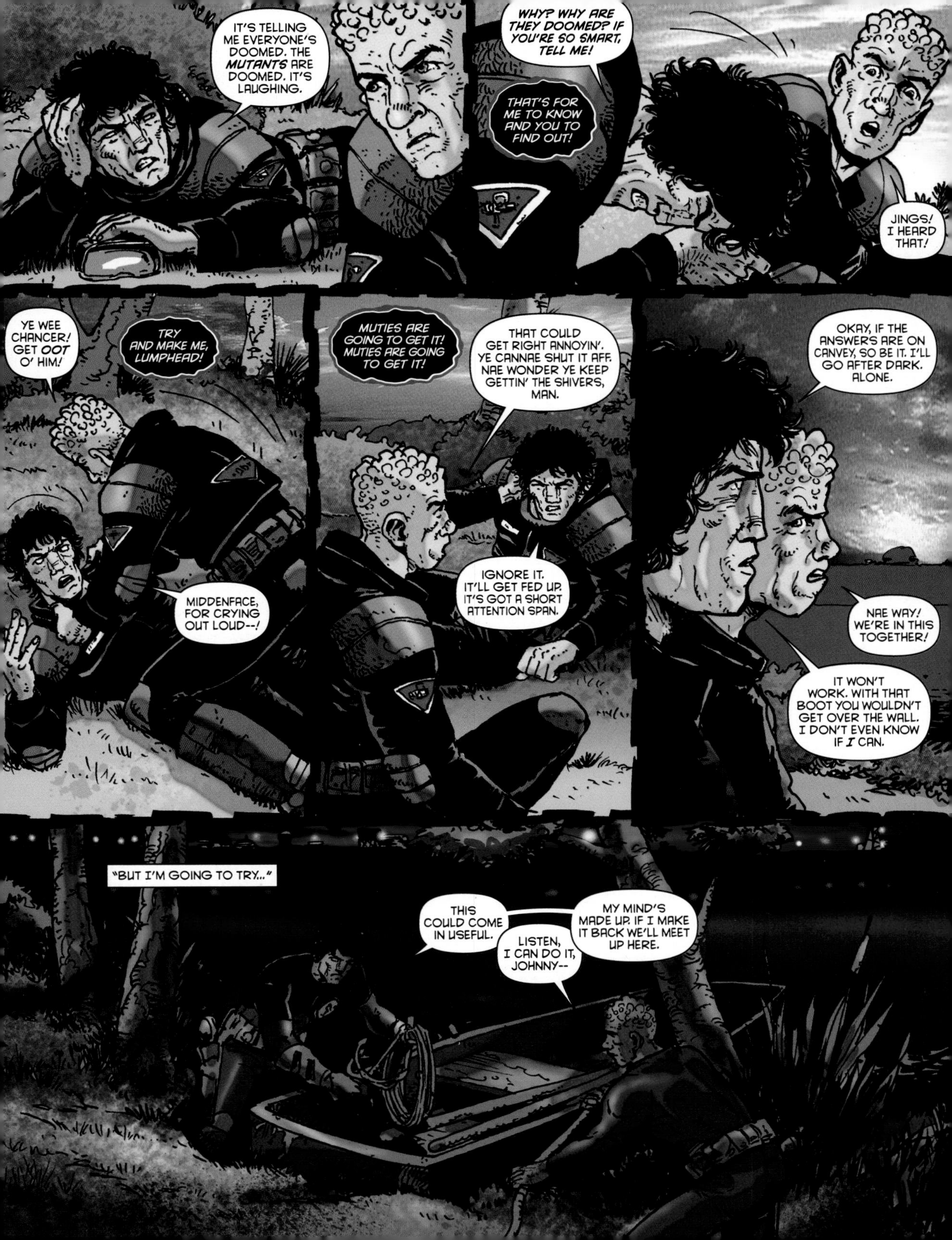

IT'S TELLING ME EVERYONE'S DOOMED. THE MUTANTS ARE DOOMED. IT'S LAUGHING.
WHY? WHY ARE THEY DOOMED? IF YOU'RE SO SMART, TELL ME!
THAT'S FOR ME TO KNOW AND YOU TO FIND OUT!
JINGS! I HEARD THAT!
YE WEE CHANCER! GET OOT O' HIM!
TRY AND MAKE ME, LUMPHEAD!
MIDDENFACE, FOR CRYING OUT LOUD--!
MUTIES ARE GOING TO GET IT! MUTIES ARE GOING TO GET IT!
THAT COULD GET RIGHT ANNOYIN'. YE CANNAE SHUT IT AFF. NAE WONDER YE KEEP GETTIN' THE SHIVERS, MAN.
IGNORE IT. IT'LL GET FED UP. IT'S GOT A SHORT ATTENTION SPAN.
OKAY, IF THE ANSWERS ARE ON CANVEY, SO BE IT. I'LL GO AFTER DARK. ALONE.
NAE WAY! WE'RE IN THIS TOGETHER!
IT WON'T WORK. WITH THAT BOOT YOU WOULDN'T GET OVER THE WALL. I DON'T EVEN KNOW IF I CAN.
"BUT I'M GOING TO TRY..."
THIS COULD COME IN USEFUL.
MY MIND'S MADE UP. IF I MAKE IT BACK WE'LL MEET UP HERE.
LISTEN, I CAN DO IT, JOHNNY--

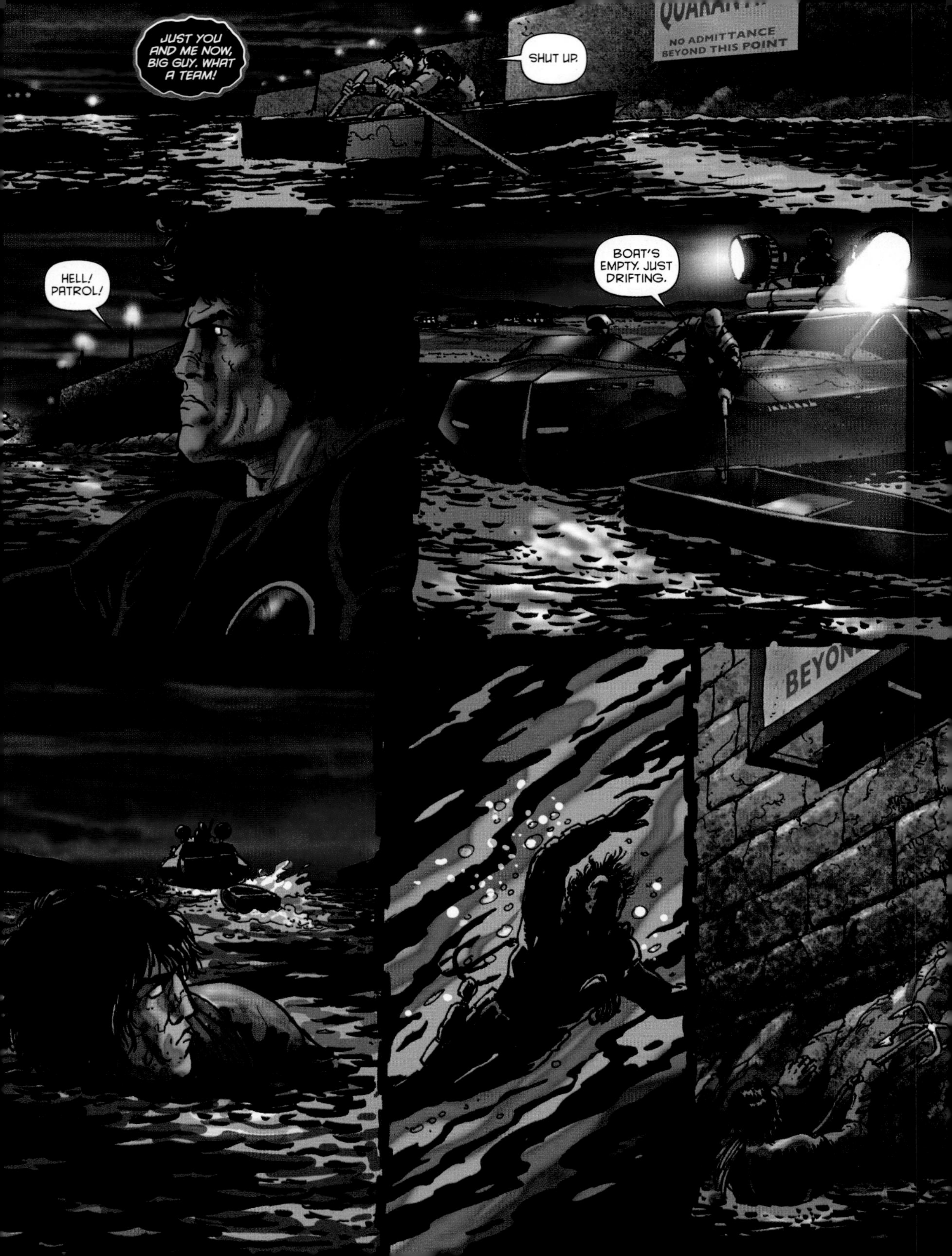

JUST YOU AND ME NOW, BIG GUY. WHAT A TEAM!
SHUT UP.
NO ADMITTANCE BEYOND THIS POINT
HELL! PATROL!
BOAT'S EMPTY. JUST DRIFTING.
BEYON

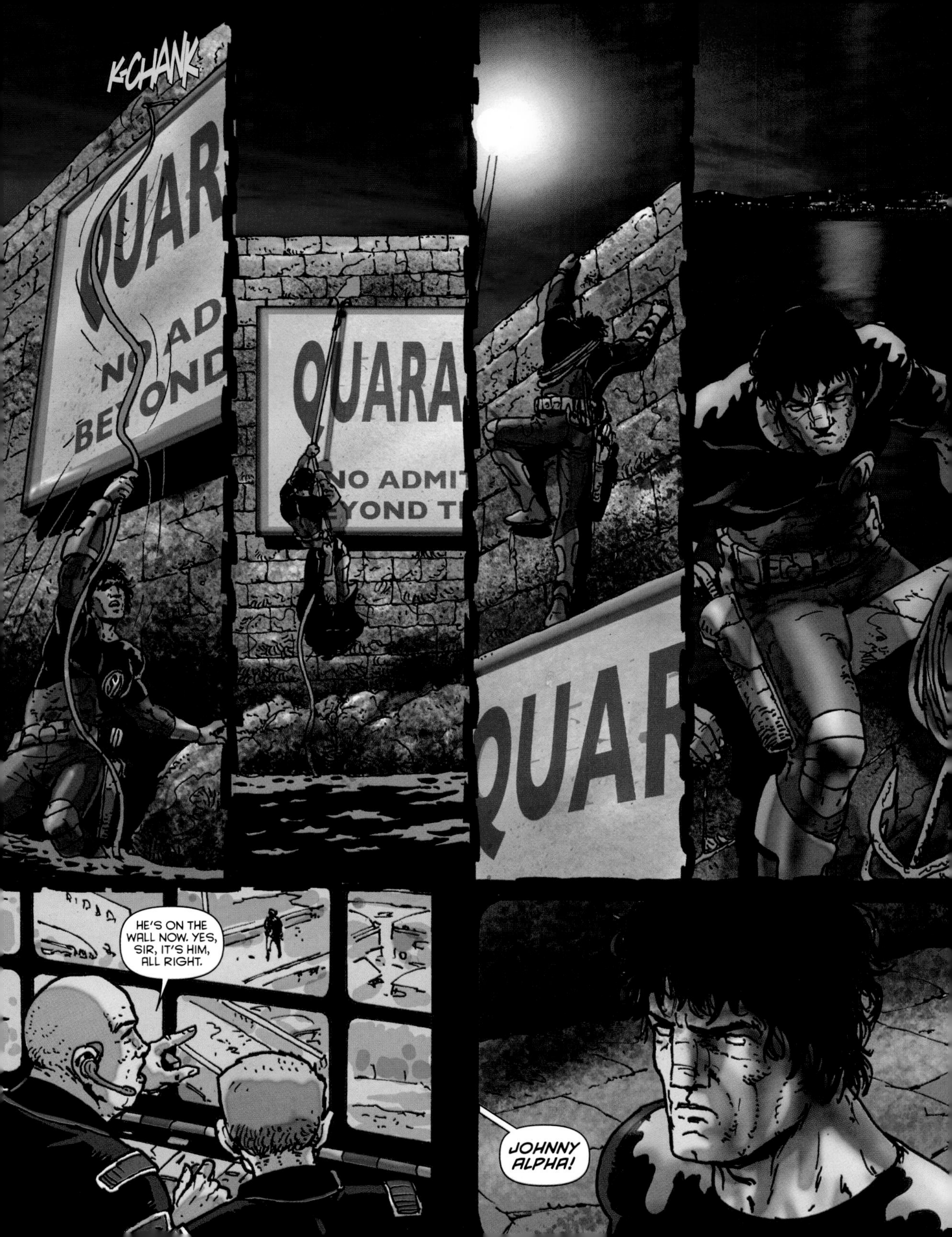
K-CHANK
QUAR
NO AD
BEYOND
QUARA
NO ADMIT
EYOND T
QUAR
HE'S ON THE WALL NOW. YES, SIR, IT'S HIM, ALL RIGHT.
JOHNNY ALPHA!

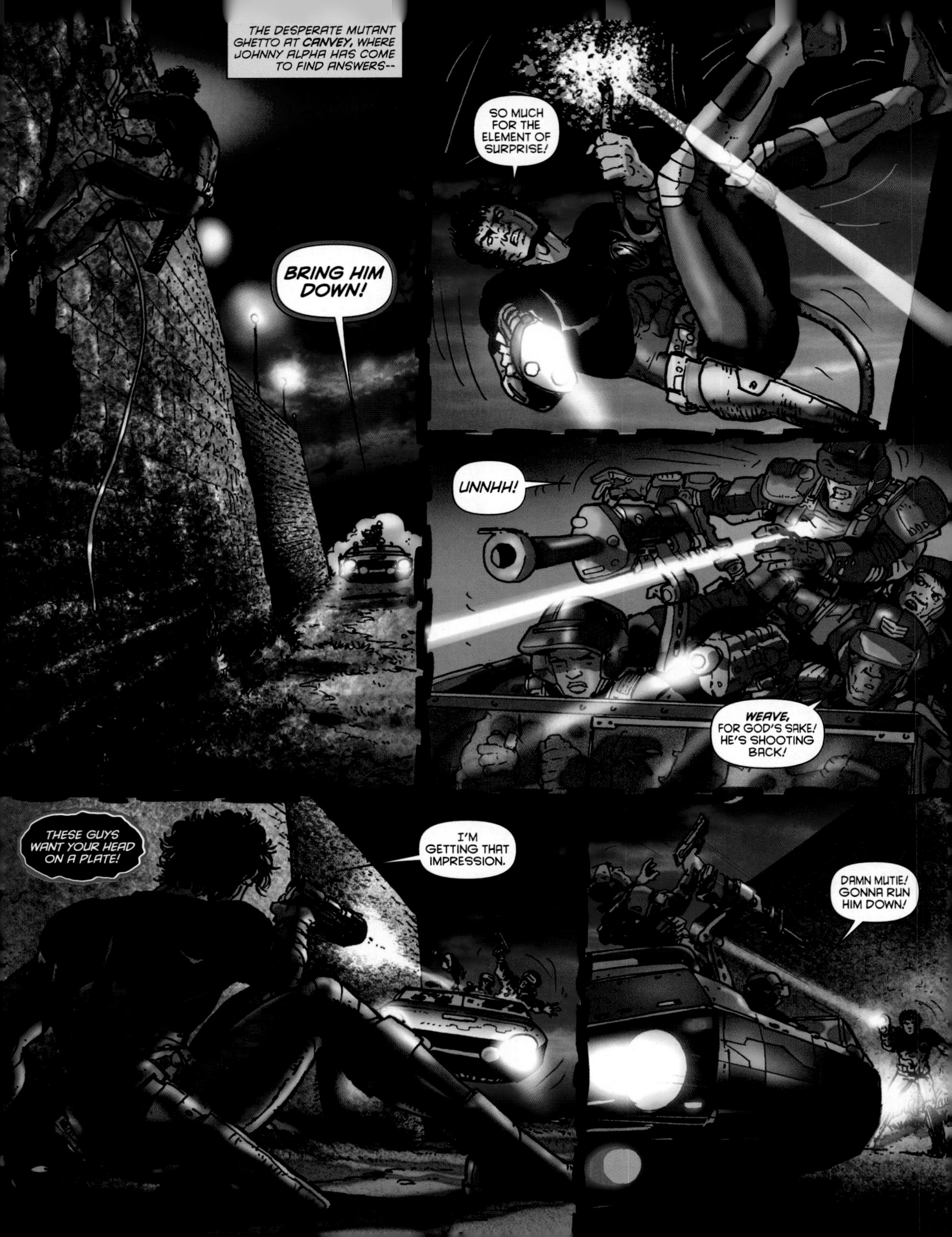
THE DESPERATE MUTANT GHETTO AT CANVEY, WHERE JOHNNY ALPHA HAS COME TO FIND ANSWERS--
BRING HIM DOWN!
SO MUCH FOR THE ELEMENT OF SURPRISE!
UNNHH!
WEAVE, FOR GOD'S SAKE! HE'S SHOOTING BACK!
THESE GUYS WANT YOUR HEAD ON A PLATE!
I'M GETTING THAT IMPRESSION.
DAMN MUTIE! GONNA RUN HIM DOWN!

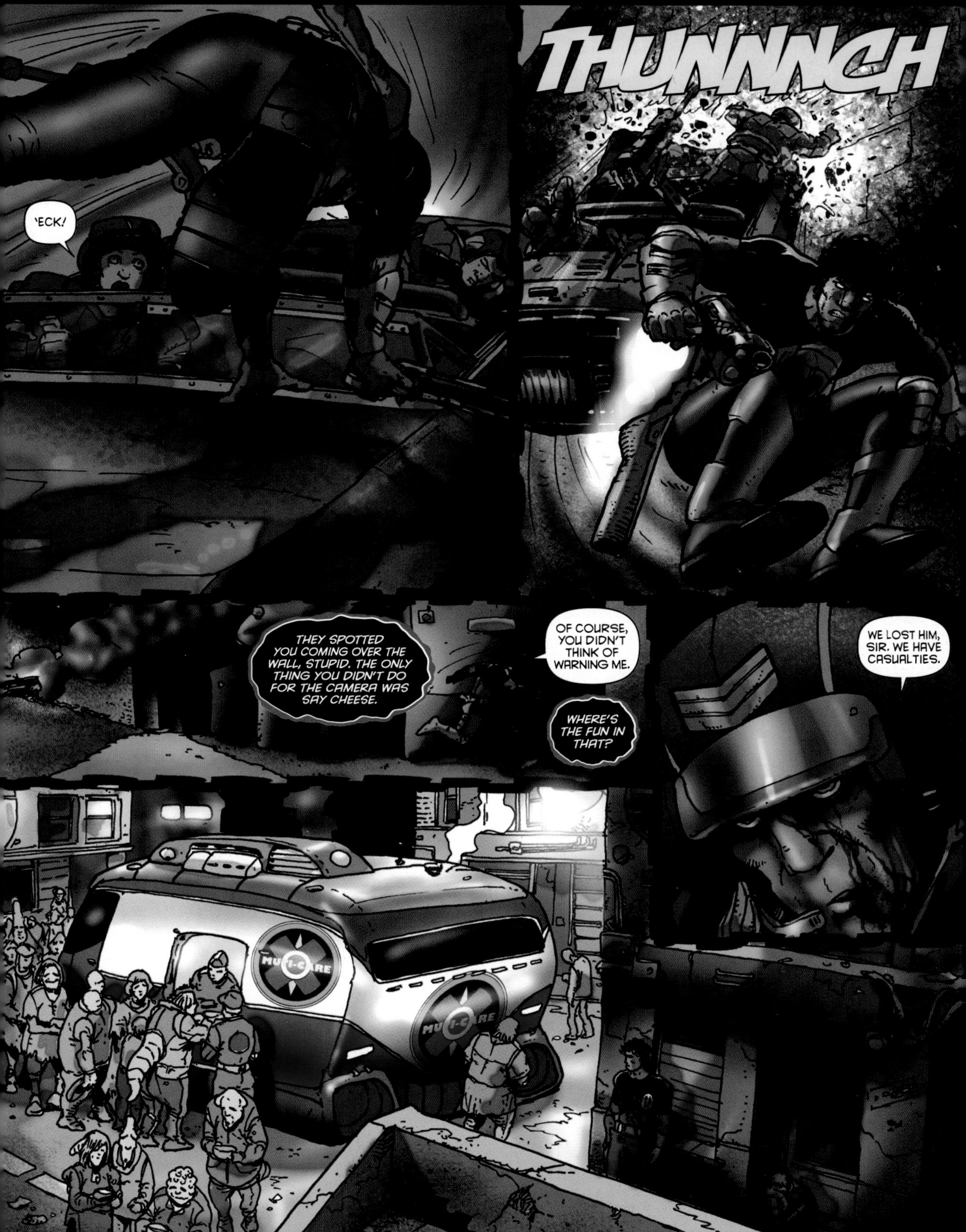
'ECK!
THUNNNCH
THEY SPOTTED YOU COMING OVER THE WALL, STUPID. THE ONLY THING YOU DIDN'T DO FOR THE CAMERA WAS SAY CHEESE.
OF COURSE, YOU DIDN'T THINK OF WARNING ME.
WHERE'S THE FUN IN THAT?
WE LOST HIM, SIR. WE HAVE CASUALTIES.
MULTI-CARE

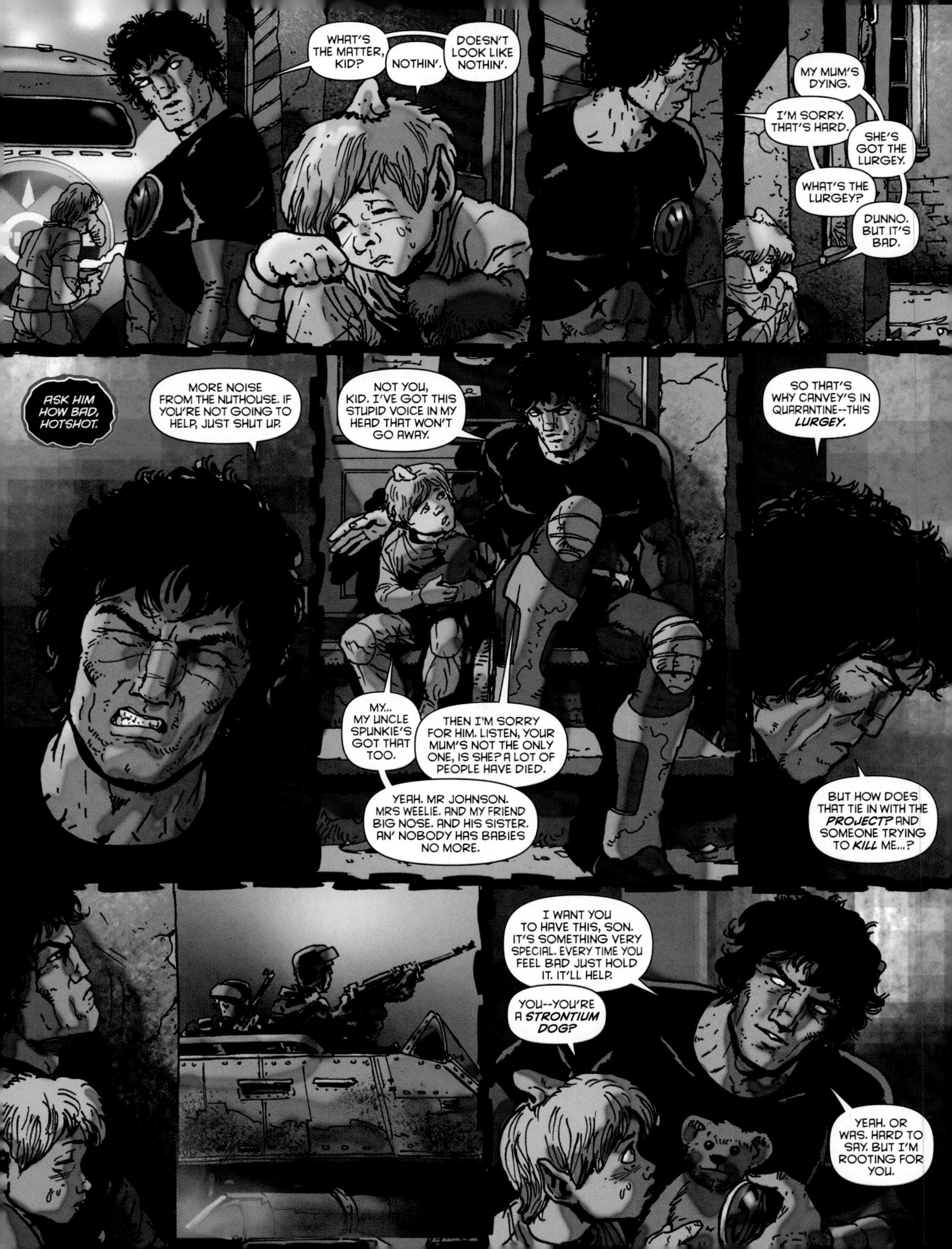
WHAT'S THE MATTER, KID?
NOTHIN'.
DOESN'T LOOK LIKE NOTHIN'.
MY MUM'S DYING.
I'M SORRY. THAT'S HARD.
SHE'S GOT THE LURGEY.
WHAT'S THE LURGEY?
DUNNO. BUT IT'S BAD.
ASK HIM HOW BAD, HOTSHOT.
MORE NOISE FROM THE NUTHOUSE. IF YOU'RE NOT GOING TO HELP, JUST SHUT UP.
NOT YOU, KID. I'VE GOT THIS STUPID VOICE IN MY HEAD THAT WON'T GO AWAY.
MY... MY UNCLE SPUNKIE'S GOT THAT TOO.
THEN I'M SORRY FOR HIM. LISTEN, YOUR MUM'S NOT THE ONLY ONE, IS SHE? A LOT OF PEOPLE HAVE DIED.
YEAH. MR JOHNSON. MRS WEELIE. AND MY FRIEND BIG NOSE. AND HIS SISTER. AN' NOBODY HAS BABIES NO MORE.
SO THAT'S WHY CANVEY'S IN QUARANTINE--THIS LURGEY.
BUT HOW DOES THAT TIE IN WITH THE PROJECT? AND SOMEONE TRYING TO KILL ME...?
I WANT YOU TO HAVE THIS, SON. IT'S SOMETHING VERY SPECIAL. EVERY TIME YOU FEEL BAD JUST HOLD IT. IT'LL HELP.
YOU--YOU'RE A STRONTIUM DOG?
YEAH. OR WAS. HARD TO SAY. BUT I'M ROOTING FOR YOU.

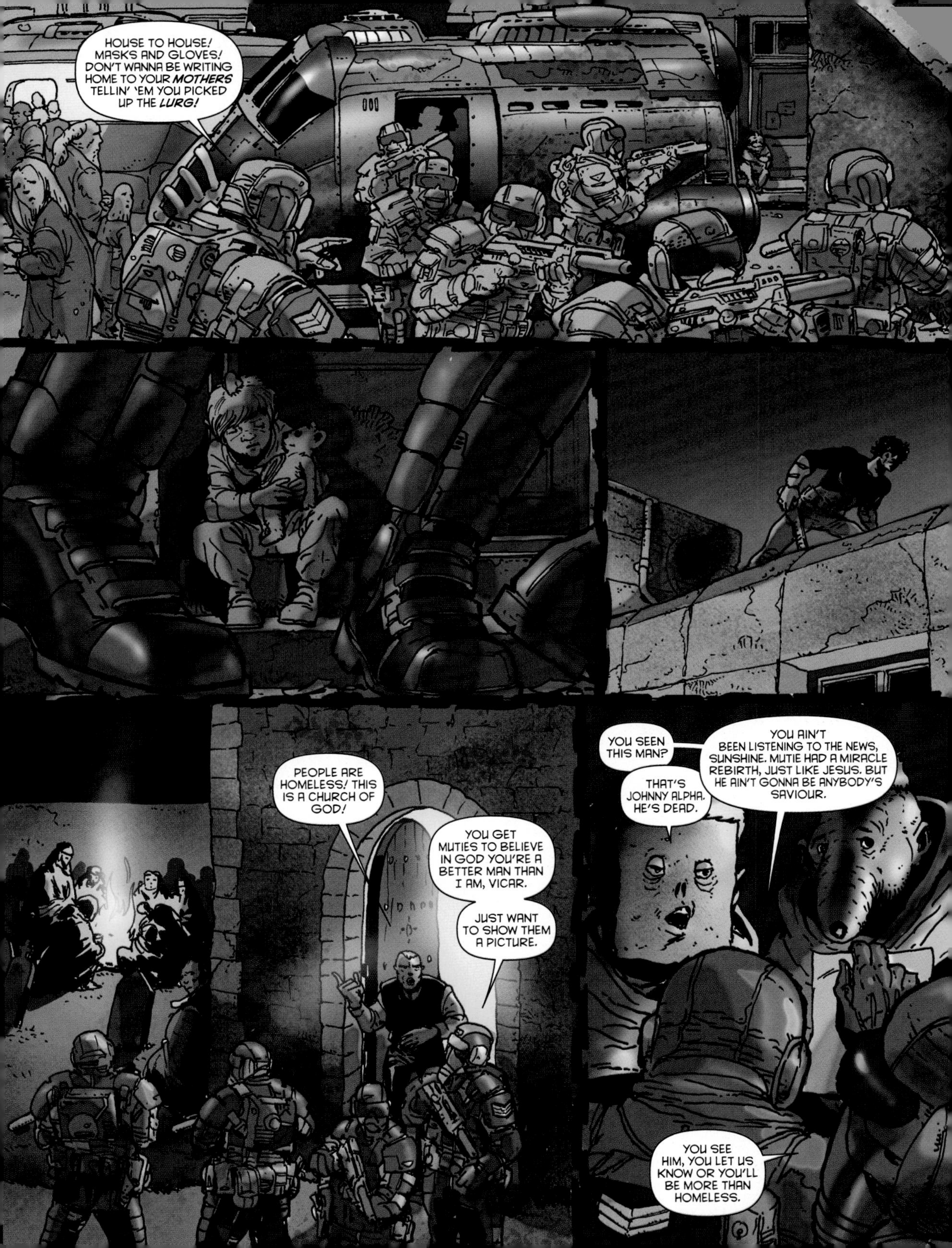
HOUSE TO HOUSE! MASKS AND GLOVES! DON'T WANNA BE WRITING HOME TO YOUR MOTHERS TELLIN' 'EM YOU PICKED UP THE LURG!
PEOPLE ARE HOMELESS! THIS IS A CHURCH OF GOD!
YOU GET MUTIES TO BELIEVE IN GOD YOU'RE A BETTER MAN THAN I AM, VICAR.
JUST WANT TO SHOW THEM A PICTURE.
YOU SEEN THIS MAN?
THAT'S JOHNNY ALPHA. HE'S DEAD.
YOU AIN'T BEEN LISTENING TO THE NEWS, SUNSHINE. MUTIE HAD A MIRACLE REBIRTH, JUST LIKE JESUS. BUT HE AIN'T GONNA BE ANYBODY'S SAVIOUR.
YOU SEE HIM, YOU LET US KNOW OR YOU'LL BE MORE THAN HOMELESS.

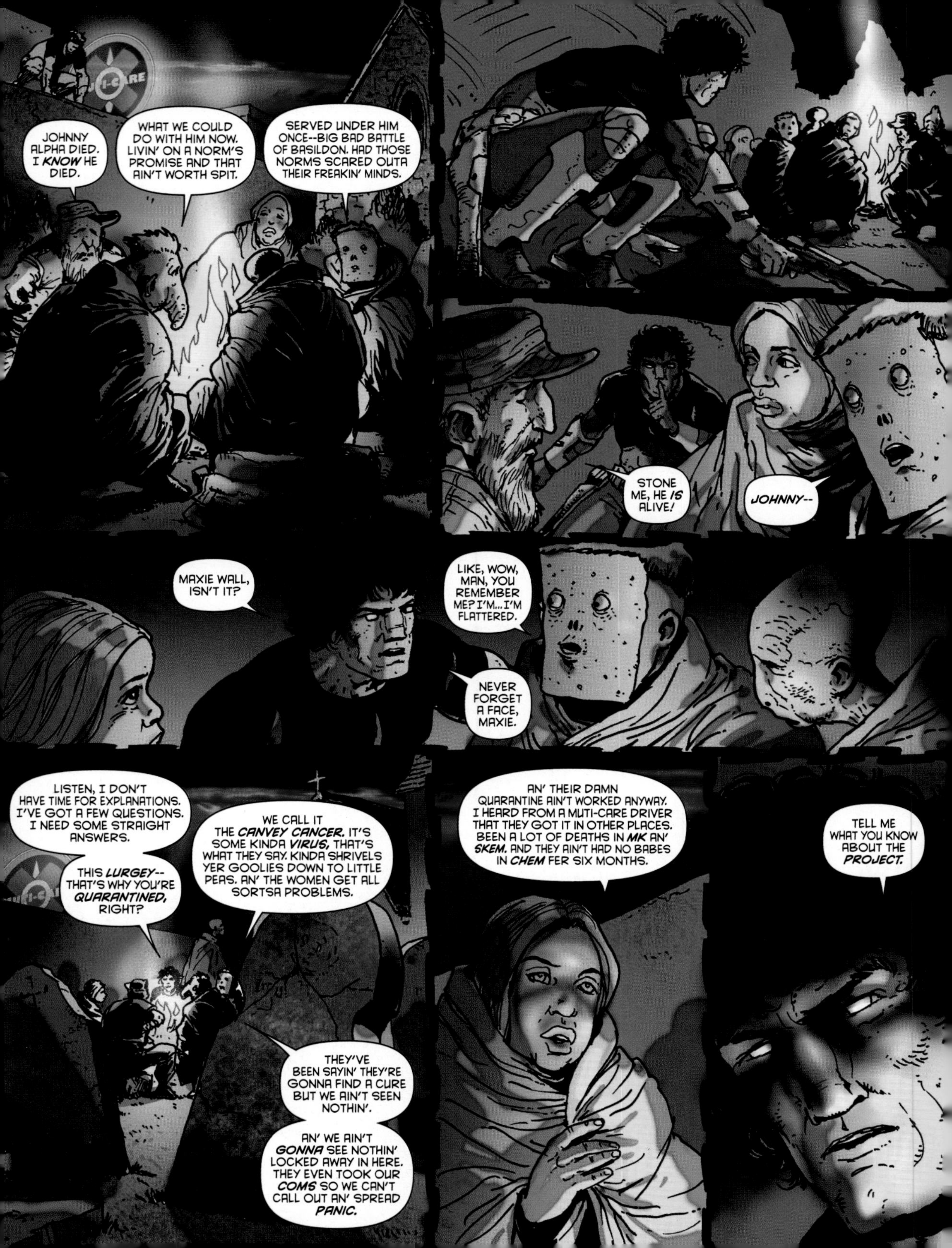
JOHNNY ALPHA DIED. I *KNOW* HE DIED.
WHAT WE COULD DO WITH HIM NOW. LIVIN' ON A NORM'S PROMISE AND THAT AIN'T WORTH SPIT.
SERVED UNDER HIM ONCE--BIG BAD BATTLE OF BASILDON. HAD THOSE NORMS SCARED OUTA THEIR FREAKIN' MINDS.
STONE ME, HE *IS* ALIVE!
JOHNNY--
MAXIE WALL, ISN'T IT?
LIKE, WOW, MAN, YOU REMEMBER ME? I'M...I'M FLATTERED.
NEVER FORGET A FACE, MAXIE.
LISTEN, I DON'T HAVE TIME FOR EXPLANATIONS. I'VE GOT A FEW QUESTIONS. I NEED SOME STRAIGHT ANSWERS.
THIS *LURGEY*--THAT'S WHY YOU'RE *QUARANTINED,* RIGHT?
WE CALL IT THE *CANVEY CANCER.* IT'S SOME KINDA *VIRUS,* THAT'S WHAT THEY SAY. KINDA SHRIVELS YER GOOLIES DOWN TO LITTLE PEAS. AN' THE WOMEN GET ALL SORTSA PROBLEMS.
THEY'VE BEEN SAYIN' THEY'RE GONNA FIND A CURE BUT WE AIN'T SEEN NOTHIN'.
AN' WE AIN'T *GONNA* SEE NOTHIN' LOCKED AWAY IN HERE. THEY EVEN TOOK OUR *COMS* SO WE CAN'T CALL OUT AN' SPREAD *PANIC.*
AN' THEIR DAMN QUARANTINE AIN'T WORKED ANYWAY. I HEARD FROM A MUTI-CARE DRIVER THAT THEY GOT IT IN OTHER PLACES. BEEN A LOT OF DEATHS IN *MK* AN' *SKEM.* AND THEY AIN'T HAD NO BABES IN *CHEM* FER SIX MONTHS.
TELL ME WHAT YOU KNOW ABOUT THE *PROJECT.*

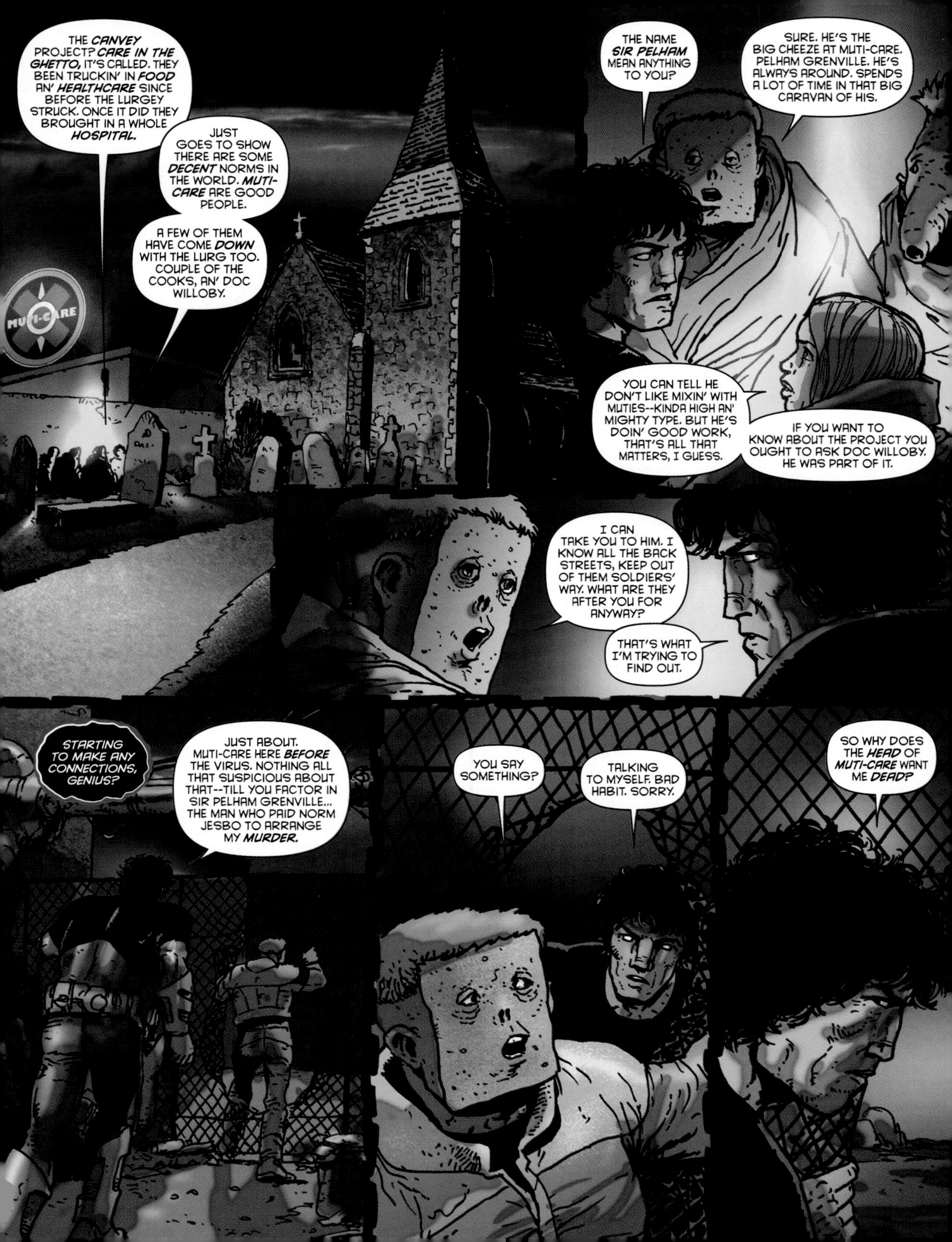
THE CANVEY PROJECT? CARE IN THE GHETTO, IT'S CALLED. THEY BEEN TRUCKIN' IN FOOD AN' HEALTHCARE SINCE BEFORE THE LURGEY STRUCK. ONCE IT DID THEY BROUGHT IN A WHOLE HOSPITAL.
JUST GOES TO SHOW THERE ARE SOME DECENT NORMS IN THE WORLD. MUTI-CARE ARE GOOD PEOPLE.
A FEW OF THEM HAVE COME DOWN WITH THE LURG TOO. COUPLE OF THE COOKS, AN' DOC WILLOBY.
MUTI-CARE
THE NAME SIR PELHAM MEAN ANYTHING TO YOU?
SURE. HE'S THE BIG CHEEZE AT MUTI-CARE. PELHAM GRENVILLE. HE'S ALWAYS AROUND. SPENDS A LOT OF TIME IN THAT BIG CARAVAN OF HIS.
YOU CAN TELL HE DON'T LIKE MIXIN' WITH MUTIES--KINDA HIGH AN' MIGHTY TYPE. BUT HE'S DOIN' GOOD WORK, THAT'S ALL THAT MATTERS, I GUESS.
IF YOU WANT TO KNOW ABOUT THE PROJECT YOU OUGHT TO ASK DOC WILLOBY. HE WAS PART OF IT.
I CAN TAKE YOU TO HIM. I KNOW ALL THE BACK STREETS, KEEP OUT OF THEM SOLDIERS' WAY. WHAT ARE THEY AFTER YOU FOR ANYWAY?
THAT'S WHAT I'M TRYING TO FIND OUT.
STARTING TO MAKE ANY CONNECTIONS, GENIUS?
JUST ABOUT. MUTI-CARE HERE BEFORE THE VIRUS. NOTHING ALL THAT SUSPICIOUS ABOUT THAT--TILL YOU FACTOR IN SIR PELHAM GRENVILLE... THE MAN WHO PAID NORM JESBO TO ARRANGE MY MURDER.
YOU SAY SOMETHING?
TALKING TO MYSELF. BAD HABIT. SORRY.
SO WHY DOES THE HEAD OF MUTI-CARE WANT ME DEAD?

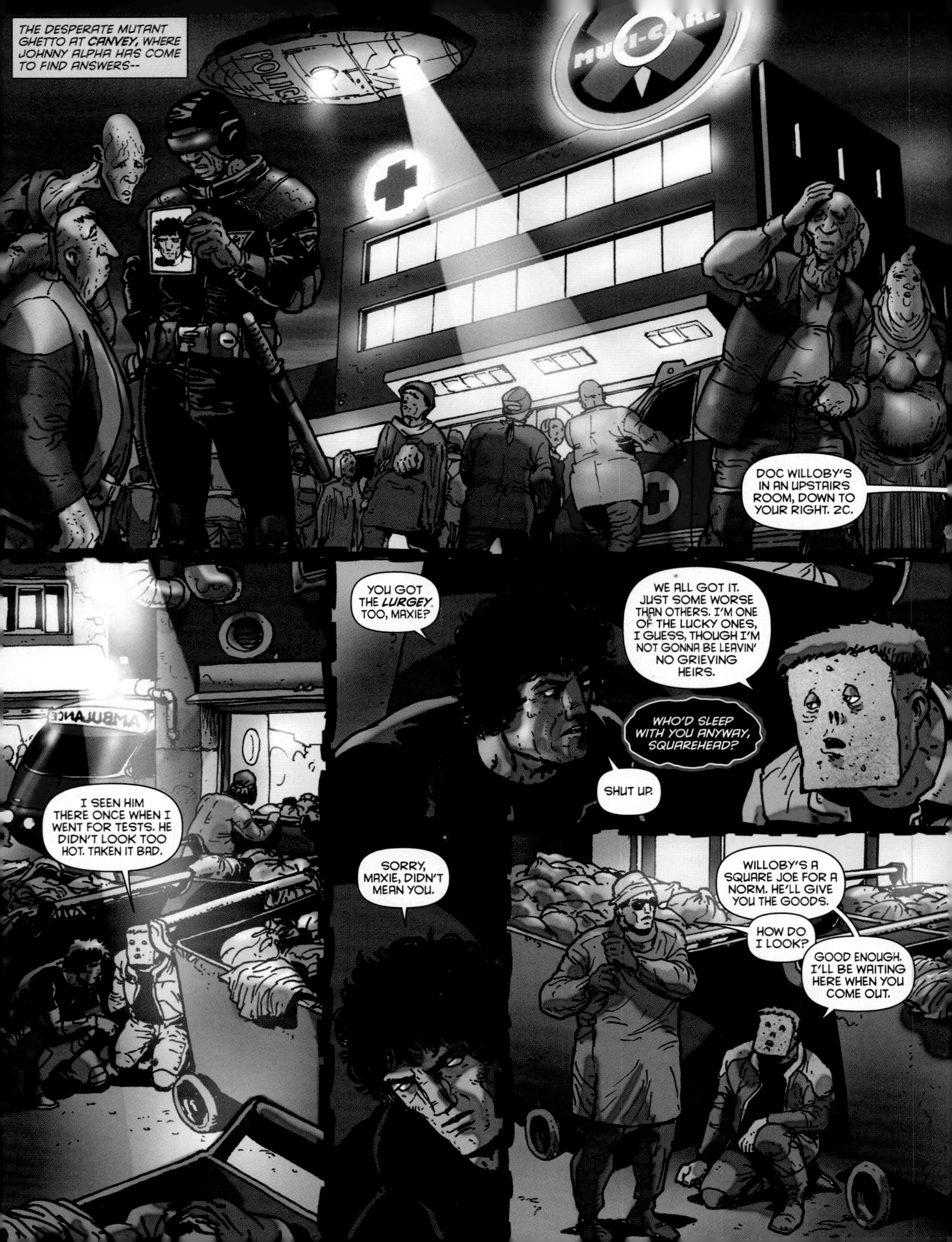
THE DESPERATE MUTANT GHETTO AT CANVEY, WHERE JOHNNY ALPHA HAS COME TO FIND ANSWERS--
POLICE
DOC WILLOBY'S IN AN UPSTAIRS ROOM, DOWN TO YOUR RIGHT. 2C.
AMBULANCE
I SEEN HIM THERE ONCE WHEN I WENT FOR TESTS. HE DIDN'T LOOK TOO HOT. TAKEN IT BAD.
YOU GOT THE LURGEY TOO, MAXIE?
WE ALL GOT IT. JUST SOME WORSE THAN OTHERS. I'M ONE OF THE LUCKY ONES, I GUESS, THOUGH I'M NOT GONNA BE LEAVIN' NO GRIEVING HEIRS.
WHO'D SLEEP WITH YOU ANYWAY, SQUAREHEAD?
SHUT UP.
SORRY, MAXIE, DIDN'T MEAN YOU.
WILLOBY'S A SQUARE JOE FOR A NORM. HE'LL GIVE YOU THE GOODS.
HOW DO I LOOK?
GOOD ENOUGH. I'LL BE WAITING HERE WHEN YOU COME OUT.

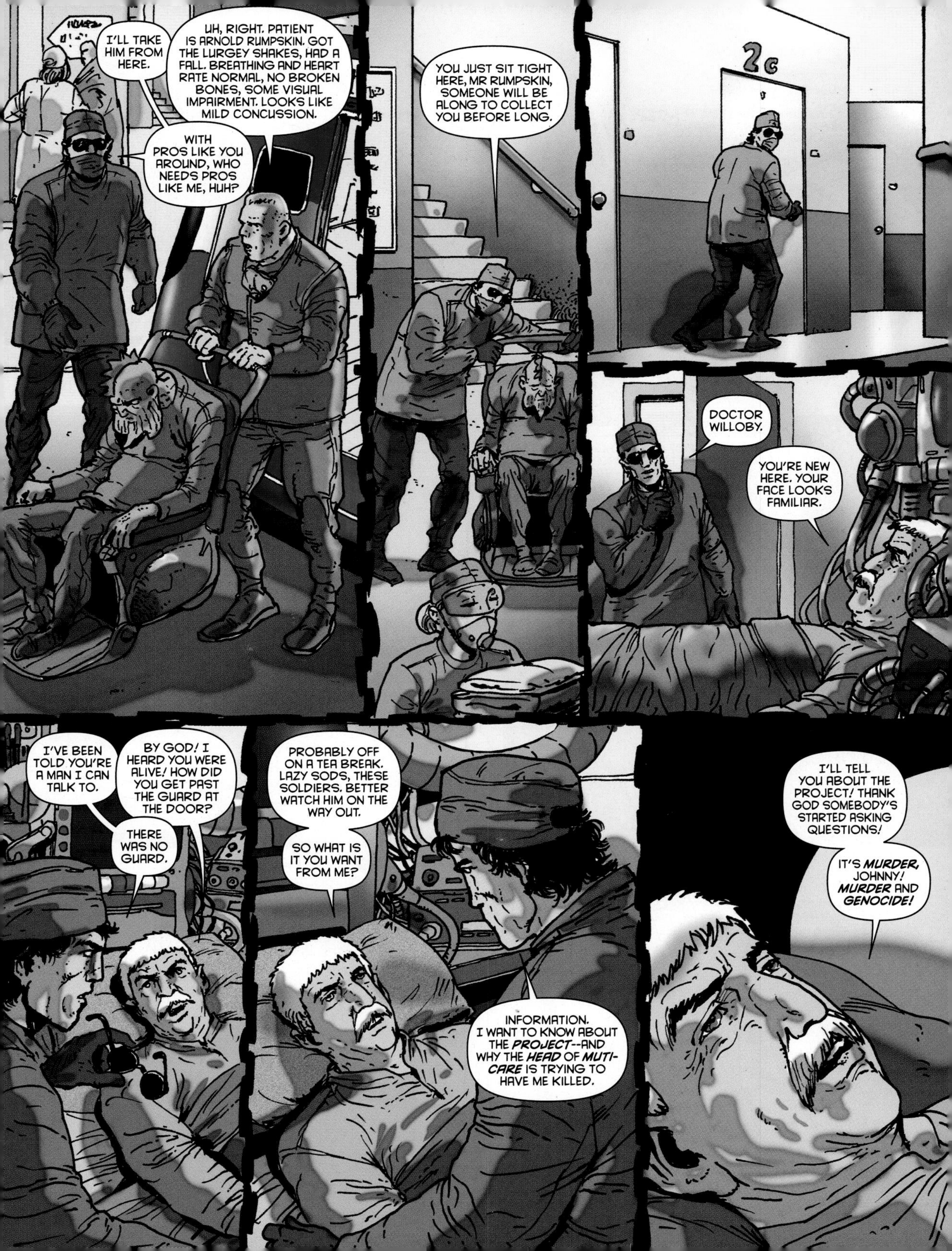
I'LL TAKE HIM FROM HERE.
UH, RIGHT. PATIENT IS ARNOLD RUMPSKIN. GOT THE LURGEY SHAKES, HAD A FALL. BREATHING AND HEART RATE NORMAL, NO BROKEN BONES, SOME VISUAL IMPAIRMENT. LOOKS LIKE MILD CONCUSSION.
WITH PROS LIKE YOU AROUND, WHO NEEDS PROS LIKE ME, HUH?
YOU JUST SIT TIGHT HERE, MR RUMPSKIN, SOMEONE WILL BE ALONG TO COLLECT YOU BEFORE LONG.
2c
DOCTOR WILLOBY.
YOU'RE NEW HERE. YOUR FACE LOOKS FAMILIAR.
I'VE BEEN TOLD YOU'RE A MAN I CAN TALK TO.
BY GOD! I HEARD YOU WERE ALIVE! HOW DID YOU GET PAST THE GUARD AT THE DOOR?
THERE WAS NO GUARD.
PROBABLY OFF ON A TEA BREAK. LAZY SODS, THESE SOLDIERS. BETTER WATCH HIM ON THE WAY OUT.
SO WHAT IS IT YOU WANT FROM ME?
INFORMATION. I WANT TO KNOW ABOUT THE *PROJECT*--AND WHY THE *HEAD* OF *MUTI-CARE* IS TRYING TO HAVE ME KILLED.
I'LL TELL YOU ABOUT THE PROJECT! THANK GOD SOMEBODY'S STARTED ASKING QUESTIONS!
IT'S *MURDER,* JOHNNY! *MURDER* AND *GENOCIDE!*

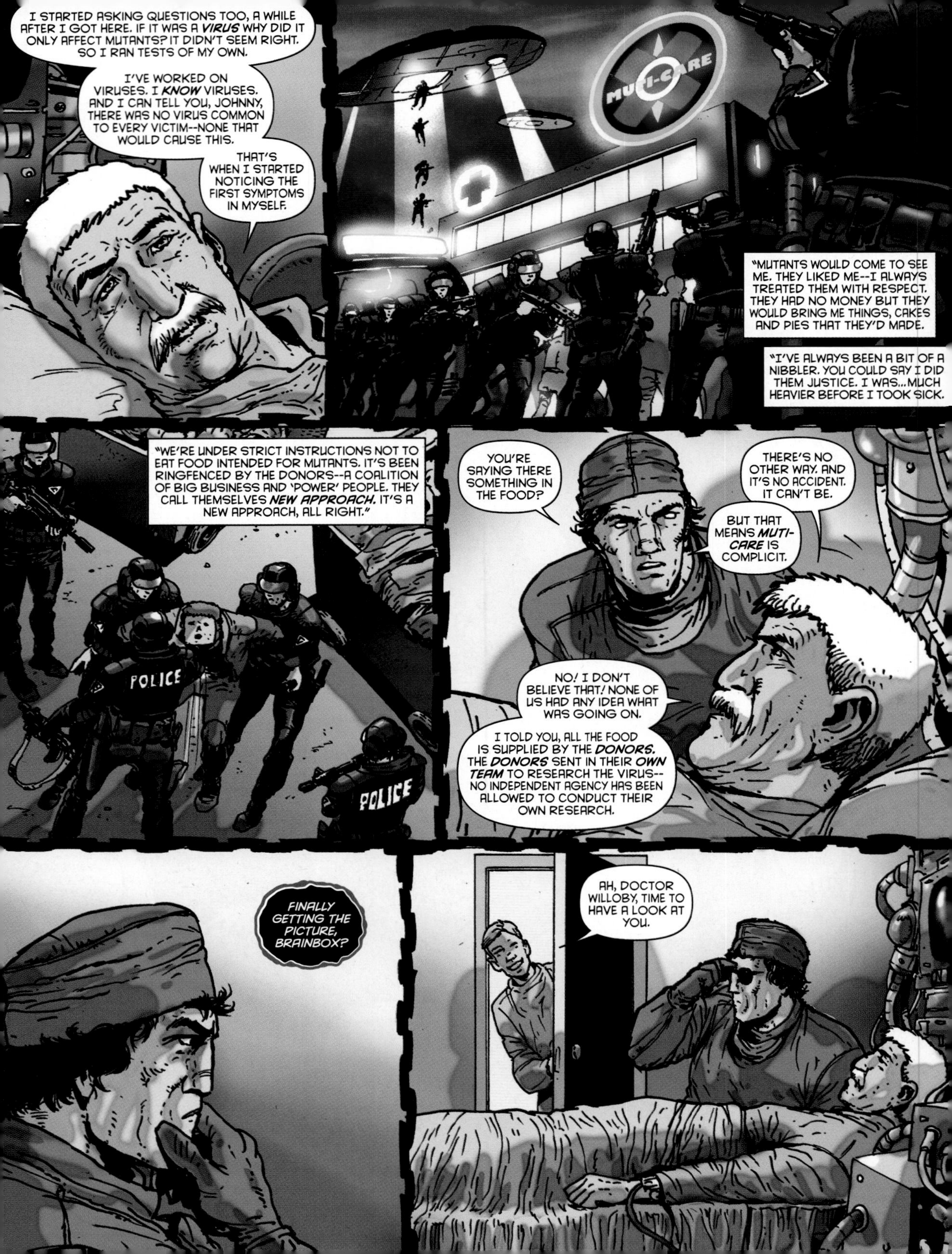
I STARTED ASKING QUESTIONS TOO, A WHILE AFTER I GOT HERE. IF IT WAS A *VIRUS* WHY DID IT ONLY AFFECT MUTANTS? IT DIDN'T SEEM RIGHT. SO I RAN TESTS OF MY OWN.
I'VE WORKED ON VIRUSES. I *KNOW* VIRUSES. AND I CAN TELL YOU, JOHNNY, THERE WAS NO VIRUS COMMON TO EVERY VICTIM--NONE THAT WOULD CAUSE THIS.
THAT'S WHEN I STARTED NOTICING THE FIRST SYMPTOMS IN MYSELF.
MUTI-CARE
"MUTANTS WOULD COME TO SEE ME. THEY LIKED ME--I ALWAYS TREATED THEM WITH RESPECT. THEY HAD NO MONEY BUT THEY WOULD BRING ME THINGS, CAKES AND PIES THAT THEY'D MADE.
"I'VE ALWAYS BEEN A BIT OF A NIBBLER. YOU COULD SAY I DID THEM JUSTICE. I WAS...MUCH HEAVIER BEFORE I TOOK SICK.
"WE'RE UNDER STRICT INSTRUCTIONS NOT TO EAT FOOD INTENDED FOR MUTANTS. IT'S BEEN RINGFENCED BY THE DONORS--A COALITION OF BIG BUSINESS AND 'POWER' PEOPLE. THEY CALL THEMSELVES *NEW APPROACH.* IT'S A NEW APPROACH, ALL RIGHT."
POLICE
POLICE
YOU'RE SAYING THERE SOMETHING IN THE FOOD?
THERE'S NO OTHER WAY. AND IT'S NO ACCIDENT. IT CAN'T BE.
BUT THAT MEANS *MUTI-CARE* IS COMPLICIT.
NO! I DON'T BELIEVE THAT! NONE OF US HAD ANY IDEA WHAT WAS GOING ON.
I TOLD YOU, ALL THE FOOD IS SUPPLIED BY THE *DONORS.* THE *DONORS* SENT IN THEIR *OWN TEAM* TO RESEARCH THE VIRUS--NO INDEPENDENT AGENCY HAS BEEN ALLOWED TO CONDUCT THEIR OWN RESEARCH.
FINALLY GETTING THE PICTURE, BRAINBOX?
AH, DOCTOR WILLOBY, TIME TO HAVE A LOOK AT YOU.

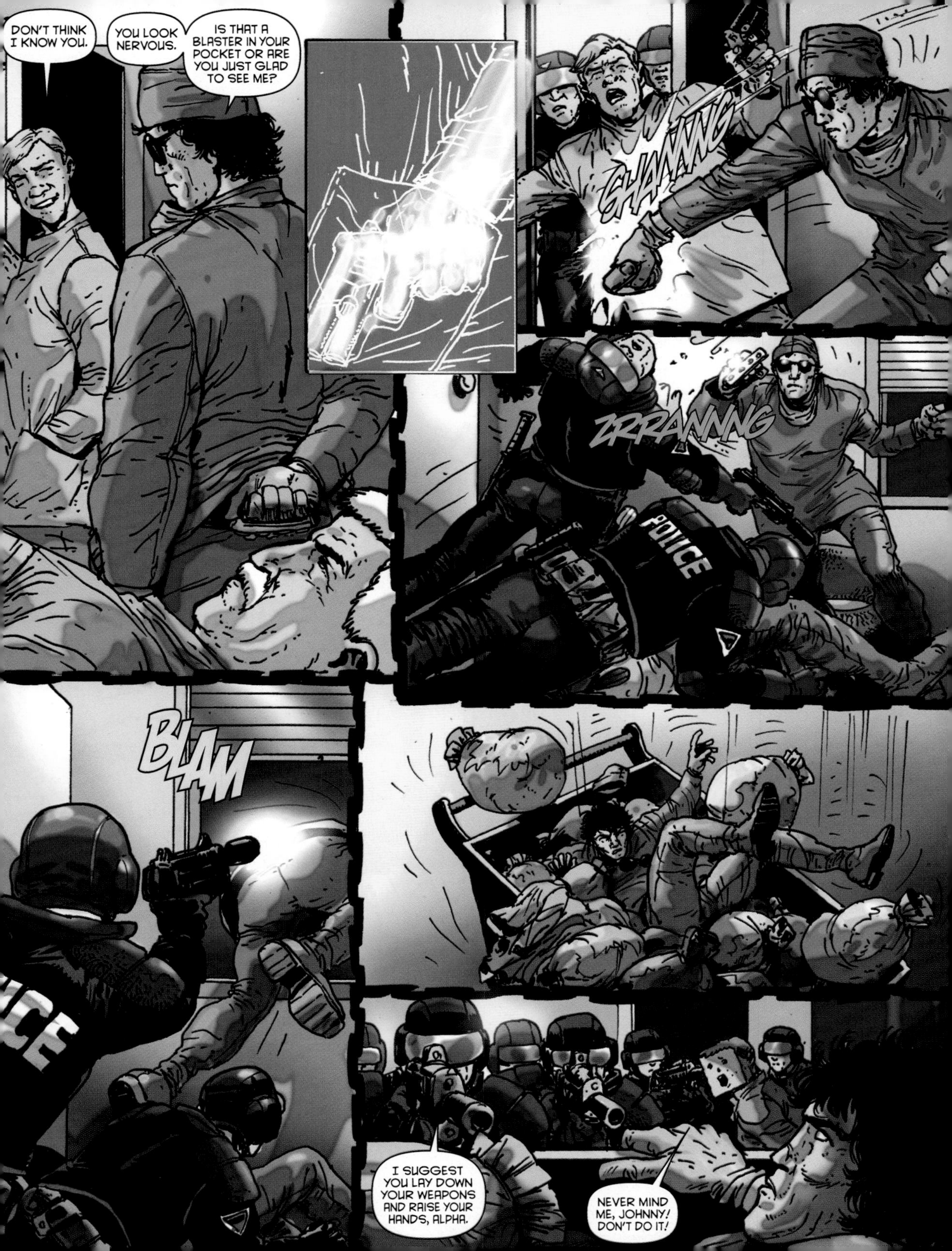

DON'T THINK I KNOW YOU.
YOU LOOK NERVOUS.
IS THAT A BLASTER IN YOUR POCKET OR ARE YOU JUST GLAD TO SEE ME?
SHANNNG
ZRRANNNG
POLICE
BLAM
I SUGGEST YOU LAY DOWN YOUR WEAPONS AND RAISE YOUR HANDS, ALPHA.
NEVER MIND ME, JOHNNY! DON'T DO IT!

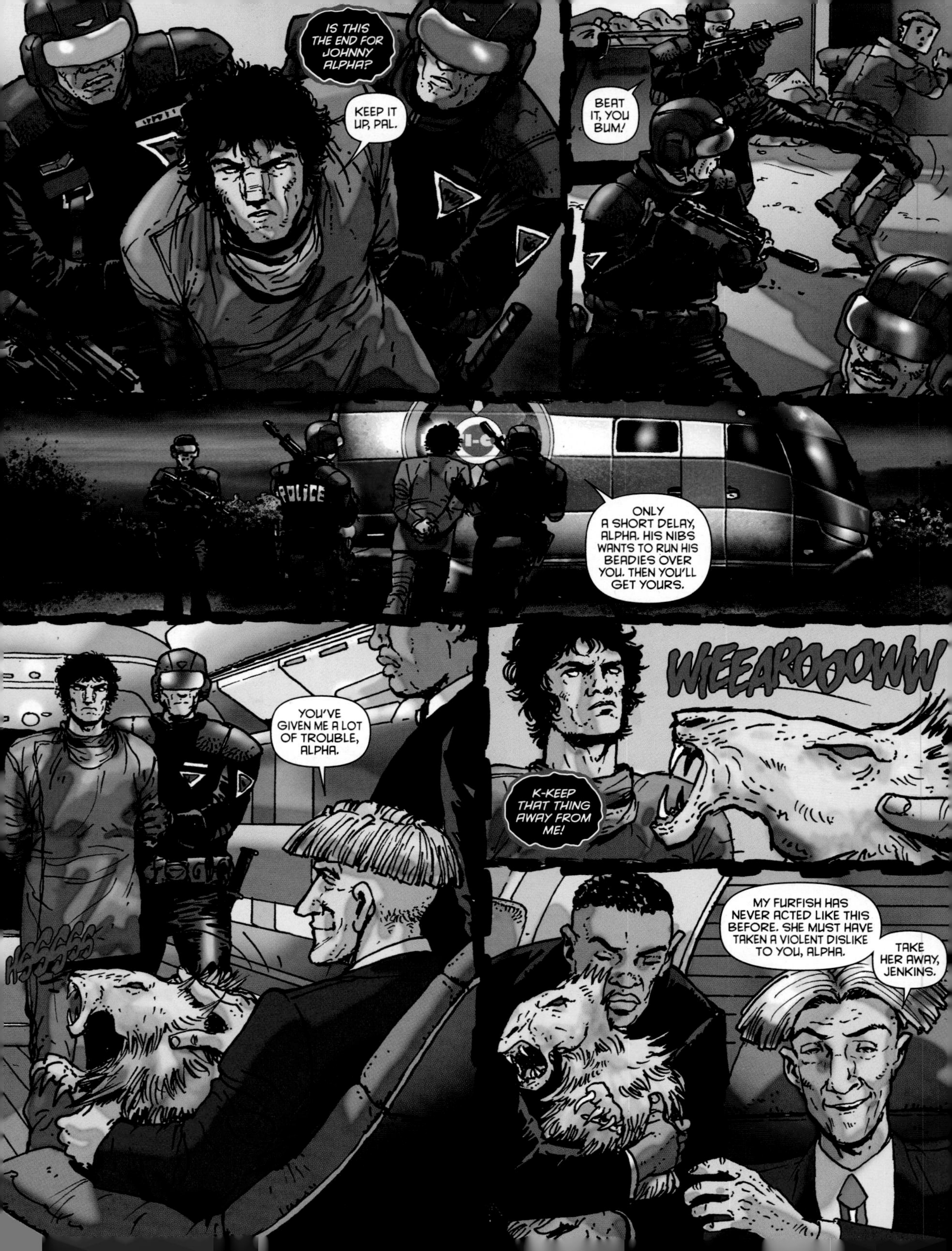

IS THIS THE END FOR JOHNNY ALPHA?
KEEP IT UP, PAL.
BEAT IT, YOU BUM!
POLICE
ONLY A SHORT DELAY, ALPHA. HIS NIBS WANTS TO RUN HIS BEADIES OVER YOU. THEN YOU'LL GET YOURS.
YOU'VE GIVEN ME A LOT OF TROUBLE, ALPHA.
HSSSSS
WIEEAROOOWW
K-KEEP THAT THING AWAY FROM ME!
MY FURFISH HAS NEVER ACTED LIKE THIS BEFORE. SHE MUST HAVE TAKEN A VIOLENT DISLIKE TO YOU, ALPHA.
TAKE HER AWAY, JENKINS.

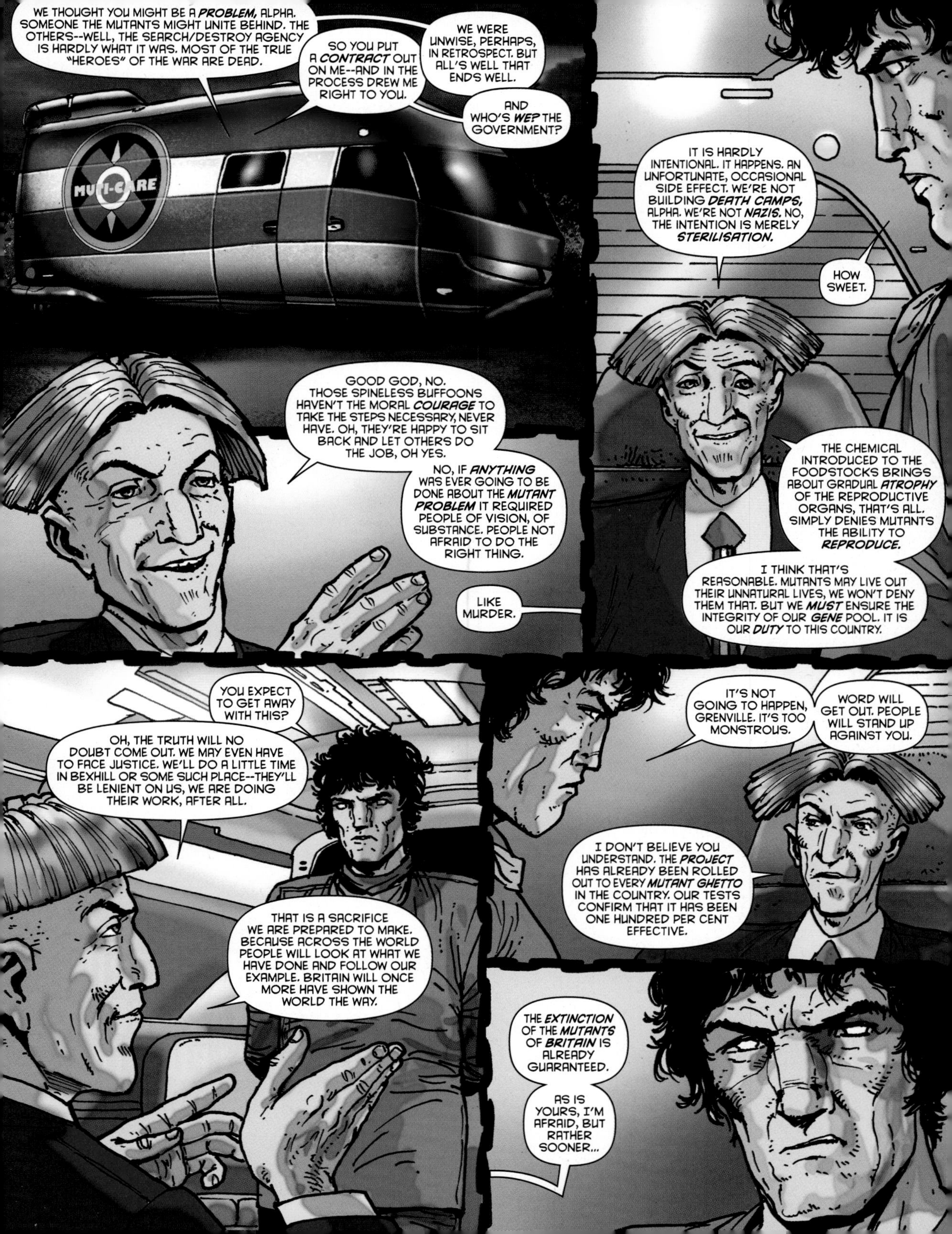

WE THOUGHT YOU MIGHT BE A ***PROBLEM,*** ALPHA. SOMEONE THE MUTANTS MIGHT UNITE BEHIND. THE OTHERS--WELL, THE SEARCH/DESTROY AGENCY IS HARDLY WHAT IT WAS. MOST OF THE TRUE "HEROES" OF THE WAR ARE DEAD.
SO YOU PUT A ***CONTRACT*** OUT ON ME--AND IN THE PROCESS DREW ME RIGHT TO YOU.
WE WERE UNWISE, PERHAPS, IN RETROSPECT. BUT ALL'S WELL THAT ENDS WELL.
AND WHO'S ***WE?*** THE GOVERNMENT?
MUTI-CARE
IT IS HARDLY INTENTIONAL. IT HAPPENS. AN UNFORTUNATE, OCCASIONAL SIDE EFFECT. WE'RE NOT BUILDING ***DEATH CAMPS,*** ALPHA. WE'RE NOT ***NAZIS.*** NO, THE INTENTION IS MERELY ***STERILISATION.***
HOW SWEET.
GOOD GOD, NO. THOSE SPINELESS BUFFOONS HAVEN'T THE MORAL ***COURAGE*** TO TAKE THE STEPS NECESSARY, NEVER HAVE. OH, THEY'RE HAPPY TO SIT BACK AND LET OTHERS DO THE JOB, OH YES.
NO, IF ***ANYTHING*** WAS EVER GOING TO BE DONE ABOUT THE ***MUTANT PROBLEM*** IT REQUIRED PEOPLE OF VISION, OF SUBSTANCE. PEOPLE NOT AFRAID TO DO THE RIGHT THING.
LIKE MURDER.
THE CHEMICAL INTRODUCED TO THE FOODSTOCKS BRINGS ABOUT GRADUAL ***ATROPHY*** OF THE REPRODUCTIVE ORGANS, THAT'S ALL. SIMPLY DENIES MUTANTS THE ABILITY TO ***REPRODUCE.***
I THINK THAT'S REASONABLE. MUTANTS MAY LIVE OUT THEIR UNNATURAL LIVES, WE WON'T DENY THEM THAT. BUT WE ***MUST*** ENSURE THE INTEGRITY OF OUR ***GENE*** POOL. IT IS OUR ***DUTY*** TO THIS COUNTRY.
YOU EXPECT TO GET AWAY WITH THIS?
OH, THE TRUTH WILL NO DOUBT COME OUT. WE MAY EVEN HAVE TO FACE JUSTICE. WE'LL DO A LITTLE TIME IN BEXHILL OR SOME SUCH PLACE--THEY'LL BE LENIENT ON US, WE ARE DOING THEIR WORK, AFTER ALL.
THAT IS A SACRIFICE WE ARE PREPARED TO MAKE. BECAUSE ACROSS THE WORLD PEOPLE WILL LOOK AT WHAT WE HAVE DONE AND FOLLOW OUR EXAMPLE. BRITAIN WILL ONCE MORE HAVE SHOWN THE WORLD THE WAY.
IT'S NOT GOING TO HAPPEN, GRENVILLE. IT'S TOO MONSTROUS.
WORD WILL GET OUT. PEOPLE WILL STAND UP AGAINST YOU.
I DON'T BELIEVE YOU UNDERSTAND. THE ***PROJECT*** HAS ALREADY BEEN ROLLED OUT TO EVERY ***MUTANT GHETTO*** IN THE COUNTRY. OUR TESTS CONFIRM THAT IT HAS BEEN ONE HUNDRED PER CENT EFFECTIVE.
THE ***EXTINCTION*** OF THE ***MUTANTS*** OF ***BRITAIN*** IS ALREADY GUARANTEED.
AS IS YOURS, I'M AFRAID, BUT RATHER SOONER...

BONUS STRIP:
WHAT IF...? MAX BUBBA
HADN'T KILLED WULF

Writer: Alan Grant
Artist: Carlos Ezquerra
Letters: Ellie De Ville

Originally published in *2000 AD* Prog 1772

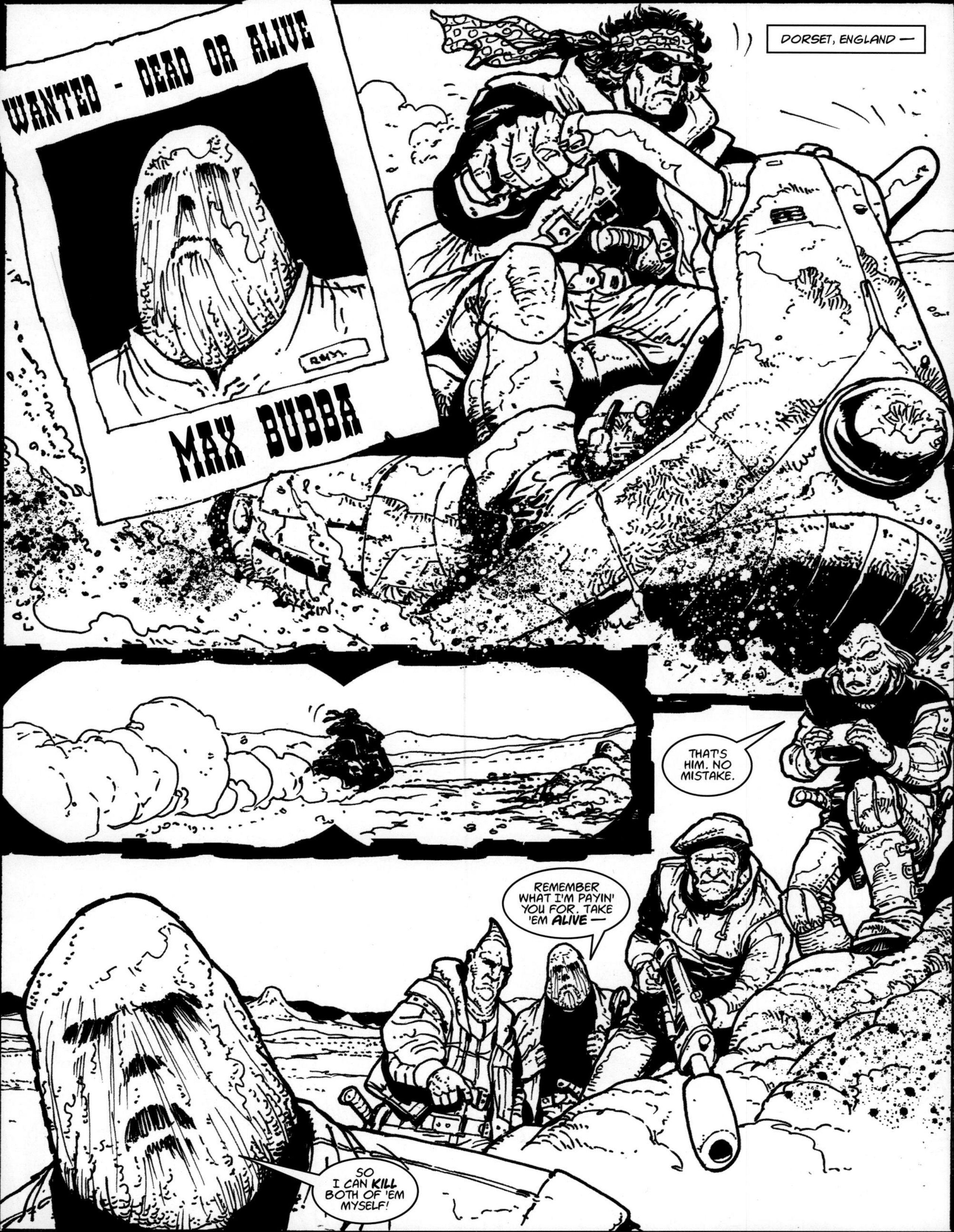

WANTED - DEAD OR ALIVE
MAX BUBBA
DORSET, ENGLAND —
THAT'S HIM. NO MISTAKE.
REMEMBER WHAT I'M PAYIN' YOU FOR. TAKE 'EM ALIVE —
SO I CAN KILL BOTH OF 'EM MYSELF!

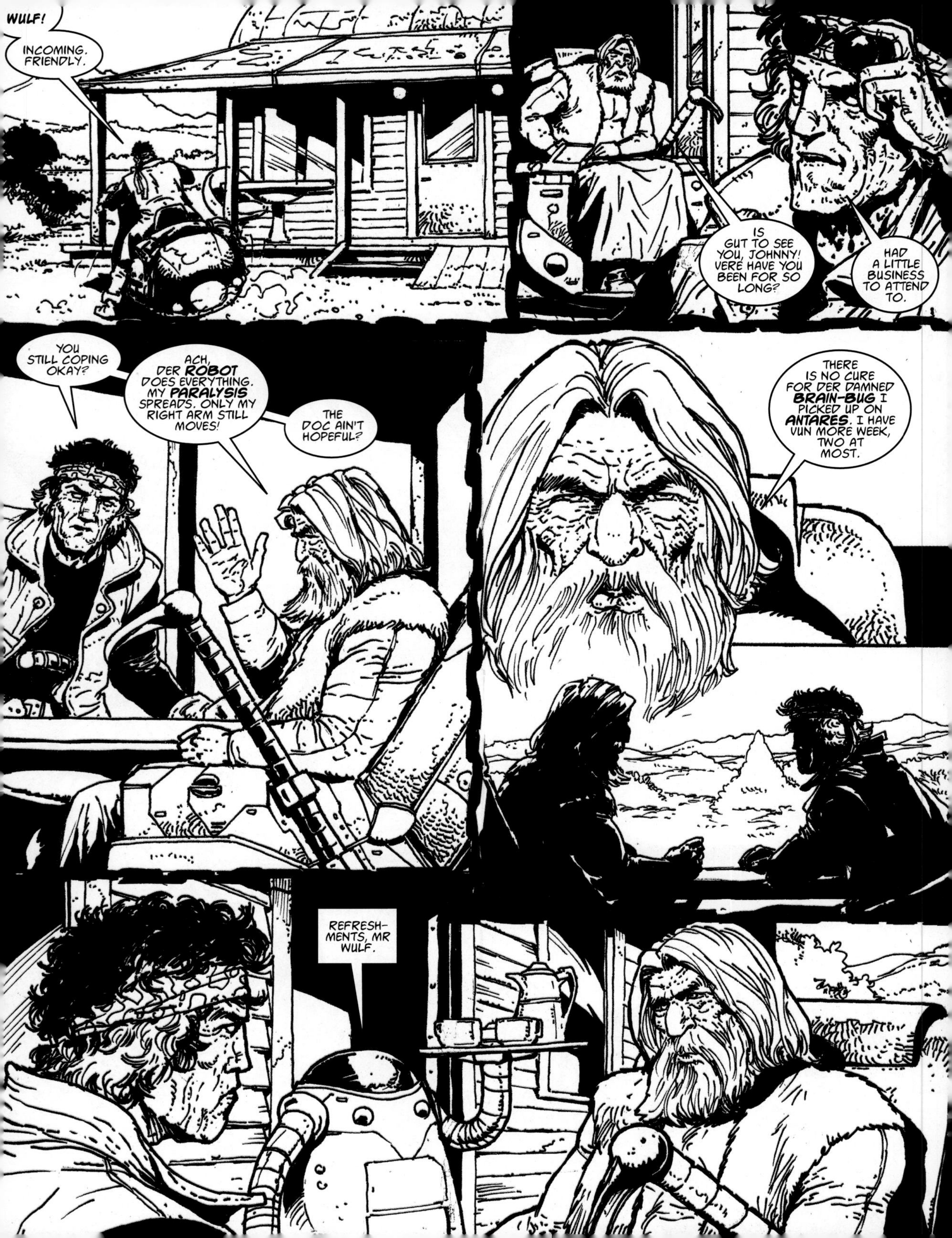
WULF!
INCOMING. FRIENDLY.
IS GUT TO SEE YOU, JOHNNY! VERE HAVE YOU BEEN FOR SO LONG?
HAD A LITTLE BUSINESS TO ATTEND TO.
YOU STILL COPING OKAY?
ACH, DER ROBOT DOES EVERYTHING. MY PARALYSIS SPREADS. ONLY MY RIGHT ARM STILL MOVES!
THE DOC AIN'T HOPEFUL?
THERE IS NO CURE FOR DER DAMNED BRAIN-BUG I PICKED UP ON ANTARES. I HAVE VUN MORE WEEK, TWO AT MOST.
REFRESH-MENTS, MR WULF.

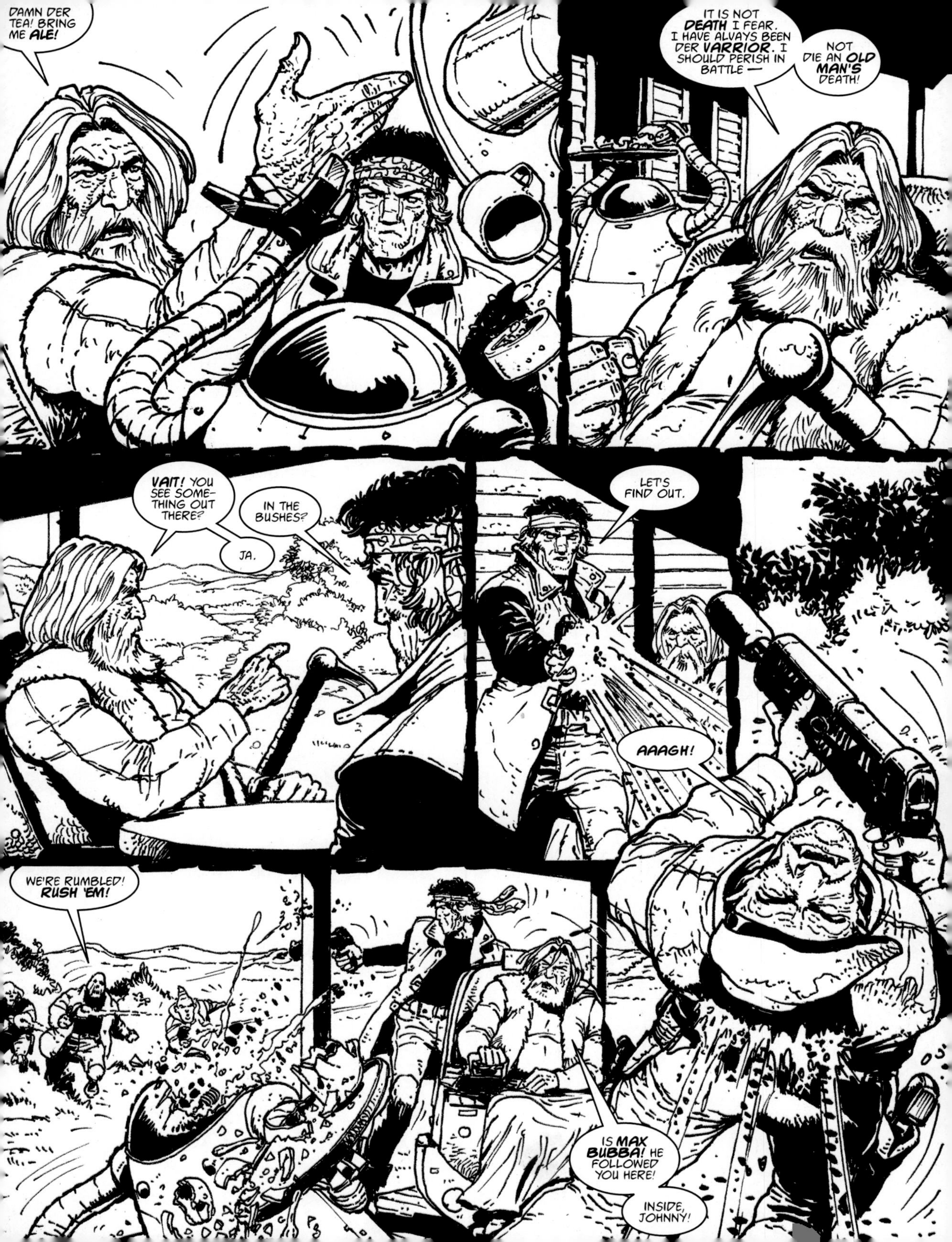

DAMN DER TEA! BRING ME ALE!
IT IS NOT DEATH I FEAR. I HAVE ALWAYS BEEN DER VARRIOR. I SHOULD PERISH IN BATTLE —
NOT DIE AN OLD MAN'S DEATH!
VAIT! YOU SEE SOME-THING OUT THERE?
IN THE BUSHES?
JA.
LET'S FIND OUT.
AAAGH!
WE'RE RUMBLED! RUSH 'EM!
IS MAX BUBBA! HE FOLLOWED YOU HERE!
INSIDE, JOHNNY!

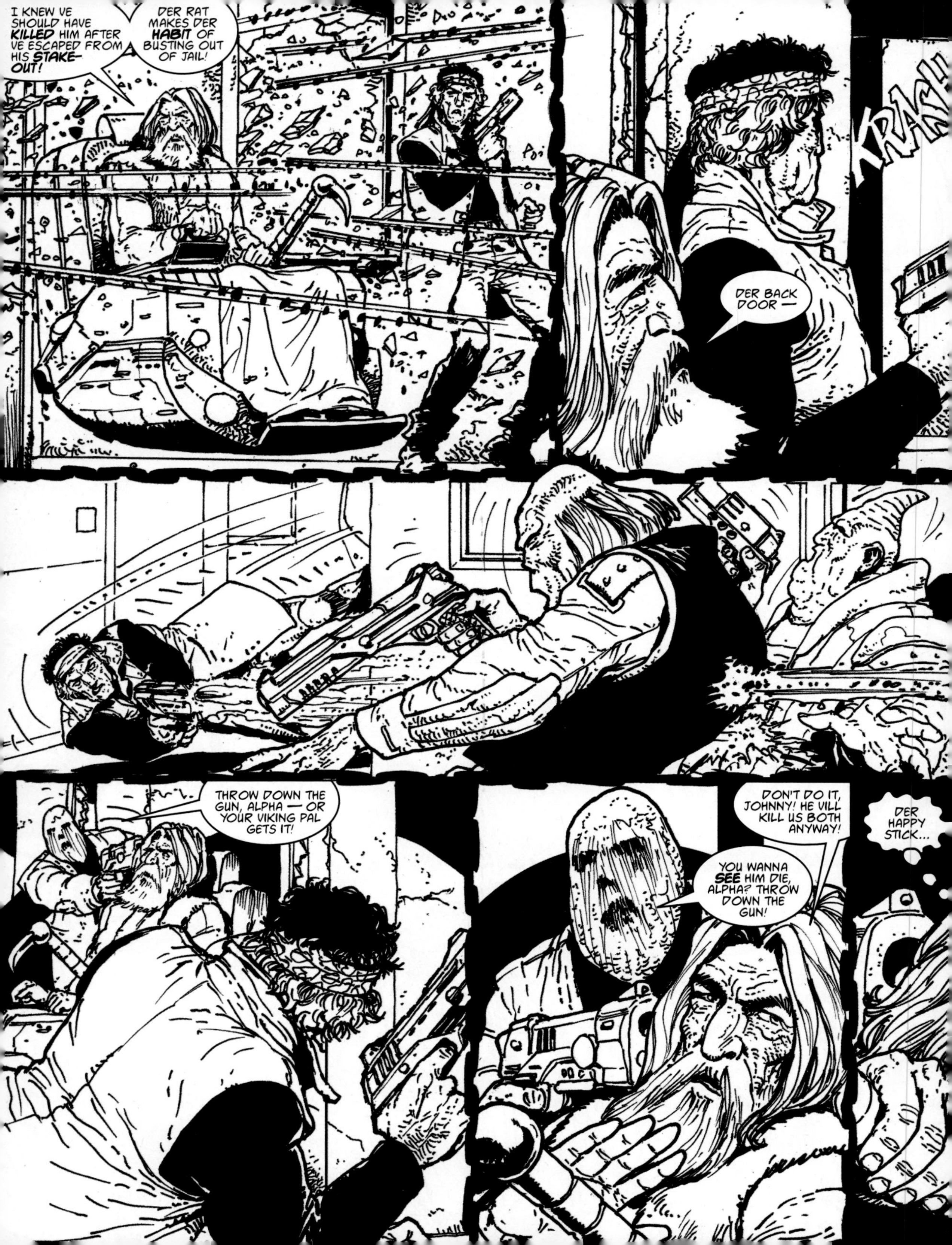
I KNEW VE SHOULD HAVE **KILLED** HIM AFTER VE ESCAPED FROM HIS **STAKE-OUT**!
DER RAT MAKES DER **HABIT** OF BUSTING OUT OF JAIL!
DER BACK DOOR —
THROW DOWN THE GUN, ALPHA — OR YOUR VIKING PAL GETS IT!
DON'T DO IT, JOHNNY! HE VILL KILL US BOTH ANYWAY!
YOU WANNA **SEE** HIM DIE, ALPHA? THROW DOWN THE GUN!
DER HAPPY STICK...

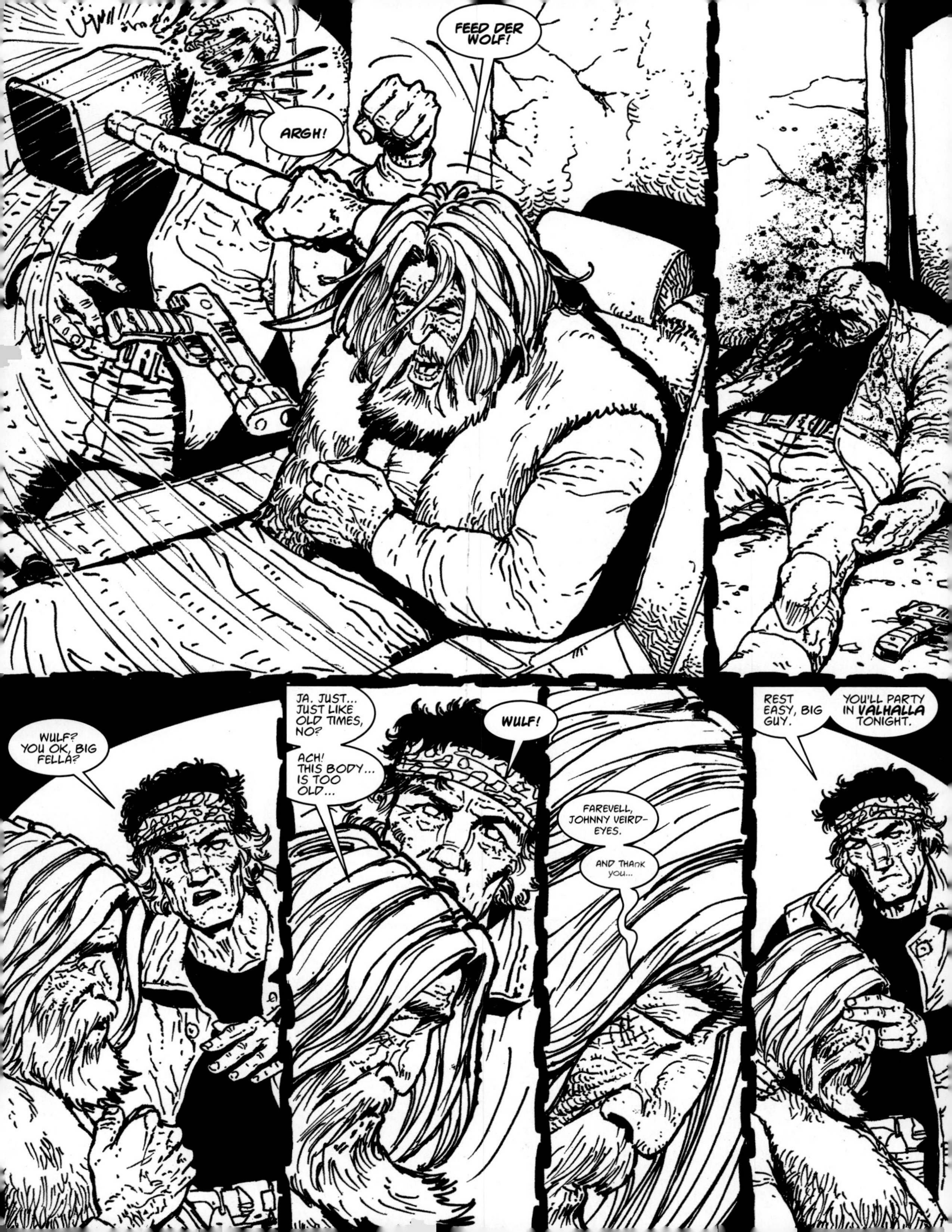
ARGH!
FEED DER WOLF!
WULF? YOU OK, BIG FELLA?
WULF!
JA. JUST... JUST LIKE OLD TIMES, NO?
ACH! THIS BODY... IS TOO OLD...
FAREVELL, JOHNNY VEIRD-EYES.
AND THANK YOU...
REST EASY, BIG GUY.
YOU'LL PARTY IN VALHALLA TONIGHT.

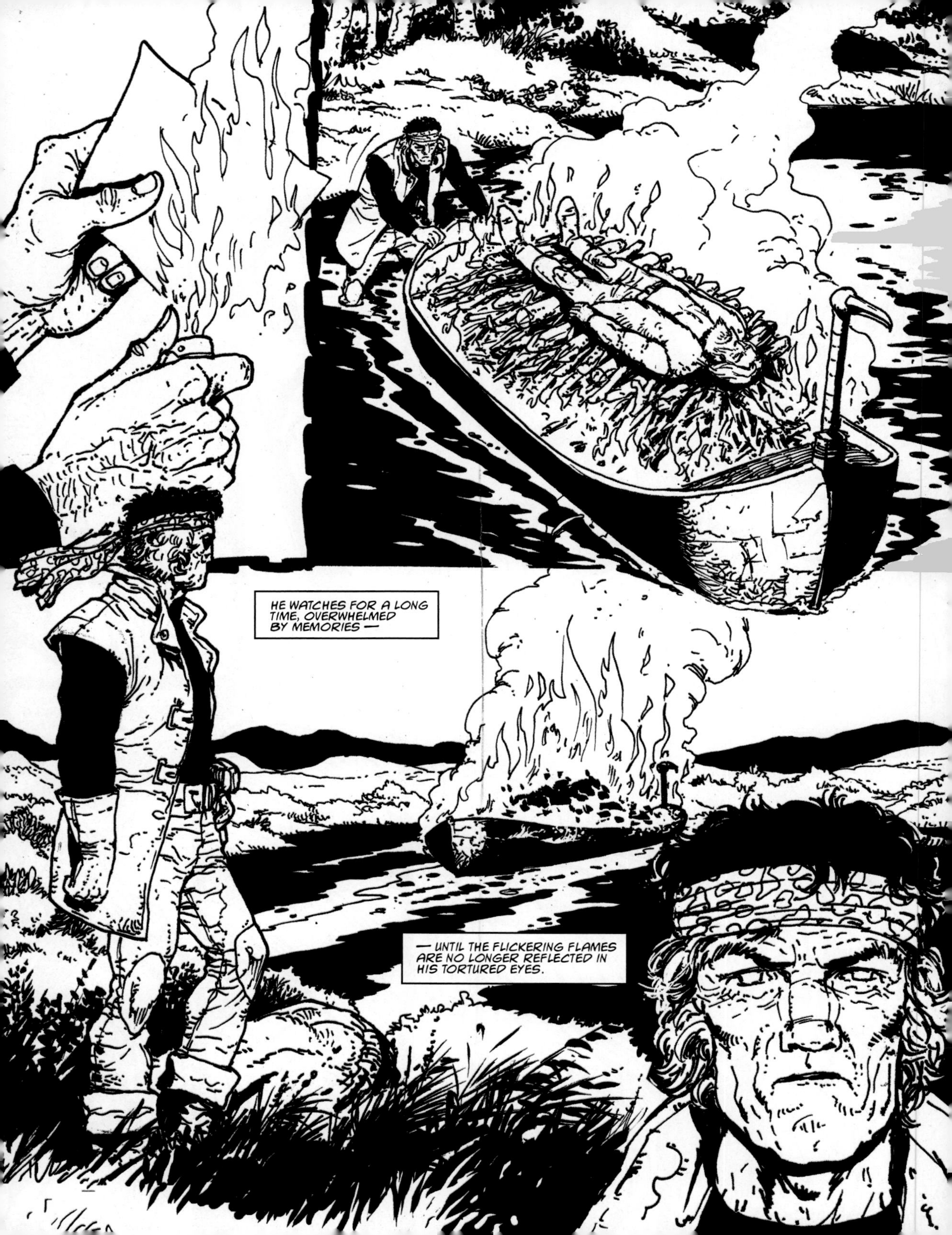
HE WATCHES FOR A LONG TIME, OVERWHELMED BY MEMORIES —
— UNTIL THE FLICKERING FLAMES ARE NO LONGER REFLECTED IN HIS TORTURED EYES.

COVERS GALLERY

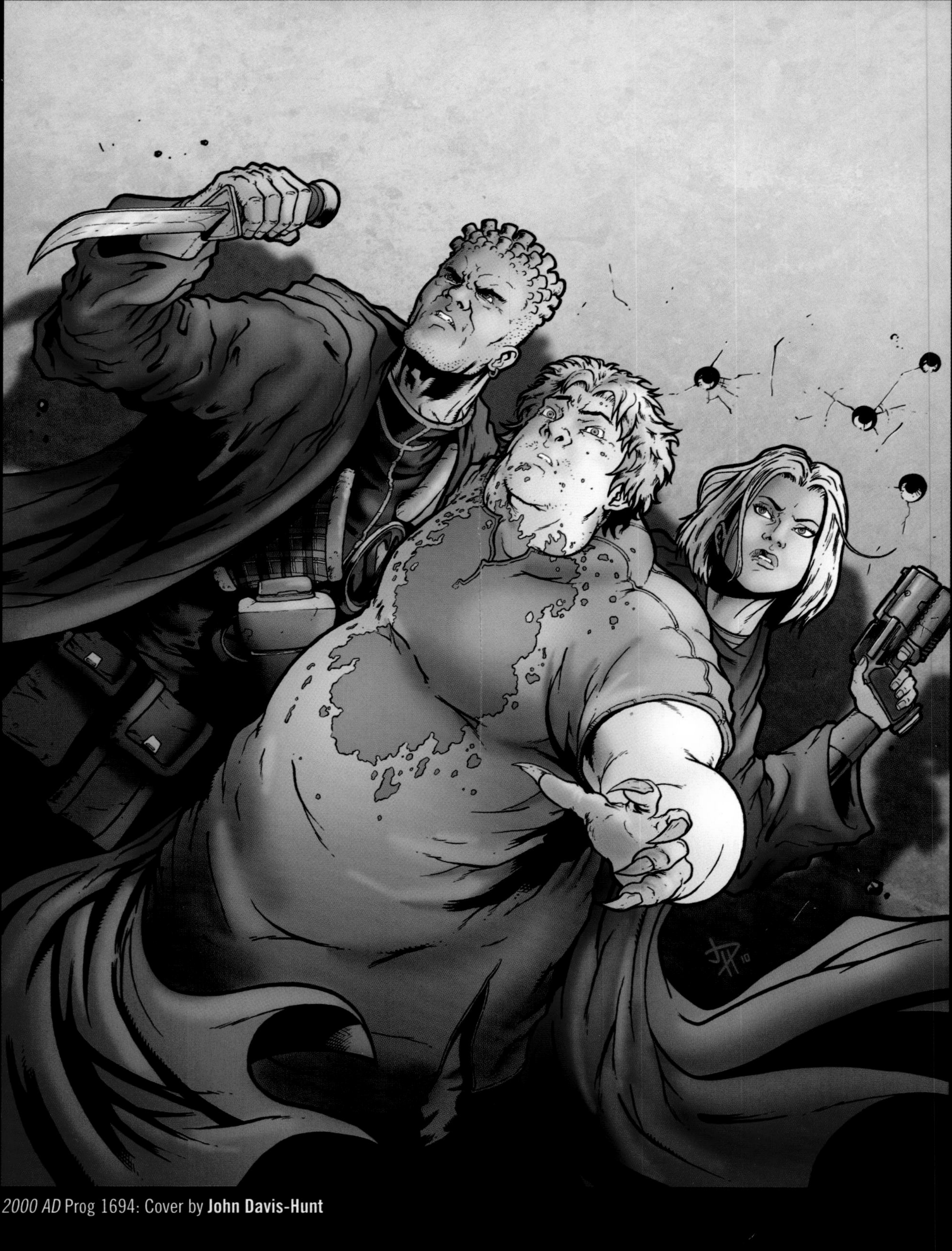

2000 AD Prog 1694: Cover by **John Davis-Hunt**

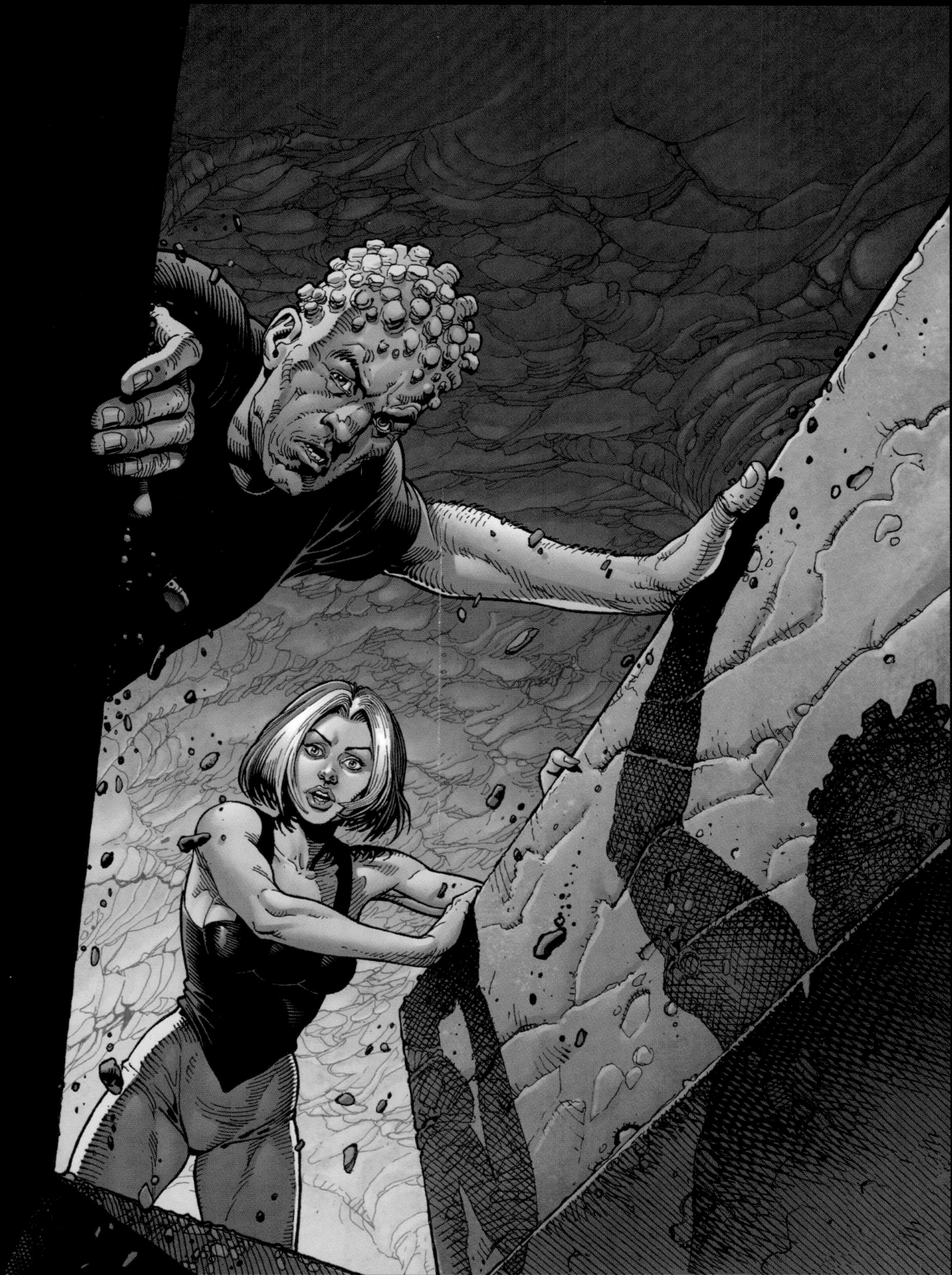

2000 AD Prog 1698: Cover by **Cliff Robinson**

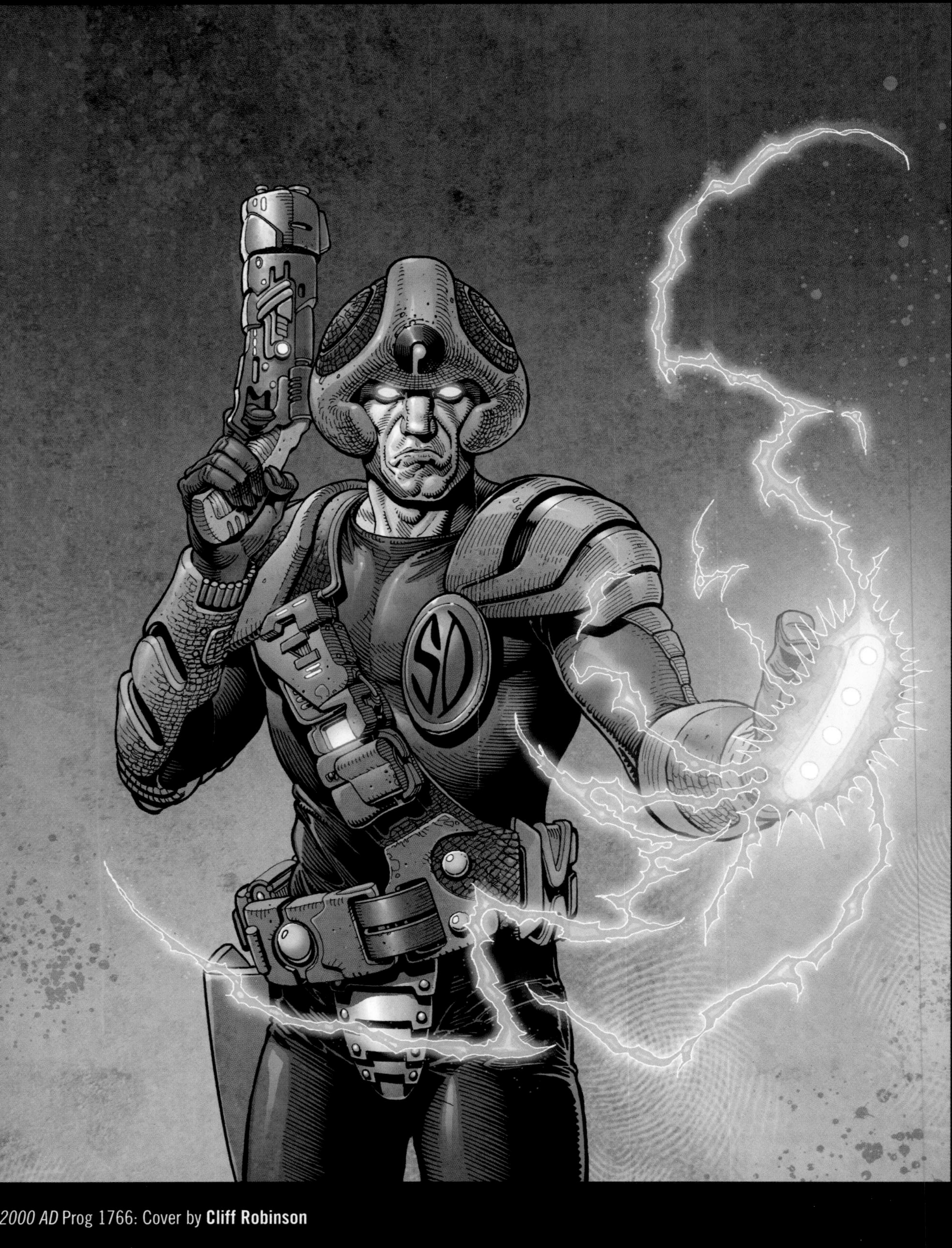
SY
2000 AD Prog 1766: Cover by **Cliff Robinson**

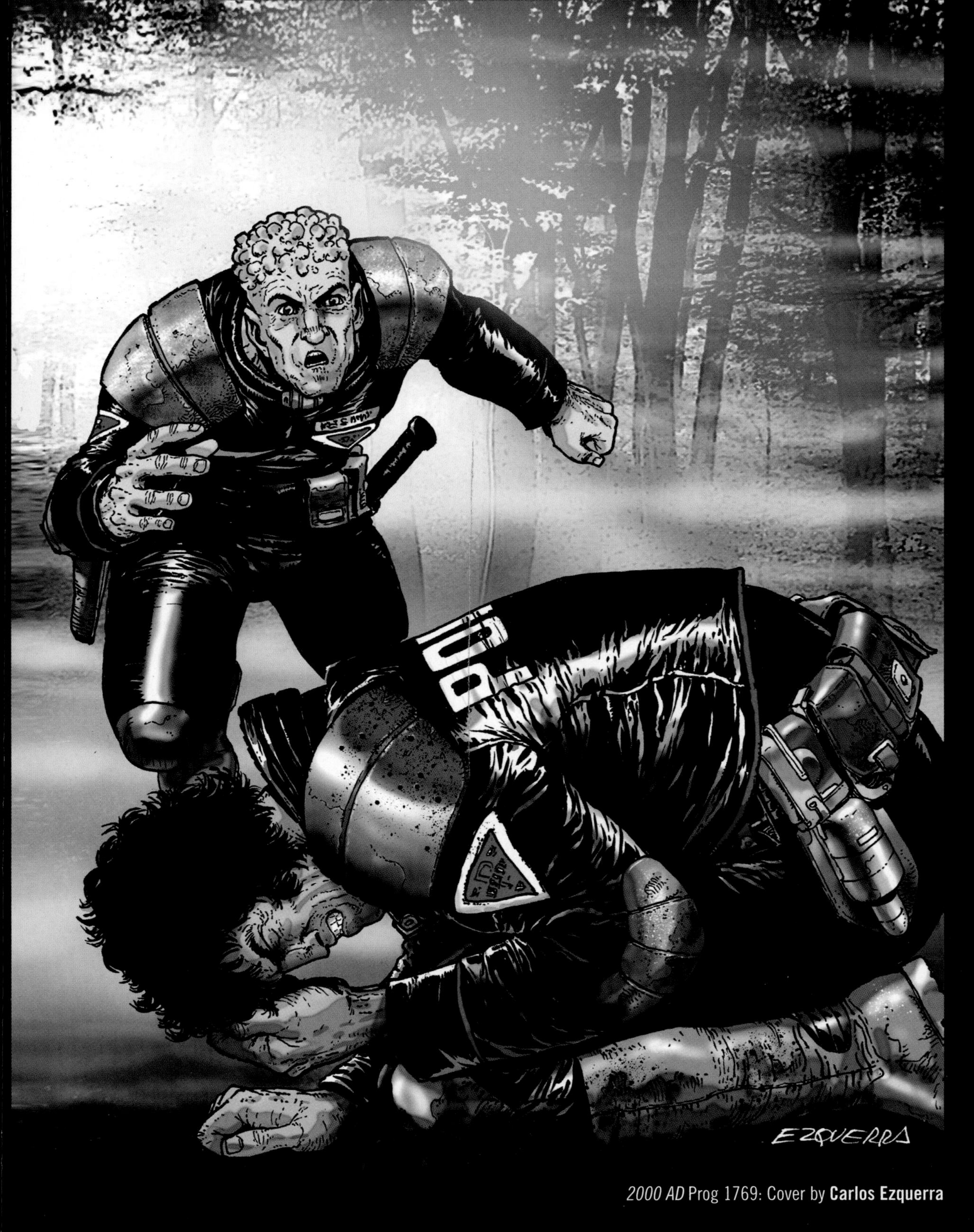
EZQUERRA

2000 AD Prog 1769: Cover by **Carlos Ezquerra**

JOHN WAGNER

John Wagner has been scripting for *2000 AD* for more years than he cares to remember. His creations include *Judge Dredd*, *Strontium Dog*, *Ace Trucking*, *Al's Baby*, *Button Man* and *Mean Machine*. Outside of *2000 AD* his credits include *Star Wars*, *Lobo*, *The Punisher* and the critically acclaimed *A History of Violence*.

CARLOS EZQUERRA

As co-creator of *Judge Dredd* **Carlos Ezquerra** designed the classic original costume as well as visually conceptualising Mega-City One. He also co-created *Strontium Dog*. He has also illustrated *A.B.C. Warriors*, *Judge Anderson*, *Tharg the Mighty*, *Al's Baby* and *Cursed Eath Koburn* amongst many others. Outside of the Galaxy's Greatest Comic, Ezquerra first illustrated *Third World War* in *Crisis* magazine, and has since become a regular collaborator with Garth Ennis, working on *Adventures in the Rifle Brigade*, *Bloody Mary*, *Just a Pilgrim*, *Condors* and *The Magnificent Kevin*. He also pencilled two special *Preacher* episodes.